C000297327
The most amazing scenic journeys in Britain

PUBLISHED B
THE READER'S DIGEST ASSOCIATION LIMITE
LONDON • NEW YORK • SYDNEY • MONTREA

The most amazing scenic journeys in Britain

Contents

Introduction

The beauty and variety of Britain's landscape makes every drive through town and country a journey of discovery. Take time out to explore the scenic routes in this guide and add a whole new dimension to holidays, days out or weekends away.

A third of all journeys in Britain today are made on motorways and trunk roads. Alongside these fast, utilitarian routes are the slower roads – winding A and B roads that fork into country lanes, which in turn meander from hamlet to cottage and on into deep countryside. These are authentic roads, created many centuries before the car, or even the horse and carriage. They once served as trade routes, communication routes, drovers' roads and pilgrim paths, and they pass through some of the most beautiful places in Britain.

The tours in this book have been specially planned to take in the very best of Britain's amazing landscape and heritage. Each of the drives begins at a touring base – a town or village selected for its scenic attractions, fine architecture and historic importance. Many of the towns are worthy of a stopover in themselves, and are well served with cafés, restaurants and shops.

The touring routes head away from the towns, passing pretty villages, nature centres, ancient monuments, museums and castles. They continue through farmland, moors, marshes and woods, climbing hilly country for spectacular views and dipping down into secluded river valleys that seem a world away from modern life.

Maps and text guide you step by step along the route, with facts and anecdotes on the history, geography, geology, legends and points of interest in the area, plus fascinating insights into flora, fauna and the lives of the famous locals.

How to use this book

The book is divided into six chapters, covering the following regions: Southwest, Southeast, Central, Northern, Wales and Scotland (see map, right). Large regional maps at the start of each chapter show the featured counties (or areas for Wales and Scotland), and the location of the touring base – the departure point – of each drive.

The drives are ordered by county (or area) within each chapter. Every drive has its own detailed touring map, showing the route and places of interest – such as gardens, stately homes, museums, adventure parks, churches,

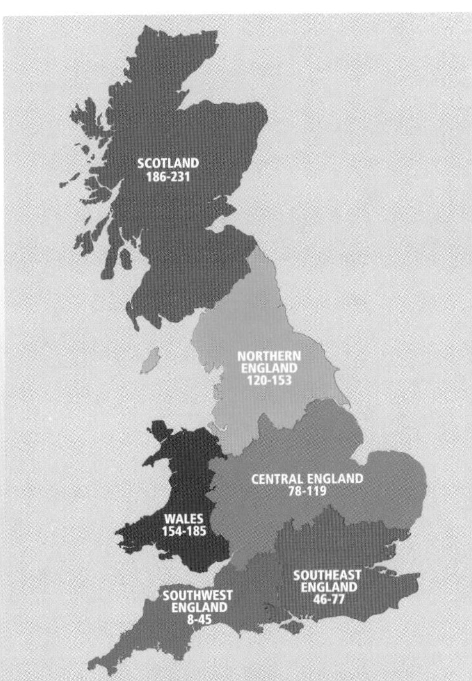

KEY TO SYMBOLS USED ON DRIVE MAPS

- Drive route
- Navigation point

ROADS

- Roundabout
- Multilevel junction
- Gradient steeper than 1 in 7
- Motorway

GENERAL FEATURES

- Car park
- Airport, airfield
- Car ferry
- Railway with station
- Built up area
- Woodland
- Lake/sea

PLACES OF INTEREST

- Abbey, priory, etc
- Ancient monument
- Arboretum
- Battle site
- Cathedral
- Church
- Country park
- Craft centre
- Garden
- Heritage railway
- Hillfort/long barrow
- House or castle in ruins
- House or castle with interesting interior
- Industrial feature
- Lighthouse
- Museum
- Natural feature
- Nature reserve
- Nature trail
- Picnic site
- Roman site
- Tourist information
- Viewpoint (all round)
- Viewpoint (directional)
- Watermill
- Wildlife park
- Windmill

monuments, viewpoints, parking and picnic areas – along the way. The touring base is highlighted in bold, and each route circles or loops the area, from time to time branching off for a detour to a place of particular interest or beauty.

The text provides clear directions and is broken down into numbered sections, each number corresponding to a number on the map to make navigation simple. Mileage is calculated and featured at the start of each drive to help you plan your tour.

Abbreviations

The following are used throughout the book:
Cadw Welsh Historic Monuments, **www.cadw.wales.gov.uk;**
EH English Heritage, **www.english-heritage.org.uk;**
NT National Trust, **www.nationaltrust.org.uk;**
NTS National Trust for Scotland, **www.nts.org.uk;**
RSPB Royal Society for the Protection of Birds, **www.rspb.org.uk;**
SWT Scottish Wildlife Trust, **www.swt.org.uk**

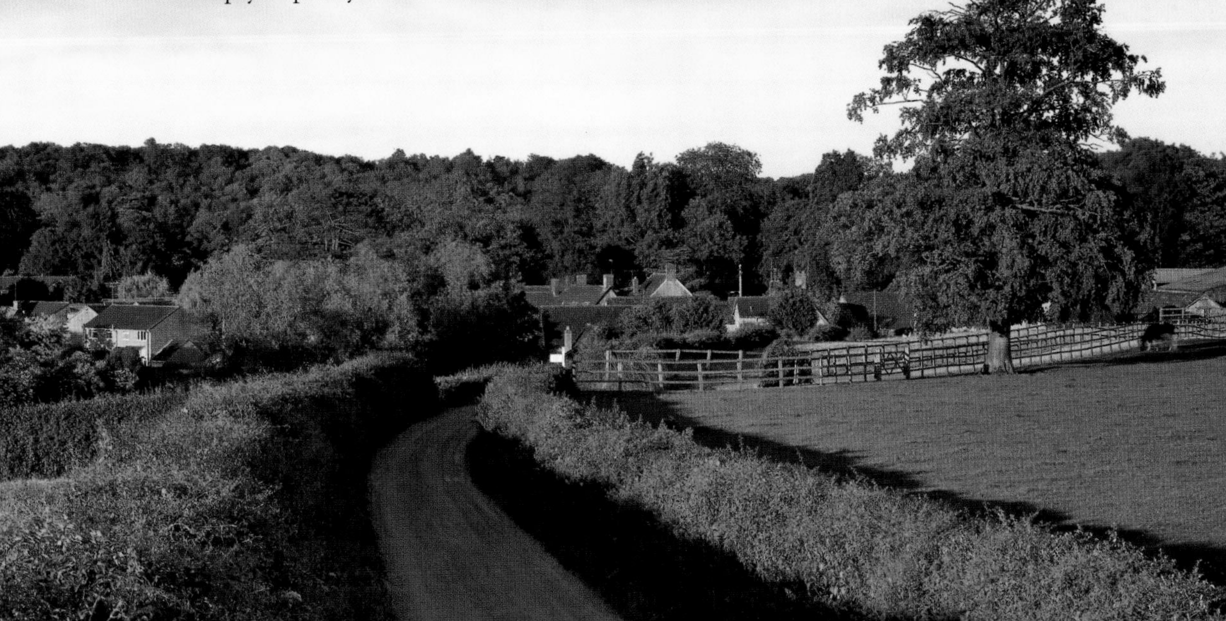

Southwest England

England's southwesterley backroads trace the region's rich history, linking sea ports to market towns and old mines to villages. High moors bear traces of the peninsula's ancient past, and provide panoramas little changed for hundreds of years.

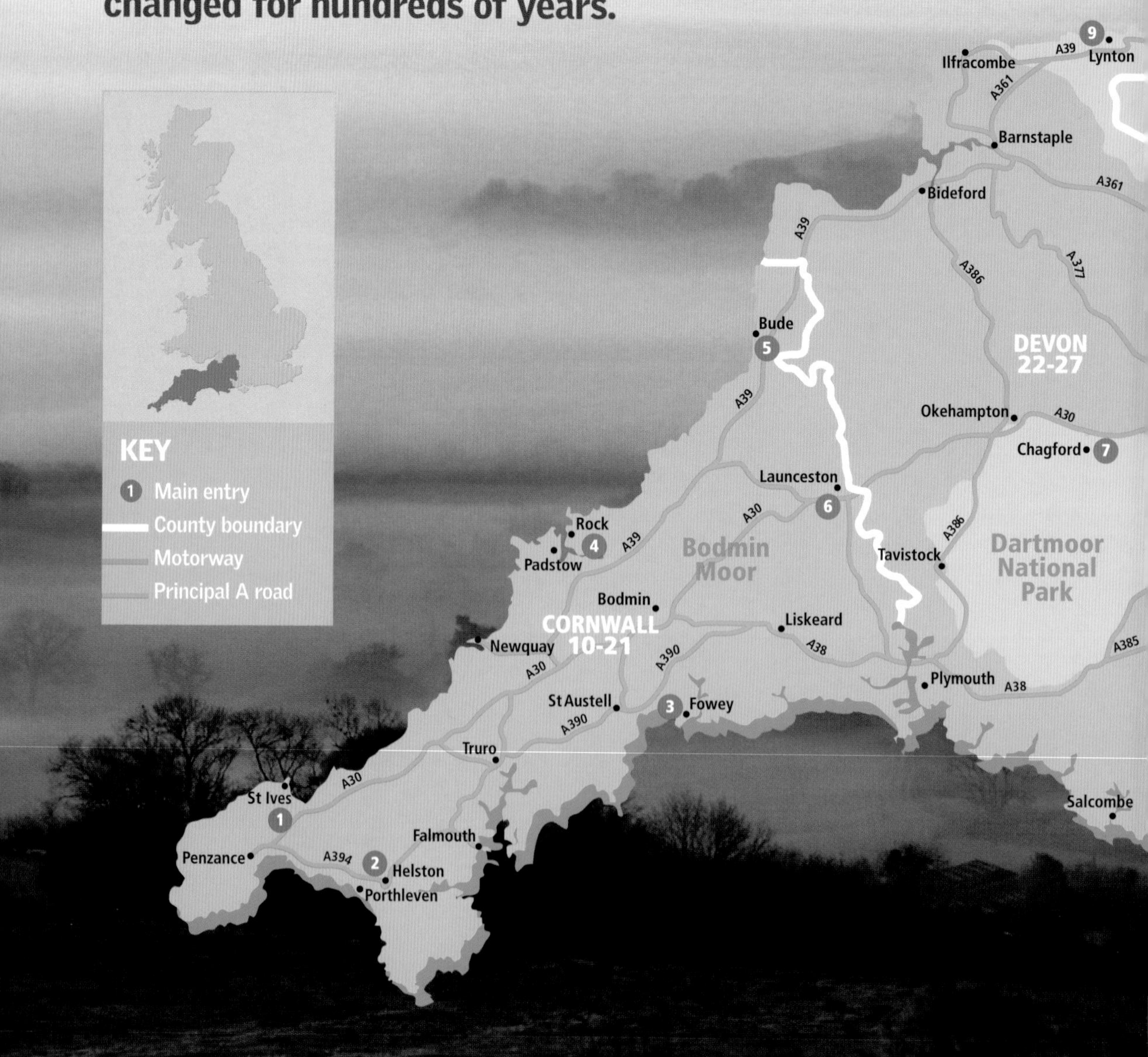

A419
Swindon
M4
A346
Bristol
Chippenham
A4
Marlborough
17
A38
A37
Bath
Bradford on Avon
Weston-super-Mare
16
A350
Devizes
A338
Trowbridge
Mendip Hills
WILTSHIRE 42-45
Minehead
Frome
15
Wells
A36
A361
Exmoor National Park
A39
A361
Warminster
Bridgwater
Somerset Levels
Glastonbury
A303
A338
14
Dulverton
SOMERSET 38-41
A37
Salisbury
Taunton
Shaftesbury
A354
A36
A396
M5
A30
A303
Yeovil
13
Sherborne
A350
A354
Tiverton
A30
Blandford Forum
Honiton
A37
DORSET 28-37
A31
A30
A35
A348
A338
Exeter
10
Lyme Regis
A35
A35
Poole
Bournemouth
Dorchester
11
Exmouth
Weymouth
12
Swanage
A38
A380
Torquay
Totnes
8
Dartmouth

CORNWALL

Stretching westward into the Atlantic, this granite-spined county is a scenic marvel, with wild coastal cliffs, picturesque ports and golden sands. Inland, the moors surrender the secrets of their plundered past.

1 ST IVES

TOUR LENGTH 41 miles

A tour of England's most westerly tip, circling the peninsula from the artists' colony of St Ives through the dramatic landscape of Land's End, passing pretty coves, an old tin mine and a lively fishing port on the way.

St Ives to Morvah

1 The charming coastal town of St Ives was once a busy centre of industry, with pilchard fishing and local tin exports its mainstays. Sandy beaches, rare on this rugged peninsula, are now the major attraction, but fishermen still use the harbour, catching fresh fish for local restaurants. The town has long been the haunt of artists and has some 30 art galleries, including the Tate St Ives.

To begin the drive, take the B3306 from the town, signposted to St Just. The road winds through gorse and scrub moors speckled with rocky outcrops. Beyond the moors, the route offers glimpses of the distant sea.

2 After about 4 miles, a right turn leads to Zennor, once a mining community, and wild, rocky Pendour Cove. The village's Wayside Folk Museum, open daily between April and September, explains the area's history. In the church is a bench dating from the 15th century, with carvings illustrating a local legend of tragic love between a man and a mermaid. Zennor Quoit, on the other side of the coast road, is the largest surviving chambered tomb in Britain.

Drive on to Morvah, a tiny moorland village with a coffee shop, art gallery and some fine views.

Morvah to Treen

3 Continue through Pendeen, where the old Geevor tin mine is now a museum. At the Trewellard Hotel, turn right to the Levant Mine and Beam Engine, perched on the cliff edge. The old tin mine beam engine has been restored to working order by the National Trust. Check opening times before visiting. Return to the coast road and turn right, climbing steeply into St Just, the westernmost town on mainland Britain and a thriving mining centre in Victorian times. Cape Cornwall juts into the sea to the west, and beyond it are the Brisons, craggy rocks where many ships have been wrecked. Continue through St Just then turn right on the B3306 and follow the signs to Land's End.

4 The wave-lashed granite headland of Land's End is the most southwesterly point on the British mainland. Visitors pay a charge to enter the area, where there are displays of Cornish history and legends. On a clear day there are stupendous views to the Isles of Scilly, about 28 miles away, from the clifftop path. Nearby Whitesand Bay is a popular surfing beach. From Land's End turn right on the B3315. After about 4 miles turn right into the small village of Treen.

Treen to Lamorna Cove

5 Return to the B3315 and turn right. Climb steeply out of a narrow valley then fork right towards Newlyn. Shortly after passing a lane to St Buryan on the left, a large ring of standing stones, known as the Merry Maidens, is visible in

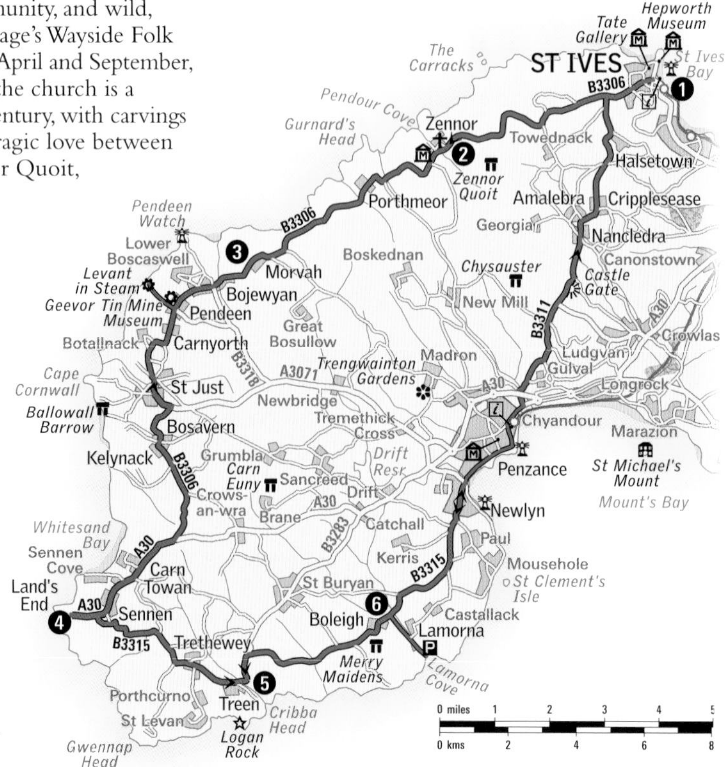

a field on the right. Local legend recounts that the circle was created when some young women dancing in the field on a Sabbath were punished by being turned to stone.

Turn right on the narrow road to Lamorna Cove, where a few cottages are grouped around the quay with rocks from the old quarry stacked up above them. The beach is sandy at low tide and paths lead along the cliffs to Mousehole (pronounced Mowzull), described by writer Dylan Thomas as 'the loveliest village in England'.

Lamorna Cove to St Ives

6 Return to the B3315 and turn right to Newlyn, which became popular with artists in the 1880s who were drawn by the special quality of light in this part of Cornwall. Newlyn retains some of its old character while maintaining its position as an important fishing port. A lively fish market takes place early each morning.

Continue ahead into Penzance. The resort town stretches along the seafront, flanked by the only promenade in Cornwall. At the far end of the bay are Marazion, Cornwall's oldest town, and St Michael's Mount (NT), a castle-topped granite crag connected to the mainland by a causeway.

From Penzance, follow the coast road past the harbour then turn left on to the B3311 towards St Ives. The road goes under the A30 and climbs steadily to a roadside parking area with splendid views of the south coast of Cornwall. Continue to a T-junction then turn right into St Ives.

CAPE CORNWALL

CORNWALL

2 PORTHLEVEN

TOUR LENGTH 49 miles

From Porthleven's charming harbour, a web of lanes crosses pasture and heath, linking old farming and fishing villages. Rocky coves and sandy beaches characterise an impressive coastline, descending in the far south to Lizard Point.

Porthleven to Loe Valley

1 Victorian ingenuity built the sturdy harbour at Porthleven, a haven in winter from savage southwesterlies. Once known for building boats, the little port still has a small fishing fleet, and attractive villas and cottages line the quay and cliffs. The Shipwreck Centre is fittingly situated in a port where, early last century, Henry Trengrouse experimented with lifeline rockets.

To begin the drive, climb out of Porthleven on the B3304 towards Helston. The road dips in and out of a wooded valley and winds between hedge-topped banks into Loe Valley on the outskirts of Helston. A car park by a lake on the left, and just before a garage on the right, leads to footpaths through the valley.

Loe Valley to Helford

2 Continue along the B3304 to a double mini-roundabout. Turn right then left into Helston and follow the wide, steep main street to traffic lights. This historic market town, a mix of old stone houses and modern buildings, was a busy port until the 13th century, when it was cut off from the sea. The town is known for its Furry (fair) Dance through gaily bedecked streets in May. Flambards Theme Park, to the south, displays aircraft and historical re-creations.

Beyond the traffic lights, continue to the double mini-roundabout and turn left on the B3297 towards Redruth. Follow the road for 3 miles, through Wendron and downhill round the S-bend into Trenear. Turn right to visit the 18th-century Poldark tin mine.

3 Return to the B3297. Turn left, and at the end of the S-bend turn left again, following a sign to Gweek. Cross the A394. The road snakes right and left. After a short distance, where the road divides, fork left through a steep dip to a T-junction and turn right to Gweek, at the head of the Helford creek. For centuries, Gweek was the main port in the area and a jumble of boats still lines the river. The nearby Cornish Seal

PORTHLEVEN HARBOUR

Sanctuary cares for injured and lost Atlantic seals. Turn right at the T-junction by Gweek Inn, cross two bridges, then immediately turn sharp left, signposted to St Keverne. The road winds round a wooded spit, then climbs to a roundabout. Turn left to Mawgan and follow the road through the village, signposted to St Martin. The road descends over an arm of Mawgan creek and climbs to St Martin.

❹ Continue to Newtown-in-St Martin, and turn left on to a minor road, signposted to Helford and Manaccan. Continue along the lane for 1½ miles to the crossroads and turn right to Manaccan. At the T-junction, turn left and follow the signposted lane to Helford. This village of thatched cottages was once an important port; its river a thoroughfare for pirates and free traders. A pedestrian ferry crosses the river, taking passengers to Glendurgan Gardens.

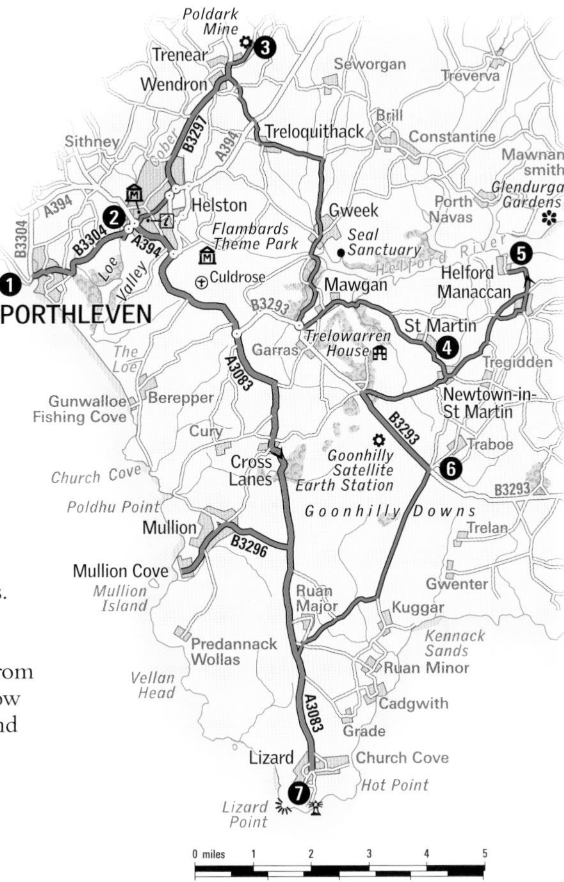

Helford to Lizard

❺ Return to Newtown-in-St Martin and from its centre turn left, signposted to Lizard. Follow the road to the T-junction with the B3293 and turn left. The road runs across flat Goonhilly Downs, dominated by the cluster of dishes of the Satellite Earth Station – once the largest in the world. A visitors' centre is on the right.

❻ Turn right at the crossroads, signposted to Ruan Minor and Lizard. Follow the long, straight road, and take the first turning on the right, signposted to Helston and Lizard. Continue to the T-junction with the A3083. Turn left towards Lizard, an Area of Outstanding Natural Beauty with one of the warmest climates in Britain. There is parking at the edge of the village beside the green on the right.

Lizard to Porthleven

❼ Take the A3083 back towards Helston, and after about 3½ miles turn left on to the B3296 to Mullion Cove. Dominated by its huge greenstone harbour walls, the cove was once a haunt of smugglers. Return to the A3083. Turn left, soon skirting the vast naval air station at Culdrose – one of the largest helicopter bases in Europe. After a right bend, turn left at a roundabout on the A394, following signs to Porthleven. Then, turn left again on the B3304, crossing Loe Valley back to Porthleven.

CORNWALL

3 FOWEY

TOUR LENGTH 54 miles

The drive from the old Cornish fishing port of Fowey turns inland, through a rolling landscape quilted with fields and dotted with wooded valleys surrounding the silvery spine of the River Fowey.

Fowey to Polkerris

1 A seaport redolent of its long history of trade, piracy and smuggling, Fowey (pronounced Foy) is a maze of tiny streets and quaint cottages. A pretty harbour looks across the mouth of the River Fowey to the village of Polruan on the opposite bank.

From Fowey, take the A3082 towards Bodmin. After ¾ mile, at the head of a layby on the right, stands the 6th-century Tristan Stone. The 2.7m (9ft) column is carved with a Christian Tau, or T-shaped cross, and bears a Latin inscription that translates as 'Drustanus, son of Cunomorus, lies here'. It honours the memory of Prince Tristan who, according to legend, had a doomed love affair with Iseult, an Irish princess betrothed to his father (or uncle, according to some versions of the story) King Mark Cunomorus of Cornwall. Continue on the Bodmin road to a mini roundabout and turn left, still on the A3082, towards St Austell.

After 1 mile turn left for Polkerris. Almost immediately take a right turn down a steep narrow lane to a car park on the right. Polkerris is a small hamlet close to a picturesque sandy cove. Until the late 19th century it was an important pilchard-processing centre; today it is a popular holiday destination.

Polkerris to Lanhydrock

2 Return to the mini roundabout near the Tristan Stone and turn left on the B3269 towards Liskeard, following it for 4½ miles. Turn right on the A390 to Lostwithiel, the capital of Cornwall in the 13th century, which became a great tanning centre.

Turn left after the Royal Talbot Inn on a minor road to Restormel Castle, which was originally built by the Normans in about 1100 as a motte and bailey. Reconstructed in the late 13th century, the castle (EH) became the property of Edward, the Black Prince, first Duke of Cornwall in 1337. Return to Lostwithiel.

3 At Lostwithiel High Street turn right. After 140m, take the third, unsignposted road on the right (B3268). The road meanders through woods and fields to join the B3269 at Sweetshouse. Turn right towards Bodmin. After 1¼ miles turn right at a mini roundabout, and right again after ¼ mile to Lanhydrock (NT). Set amid parkland, the house was built by the influential Robartes family in the 17th century. Much of it was rebuilt after a fire in 1881, but a few original features remain. The house is open February to November; the garden all year.

Lanhydrock to Talland

4 Continue to a junction with a minor road and turn right. The road crosses the Fowey by Respryn Bridge and, after 3 miles, meets the A390. Turn left towards Liskeard, and beyond Middle Taphouse turn right on the B3359 towards Looe. After 2½ miles, turn left on a lane to the Forestry Commission Deerpark, a good spot for picnics.

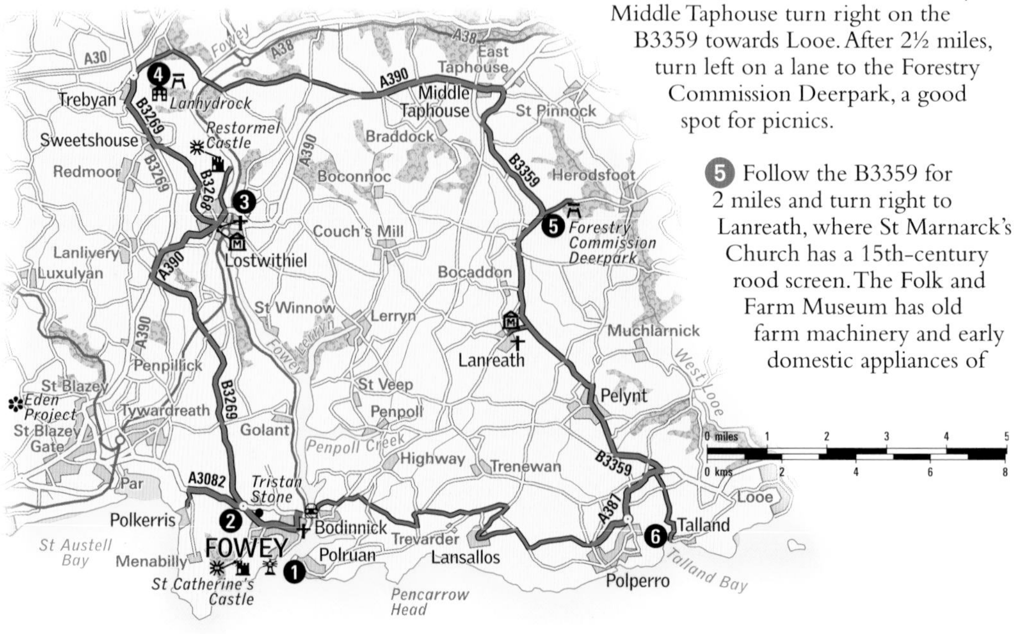

5 Follow the B3359 for 2 miles and turn right to Lanreath, where St Marnarck's Church has a 15th-century rood screen. The Folk and Farm Museum has old farm machinery and early domestic appliances of all kinds. Return to the B3359 and go through Pelynt to the junction with the A387. Turn right, and immediately left to Talland. The road becomes a steep single track. At the bottom, bear left at the telephone box and turn right into the car park for Talland Bay, a sand and shingle beach with abundant rock pools at low tide.

Talland to Fowey

6 Return to the A387 and turn left to Polperro, curving down to a mini roundabout on the edge of the little resort. Turn right towards Lansallos. After 1½ miles of winding, narrow roads, turn right at a T-junction to Lansallos, then take the first turning on the left into the village, where the medieval St Ildierna's Church has twice been struck by lightning.

A mile beyond the village turn left towards Polruan. The road passes a left turn to Trevarder and after 1 mile bends left. About 250m later, turn right to Bodinnick. The road bends sharply right to a T-junction. Turn left and descend into Bodinnick, from where a car ferry to Fowey operates from dawn to dusk.

VICTORIAN GARDENS BLOOM IN SPRING

LANHYDROCK

CORNWALL

4 ROCK

TOUR LENGTH 54 miles

Surfing towns, traces of old local industry and geological marvels on a drive that skirts Bodmin Moor. Much of the land is imbued with myth, as the route passes through the heart of King Arthur's country.

Rock to Pentireglaze

1 The cheerful village of Rock, lining the northern shore of the Camel estuary, has long been popular with yachtsmen, waterskiers and windsurfers. It is linked by foot ferry to the small resort of Padstow across the estuary, with its narrow streets and busy harbour.

From the quay take the road uphill, and opposite the garage turn left to Trebetherick. Cone-shaped Brea Hill dominates the view on the left. At the top of the hill in Trebetherick, a narrow road leads to Daymer Bay. A path off this road leads to St Enodoc Church, burial place of Sir John Betjeman. Keep on through Trebetherick and Polzeath. Just beyond Polzeath turn left on the road signposted to Lundynant Caravan Park, and continue straight to Pentireglaze.

Pentireglaze to Boscastle

2 Beyond Pentireglaze, turn left at the T-junction, then at the junction with the B3314 turn left towards Delabole. After 1 mile, a road on the left leads to Long Cross Victorian Gardens, which offer pleasant walks. Continue past St Endellion Church on the left, then turn left on the B3267 for Port Isaac, where extremely narrow streets lead almost vertically down to the tiny harbour.

3 From Port Isaac descend into Portgaverne, then climb to the junction with the B3314 and turn left to Delabole, where a tour of the slate quarry explains the history of this major Cornish industry.

4 At the crossroads beyond Delabole turn left to Trebarwith, where the beach is scattered with strange rock formations. At the junction in Trebarwith turn right and continue into the valley, then turn left and immediately right to climb to Treknow. At the T-junction above the village turn left, then follow the road through Treven to Tintagel, where Cornwall's mystical past and the legendary deeds of King Arthur sit uneasily with the trappings of modern tourism. From Tintagel, take the road to Bossiney, then to Boscastle. The harbour of this medieval village was famous for its narrow passage – ships had to be towed in with ropes braced around posts on the shores to keep them mid-channel when seas were high. The village was devastated by flooding in 2004 but has now been superbly restored.

Boscastle to Poley's Bridge

5 From Boscastle turn left on the B3266, signposted to the ancient town of Camelford on the edge of Bodmin Moor. Continue to the crossroads with the B3314. On the left is the British Cycling Museum, open Sundays to Thursdays, housed in Camelford's former station, and ½ mile to the right is the Delabole Wind Farm. Continue to Camelford to visit the North Cornwall Museum and Gallery, which records 100 years of working life in the area.

6 Leave Camelford on the A39 heading towards Wadebridge. Turn left on the B3266 towards Bodmin and after about 3 miles turn left signposted to St Breward.

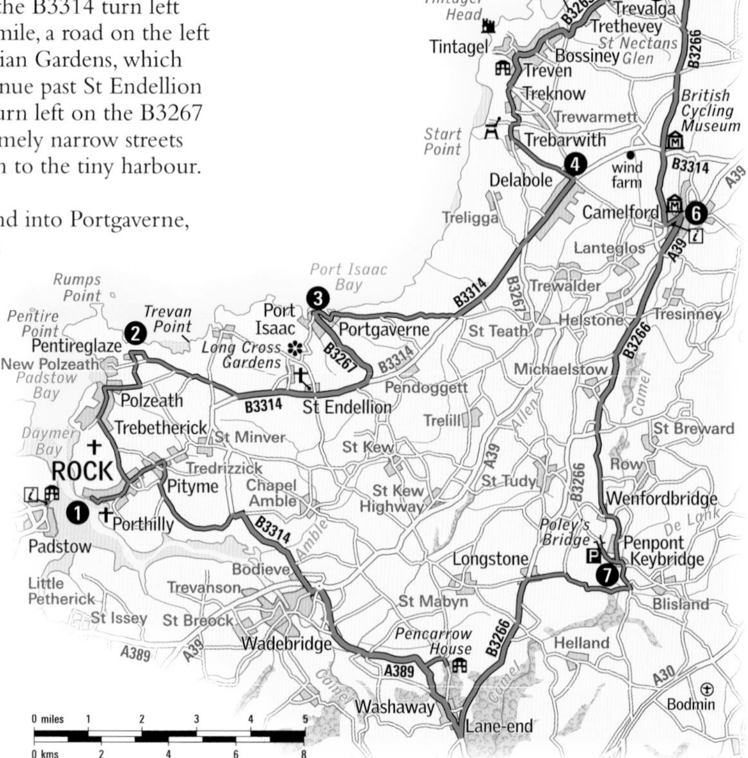

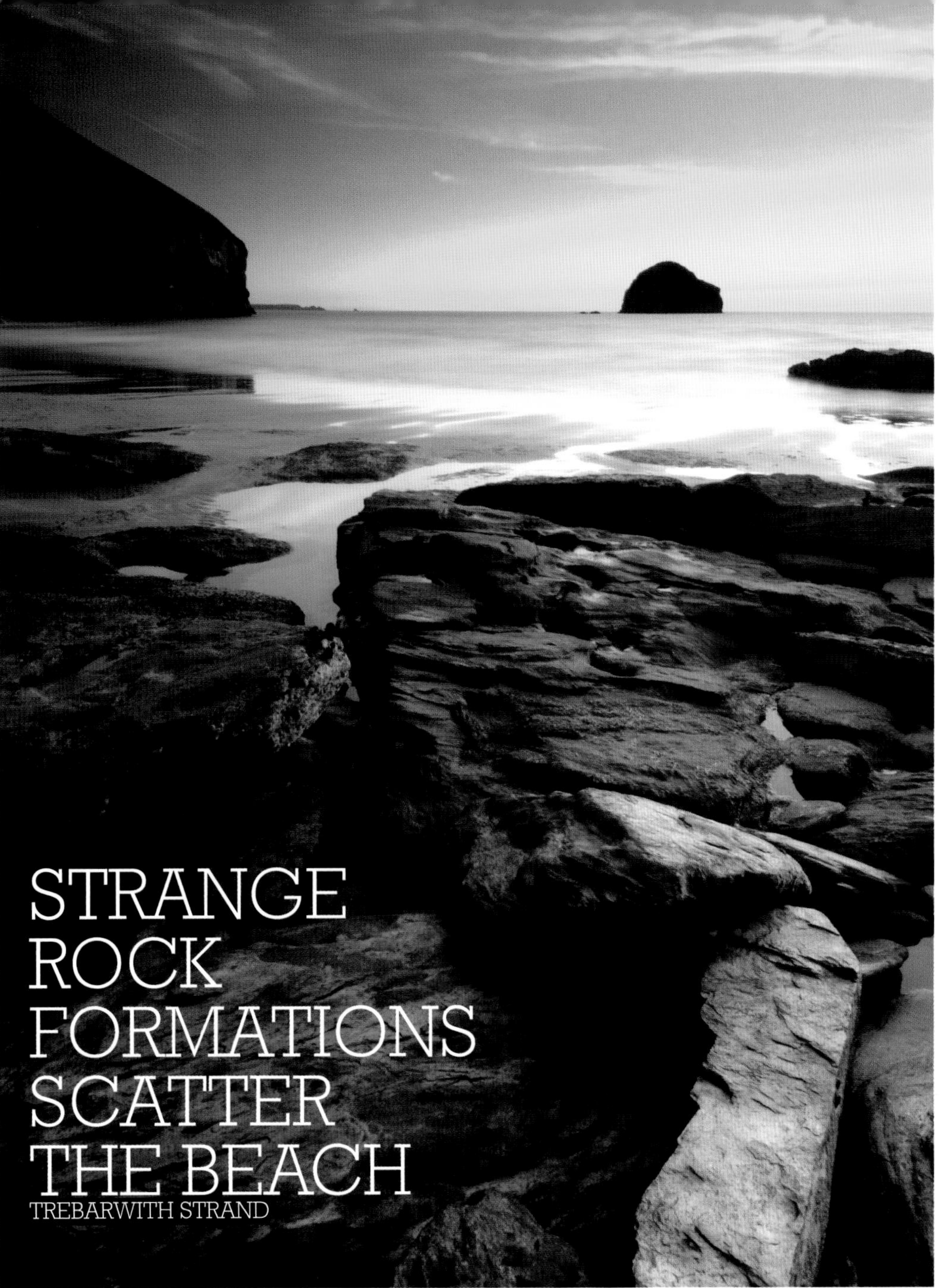

STRANGE ROCK FORMATIONS SCATTER THE BEACH
TREBARWITH STRAND

At the T-junction in Wenfordbridge, turn left and cross the River Camel. Fork right towards Blisland, climbing through Penpont. Where the road forks, bear right to Keybridge, and turn right for Poley's Bridge car park. From here, walkers and cyclists can take the Camel Trail – 17 miles of disused railway – to Camelford, through the Camel Valley.

Poley's Bridge to Rock

7 Return to Keybridge and keep straight on at a junction to cross the De Lank river. After about ½ mile, turn right on to a road signposted to St Mabyn. Cross the Camel Trail and river, then go on to Longstone. Turn left at the T-junction on to the B3266 and go through woods around the hamlet of Washaway. At the T-junction with the A389 turn right towards Wadebridge. After 2 miles, a minor road on the right leads to Pencarrow House, open spring to autumn, Sundays to Thursdays, set in formal and woodland gardens. Continue on the A389 to a roundabout. Take the first exit, then turn right on to the B3314 towards Rock. Just beyond Gutt Bridge turn left at a campsite sign. Bear right to Pityme, and turn left to return to Rock.

CORNWALL

5 BUDE

TOUR LENGTH 51 miles

A leisurely drive from the pretty surfing town of Bude on the Atlantic Heritage Coast, through hidden valleys, scattered hamlets and churches with holy wells. Stop off at the lovely North Devon village of Clovelly, or picnic at the Tamar Lakes.

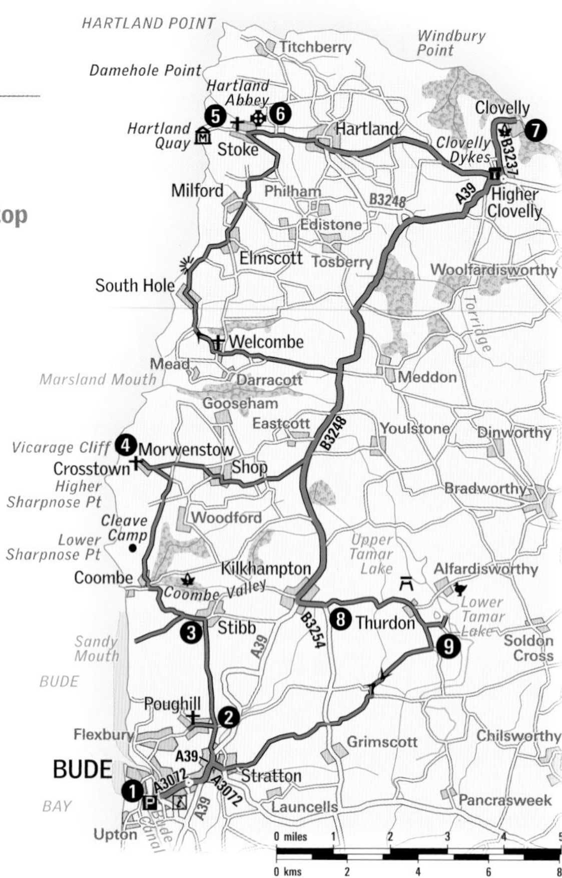

Bude to Morwenstow

1 Golden beaches facing the Atlantic were the foundation of Bude's prosperity. In the early 19th century, the harbour and canal were developed to transport sea sand, valued as a sweetener for acid soils. Today these beaches are a mecca for surfers. The coast north and south remains wild and unspoilt.

Start the drive at the car park by Bude canal. Built in the 1820s, the canal was an impressive feat of engineering, flowing for 35 miles from Bude to Holsworthy in the east and south to Launceston. Incline planes carried boats 130m (430ft) above sea level just after leaving Bude in a distance of just 6 miles. The canal was closed in 1891 after the railways rendered it obsolete. Today a stretch of 2 miles remains open from Bude to Helebridge and canal paths are being restored for walkers.

To begin the drive, follow the A3072 to a T-junction with the A39 and turn left towards Bideford. Beyond the junction where the A3072 joins from the right, fork left on a minor road signposted to Coombe Valley.

2 Turn left at the crossroads to Poughill (pronounced poffil), where the 14th-century parish church of St Olaf has carved Tudor pews and frescoes. Return to the crossroads and turn left.

3 At Stibb, turn left and after ½ mile turn left again to Sandy Mouth beach. At low tide, golden sands surround extraordinary rock formations beneath the folded and eroded strata of the cliffs. Return to the T-junction and turn left into Coombe Valley, where a watermill and cottages stand by a stream. The road winds out of the valley past Cleave Camp satellite-tracking station. Keep straight on at the crossroads and follow the road through Crosstown to Morwenstow.

Morwenstow to Stoke

4 At Morwenstow, follow the signs for Bideford. Turn left on the A39, and after 2 miles turn left on a minor road to Welcombe, which is in Devon. Opposite the church is St Nectan's Well, a holy spring housed in a medieval structure but dating back to before the Norman Conquest. Continue along the lane, which dips into a coomb. Turn right and follow a hedged lane to Elmscott. Turn left at Elmscott Farm for Stoke and Hartland. Continue straight on at the crossroads at the bottom of the valley. Go up the other side and turn right at the crossroads. Fork left for Stoke and Hartland Quay. Follow the road to the next junction and turn left. Continue into Stoke.

5 Turn left for the car park near St Nectan's Church, which is largely 14th century. The tower may have been built as a landmark for seafarers – at 39m (128ft), it is visible for miles and has given the church the name 'Cathedral of North Devon'. Just 100m from the church down a small path is a spring, also known as St Nectan's Well, housed in a wellhead structure with an arched door.

Stoke to Bude

6 Return along the main street of Stoke; turn left for Hartland. Hartland Abbey, to the left, is a Gothic mansion built on the foundations of a medieval monastery. Keep straight ahead in Hartland on the B3248, turn left on the A39 and left again at the roundabout to Clovelly.

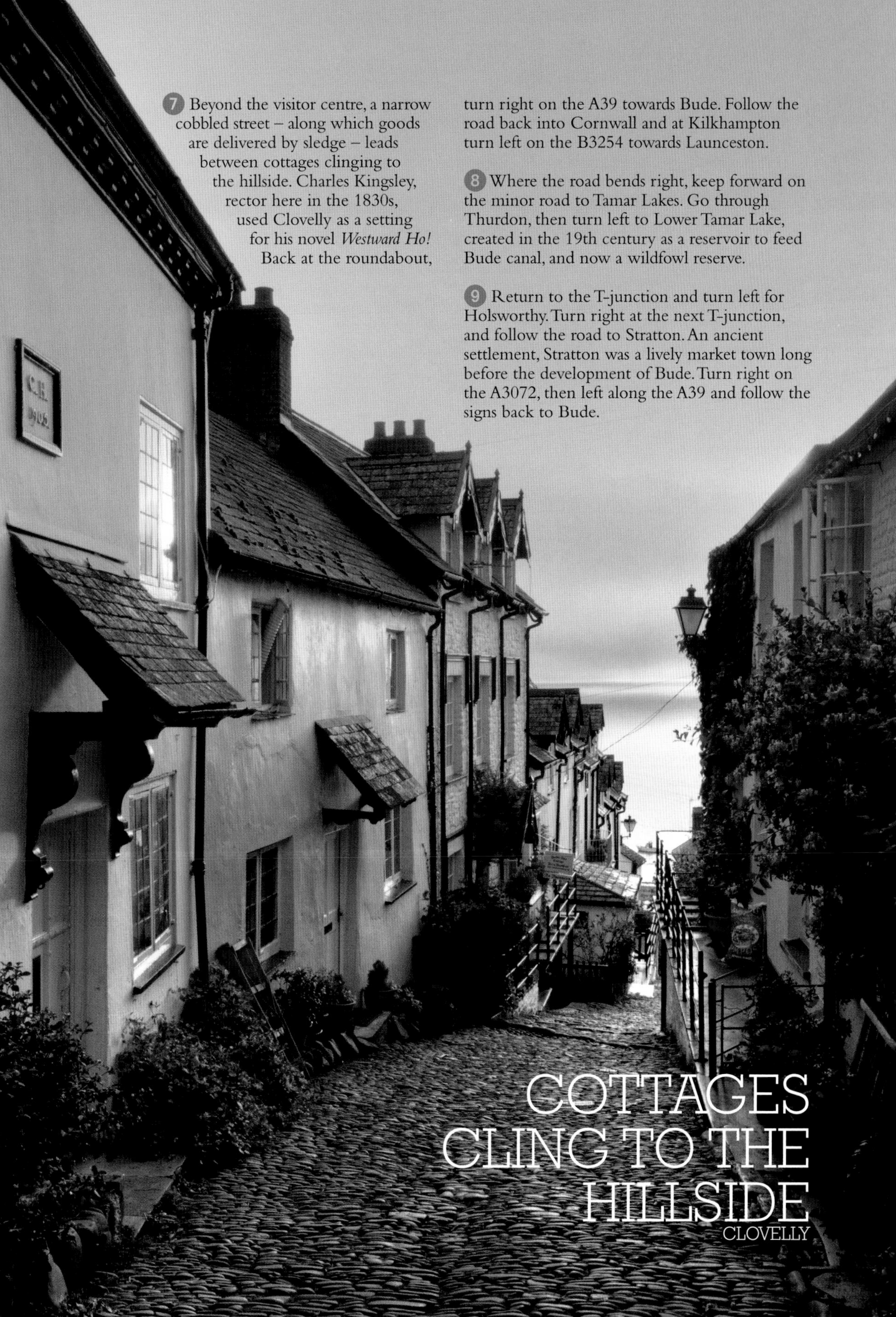

7 Beyond the visitor centre, a narrow cobbled street – along which goods are delivered by sledge – leads between cottages clinging to the hillside. Charles Kingsley, rector here in the 1830s, used Clovelly as a setting for his novel *Westward Ho!* Back at the roundabout, turn right on the A39 towards Bude. Follow the road back into Cornwall and at Kilkhampton turn left on the B3254 towards Launceston.

8 Where the road bends right, keep forward on the minor road to Tamar Lakes. Go through Thurdon, then turn left to Lower Tamar Lake, created in the 19th century as a reservoir to feed Bude canal, and now a wildfowl reserve.

9 Return to the T-junction and turn left for Holsworthy. Turn right at the next T-junction, and follow the road to Stratton. An ancient settlement, Stratton was a lively market town long before the development of Bude. Turn right on the A3072, then left along the A39 and follow the signs back to Bude.

COTTAGES CLING TO THE HILLSIDE

CLOVELLY

CORNWALL

6 LAUNCESTON

TOUR LENGTH **54 miles**

Set in a vale between Bodmin Moor and Dartmoor, Launceston's untamed landscape contrasts with the lower reaches of the River Tamar, which winds to Plymouth Sound through quiet tidal creeks.

Launceston to Minions

❶ For several centuries after the Norman Conquest, Launceston was the most important town in Cornwall, with an abbey, a mint and a thriving market. Its castle survives as a hilltop ruin, and the town's history is recalled at the Lawrence House Museum.

From the centre of Launceston, follow the signs for Bodmin, passing under the A30. At a roundabout take the B3254 through South Petherwin and across the River Inny, Bodmin Moor looming ahead. At the crossroads turn left on the B3257. After 2½ miles turn right on a minor road to the riverside village of Rilla Mill.

❷ From Rilla Mill, continue on the minor road, straight over the crossroads at Upton Cross, to Minions, a former mining centre and, at 300m (980ft) above sea level, the highest village in Cornwall. A car park on the right just before the village, beyond an old railway bridge, gives access to the high moorland, and sites of natural, geological and archaeological interest. Close to the car park, the Heritage Centre in an old mining engine house provides local information.

Minions to Cotehele Quay

❸ Drive back to Upton Cross and turn right on the B3254, passing the ruined mines and spoil heaps of

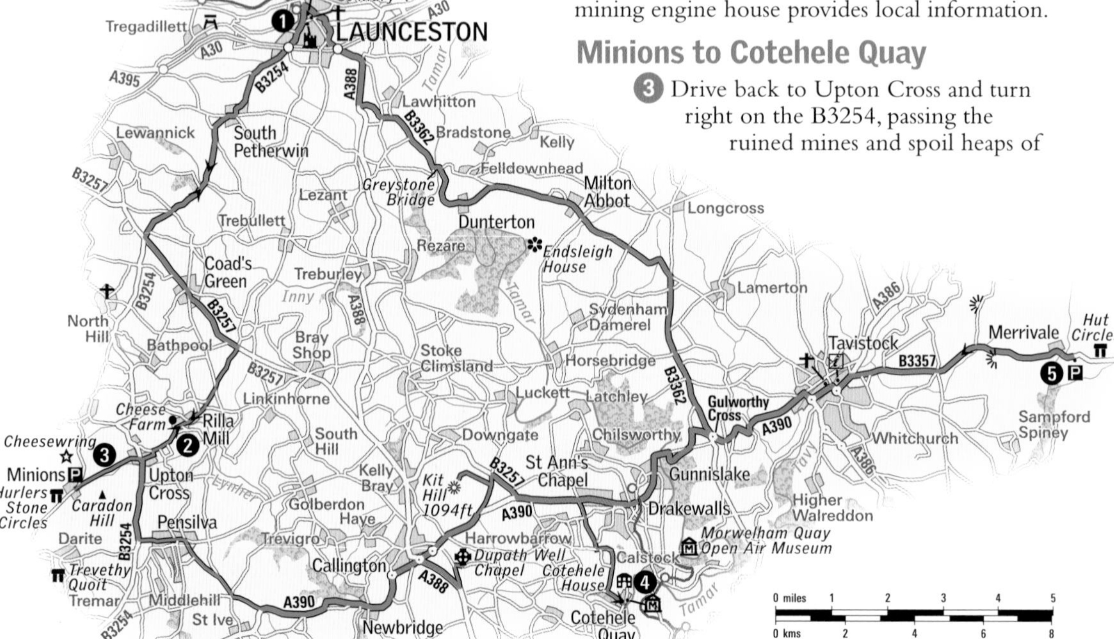

PREHISTORIC TRACES AT MERRIVALE

Caradon Hill. A mile farther on, turn left to Pensilva and follow the signs to Callington, turning left on the A390. Bypassing Callington village, take the third exit at a roundabout signposted Tavistock and Launceston. At a second roundabout take the third exit – the A388 – signposted to Plymouth and Saltash. Follow the A388 for approximately 1 mile. Take a left, then right turn along a small road to Dupath Well, a medieval shrine beside a sacred spring. The tiny chapel may have been built to sanctify a pagan site and was probably used for baptisms. Return to the A388 and turn right to Launceston. At the roundabout take the third exit to Tavistock. Continue along the A390 for 1 mile, fork left on a minor road and turn left to the summit of Kit Hill. Follow the B3257 back to the A390 and continue to St Ann's Chapel. Turn right on a minor road to Cotehele, following the signs through narrow lanes to Cotehele House. Continue along the lane to the museum and gallery at Cotehele Quay.

Cotehele Quay to Merrivale

4 Return to the A390 and go on to Tavistock, in Devon, thought to be the birthplace of sailor and navigator Sir Francis Drake (1540–96). A canal-side walk begins near his statue in Plymouth Road. From the town centre follow the signs to the B3357 towards Princetown. As the road climbs to Dartmoor, a car park on the right offers views south towards Plymouth Sound and back over the town to Bodmin. Continue through Merrivale to the National Trust car park on the right, ¼ mile beyond the Dartmoor Inn. From there, paths lead through one of Dartmoor's best-preserved prehistoric landscapes.

Merrivale to Launceston

5 Follow the B3357 back to Tavistock, taking the third exit at the roundabout for Town Centre. At traffic lights, go on to the mini roundabout, taking the first exit to the B3362. At a further roundabout take the first exit – the B3362 – towards Launceston. At Gulworthy Cross roundabout take the third exit signposted Milton Abbot. A mile south is Endsleigh House, built by the 6th Duke of Bedford in 1810. The house is now a hotel but the gardens are open to the public.

Continuing along the B3362, cross the Tamar back into Cornwall over the 15th-century Greystone Bridge and turn right on the A388 to return to Launceston.

DEVON

From meandering estuaries and tranquil backwaters of the south, the county's roads cross the moors to the wild and rugged north, characterised by deep wooded valleys and narrow, isolated coves.

7 CHAGFORD

TOUR LENGTH 45 miles

Courted by fierce rocky tors and the gentle River Teign, this circular tour reveals a landscape that shifts from high moorland to green valleys. Many of Dartmoor National Park's greatest natural and architectural attractions lie on the route.

Chagford to Bellever

❶ The views from Chagford's narrow streets are a constant reminder that the town stands on a scenic threshold. In one direction are the sheltered fields and woods of the Teign valley; in the other is the treeless, wild terrain of Dartmoor – the highest land in southern England. From one side, rolling, deep-folded countryside beckons seductively; from the other, jagged windswept tors look haughtily down.

From Chagford follow minor roads signposted to Postbridge until you reach a T-junction with the B3212, about 3 miles distant. Turn right. The road climbs uphill over a cattle grid, on to a long archaeological remains, from standing stones to medieval field systems and 17th-century mine workings. Continue into Postbridge.

❷ Postbridge is a hamlet with a shop, inn and information centre and a complete clapper bridge, built in the 1780s, just downstream of the road bridge over the East Dart river. Its granite slabs and piers had to bear the weight of strings of packhorses laden with tin ore.

Take the first left after the clapper bridge to Bellever. Turn left at the T-junction in the hamlet, then almost immediately take a track on the right, by a sign for 'High Dartmoor – Bellever', to a car park. From here, paths lead up on to the moors, where there are abundant traces of the region's prehistoric settlers.

Bellever to Manaton

❸ Return to Postbridge and turn right on the B3212 for ¾ mile, then take a minor road on the right signposted to Widecombe in the Moor. The fair, immortalised in a folk song, takes place on the second Tuesday in September. The village's 14th-century St Pancras Church, known as 'the cathedral of the moor' because of its large interior, contains a painted rood screen and eye-catching carved roof bosses. The huge tower is a later addition, said to have been built with donations from tin miners.

❹ Take the B3387 towards Bovey Tracey. The road climbs from the sheltered East Webburn valley to Haytor Rocks. From the car park on the right just beyond Haytor, walk up to the rocks for one of the finest views in southern Britain. Back on the road, continue downhill towards the Bovey valley, turning left towards Manaton at the bottom of the hill. Less than a mile farther on, a narrow road on the left leads to a car park in Yarner Wood National Nature Reserve, which is a haven for small birds.

Continue over Trendlebere Down to Manaton. The car park, a right turn at the minor crossroads in the centre of the village, signposted to the parish hall, is a popular starting point for many fine and bracing Dartmoor walks.

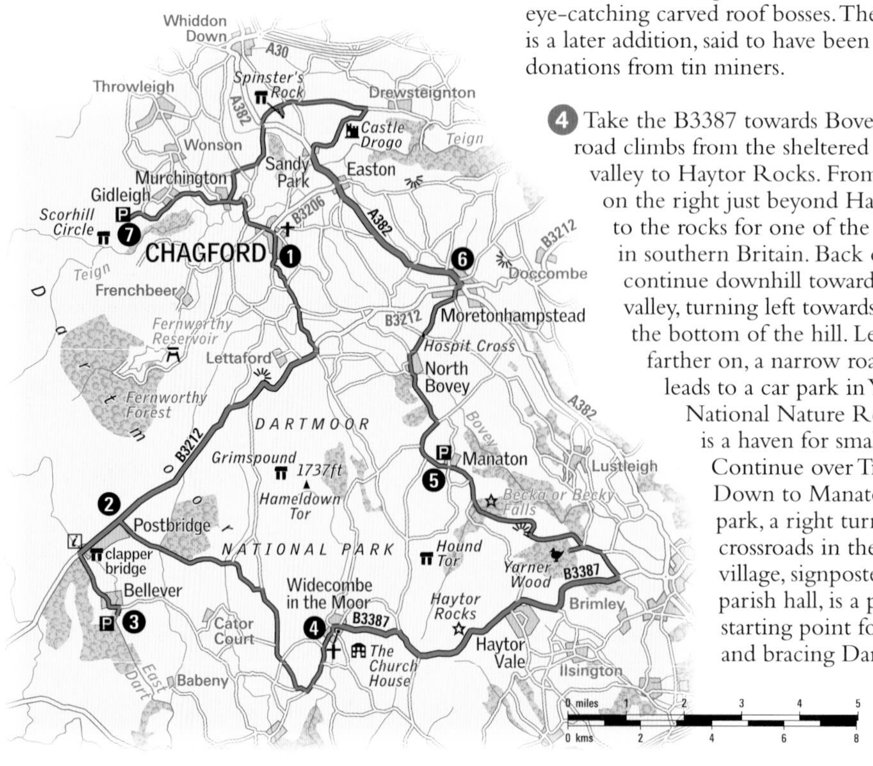

WIDECOMBE IN THE MOOR

Manaton to Scorhill

5 Drive back to Manaton crossroads and turn right to North Bovey, a typical Devon village with thatched cottages grouped around a green. Continue along the lane signposted to Moretonhampstead, where there has been a settlement since Saxon times. It was an important staging post in the days of horse-drawn transport. The charming town lies in the Wray valley and was largely rebuilt after a disastrous fire in the 19th century – although some fine almshouses dating back to the 17th century survived.

6 From Moretonhampstead town centre, take the A382 towards Exeter. At a minor crossroads in the hamlet of Sandy Park, a short distance beyond the bridge over the Teign, turn right to Castle Drogo, a 20th-century house (NT) designed by the architect Sir Edwin Lutyens and one of his most remarkable works. Billed by the National Trust as 'the last castle to be built in England', it has a medieval look combined with more modern comfort. Continue to a T-junction and turn left, then where the road divides fork left on to a lane. The road passes Spinster's Rock, a tomb dating from between 3500 and 2500 BC. Cross the A382 and follow the signs towards Gidleigh. Turn right at the T-junction in Murchington, and keep straight on to Scorhill. A footpath from the car park leads up to Scorhill Circle, a ring of 23 standing stones erected in the Bronze Age. Several cairns lie close by, and the entire landscape is scattered with remnants of its ancient inhabitants.

Scorhill to Chagford

7 Return past Gidleigh to Murchington T-junction, then follow the signs to Chagford. The lane drops then climbs steeply before a final descent to Chagford's ancient bridge over the River Teign.

DEVON

8 TOTNES

TOUR LENGTH 71 miles

Explore the lush tranquillity of south Devon, where sub-tropical plants flourish in the mild climate of the Kingsbridge estuary. The rugged headlands of Bolt Head, Prawle Point and Start Point provide a dramatic contrast to the gentler fringes of Start Bay.

Totnes to Harford Moor

1 The remains of a Norman castle set on a grassy mound overlook the River Dart in the charming market town of Totnes. The river meanders between orchards and rich red farmland before reaching the sea at Dartmouth.

To begin the drive, take the A385 signposted to Plymouth and drive to Dartington. The Dartington Cider Press Centre, shops and restaurants set in converted stone farm buildings, specialises in British artefacts, including jewellery, pottery and Dartington glassware. The gardens at medieval Dartington Hall are open daily. Continue on the A385 for 2 miles to Tigley, then turn left on the road signposted to Harberton. After ½ mile, bear left at the T-junction and then turn right at the crossroads, towards Plymouth.

2 At Avonwick take the left fork signposted to Ugborough (A3121). After nearly 3 miles take a right turn into Ugborough, a village of slate-roofed, whitewashed houses round a wide square. St Peter's Church, which fills the south side of the square, has a superb 15th-century screen painted with saints. Drive through the square, go straight over the road at the bottom, then fork right to Bittaford. Go under the A38 and turn left at the next junction on the B3213 towards Ivybridge. After 1½ miles turn right, signposted Harford, up Cole Lane, the next right turn after the road to the station. After ½ mile turn right over the railway bridge towards Harford and Lukesland.

KINGSBRIDGE ESTUARY

The lane winds for 2¼ miles between steep, tree-lined banks, with the swell of Dartmoor rising to the right and the slopes of Hanger Down to the left. In Harford, turn right at the church towards Harford Moor. A gate gives access to a gravelled parking area and the moor – with spectacular views. If the weather is good, you can see as far as the South Devon coast.

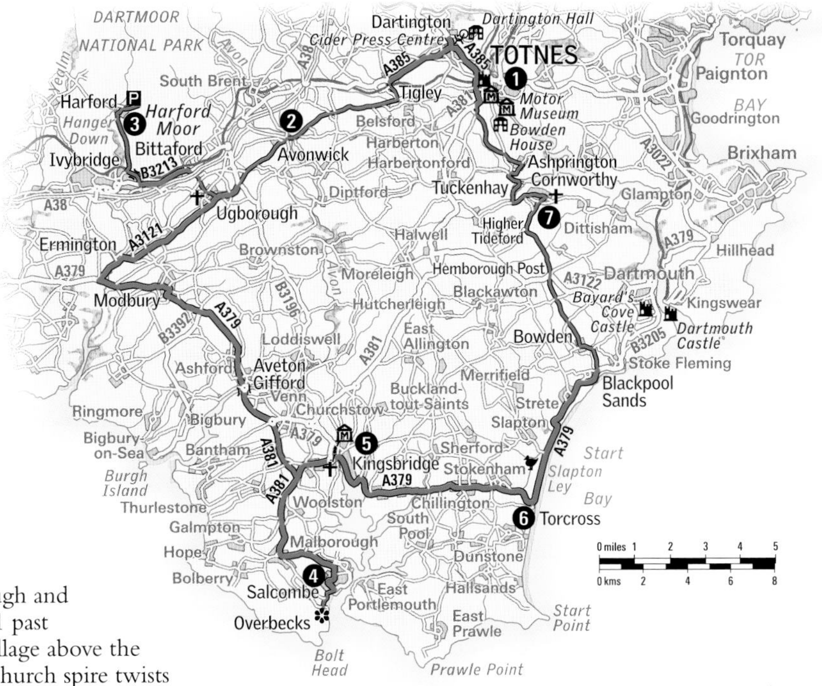

Harford Moor to Salcombe

3 Return to Ugborough and turn right on the A3121 past Ermington, a hillside village above the Erme river, where the church spire twists like a jester's cap. Turn left on the A379 to Modbury, noted for its many antiques shops. Most of the houses along Modbury's steep main street are Georgian, many of them slate-hung on the upper floors in the local style. Continue for 4 miles, skirting Aveton Gifford, where the road crosses the River Avon by a medieval causeway; 1¼ miles farther on go straight ahead at a roundabout signposted A381 to Salcombe. After 1½ miles turn right at a T-junction on the A381 to Salcome, at the mouth of the Kingsbridge estuary, where the harbour is filled with yachts and dinghies. Narrow streets along the waterfront are lined with small boatyards. With the harbour to your left, follow the coast road signposted to Sharpitor, and continue to Overbecks Museum and Garden (NT). The sub-tropical coastal garden has lovely views and surrounds a fine Edwardian house that was home to the inventor, Otto Overbeck. The House serves as a museum for his collections and inventions, including health-giving machines and musical instruments.

Salcombe to Slapton Ley

4 From Salcombe follow the A381 to Kingsbridge, which stands at the head of a deep estuary cut by a host of tiny creeks and fed by many small streams. The estuary ends at a small harbour, from which Fore Street, lined with a medley of old buildings, rises steeply to the top of the town. Just beside St Edmund's Church is The Shambles, a covered walk. The Cookworthy Museum of Rural Life is named after William Cookworthy, who was born in the town in 1705. Cookworthy was first Englishman to discover the English source of China clay, and learn the Chinese secret of making true porcelain.

5 From Kingsbridge follow the A379 towards Dartmouth to Torcross, a former fishing village protected from the waves by a massive boulder wall. The road runs along a shingle bank dividing the freshwater lake of Slapton Ley from the sea.

Slapton Ley to Totnes

6 Continue on the A379, following Start Bay as far as the golden crescent of Blackpool Sands. Turn left after a stone bridge on a road marked 'No through road for vehicles over 6ft wide'. In Bowden turn right, signposted to Halwell. Go straight on at the crossroads (no signs), and at the next junction turn right, then first left for Hemborough Post. At a T-junction turn right and after 50m, on a bend by a pub, turn left and follow signs to Higher Tideford, Cornworthy, Tuckenhay and Ashprington.

7 At Cornworthy the remains of an abbey gatehouse loom above the road, with the tower of St Peter's Church ahead. Tuckenhay stands at the top of a quiet tidal creek of the River Dart; former mills and wharves used for exporting road stone are reminders of the village's once thriving rural industry. At Ashprington follow the road as it makes a sharp dogleg turn to the left. After 2 miles turn right on the A381 to Totnes.

DEVON

9 LYNTON

TOUR LENGTH 37 miles

The coastline around Lynton is dramatic. Steep escarpments tower above the shore. Rocky coves are isolated by steep slopes cloaked in oak woods. Inland lie wild moors, tumbling streams and lush wooded valleys.

Lynton to Malmsmead

1 Perched on cliffs high above its sister village of Lynmouth, Lynton has prospered in spite of its inaccessibility. Two hundred years ago, Romantic poets Wordsworth, Shelley and Coleridge were attracted to the tiny hamlet in a wild setting. By the middle of the 19th century, Lynton had become a thriving holiday resort. Today, it is still charmingly Victorian and the cliff railway, built in 1890, remains in constant use. Explore the town on foot from the car park in Cross Street.

For the drive, turn right opposite the town hall, follow the road downhill to a T-junction and turn sharp left on the B3234 into Lynmouth, with its picturesque harbour and thatched cottages. In 1952, the village was devastated by a flood that swept away buildings and bridges and claimed 34 lives. Turn left over the East Lyn river on the A39, signposted to Minehead, climbing up Countisbury Hill, 305m (1,000ft) above the sea. Continue to County Gate, where there are superb views of the hills and wooded valleys fringing Exmoor.

2 About ¼ mile farther on from County Gate, turn right to the hamlet of Oare, in Somerset. The novelist R.D. Blackmore's grandfather was rector of the 15th-century church here and this is where Blackmore's fictional heroine, Lorna Doone, was shot during her wedding ceremony. Turn right at the T-junction in front of the church and continue to Malmsmead. Cross the 17th-century packhorse bridge over Badgworthy (pronounced badgery) Water.

Malmsmead to Hunter's Inn

3 Continue along the lane, following the East Lyn river through a steep-sided valley of oak woods. At a crossroads in Brendon, a village of whitewashed cottages, go straight ahead.

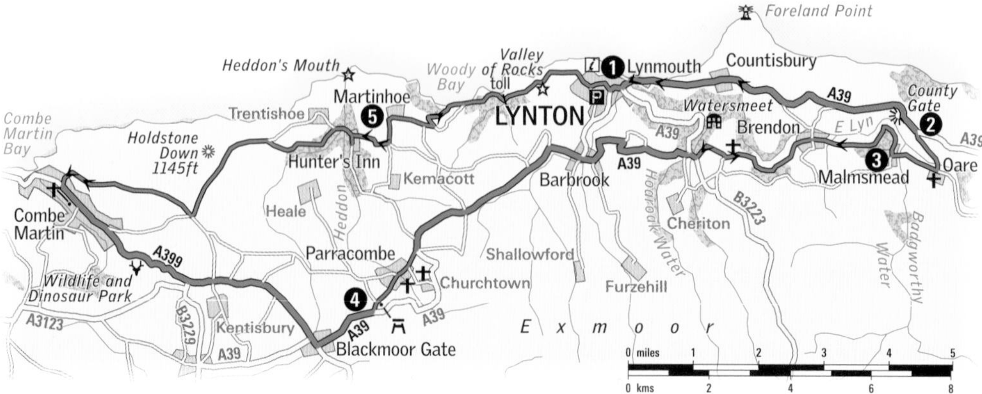

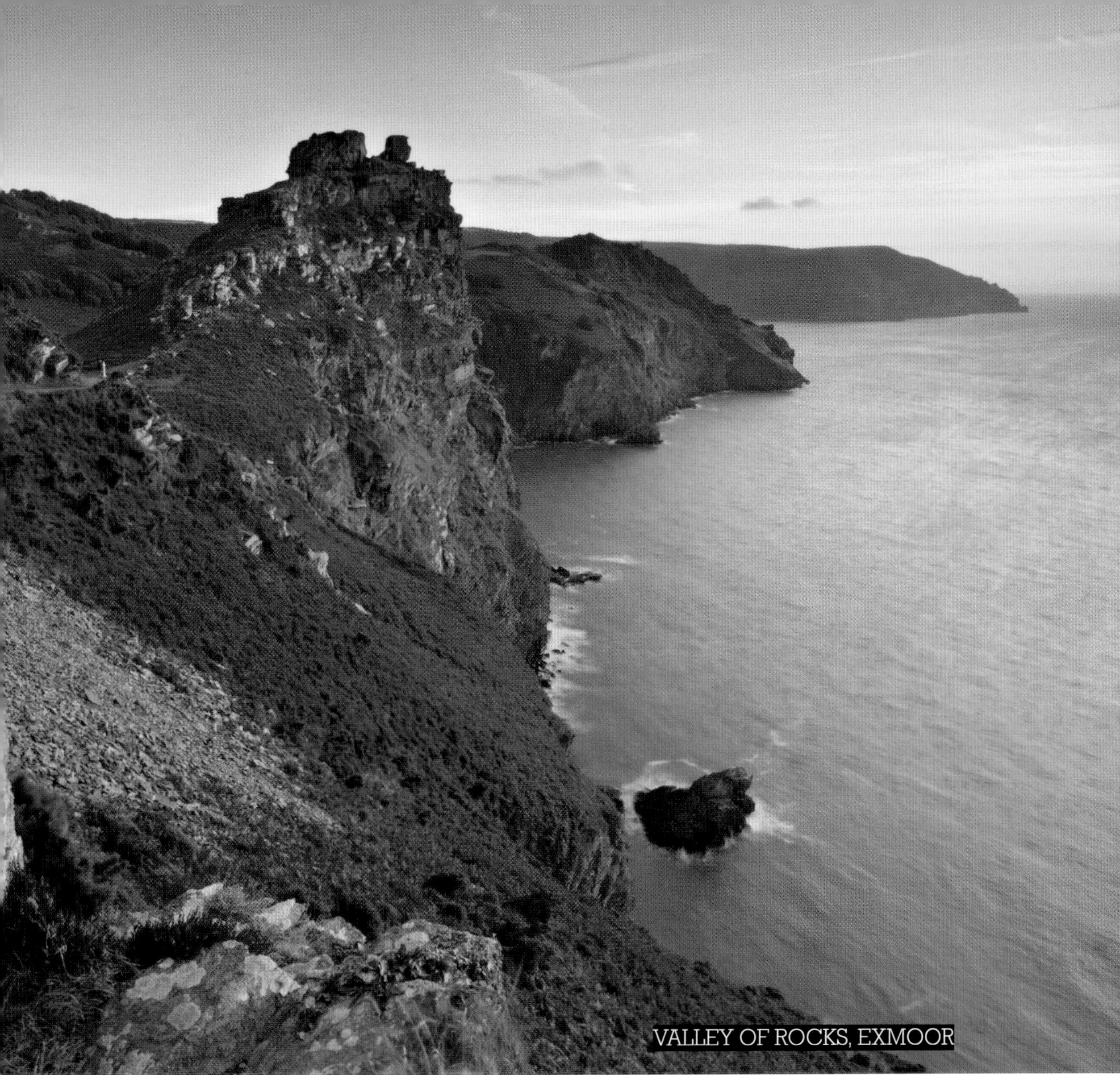
VALLEY OF ROCKS, EXMOOR

Climbing from the valley, the road passes Brendon church, 3 miles distant. Turn right at the T-junction. At the bottom of the hill, turn right and immediately left on the A39. After 6 miles, turn right to Parracombe. Reached by a bridleway from the village is St Petrock's Church – its Georgian interior almost unchanged for two centuries.

4 Follow the road through Parracombe back on to the A39 and turn right. At Blackmoor Gate turn right on the A399 towards Combe Martin. After 3½ miles, the Wildlife and Dinosaur Park combines commercial attractions with wildlife conservation.

Continue to Combe Martin, where the Pack o' Cards inn is rumoured to have been built as early as 1690. It has 52 windows arranged over four storeys, each with 13 doors. Turn right up Shute Lane, 100m beyond the inn. From here, the lanes towards Lynton are narrow, tortuous and sometimes very steep. After 2 miles, turn left at a crossroads, signposted to Hunter's Inn, a lodge set in the heart of the beautiful Heddon Valley, one of the deepest valleys in England. From Holdstone Down there are views along the coast before the road descends into a wooded valley.

Hunter's Inn to Lynton

5 Take the unmarked lane to the right of Hunter's Inn. After climbing steeply from the valley, turn left for Woody Bay, past Martinhoe. Keep left at the fork, then turn sharp left down hairpin bends to pass the Woody Bay Hotel. The steep and narrow lane winds on through oak woods high above the sea to a toll road through the Valley of Rocks, where extraordinary jagged rock formations were created during the most recent Ice Age. Beyond the valley car park the road returns to Lynton.

DORSET

The Channel tides wash ancient treasures from the county's southern coast, creating beaches of World Heritage wonder. To the north, a gentle landscape still bears the scars of the early English tribes.

10 LYME REGIS

TOUR LENGTH 57 miles

Marine wildlife and abundant beach fossils are a feature of the West Dorset Heritage Coast, accessible from the southern stretch of the drive. Inland, the route crosses into the East Devon countryside, extending to picturesque Branscombe.

Lyme Regis to Netherbury

1 Lyme Regis became a fashionable seaside retreat in the late 18th and early 19th centuries. Fossil-hunters are drawn to the shores around Lyme, which are made up of loose blue lias, a kind of limestone that is rich in fossils.

Follow the A3052 from Lyme Regis towards Charmouth. Where the road meets a roundabout leading to the A35, turn right on a minor road to the village, and just beyond it, fork right along Stonebarrow Lane. On the right, after a cattle grid, is a car park that gives access to walks along the Charmouth cliffs and up to Golden Cap, the highest point on England's south coast.

2 Return to the junction at the end of Stonebarrow Lane and turn right. At the A35, turn right then immediately left to Whitchurch Canonicorum. The Church of St Candida and Holy Cross, dating from the 12th century, is the only parish church in England to contain the bones of its patron saint, a Saxon woman said to have been killed by Danish raiders.

Go straight on at the village crossroads, signposted to Shave Cross. Following signs to Bridport, turn left on the A35 through Chideock. Turn left on the B3162 to Bridport. The town has been a rope-making centre since medieval times, but 'Bridport daggers', or hangmen's nooses, are no longer made. Go straight on through Bridport, then turn left on the A3066 towards Beaminster.

3 After 4 miles, turn left to Netherbury. The village once had the greatest number of cider orchards in West Dorset. Today it continues the cider making tradition with its Netherbury cider, made from apples grown in an orchard bordering the River Brit and sold in local free houses. The second turn on the right by the bus shelter leads to the Netherbury village hall car park.

Netherbury to Birdsmoorgate

4 Return from Netherbury to the A3066 and turn left to Beaminster. Beaminster (pronounced Beminster) was rebuilt in honey-coloured stone after three fires, the most recent in 1781. Turn left on the B3163 to Broadwindsor. In the village centre take the B3164 towards Lyme Regis. The road climbs past Pilsdon Pen, one of the highest

VIEWS SOUTH ACROSS MARSHWOOD VALE

LEWESDON HILL FROM PILSDON PEN

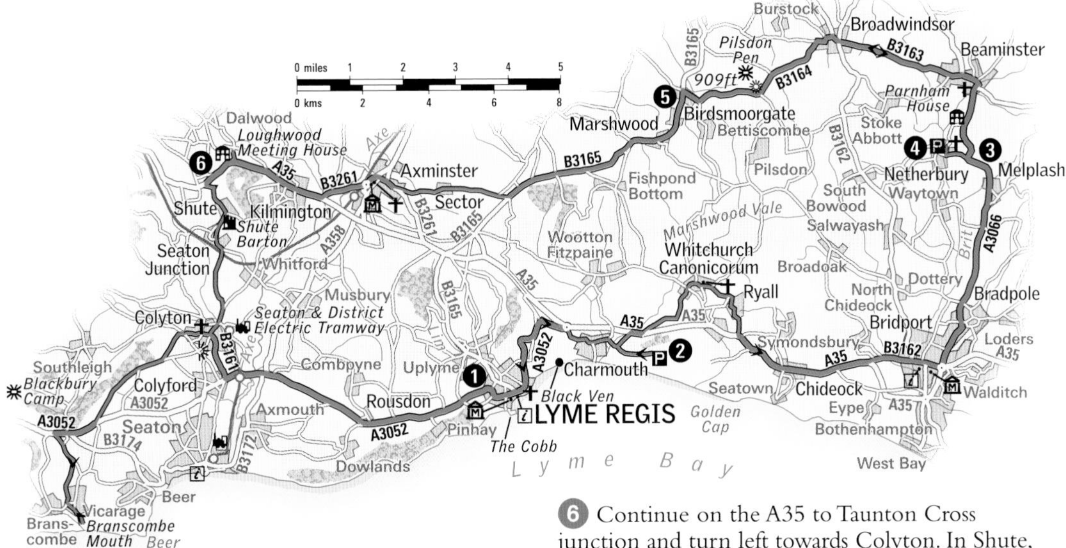

hills in Dorset at 277m (909ft), with views south across Marshwood Vale to Golden Cap, and inland to the Mendip Hills.

Birdsmoorgate to Branscombe

5 Turn left on the B3165 towards Lyme Regis. After 5 miles, turn right to Sector and continue to Axminster. The museum next to St Mary's Church includes a display on the history of carpet-making in the town. Continue past the church to a roundabout. Go straight ahead on the B3261, then right on the A35 towards Honiton. Just after a sign for Studhayes Cross, turn right to Loughwood Meeting House. This simple thatched building was put up in 1653 by Baptists from the nearby village of Kilmington.

6 Continue on the A35 to Taunton Cross junction and turn left towards Colyton. In Shute, turn left to Shute Barton (NT), a 14th-century turreted manor house with a Tudor gatehouse. Return to the road through Shute and continue to Colyton. The road leads past the northern terminus of the Seaton Tramway, which runs beside the Axe estuary. Turn right into Queen Street and follow signs for Sidmouth, turning right onto the A3052 after 3 miles. After the junction with the B3174 to Beer, take the second left signposted to Branscombe. Then at the first signposted junction turn right to Branscombe, believed to be England's longest village.

Turn right just beyond the Mason's Arms on a road marked 'Beach' to reach Branscombe Mouth on the South West Coast Path, a popular spot for walkers. For Lyme Regis, return to the A3052, turn right and follow the road through Colyford and over the River Axe.

DORSET

11 DORCHESTER

TOUR LENGTH 49 miles

From Dorset's handsome county town to the enigmatic Chesil Beach and Fleet Lagoon, the road continues, taking in heaths, forest and timeless villages of stone nestling deep in the southern countryside.

Dorchester to Abbotsbury

1 Dorchester's Roman legacy is still visible in the modern town. The sloping High Street forms part of the grid plan of the 1st-century settlement of Durnovaria; the Walks follow the line of the Roman ramparts. There is also evidence of earlier occupation in Maumbury Rings, a Neolithic henge, where the Romans created an amphitheatre, and the massive Iron Age hillfort of Maiden Castle to the south. Much later, another citizen left his mark. Dorchester is the 'Casterbridge' of Thomas Hardy's novels. Hardy lived there, at Max Gate, and his study is re-created in the Dorset County Museum.

Begin the drive following the B3150 towards Honiton. After 1 mile, turn left at a roundabout, signposted to Martinstown. At a T-junction turn right on the B3159 and go through the village. Where the road bends sharp right, turn left on a minor road leading past the Hardy Monument, a memorial to Admiral Thomas Masterman Hardy, Lord Nelson's flag captain at the Battle of Trafalgar in 1805.

2 Continue straight on at the crossroads and follow the road into Abbotsbury. Just west of Abbotsbury, signposted from the B3157, are sub-tropical gardens. At the end of the road is Chesil Beach, an 18 mile shingle bank comprising an estimated 180 billion pebbles. The bank encloses a lagoon called The Fleet.

Abbotsbury to Osmington

3 Return to the B3157 and turn right towards Weymouth. Where the road bends right in Portesham, go straight ahead on a minor road signposted to Dorchester. Take the first turn right, signposted to Upwey. Continue to a T-junction and turn right on the B3159 into Upwey, where

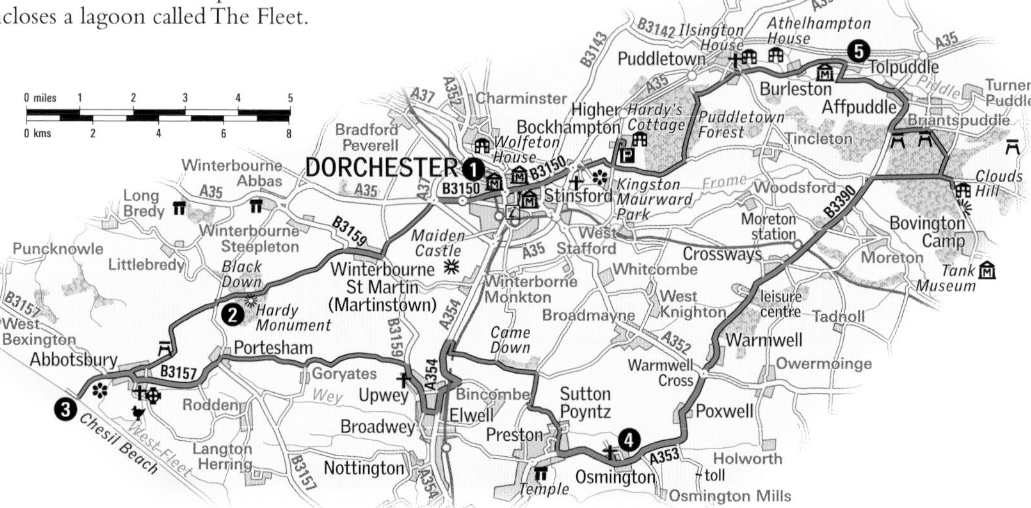

CHESIL BEACH

the Church of St Laurence has Jacobean carvings. The village takes its name from the River Wey – the source is a spring in the hill behind the village's wishing well. George III was a regular visitor to the well, which was famed for its medicinal waters. The seating dates from 1887 and was built to commemorate Queen Victoria's Golden Jubilee.

Follow the road to the A354 and turn left, then take the second right turn, signposted to Came Down. At the crossroads, turn right towards Preston, then fork left to Sutton Poyntz. Turn left at the T-junction on the A353 and continue to Osmington.

Osmington to Higher Bockhampton

4 Carry on through Osmington to the roundabout and go straight ahead on the B3390, continuing for some 5 miles. After a watercress farm on the left, turn right at the crossroads and right again to Clouds Hill. T.E. Lawrence bought the house (NT) in 1925 when he was stationed at nearby Bovington Camp. There he wrote *The Seven Pillars of Wisdom,* his epic account of his time in the East. The house is open from March to November, noon to 5pm (or dusk).

Go back to the T-junction and turn left then first right. Turn left towards Briantspuddle and at the crossroads turn left to a T-junction with the B3390. Turn right into Affpuddle and left into Tolpuddle. The Tolpuddle Martyrs held protest meetings in 1833 under the sycamore tree that still stands on the village green. A museum in the TUC Memorial Cottages of 1934 tells the Martyrs' story.

5 At the T-junction, just after the Martyrs Tree, turn left, passing the Tudor Athelhampton House on the right. Continue to Puddletown – 'Weatherbury' in Hardy's 1874 novel *Far from the Madding Crowd*. The Church of St Mary has a fine oak roof and a gallery, and Ilsington House displays a varied art collection.

Just after pedestrian traffic lights, turn left and go straight ahead on New Street. Immediately after the pedestrian crossing, turn left into Coombe Road and continue through Puddletown Forest and along Rhododendron Mile to the T-junction. Turn right, then right again at the crossroads towards Higher Bockhampton.

Thorncombe Wood car park is convenient for a visit to Hardy's Cottage (NT) where the writer was born and lived until the age of 34. Return to the crossroads, turn right and at the roundabout go straight ahead to drive back into Dorchester.

Signs of the times

Finding the way is easy today. Centuries ago the odd stone cross or timber post were all the help a lonely traveller could expect.

In 20 BC, the Emperor Caesar Augustus erected a gold-encased milestone near the centre of imperial Rome. It marked the centre of the civilised world, the place to which all roads led. It was the Romans who first introduced road signs into Britain following the Conquest in AD 43, in the shape of the milestones they placed along their superb road system. But when the Romans left Britain four centuries later, travellers were pretty much left to their own devices for the next 1,000 years. It was so dangerous to cross open country that the monastic communities took it upon themselves to set up stone crosses as waymarkers for wanderers. In the far west these were generally Celtic crosses with wheel heads, such as the ancient example that still stands at Rospletha near St Levan's, a few miles from Land's End. More easterly crosses tended to be Latin crosses with short crossbars – for example, the much-eroded Bennett's Cross on the Two Moors Way across Exmoor, or Nun's Cross on Dartmoor near the grim prison.

Wooden pointers

After the Dissolution of the Monasteries in the 1530s the old waymarks became neglected, and many travellers lost their lives in wild places. Some parishes erected inscribed timber posts as markers, but most folk were illiterate and still relied on landmarks. In 1667, under order of the local justices, guide-posts showing the way and distance to the nearest market town were erected on the moors where routes crossed, and this initiative soon spread widely across the country.

One of the oldest stands beside the A422 at Wroxton in Oxfordshire, carrying four sundials and the inscription: 'First given by Mr Fran. White in the year 1686'. Another venerable guide-post, on a crossroads in the Cotswolds just south of Chipping Campden where the B4081 meets the A44, points the direction with a finger. Erected by Joseph Izod in 1699, this is the oldest known fingerpost in Britain – although it's almost certainly a replacement for the original wooden finger, which would have rotted away after three centuries of exposure.

Fingerposts persisted along the roads, but the milestone was soon to make a return. By the 1740s many of the recently formed turnpike trusts were marking every mile of their new, well-surfaced highways with milestones. In 1773 the General Turnpike Act required trustees to erect signs informing travellers of the distance to the nearest town, and often to London. Even nowadays, where a newer road may have superseded a turnpike, the course of the old through route is often marked by a line of these evenly spaced milestones. Several still stand in the hedges along the old coaching road over Charnage and Mere Downs in Wiltshire, each stone inscribed 'XX miles from Sarum, XCIX from London'.

The old fingerposts still point the way at minor road junctions

EAST LULWORTH, DORSET

New directions

Milestones, guide-posts and fingerposts were good enough in the days of horse transport, but once the 20th century and the age of the motor car had dawned, the nation's system of road signs required a complete overhaul. At first, warning symbols, mileage indicators and directional posts were installed piecemeal by cycle clubs and voluntary motoring organisations, such as the Automobile Association (AA) and the Royal Automobile Club (RAC). Then the Motor Car Act of 1903 put the onus on local authorities. After the First World War, the now familiar black and white fingerposts were introduced by the Ministry of Transport, although county councils could design the 'fingers', posts and decorative finials on the top as they pleased – West Country posts, for example, were red with white lettering. Different councils chose finials in ring, ball or triangular shapes. Somerset County Council went for tetrahedral or pyramid-shaped finials; one can still be seen between Wells and Wookey Hole, and another opposite the Castle of Comfort Inn on the old hill road from Wells to Bristol.

By the 1960s these 'traditional' road signs had once more become inadequate to deal with increased traffic, and a government report of 1963 signalled the introduction of the European-style signs – large, colourful and easy to read – that are so familiar today. But the old fingerposts, as fit for purpose as ever for walkers, cyclists and slow-going drivers, still point out the way at minor road junctions. In fact, in 2005 English Heritage joined forces with the Department for Transport in asking local authorities to retain and repair these traditional fingerposts, now valued as 'attractive items of street furniture', which are 'unobtrusive and compatible with local character'.

Some road signs had to be changed to keep up with the times, though. Symbols showing a transmitting beacon and a lorry cancelled by a red stripe had to be installed at St Hilary, near the M4 in the Vale of Glamorgan, because so many drivers, misled by their onboard satellite navigation systems, were getting their monster trucks stuck fast in the narrow lane. It happens in the West Country, too. One Czech lorry driver got his vehicle so firmly wedged in a lane at Ivybridge in Devon that he couldn't open the doors. He spent three nights trapped in his cab before he was rescued. If he had just stuck to the road atlas and the fingerposts, this alarming catastrophe would never have happened.

DORSET

12 SWANAGE

TOUR LENGTH 46 miles

The double-looped drive from Swanage explores Dorset's Isle of Purbeck, from the hilltop ruins of Corfe Castle to the beautiful Lulworth Cove. Stranger attractions include the ghost village of Tyneham, a decaying monument to wartime command.

Swanage to Corfe Castle

1 The Isle of Purbeck has traded its marble since the Middle Ages, and until the 19th century Swanage was a busy port at the centre of this local industry. But since the arrival of the railway in 1895, Swanage has earned its living as a seaside resort. Its long sandy beach is safe and popular and the town is an excellent base for exploring the area, with its stunningly beautiful coastline, the dramatic ruins of Corfe Castle at its heart, and lovely old stone villages in and around its peaceful hills.

To begin the drive, head north along the seafront, following signs to Studland, and climb through the outer fringes of Swanage into the hills. Bear right and then turn right on the B3351 into Studland. Ahead are sandy beaches and the heath, a National Nature Reserve where golden-ringed dragonflies, blue marsh gentians and magenta Dorset heather are found.

2 Return on the B3351, climbing towards Corfe Castle with the Purbeck ridge to the left and, to the right, superb views of Purbeck woodland, Poole Harbour and its islands.

The road winds on until craggy Corfe Castle (NT) appears through a gap in the ridge. Built by William the Conquerer, the castle became a royal residence and prison in the reign of King John (1199-1216). Sold to the Bankes family in 1635, it withstood a seige in 1643 during the Civil War, Lady Mary Bankes, wife of Charles I's Lord Chief Justice, holding off the Parliamentarians for six weeks. But the castle could not be saved; it was destroyed after a second seige in 1646. Go under the railway bridge into the village of attractive houses with roofs tiled in Purbeck stone. Park in the castle car park to explore the village and castle.

Corfe Castle to Worth Matravers

3 From the car park turn right, skirting the base of the conical castle mound, and take the winding and wooded road to Church Knowle, a village of pretty stone-and-thatch houses. Continue to

LULWORTH COVE

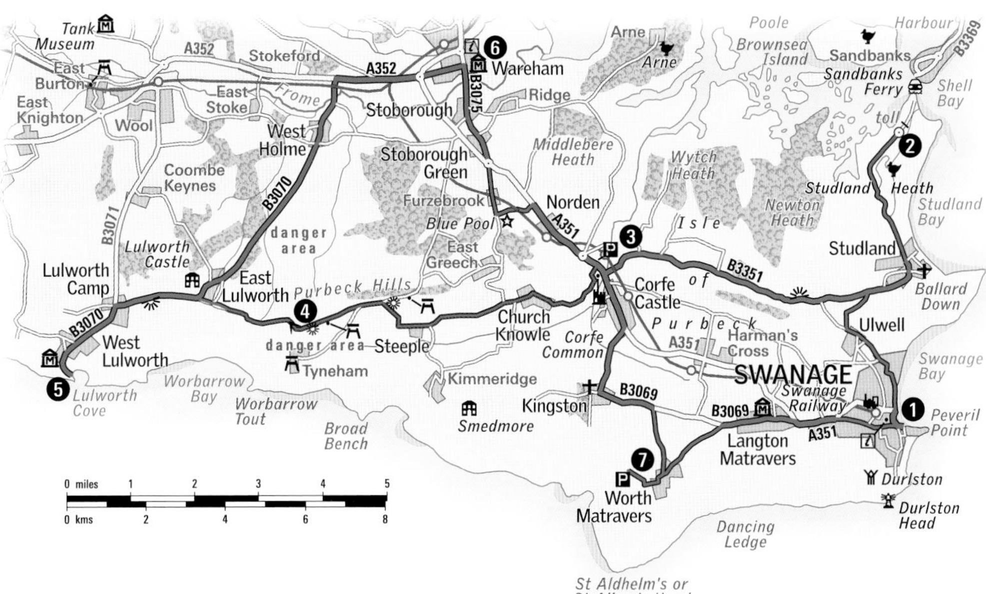

Steeple, tucked away to the left, from where the road climbs to a junction. Turn left towards East Lulworth. The road runs through Ministry of Defence land that may be subject to diversions during army manoeuvres. The village of Tyneham, off to the left, was commandeered as an army training ground during the Second World War. It was never returned to the parishioners and is now a ghost village, its buildings crumbling to ruins. The church is a museum, open to visitors most weekends.

❹ Continue along the crest of the hill past a picnic spot on the right before dropping down to East Lulworth. Lulworth Castle, designed as a hunting lodge early in the 17th century with fine views from its 30m (100ft) tower, stands in trees ahead. At the junction in East Lulworth, turn left and left again to Lulworth Camp. At the crossroads turn left on the B3070 to West Lulworth and Lulworth Cove. The circular little bay and weird rock formations attract many summer visitors. From its car park, a 1½ mile clifftop walk leads to Durdle Door, a dramatic limestone arch jutting out to sea.

❺ Return to East Lulworth and take the B3070 (also subject to diversions) to Wareham, through forest and across sandy heathland. Cross the River Frome and turn right on to the A352 for Wareham, going straight on at the roundabout for the town centre. The old town, built in Saxon times to guard the entrance to Poole Harbour, is still largely contained within its walls. The Saxon church of St Martin's, with its fragmented frescoes, houses an effigy of Lawrence of Arabia, recumbent in Arab dress. It was sculpted from Purbeck marble by official war artist Eric Kennington. Originally intended for St Paul's Cathedral or Westminster Abbey, the effigy was presented to St Martins by Lawrence's brother in 1939.

❻ Turn right on the B3075, recrossing the River Frome. Go through Stoborough to a roundabout. To visit the beautiful Blue Pool, take the second exit, to Furzebrook, cross over the railway and just beyond Furzebrook turn left. The pool is open from early March to the end of November from 10am to 5pm – later in summer. At other times, take the A351 to Corfe Castle.

Follow the A351 through Corfe Castle village and bear right on to the B3069, which rises steeply upwards to Kingston. Turn left along the crest towards Langton Matravers. Take the first turning right and right again at the Square and Compass pub. This unique pub has its own fossil museum, with specimens from Purbeck and farther afield.

Go through Worth Matravers. Challenging coastal walks begin close to the village. Take a left turn on the track just as the road bends sharp right at Renscombe Farm for the car park and access to pathways.

Worth Matravers to Swanage

❼ Retrace the route back through Worth Matravers and go straight on past the Square and Compass to the B3069. Turn right for Langton Matravers, where the Coach House museum tells the story of Purbeck marble, which is used to decorate many churches and cathedrals including Westminster Abbey. From Langton Matravers, turn right on to the A351 back to Swanage.

DORSET

13 SHERBORNE

TOUR LENGTH 39 miles

A two-county tour, beginning in the beautiful Dorset town of Sherborne, slipping into Somerset at Stoford and back again just past South Cadbury. The countryside has a timeless flavour, its verdant hills and valleys set with tranquil villages of honey-coloured stone.

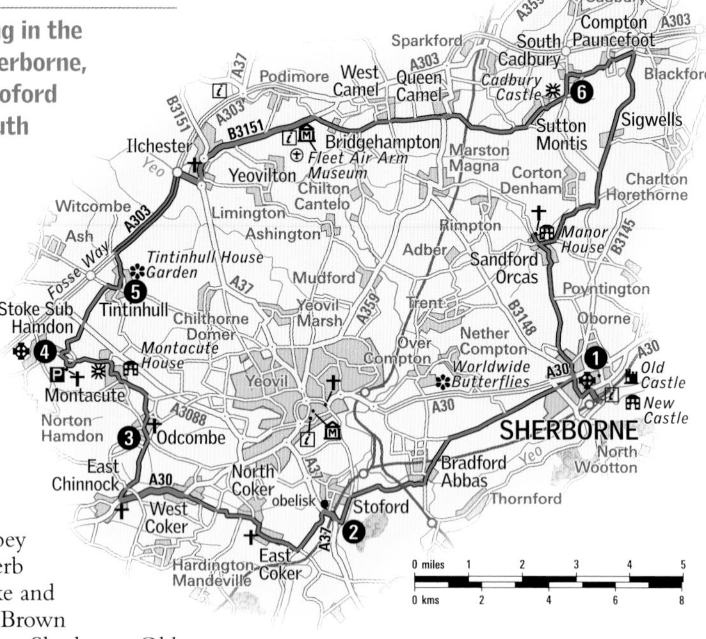

Sherborne to Stoke Sub Hamdon

1 Sherborne retains in miniature the air of the cathedral city that it was in Saxon times. Its narrow streets are lined with medieval buildings, dominated by the abbey church of St Mary, with its superb 15th-century fan vaulting. A lake and gardens designed by Capability Brown separate the ruins of 12th-century Sherborne Old Castle from Sherborne New Castle, built in 1594 by Sir Walter Raleigh. Relics of more ancient times, particularly Iron Age hillforts, dot the nearby wooded hills above villages built of locally quarried hamstone.

Join the A30 towards Yeovil and fork left towards Bradford Abbas, crossing over the A352. At the fork bear left to pass Bradford Abbas. After crossing the bridge over the River Yeo, turn right through Clifton Maybank to Stoford. At the T-junction around 50m after the narrow bridge, turn left towards Melbury to meet the A37.

2 Turn right, over the railway, to a junction below a stone obelisk, one of four follies marking the boundaries of privately owned Barwick Park. Turn left at the junction towards Sutton Bingham. After an avenue of oaks, turn right to East Coker, its thatched cottages clad with roses and wisteria. The ashes of the poet T.S. Eliot, who died in 1965, are buried at St Michael's Church.

About ¼ mile beyond East Coker, turn left towards West Coker and descend to a crossroads. Take the road ahead to West Coker. At the junction with the A30 turn left, signposted to East Chinnock. Pass under a bridge and turn right opposite a church on to a steep road, following signs to Odcombe.

3 Turn left through the village, signposted to Stoke Sub Hamdon. At the next crossroads turn right and follow the signs to Montacute. The hamstone Montacute House (NT) was built in the 1590s by Sir Edward Phelips, Speaker of Parliament and prosecutor of Guy Fawkes after the Gunpowder Plot of 1605.

Follow the road through the village towards Stoke Sub Hamdon. Soon after the school on the right, bear left on to a slip road to the left of St Mary's Church at East Stoke where it's possible to park. Footpaths lead to some disused quarries from which the honey-gold limestone known as hamstone was cut. Energetic walkers can take the track past woodland to the conical St Michael's Hill, at Montacute. St Michael's Tower on the top, built in 1760 as an observatory, is privately owned but is open to the public. A spiral staircase winds to the top of the 13m (45ft) tower, which overlooks south Somerset. The windows are barred but still give lovely views.

Stoke Sub Hamdon to South Cadbury

4 Turn left on to the main road. After around 300m turn sharp right on Windsor Lane, then first left on to a winding lane that passes under the A3088. At the junction turn right to the honey-stoned Domesday village of Tintinhull. Turn left into St Margaret's Road, passing 13th and 14th-century St Margaret's Church, and bear left at the junction. Turn right on Queen Street for Tintinhull House Garden (NT), where formal garden 'rooms' are divided by walls and hedges of box and yew.

MONTACUTE HOUSE

5 Return to the junction and turn right. At the junction with the A303 turn right. After 1 mile follow the signs into Ilchester and take the B3151 towards Sparkford. Pass the Royal Naval Air Station at Yeovilton on the right and then turn right to the Fleet Air Arm Museum, where the many exhibits include the prototype Concorde 002. At the next junction turn right and follow the hedged road to Queen Camel. At the junction bear left then right and follow the road into Sutton Montis. Turn right on the hedged road to South Cadbury. The hillfort, built around the 3rd century bc, was refortified by the Britons in the late 5th and early 6th centuries ad as a defence against the Saxons. This was the time of the legendary Kind Arthur, and Cadbury Castle is one of the purported sites of Camelot. A timber feasting hall, fit for a king, is one of the discoveries on the site.

South Cadbury to Sherbourne

6 Follow the road from South Cadbury to Compton Pauncefoot. Continue beyond the village on Hockley Lane for ½ mile to the junction and turn sharp right. Continue for 3 miles through the rolling countryside on the Somerset/Dorset border, and beyond a sharp right bend, fork right, signposted to the ancient village of Corton Denham. Follow the signs to Sandford Orcas. At the T-junction in the village, turn right to see two lovely hamstone buildings: the reputedly haunted Sandford Orcas Manor House, built in the 1550s by Edward Knoyle, and St Nicholas Church, dating from the 13th century. The font is Norman, although its cover is of a later date, and the south chapel, which was added in the 15th century, has a beautiful carved oak ceiling with square panels. Return to the village junction and continue ahead to Sherborne.

SOMERSET

Rising above the watery Somerset Levels, the Mendip Hills are punctured by atmospheric limestone caverns and the great gorge at Cheddar. Medieval towns and ancient sites stretch away to Exmoor in the west.

14 DULVERTON

TOUR LENGTH 48 miles

This tour of the Exmoor National Park passes tiny villages of thatched cottages, dotted among sylvan valleys and lonely heaths, while taking in some fine coastal views.

Dulverton to Winsford

1 Dubbed the 'southern gateway' to Exmoor, Dulverton lies in the wooded Barle valley. Narrow streets cluster on the east side of a bridge dating from the Middle Ages, when the woollen industry flourished. Follow the B3223, signposted to Lynton, hugging the River Barle for 1 mile. The narrow road bends right signposted Tarr Steps, climbing out of woods on to moorland grazed by sheep and ponies. Cross a cattle grid and turn left to Tarr Steps. Follow the road down to a T-junction and turn left to a car park. A short walk leads to the oldest and longest clapper bridge in the country.

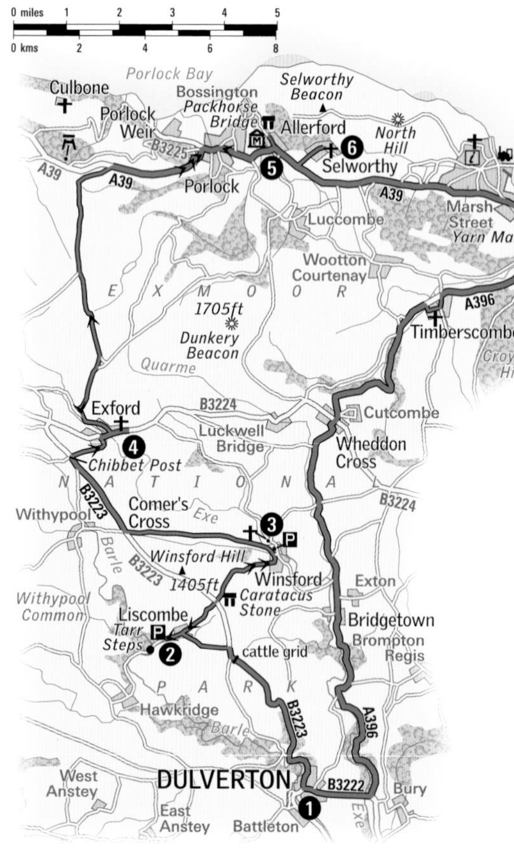

2 Return up the lane, fork left and at a crossroads with the B3223 go straight on and continue to Winsford. Pass the Old Oak inn, turn right by the memorial cross. Immediately left is a car park, opposite a garage – a popular starting point for walkers exploring the surrounding countryside.

Winsford to Selworthy

3 With the memorial cross on your left, drive on through a ford to reach the B3223 at Comer's Cross. Turn right on to the B3223. At the next crossroads, Chibbet Post, turn right and descend to Exford. Turn right across the bridge over the River Exe and follow the B3224 for ½ mile uphill towards Taunton to visit the mainly 16th-century church of St Mary Magdalene. Return down the B3224. At the Crown Hotel fork right to Porlock.

4 After ½ mile the road climbs on to the moor. Dunkery Beacon, the highest point on Exmoor, is on the right. At the T-junction, turn right on to the A39 for the steep descent to Porlock. Porlock Weir is 1½ miles west on the B3225; from there, a 2 mile footpath leads to England's smallest church, at Culbone. Climb steeply out of Porlock on the A39. Turn left into Allerford.

5 Return to the A39. Take the next left turning to the National Trust village of Selworthy. The creamy yellow, cob-walled cottages, with tall round chimneys, protruding bread ovens and thatched roofs, were built by Sir Thomas Acland in 1828 for retired Holnicote estate workers. One is a tearoom, another a National Trust shop.

Selworthy to Dunster

6 Return to the A39 and turn left, bypassing the busy resort of Minehead. About a mile beyond Minehead, turn right at the traffic lights on the A396 to Dunster. Pass the octagonal yarn market and turn right below the Norman castle along Church Street and into West Street. Turn left into Park Street; the village car park is on the left.

Dunster to Dulverton

7 Continue on the A396 to Timberscombe; turn left into the village. Follow the road to the right, back to the A396. At Wheddon Cross crossroads, go straight on, dropping down into the valleys of the Quarme and Exe. The road winds beside the Exe for 5 miles before a sharp right turn onto the B3222 leads over the river and back to Dulverton.

15 WELLS

TOUR LENGTH 39 miles

Rising from a low-lying plain, the Mendip Hills, with their spectacular limestone caves and deep gorges, cut a broad swathe through Somerset. Southeast of the range is Wells, a medieval jewel of a city, and Glastonbury, with its aura of ancient otherworldliness.

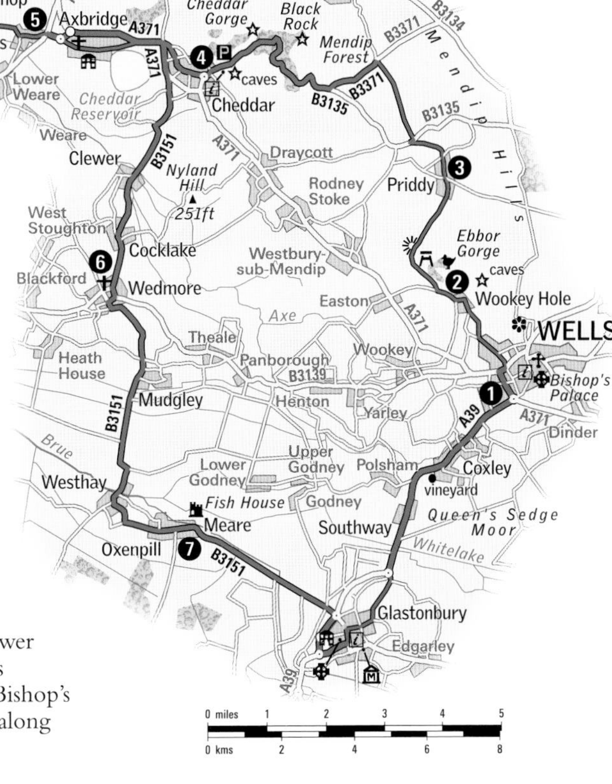

Wells to Priddy

❶ Wells is England's smallest city, dominated by its awe-inspiring cathedral. Its west front features around 400 carved figures that were originally brightly painted with gold detailing. The nave is dominated by mighty scissor arches, built to support the central tower, which was heightened and given a spire in 1338. The weight of the tower caused supporting pillars to sink; the arches proved the building's elegant saviour. The Bishop's Palace and 14th-century church buildings along Vicar's Close add to the city's medieval atmosphere.

Leave Wells on the one-way High Street; follow signs to Glastonbury. Within a mile turn right on Wells bypass. Turn right at the T-junction towards Bath, then immediately left at the sign for Wookey Hole. Drive through the village to the caves, inhabited between 35,000 BC and 12,000 BC. Three caves are open to the public, in one of which is the rock formation said to be the legendary Witch of Wookey. A hand-made paper mill still operates, using raw cotton and original Victorian machinery. As you leave Wookey Hole, a signpost warns that the narrow lane out of the village is 'unsuitable for charabancs'.

❷ About ¼ mile beyond the sign, fork right up a steep lane, marked only with a weight-limit sign. To the right Ebbor Wood hides a dramatic ravine, and the Mendip escarpment slopes away to the left. At the top of the hill, where the lane widens, stop at the car park on the left, from where the views stretch south to the Blackdown Hills and west around Bridgwater Bay to Exmoor. Sea mist sometimes seeps into the Levels from the Bristol Channel, marooning the hilltops.

Priddy to Cheddar Gorge

❸ In the village of Priddy, 2 miles farther on, the village green is the site of a busy sheep fair held every August since 1348, when drovers abandoned Wells to the Black Death and herded their flocks to this airy spot. A thatched stack of sheep hurdles is a reminder of the fair's medieval history. Drive through Priddy with the green on the left, and pass a campsite sign. Barely a mile farther on, turn right on to the B3135 and immediately left towards Charterhouse.

At the crossroads with the B3371, turn left to Cheddar, then right at the next T-junction, continuing ahead into Cheddar Gorge. The Waterworks car park, the first large layby on the right, has an information board and views of the gorge. In parts, the buckled limestone crags loom almost 152m (500ft) over the winding road. Within, a complex of caverns, etched by water and adorned with mineral marvels in the form of fabulously shaped stalagmites and stalactites, were once inhabited by prehistoric people. Today they are home to horseshoe bats. Visitors can purchase genuine cave-aged Cheddar cheese, made and stored as it was a century ago. Cox's Cave and Gough's Cave are open to the public every day except Christmas Eve and Christmas Day. Jacob's Ladder is a flight of 274 steps up the side of the gorge, leading to walks through rare limestone grassland, heath and woodlands where the Cheddar pink flourishes, a plant that is found only in the Mendips. ▷

SOMERSET

Cheddar Gorge to Compton Bishop

4 Continue along the B3135 to a mini-roundabout where the road emerges from the gorge. Bear right towards Axbridge. On meeting the A371, turn off by the petrol station at the junction and turn right towards Axbridge. Turn left on the road signposted to Axbridge town centre. Go through the town centre to rejoin the A371, signposted to Bridgwater and Exeter, immediately before the crossroads with the A38. Continue ahead through Cross; 1 mile along Webbington Road turn left on a small side road, Rackley Road. Parking is available about 100m down on the verge. Footpaths wend their way along the banks of the River Yeo, and other tracks to Wavering Down offer superb views of the prominent landmark of Glastonbury Tor.

Compton Bishop to Meare

5 Return to the junction with the A38, go straight across and follow the A371 towards Wells. South of Cheddar, take the B3151 to Wedmore, one of Somerset's finest small towns, set on a low ridge above the Levels. The town is a rich mix of Elizabethan, Georgian and later buildings. Alfred the Great signed a peace treaty here in AD 878 after repelling the Danish invasion of Wessex, a story told in modern stained glass in the Church of St Mary.

6 Continue on the B3151, Grants Lane, from the centre of Wedmore, following signs to Meare and Glastonbury. The road descends from the ridge to the Somerset Levels and runs between flood drainage channels. The villages of Westhay, Oxenpill and Meare merge across the flat land, with only the imposing Abbot's Fish House standing out in Meare.

Meare to Wells

7 Follow the B3151 to Glastonbury, the Avalon of Arthurian legend, hiding place of the Holy Grail and home to the world's largest annual music festival. Joseph of Arimathea is believed to have built England's first Christian church here, a little wooden chapel that was the forerunner of the abbey. By Saxon times, Glastonbury was one of the greatest centres of faith and learning in the land. Long before this, the tor was significant to the Celts, who constructed a path that spiralled to the top in the form of a labyrinth. The abbey ruins, tor and well attract many tourists. From Glastonbury town centre follow the signs for Wells, joining the A39 for the last few miles.

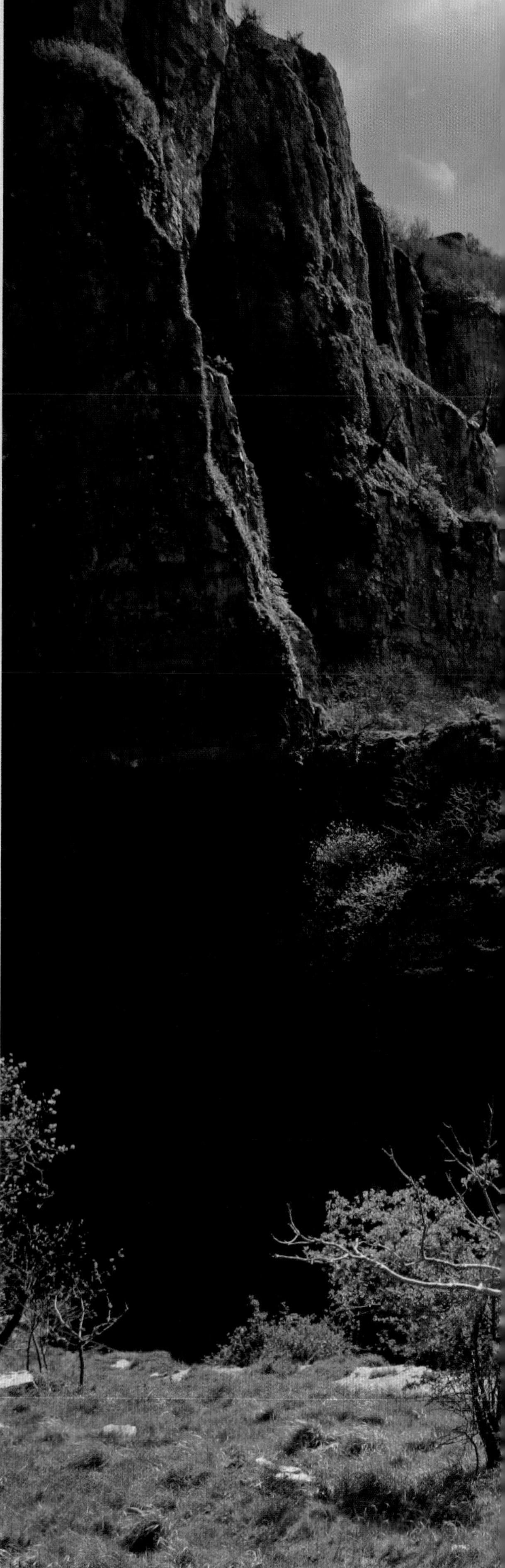

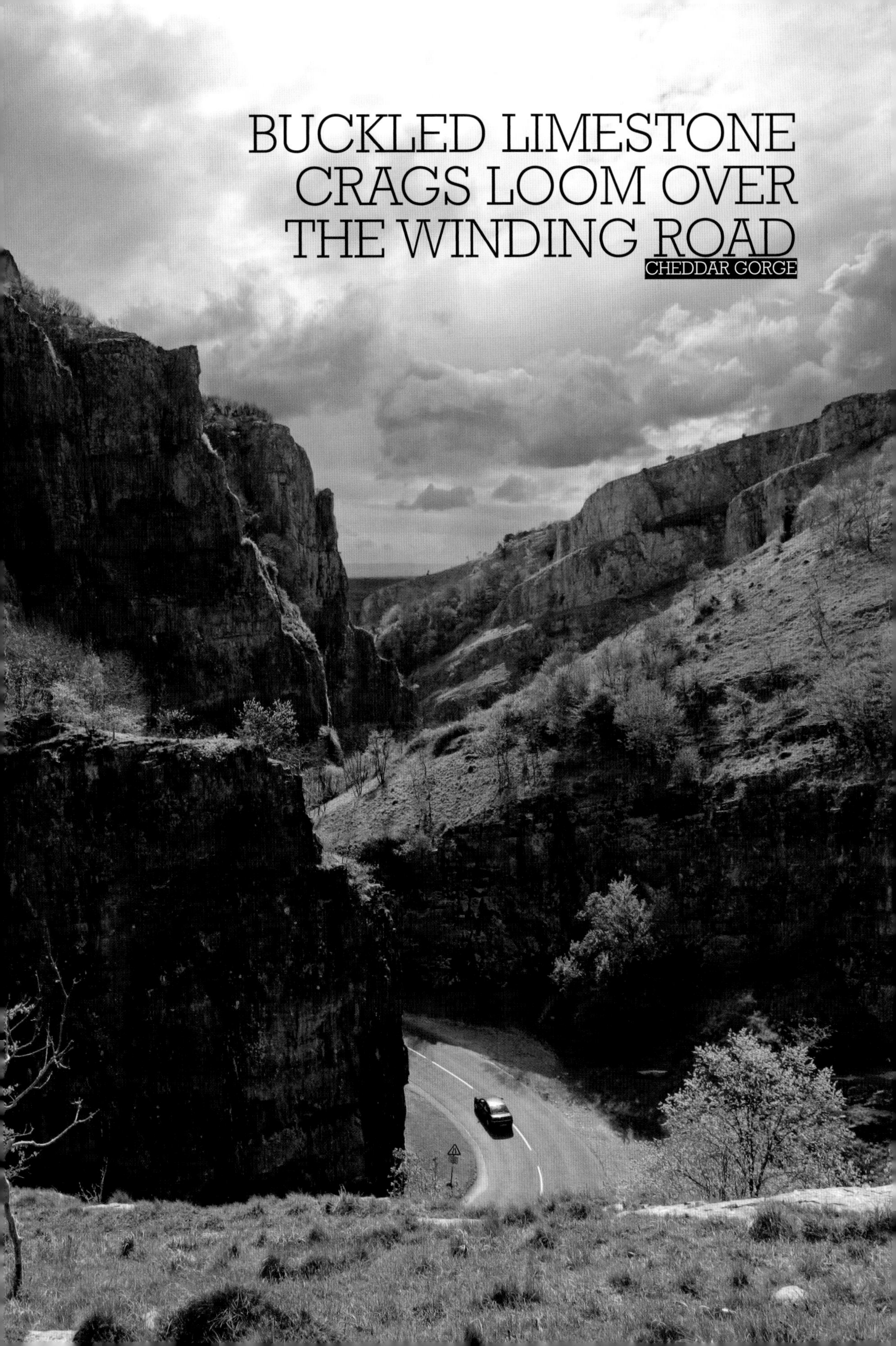
BUCKLED LIMESTONE
CRAGS LOOM OVER
THE WINDING ROAD
CHEDDAR GORGE

WILTSHIRE

The roads in England's most enigmatic county traverse a landscape both familiar and otherworldly, skirting fields of flax, rape and wheat to glimpse chalk hill carvings and the monuments of a forgotten people.

16 BRADFORD-ON-AVON

TOUR LENGTH 53 miles

A honey-coloured haven on the edge of the Cotswolds, Bradford-on-Avon was once a flourishing textile centre. Old manor houses and glorious limestone downs also lie within the compass of this drive, which strays into Somerset and Gloucestershire.

Bradford-on-Avon to Hinton Charterhouse

1 The mellow limestone buildings of Bradford-on-Avon rise from the banks of the river, where a scattering of 19th-century cloth mills recalls a past closely woven into the textile manufacturing industry. Further evidence is seen in the old clothiers' houses and weavers' cottages that line the hillside terraces. Follow the A363 over the bridge across the Avon. Continue on the B3109, passing a 14th-century tithe barn on the right. Cross the Kennet and Avon Canal over a humpback bridge and after 1 mile turn right to Westwood. At a T-junction turn right into Westwood. On the left is Westwood Manor (NT), a 15th-century stone manor house with a topiary garden, open a few afternoons a week in summer.

2 Descend a steep hill with views over the Avon valley. Just beyond Freshford, in Somerset, turn left towards Frome and Warminster. Continue up the other side of the valley and turn left on the A36, then take a right turn signposted to Hinton Charterhouse. In the village, go straight across the B3110, following the road to Wellow.

MELLOW BUILDINGS RISE FROM THE BANKS OF THE RIVER

BRADFORD-ON-AVON

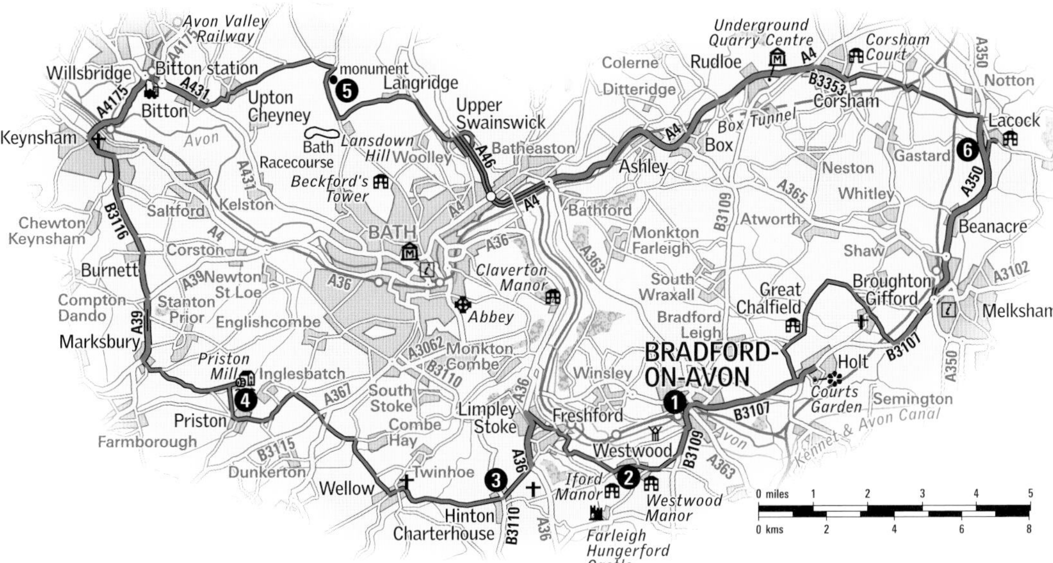

Hinton Charterhouse to Lansdown Hill

❸ Continue to a T-junction by the Rose and Crown. Turn right on the B3110 and then left to Wellow, where the Gothic church of St Julian contains some late 15th-century wall paintings. In the village turn right towards Bath and Combe Hay. Turn left on the road signposted to Dunkerton and cross the A367 at the Titfield Thunderbolt pub. Cross the B3115 on the road signposted to Priston Mill. At the next crossroads turn left for Priston and follow the signs to the early 18th-century watermill.

❹ Returning from the mill, fork right to Bath. At the next junction bear right and continue to Marksbury. Turn right on the A39. After 1 mile turn left on to the B3116 to Keynsham, and turn right by the church on the A4175 to Bitton. Just touching Gloucestershire, the road crosses the Avon by a lock and weir. At a roundabout in Willsbridge, turn right on the A431 towards Bath. To the left is Bitton station, the main stop on the Avon Valley Steam Railway. Just beyond Bitton, turn left on to the lane to Upton Cheyney; 2 miles beyond the village turn right at the junction. Opposite Bath Racecourse entrance turn left, signposted to Langridge, now back in Somerset. Park in a layby on the immediate right and follow footpaths across the racecourse (not on race days) and behind the golf club for a pleasant walk up Lansdown Hill.

Lansdown Hill to Lacock

❺ Follow the narrow road down through Langridge. Turn right at a T-junction and go through Upper Swainswick. At the T-junction turn right then left to join the Batheaston bypass towards Bath. Follow the A4 towards Chippenham, crossing back into Wiltshire from Somerset, through Box and past the towering portal of Box Tunnel, which is 1¾ miles long and was the world's longest railway tunnel when Brunel built it in 1837. Continue to Corsham. The Underground Quarry Centre, once a source of Bath stone, is on the right. In Corsham, turn right on the B3353 towards Melksham, passing behind Corsham Court, a 16th-century mansion, and follow the signs to Lacock. Turn right on the A350 and after ¾ mile turn left to Lacock. The unspoilt village of irregular, terraced stone and timber-framed buildings, with its broad streets, has been the setting for several television period productions. The village grew up at the gates of Lacock Abbey (NT), which retains its 13th-century cloisters and houses the Fox Talbot photographic museum.

Lacock to Bradford-on-Avon

❻ Rejoin the A350 towards Warminster. In Melksham, turn right on the B3107. After 2 miles turn right to Broughton Gifford; turn left by The Bell pub to cross the common. Turn left to Great Chalfield, where a moated manor (NT) with gabled façades and mullioned windows stands between the church and stables. With the manor on the right, follow the narrow road through farmland. Turn left to Holt, and left again at the T-junction beyond the manor gates. At the B3107, opposite the Tollgate Inn, turn left into Holt, where until the late 18th century cloth weavers settled disputes at The Courts (NT), now enjoyed for their fine gardens. Follow the B3107 back to Bradford-on-Avon.

WILTSHIRE

17 MARLBOROUGH

TOUR LENGTH 46 miles

Drive the sweeping chalk downland through the heart of Wiltshire, from the lovely town of Marlborough past the ancient monument of Avebury. Explore industrial heritage in Crofton, and the old forest of Savernake.

Marlborough to Avebury

1 Set in the peaceful Kennet valley, Marlborough is a town of ancient alleys, Georgian façades and coaching inns lining a wide and handsome main street. Two Roman roads crossed at Marlborough, and its prominence continued from Norman times, when William the Conqueror built a castle to the west, and a market town developed outside the castle walls. On the same site, the 6th Duke of Somerset built his graceful Castle House, now the centrepiece of an independent school.

Take the A4 towards Calne, and after 1 mile turn left on a minor road to Manton. Follow the road round to the right through the village. Just beyond Lockeridge is an area of land to the right liberally scattered with sarsen stones, or 'grey wethers' – the curious boulders left isolated on the land as the local geology evolved.

One mile farther on, turn right for East Kennett. Shortly after the village, turn left to rejoin the A4, which passes the great prehistoric mound of Silbury Hill. At Beckhampton roundabout turn right on to the A4361 to Avebury Stone Circle. Turn left for the National Trust car park.

Avebury to Ogbourne St George

2 Continue on the A4361 as it bends left to pass through the stone circle. After 4 miles, beyond Winterbourne Monkton, turn right on a minor road to Hackpen Hill, a downland route with views of a 27m (90ft) long white horse, cut into the hillside in 1838 to mark Queen Victoria's coronation. Just beyond the point where the road crosses the Ridgeway is a viewpoint parking area.

3 A couple of miles farther on, just after a telephone box and a right turn to Rockley, turn left on an unmarked minor road that twists over the hill and descends to Ogbourne Maizey, a village of brick, flint and thatch. Turn left on the A346 and, beyond Ogbourne St Andrew and Southend, turn left on a minor road and left again into Ogbourne St George.

Ogbourne St George to Great Bedwyn

4 Drive out of the village, turn left at the junction, go under the A346 and carry on to Aldbourne. The road leads over Round Hill Downs and through Woodsend. In Aldbourne, where the village green has an old pump, turn right on to the B4192. After 2 miles, just beyond Preston, turn right on to an unmarked road to Ramsbury, a cathedral town in Saxon times. Turn right at a T-junction to the village centre, then left by the Bell Inn towards Hungerford. Turn right to cross the Kennet and continue to Froxfield, where the almshouses are 17th century. Turn right on to the A4 towards Marlborough,

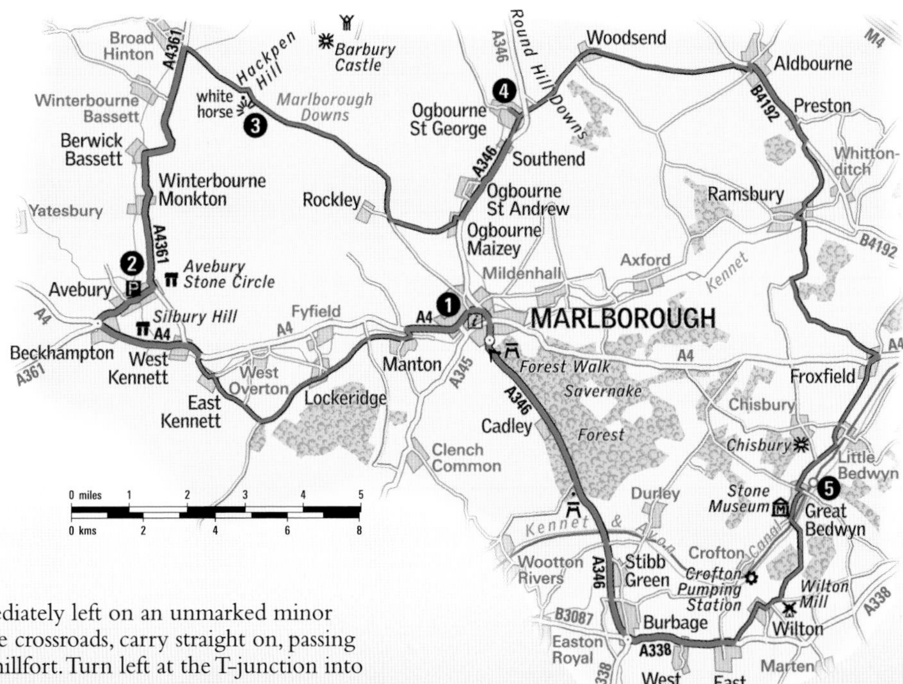

then immediately left on an unmarked minor road. At the crossroads, carry straight on, passing Chisbury hillfort. Turn left at the T-junction into Great Bedwyn.

Great Bedwyn to Marlborough

5 From the village centre take the road signposted to Crofton, passing Bedwyn Stone Museum. Follow the road over the Kennet and Avon Canal. Crofton Pumping Station is on the right, built to provide water to the summit of the Kennet and Avon Canal. One of its two Cornish beam engines, installed in 1812, is the oldest working beam engine in the world still in its original location.

Go through Wilton and East Grafton, and turn right on the A338 towards Salisbury. At the roundabout take the A346 towards Marlborough, skirting Burbage before entering the Savernake Forest, an ancient royal hunting ground replanted in the 18th century with oaks and beeches. For a car park and picnic spot, take the first left to Wootton Rivers and carry on for around 250m. Rejoin the A346 to return to Marlborough.

AVEBURY AT DAWN

Southeast England

The byways of the southeast wind through weald and downland, skirting castle grounds and grand gardens, stately homes and parks. Country towns and villages, with their characterful buildings, reflect centuries of local tradition.

BEDFORDSHIRE
48-49
ESSEX
50-51
BUCKINGHAMSHIRE
HERTFORDSHIRE
SURREY
70-73
KENT
58-63
SUSSEX
74-77
The Chilterns
The North Downs
The South Downs
The South Downs
Bedford
Biggleswade
Milton Keynes
Ampthill
Leighton Buzzard
Stevenage
Hertford
Aylesbury
Tring
St Albans
High Wycombe
Beaconsfield
Watford
Maidenhead
Windsor
Saffron Walden
Harwich
Colchester
Braintree
Clacton-on-Sea
Harlow
Chelmsford
Maldon
Brentwood
Basildon
Southend-on-Sea
Gravesend
Rochester
Chatham
Margate
Canterbury
Westerham
Maidstone
Royal Tunbridge Wells
Wye
Ashford
Dover
Folkestone
Cranbrook
Woking
Guildford
Shere
Dorking
Reigate
Farnham
Haslemere
Crawley
Crowborough
Haywards Heath
Petersfield
Rye
Lewes
Arundel
Chichester
Bognor Regis
Worthing
Brighton
Bexhill-on-Sea
Hastings
Eastbourne

BEDFORDSHIRE

The landscape of rural Bedfordshire typifies that of the shires. Its gentle, undulating farmland alternating with swathes of broadleaved woodland rises in the south to the beautiful chalk downs of the Chilterns.

1 AMPTHILL

TOUR LENGTH 63 miles

A tour around the patchwork landscape of the Chilterns from Bedfordshire to Hertfordshire, encircling the busy town of Luton. The journey passes handsome villages, grand houses and great English estates with magnificent grounds.

Ampthill to Woburn

1 The lovely buildings lining Ampthill's streets invite closer scrutiny, especially those in Church Street – where the National Trust's Avenue House has survived almost unchanged since the early 19th century, earning a reputation as a 'microcosm of Regency living'. Nearby, elegant Dynevor House, built in 1725, and Brandreth House, 70 years younger, face one another across Church Square. But the town is not solely a Georgian time capsule. Several buildings, including the Feoffee Almshouses, date from Tudor times, while St Andrew's Church dates back to the 14th century.

Leave Ampthill on the B530, Woburn Street, and continue to a T-junction. Turn right on the A507 and after 4 miles turn left. Follow the road over the M1 to the village of Ridgmont. Continue straight on, alongside the boundary wall of Woburn estate, to a roundabout in Husborne Crawley. Take the A4012 to a T-junction on the edge of Woburn. Drive into the village centre. Turn left at the crossroads into Park Street for a car park to explore this Georgian village on foot.

Woburn to Whipsnade

2 Return to the village centre crossroads and turn left on the A4012 to the junction with the A5 in Hockliffe. Turn left, then immediately right, towards Leighton Buzzard, on a continuation of the A4012. A mile farther on turn left on a minor road to Eggington. Follow the road past the entrance to Eggington House, on left, then immediately turn left to the village of Stanbridge. Turn right at the T-junction opposite the village church, then left on a minor road towards Totternhoe. At the junction with the A505 turn left then immediately right on minor road into Totternhoe, an ancient defensive site at the foot of the Chiltern Hills. At a T-junction on the far side of the village turn left – unless you wish to visit St Giles Church, which lies a short distance in the other direction and contains a stained-glass window by the 20th-century artist John Piper.

3 Continue to the B489. Turn right and continue for 1½ miles to a roundabout, then turn left on the B4506. Take the first road on the left – the B4540 – leading uphill past the entrance to Whipsnade Wildlife Park.

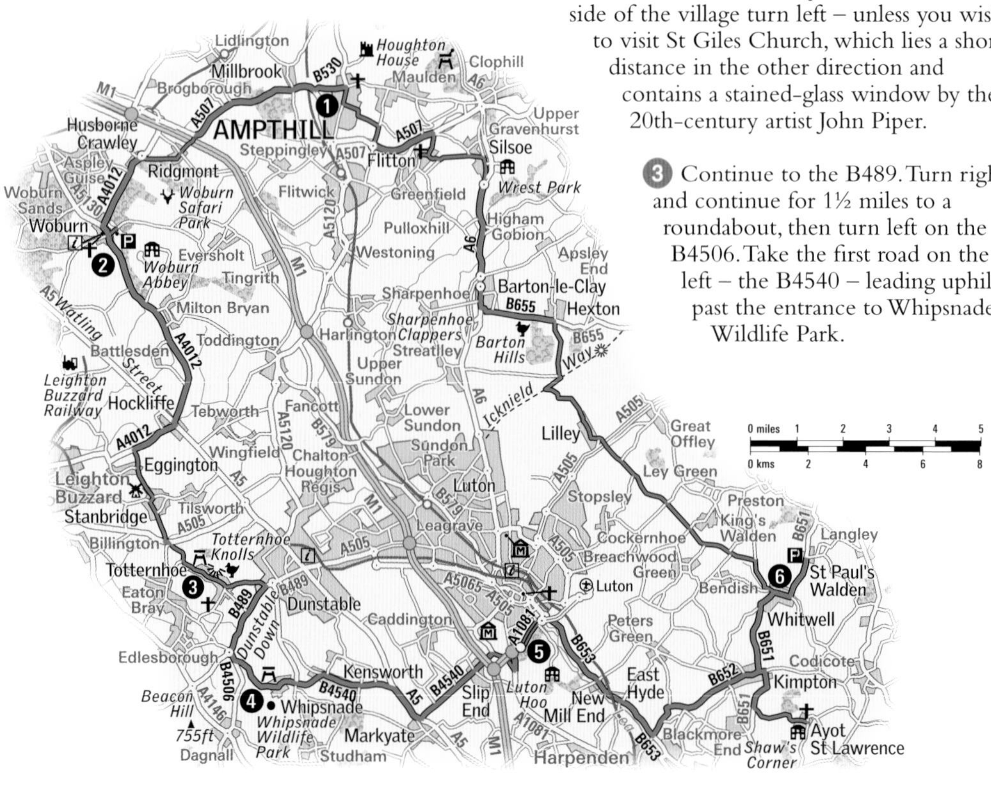

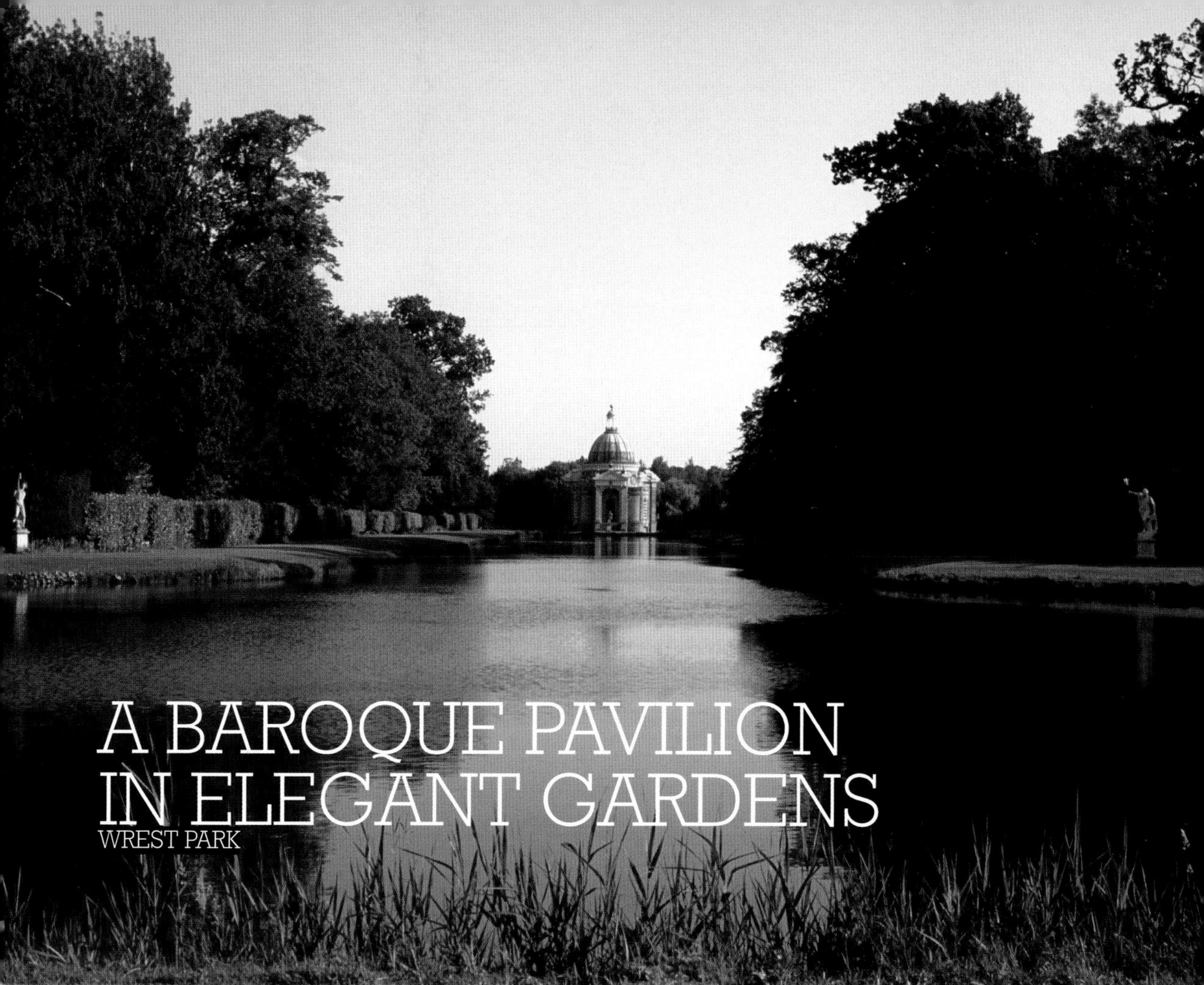

A BAROQUE PAVILION IN ELEGANT GARDENS

WREST PARK

Whipsnade to St Paul's Walden

4 Turn left out of the car park on the B4540. At a T-junction turn right on the A5; continue for ½ mile, then turn left on the edge of Markyate. At a T-junction 2 miles farther on, just beyond the M1 underpass, turn right, under the motorway spur into Luton, to a T-junction. Turn left on the A1081, which passes the entrance, on the right, to Luton Hoo, a magnificent 18th-century mansion, which was restored after a fire in 1903 by the diamond magnate Sir Julius Wernher. This Grade I listed building featured in the 1994 film *Four Weddings and a Funeral,* and opened in 2007 as a luxury hotel.

5 Continue to the multiple roundabout and turn right on the B653. At a crossroads on the edge of Harpenden turn left on the B652 to Kimpton. Drive through the village and turn right on the B651, then take the first minor road on the left to the tiny Hertfordshire village of Ayot St Lawrence, where the writer George Bernard Shaw lived for more than 40 years. His Arts-and-Crafts house, Shaw's Corner (NT), is open March to November. Visitors can stroll the gardens and see Shaw's revolving writing hut.

Return to the centre of Kimpton and turn right on the B651 through Whitwell to St Paul's Walden. Walkers can explore the surrounding countryside from the village's paths.

St Paul's Walden to Ampthill

6 Return to Whitwell and in the village centre turn right, off the B651. Carry straight on along a minor road for 6 miles to a crossroads in Hexton and turn left on the B655 to a T-junction in Barton-le-Clay. Turn right and go straight ahead at the roundabout on the A6 towards Bedford. At a roundabout take the first exit to Silsoe, where Wrest Park (EH), the ancestral home of the de Grey tea dynasty, is located. The early 18th-century formal gardens were inspired by the gardens of Versailles, with pavilions designed by the Baroque architect Thomas Archer (1668-1743). The present house dates from 1839; access to the house is limited so check opening times before visiting. From Silsoe High Street, take the first minor road on the left, heading west, to Flitton, whose Church of St John the Baptist contains numerous effigies of the de Greys. Turn right in Flitton to reach the A507, then turn left. Take the second minor road on the right to Ampthill.

ESSEX

As the capital's northern fringes fade into rural quiet, Essex comes into its own as a touring destination. Winding country roads retain the pattern of times gone by, while the countryside brings many delights and surprises.

2 SAFFRON WALDEN

TOUR LENGTH 31 miles

Drive through gentle countryside dotted with woods and sleepy, characterful villages and up onto the chalkland ridge, visiting the hilltop village of Great Chishill at Cambridgeshire's southernmost tip.

Saffron Walden to Newport

1 The market town of Saffron Walden is named after the dye obtained from the October flowering crocus, grown here in great quantities during the Middle Ages to supply the wool trade. Past prosperity is evident from the abbey-like proportions of St Mary's Church, the remains of a Norman Castle, the timbered shops, old houses and the pastel-hued marketplace – one of the first to be built in the county – filled with stalls on Tuesdays and Saturdays.

Drive along the High Street, which becomes London Road beyond the war memorial. Follow signs to Audley End. A Jacobean mansion of quite startling opulence, Audley End (EH) is set in a park and laid out by Capability Brown, with temples, obelisks and a bridge by Robert Adam. Audley End village has a single street of old cottages and the Almshouses of St Mark's College.

Turn left on the B1383 to Newport. At the entry to the village, a large boulder on the left, hollowed at the top, is a vestige of the medieval leper hospital. Its inmates left money in the hollow of the stone (actually a glacial deposit of the last Ice Age) to pay for food.

Just before the B1383 goes under a railway bridge, branch left down a side street passing Crown House with its fine pargeting on the left and creeper clad Viaduct Cottage. Continue under the railway bridge past Priory Cottage and turn left back onto the B1383 at the toll bridge. The charges, still listed on the old Toll House include 'For every ass … ½d.'

AUDLEY END HOUSE

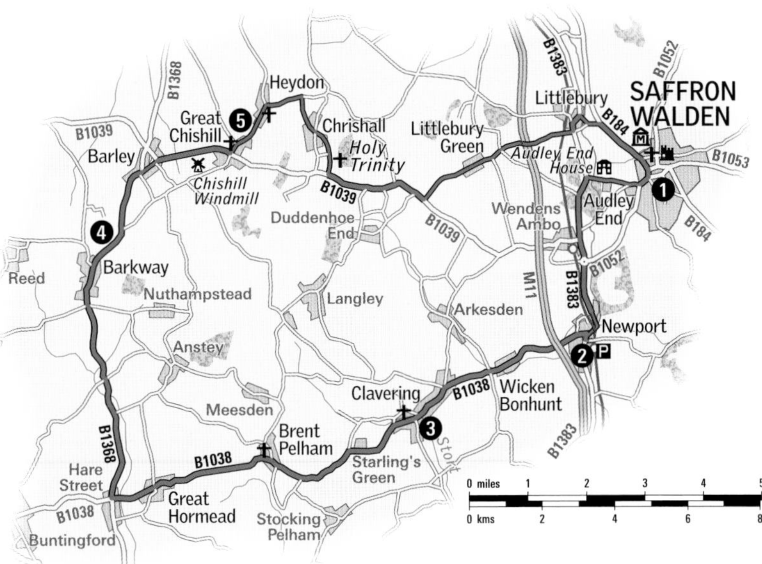

Newport to Clavering

2 From Newport take the B1038, following signs to Buntingford and Clavering. Continue under the M11 through Wicken Bonhunt, whose early 17th century Brick House is decorated with a bust of a Roman Emperor. The Domesday village of Clavering, which has houses dating back 500 years, is announced by The Cricketers inn and a village green. Behind the battlemented flint church of St Mary and St Clement, grassy mounds and a dry moat mark the site of a castle thought to have been built before the Norman Conquest and therefore one of England's oldest castle sites.

Clavering to Great Chishill

3 Continue on the B1038 across the Hertfordshire border, where the road curves right to Brent Pelham, a partly thatched village with stocks and a whipping post. The thick walls of St Mary's Church contain the grave of Piers Shonks, said to have been mortally wounded while slaying a dragon.

Continue on the B1038 through Great Hormead. At the next junction turn right on the B1368 signposted to Barkway and Barley. Pylons soon give way to rolling farmland distantly dotted with woods. Two aircraft navigation beacons, one civil, one RAF, stand sentry over the entrance to Barkway, a handsome village strung out along what was a turnpike road to Cambridge. The old mound of Periwinkle Hill in the village centre, west of the London-Cambridge road, is thought to have been the location of a Norman motte-and-bailey fortress, giving northward views as far as the city of Ely.

4 Keep on the B1368, ignoring a minor slip road to Great Chishill and passing a stud farm and the Chequers pub on the left. Just beyond, another pub sign, depicting a fox hunt, straddles the road. Drive beneath it and into Barley. Go along the village street to join the B1039 as it climbs to the hilltop village of Great Chishill – at 146m (480ft) the highest point in Cambridgeshire The sails of Great Chishill post mill stand out against the sky.

Great Chishill to Saffron Walden

5 Drive on to Heydon just under a mile away. Turn right by the church, and then after ½ mile turn right again on Abram's lane, to Chrishall (pronounced 'krissul'). Go over Chrishall crossroads along Church Road to Holy Trinity Church with its distinctive chequerboard flint tower. The church stands some way from present-day Chrishall as the original village around it was wiped out by the Black Death and a subsequent fire during the 14th century. The site of the plague pit in the churchyard is said to be haunted. Remains of a medieval castle lie in the woods behind.

At the junction beyond the church turn left on the B1039. Take the second turning on the left to Littlebury Green. Go straight on at the next crossroads, passing between broad open fields and continue over the M11 to the pretty village of Littlebury. In Littlebury turn left on the B1383 signposted to Great Chesterford and Cambridge. Just after the Queen's Head Hotel, turn right towards Saffron Walden. Drive past the long red wall of Audley End estate, turning right on the B184 for Saffron Walden.

HAMPSHIRE & ISLE OF WIGHT

Ancient settlements, historic hamlets and the wild beauty of the New Forest make Hampshire one of southern England's loveliest counties. Across the water, the Isle of Wight's western tour offers spectacular views.

3 NEW ALRESFORD

TOUR LENGTH 78 miles

From the Georgian splendour of New Alresford through Hampshire's chalk downland, past rural villages and through the remote Test valley, this tour offers a nostalgic glimpse of a gentle English past.

New Alresford to Stockbridge

1 New Alresford (pronounced Alsford) was 'new' in 1200, when it was laid out by Bishop de Lucy of Winchester alongside the Alre, a tributary of the River Itchen. Broad Street, with its colour-washed Georgian houses, shops and inns is particularly elegant. The Watercress Line, the popular name of the Mid Hants Railway, which runs steam trains between New Alresford and Alton, reflects an important local industry.

Take West Street, the B3047, towards Winchester. Just before a roundabout at the junction with the A31, turn right to Ovington. Nearly 2 miles farther on, turn right and cross a pair of bridges to Itchen Abbas, where Charles Kingsley wrote *The Water Babies*. Recross the river and turn right, skirting Avington Park, to Avington village, then turn right to Easton, a thatched village with a Norman church and plenty of clipped yew.

2 At the Chestnut Horse turn right to cross the Itchen, then left on the B3047. Go through Abbots Worthy, turn left on the A33, then immediately right into Kings Worthy. Go under the A34, then turn right, signposted to Headbourne Worthy. At the next junction, turn left and follow signs to Littleton, crossing the B3420 into Harestock Road. At the junction with the B3049 turn right for Stockbridge. Immediately before a roundabout at the edge of Stockbridge, turn left on the A3057 for Romsey – or go straight on to the centre of the village. Stockbridge means 'river crossing' and the Test has been bridged here since prehistoric times. Today its one main street is lined with antiques shops and inns.

Stockbridge to Cheriton

3 Follow the A3057 to King's Somborne. About ½ a mile beyond King's Somborne, turn right, following signposts to Horsebridge and Houghton. In Horsebridge turn right by John O'Gaunt pub and cross the Test. Just before Houghton turn left on a narrow road, which crosses remote farmland with stretches of woodland and good views over the valley. After 2½ miles, a left turn leads to Mottisfont Abbey (NT), a mainly 18th-century house built around the remains of a 12th-century priory. It has an outstanding collection of old-fashioned roses. The park and woodland offer pleasant walks.

4 Turn right on the A3057 and follow it to Romsey. Fork right to the town centre, passing the entrance to the Norman abbey on the right. Opposite is King John's House, one of the oldest surviving dwellings in England. Despite its name, it is thought to have been built in 1240, some 25 years after the king's death. Tours are available; entrance to the period garden is free.

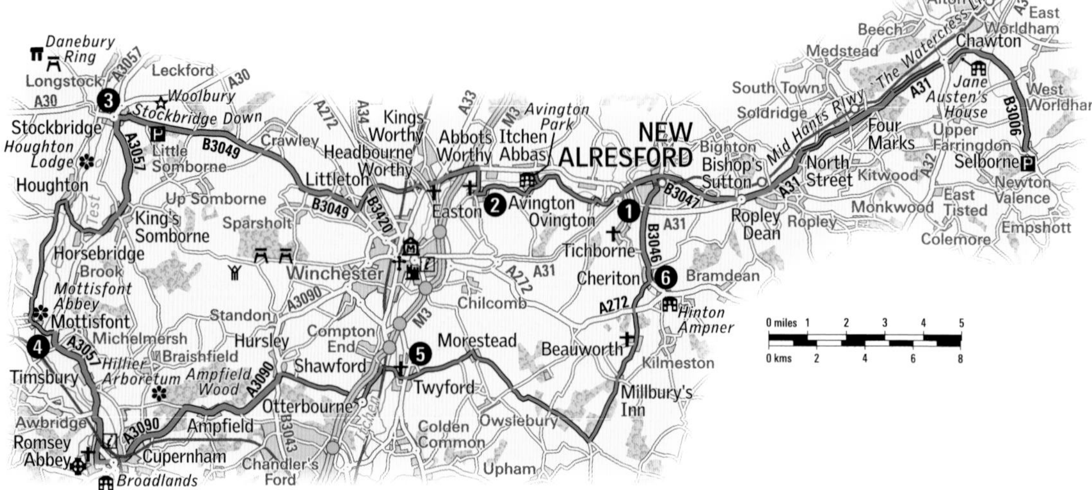

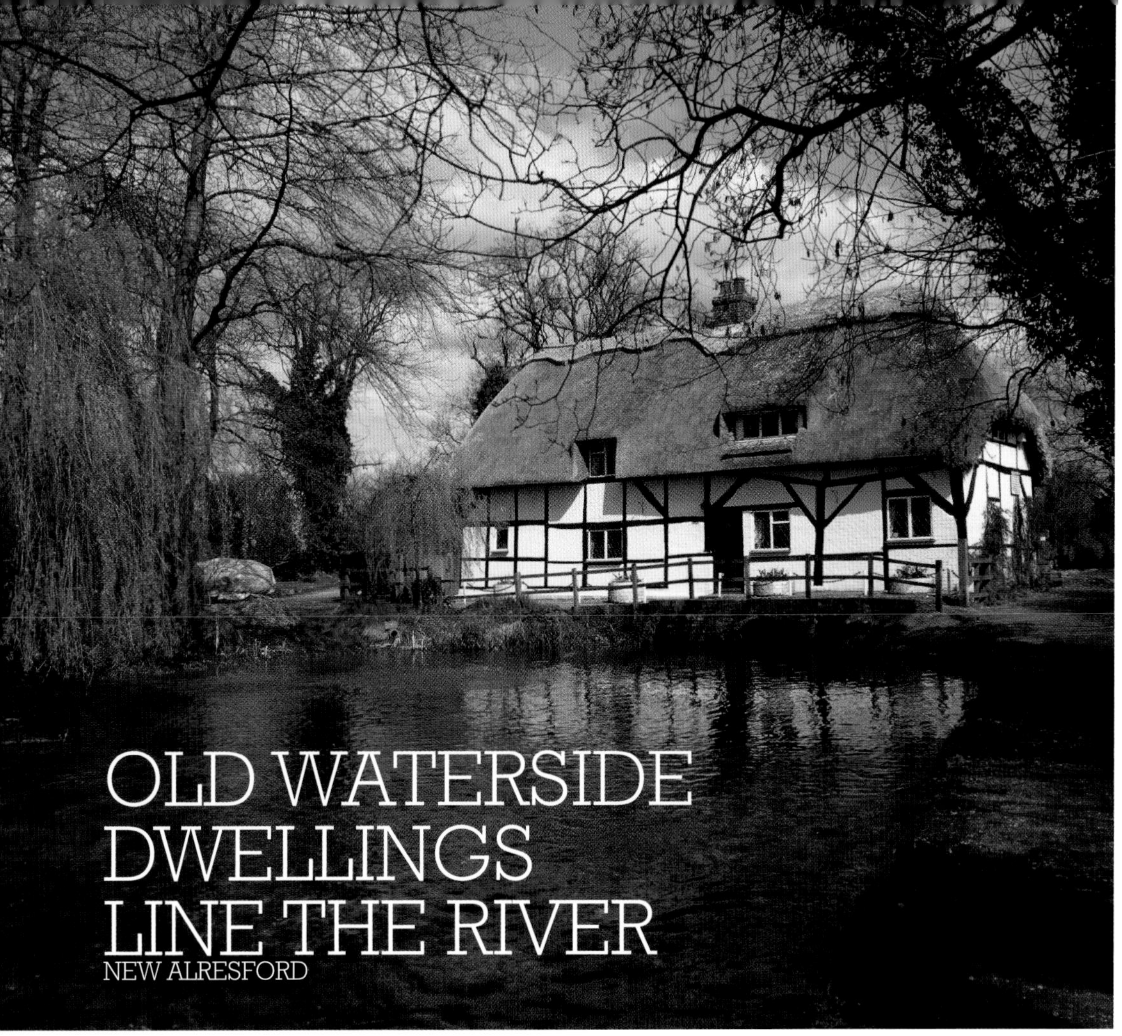

OLD WATERSIDE DWELLINGS LINE THE RIVER
NEW ALRESFORD

Follow signs out of Romsey for Winchester on the A3090, which leaves Romsey through Cupernham, then enters Ampfield Wood. On the outskirts of Hursley, at a second set of part-time traffic lights, turn right to Otterbourne.

At the edge of Otterbourne, turn left at roundabout towards Winchester, then right after 1¼ miles towards Twyford. Cross the Itchen Navigation canal and river, with views of Twyford church. The current building dates from 1878, but according to tradition, the site marks the spot of a Druid temple. Twelve 'Druid' stones were found below the old Norman tower, and were retained as the foundations of the 19th-century building. The yew tree in the churchyard is believed to be 1,000 years old.

5 At the traffic lights in Twyford, cross the B3335 and continue past Twyford waterworks to a junction by the pond in Morestead. Turn right and follow the road across the downs. At a third crossroads, turn left to Cheriton, passing through Beauworth (pronounced bew-worth), a village with thatched cottages, fine brick-and-flint houses and a church with a pretty bellcote. Cross the A272 to Cheriton.

Cheriton to Selborne

6 To return to New Alresford, follow the B3046 from Cheriton. From New Alresford take the B3047 towards Alton, passing through Bishop's Sutton. At the roundabout beyond Bishop's Sutton turn left on the A31 and continue to Four Marks. At over 182m (600ft) above sea level, Medstead and Four Marks station, on The Watercress Line, is the highest station in southern England. At roundabout beyond Four Marks, take the third exit into the village of Chawton.

On the left is the 17th-century house where Jane Austen lived with her mother and sister and her friend Martha from 1809 until the novelist's death in Winchester in 1817. Drive through the village to the B3006 and continue to Selborne. The Wakes, on the main village street, is the former home of the naturalist Gilbert White and is now a museum. White was born in Selbourne in 1720 and spent most of his time in the village as a clergyman. On the village green is St Mary's Church – White's grave is on the north side of the church, and inside the church two stained glass windows honour him. Walkers can explore the surrounding countryside on paths leading from the village.

HAMPSHIRE & ISLE OF WIGHT

4 BROCKENHURST

TOUR LENGTH 59 miles

An enchanting drive through the New Forest, a unique landscape of pasture, open heath and forest glades that has changed little in the past 1,000 years.

Brockenhurst to Woodgreen

❶ Brockenhurst is an ancient settlement of great charm, with thatched cottages overlooking little greens. Take the B3055 towards Beaulieu (pronounced bew-lee), passing the gatehouse of Brockenhurst Park. At the T-junction, turn right on the B3055, first through woodland for about 4 miles, then across open heath to Hatchet Pond on the right. At the junction beyond the pond, bear left on the B3054 to Beaulieu.

❷ Where the road forks in Beaulieu bear left on the B3056, passing a millpond on the Beaulieu river with views across to Palace House. A right turn leads to the house, Beaulieu Abbey and the National Motor Museum. Continue to Leygreen Farm and turn right on a minor road signposted to Ipley Cross. Follow the road for about 3½ miles to a T-junction just beyond the Bold Forester pub at the edge of Marchwood. Turn left on the road signposted to Colbury to the junction with the A35, passing the New Forest Otter, Owl and Wildlife Park and Longdown Activity Farm.

❸ Turn left on the A35 and go through Ashurst to the railway bridge. Cross the bridge and at once turn right to Woodlands. At a T-junction in Woodlands turn left into Bartley Road. Just before the junction with the A336, turn left into Chinham Road. Continue through woodland to the A337.

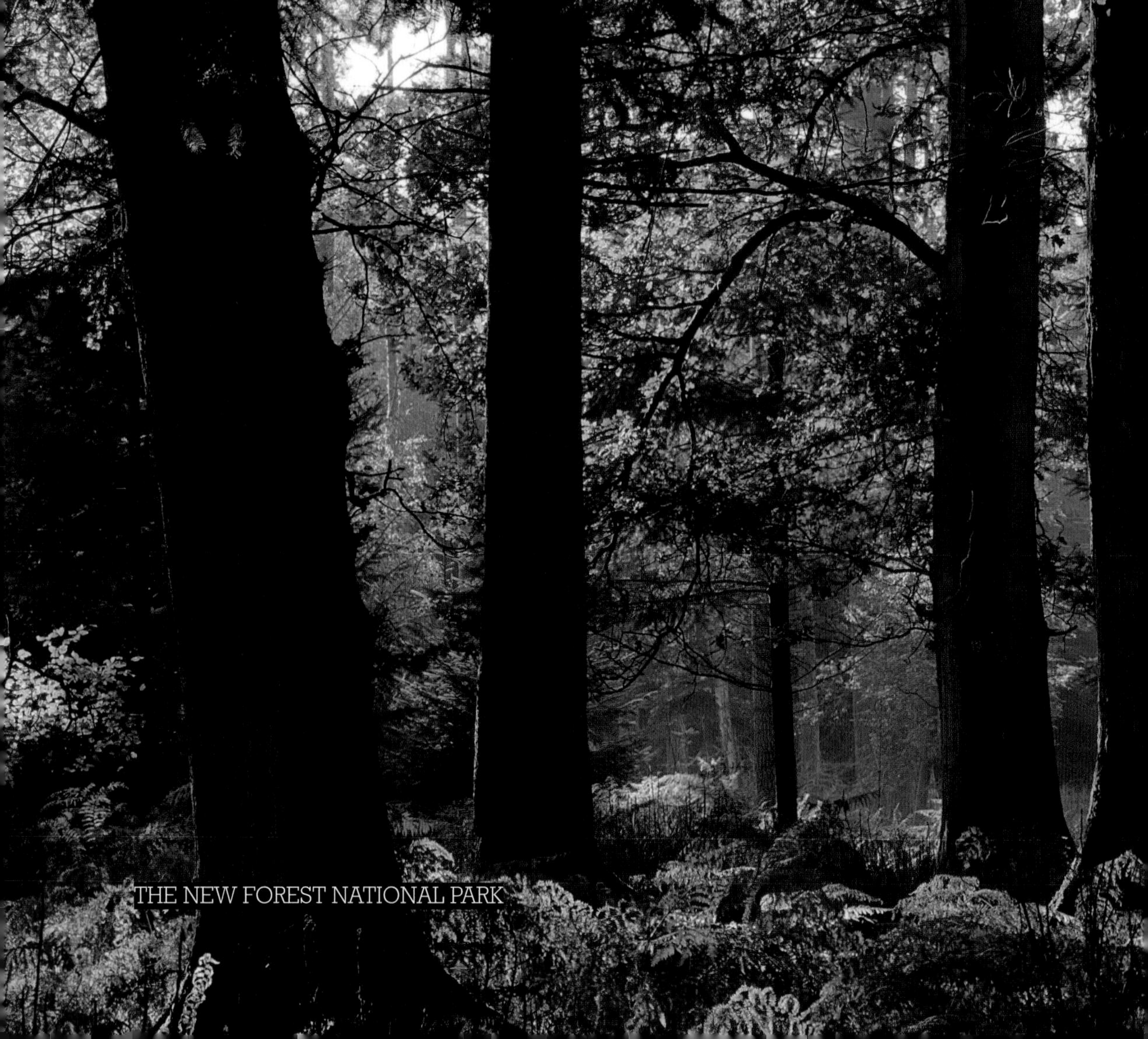

THE NEW FOREST NATIONAL PARK

4 Go straight on at the junction, then fork left towards Minstead. At the next T-junction, go right into Lyndhurst Road and continue to Minstead. About ½ mile beyond Minstead a left turn leads to the landscaped Furzey Gardens with 16th-century cottage and tearoom. At a junction with the A31 turn left, following signs to the Rufus Stone, which marks the spot where William II (1087-1100) son of William the Conqueror, was mysteriously killed by an arrow. Turn left on the B3078 towards Fordingbridge. Where the road forks, bear left to continue on the B3078 across heathland to Godshill. There are wide views from the summit of the flat-topped hill. At the junction in Godshill turn right to Woodgreen.

Woodgreen to Burley

5 Turn left past the post office and cross the Avon into Breamore. At a T-junction turn left on the A338. Continue to Fordingbridge and follow signs to Alderholt. At a junction on Alderholt's outskirts turn left into Hillbury Road, signposted to Ringwood. Continue for 5 miles, through Ringwood Forest to a junction with the B3081 and turn left towards Ringwood. At a T-junction with the A31 turn left towards Southampton, then follow signs to Ringwood. From Ringwood, continue on the A31 for about 2 miles, to Picket Post, then take the slip road on the left to Burley.

Burley to Brockenhurst

6 From Burley, follow the Brockenhurst road. Where the road forks, bear right, following signs to Southampton and the A35. Turn left on the A35 and continue for about 5 miles, with open heathland on the left and woods on the right, to a crossroads. Turn right on a minor road to Rhinefield, and continue on Rhinefield Road to return to Brockenhurst.

HAMPSHIRE & ISLE OF WIGHT

5 YARMOUTH

TOUR LENGTH 43 miles

An island drive, taking in manors, castles and sculptural wonders of nature. Hanover point has fine sea views across beaches where dinosaurs once roamed.

Yarmouth to Godshill

1 A distinctly salty atmosphere pervades Yarmouth, where the arrival of a ferry from Lymington, on the mainland, brings a fleeting bustle of traffic before the tightly bunched streets resume their customary quietness. The arcaded town hall of 1673 presides over the central square, and nearby is Yarmouth Castle (EH), dating from 1547. Yacht masts bob in the Yar estuary, whose rich variety of birdlife includes cormorants, herons and teal. Local walks include a stroll along the 190m (630ft) Victorian pier, or an excursion along the path of an old railway track beside the River Yar with its 18th-century tide mill.

Take the A3054 towards Newport. About 100m after the traffic lights at Shalfleet turn left to the Hamlet of Newtown. Founded as 'new town' in 1218 by the Bishop of Winchester, Newtown was razed by French invaders in 1377, but continued as a busy port up until the 18th century; the old Town Hall (NT) of 1699 is a reminder of past wealth. A left turn just after the Old Town Hall leads to a car park with access to the marshes of Newtown National Nature Reserve, whose breeding birds include Brent geese, teal and wigeon.

2 Continue towards Newport and after 1 mile bear left, signposted to Cowes, then take the next right, signposted to Newport. Turn right at a T-junction, go left on the A3054, and then first right to Carisbrooke, dominated by the 15th-century tower of St Mary's Church. Turn left on the B3401, then right up Cedar Hill, following the sign for Carisbrooke Castle (EH). Within the castle, the donkey wheel, used for drawing water by donkey power, is still in working order.

From the top of Cedar Hill, turn left along Whitepit Lane. Go straight on down Shide Road, then turn right onto the A3020, signposted to Shanklin, and right again to Godshill. Pretty thatched cottages surround Godshill's 15th-century All Saints Church, which has a medieval wall-painting of Christ crucified on a cross of lily plants. Park near the Old Smithy opposite the Griffin Pub to explore Godshill – and its model village – on foot

Godshill to Niton

3 Turn right out of the car park. Where the road bends right, turn left, following signs to Chale and Ventnor. At Whitwell turn right by the church to reach Niton, once a haunt of smugglers, who frequented the Buddle Inn. Follow signs for Ventnor, Blackgang and then for the village centre.

Niton to Alum Bay

4 From Niton take the A3055 to Blackgang. Blackgang Chine is a narrow cleft in the cliff plunging 120m (400ft) to the shore. It was once rife with smugglers but is now home to a theme park. At Chale, fork right on the B3399 to

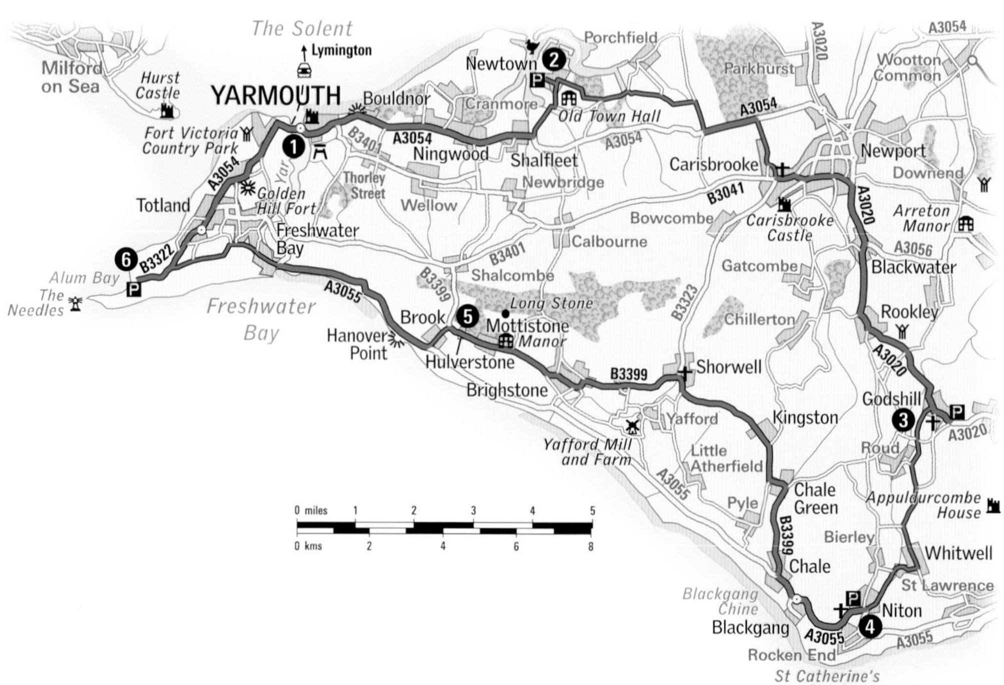

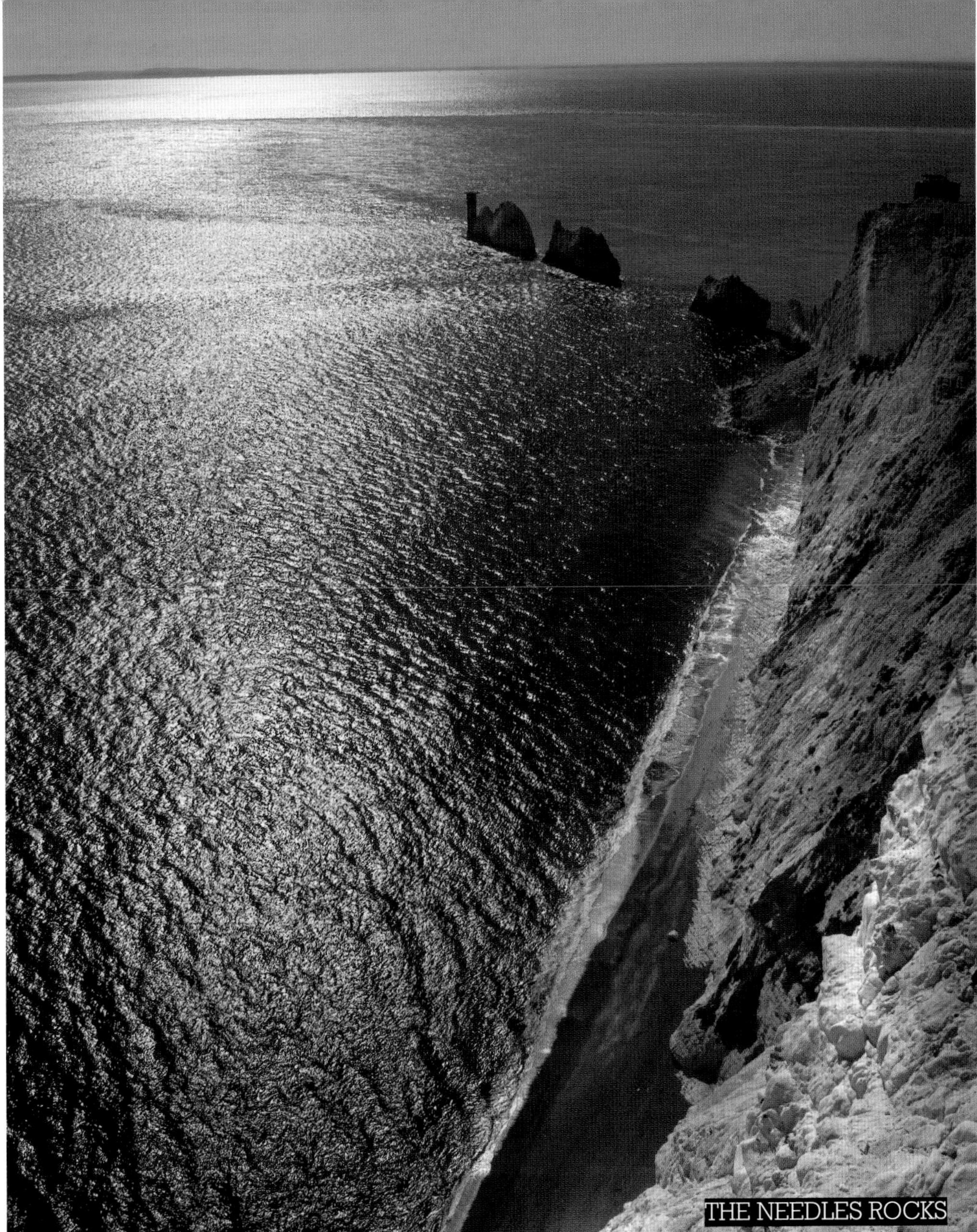
THE NEEDLES ROCKS

Shorwell (pronounced Shorrel). The village has three manor houses and thatched cottages with walls of orange-coloured stone. Turn left on the B3399 to Brighstone (pronounced Bristun), and then to Mottistone.

Mottistone manor garden (NT) is set in a sheltered valley sloping down to an L-shaped manor house dating from the 16th century. A path from the road climbs to the Long Stone, a 3.9m (13ft) high greensand stone thought to have formed part of long barrow of about 2500 BC.

5 Go through Hulverstone Village, turn left, signposted to Ventnor, then right on the A3055 towards Freshwater. The road passes Hanover Point, where the petrified stumps of a prehistoric forest are visible at low tide. Keep on the A3055 to Freshwater Bay, a fashionable 19th-century resort. Continue to Alum Bay, where the multicoloured cliffs display 21 different colours of sand. The chairlift at Needles Park provides rides from the clifftop to the beach, with views of The Needles rocks out to sea.

Alum Bay to Yarmouth

6 From Alum Bay join the B3322. Follow signs to Yarmouth, through Totland, keeping straight on to join the A3054. Off to the right is Golden Hill Fort, built in 1863-9 as a barracks. On the coast shortly before Yarmouth is Fort Victoria Country Park, which has an aquarium. The fort was built in the mid 19th century as part of the Solent defences.

KENT

Three tours, chosen for their glorious wealden views, show the county of Kent at its best. The roads rise and fall through a landscape once thick with forest, that now boasts some of the region's finest houses and castles.

6 WESTERHAM

TOUR LENGTH 52 miles

Setting off from the old town of Westerham, home of Winston Churchill, the drive winds through the Medway Valley to the fringes of East Sussex's Ashdown Forest. Pause for a stroll through the county's gardens, or enjoy a gourmet tea shop tour.

Westerham to Knole Park

1 Wooded hills, rolling parkland and open heath characterise the undulating countryside around Westerham, a small town on the North Downs. Busy throughout the year, the town is particularly lively in summer, when visitors arrive to pay homage to its best-known historical characters: General Wolfe, born there in 1727, whose childhood home, Quebec House, is now a museum of his life; and Sir Winston Churchill, who lived at nearby Chartwell for more than 40 years. Both men are commemorated by statues on Westerham's green.

For the drive, take the A25 to Brasted, and just beyond the village turn right on the road to Ide Hill. After 2 miles turn right to Emmetts Garden, open in summer. The garden (NT) has rare trees, including a 30m (100ft) Wellingtonia.

2 Beyond Ide Hill turn left on the B2042, then fork right beside Goathurst Common. The road undulates through woodland to a T-junction. Turn left, cross the A21 and turn right. Go straight on at Hubbard's Hill, continuing to a T-junction at Riverhill. Turn right, then fork first left through a wooded area. Take the second road on the right through woods. Turn right at a T-junction, then left into One Tree Hill car park. Footpaths lead from the car park to Knole Park. Thomas Bourchier, the Archbishop of Canterbury, built Knole in 1454 as a residence for himself and future archbishops. It passed from the church to Henry VIII in 1538 and then from the crown into private ownership when Elizabeth I gave it

HEVER CASTLE

to the Sackville family in 1566. It houses fine collections of furniture, tapestries and portraits. (Access to Knole for drivers is via the main entrance in Sevenoaks.)

Knole Park to Ashdown Forest

3 From the car park turn left on a winding lane. At a T-junction turn left on the B245 and take the first right, signposted to Penshurst Place and Hever Castle. Follow signs for Penshurst Place, turning right at the next T-junction to Leigh (pronounced Lye). Just beyond the village, fork left; the road becomes the B2176. The road snakes down to Penshurst, passing Penshurst Place in parkland on the left. The medieval manor house, birthplace of the 16th-century soldier, courtier and poet Sir Philip Sidney, has a spectacular Great Hall with a chestnut roof, an armour collection and a toy museum. The house is open daily from April to September.

4 In Penshurst turn right on the B2188 and continue through farmland to Fordcombe. Beyond the village turn right at a T-junction on the A264, then take the first, partly hidden left turn, to Groombridge. The narrow lane descends to a cluster of cottages, pub and church around a green. Turn right at the T-junction on the B2110, passing Groombridge Place on the left. Fork right at a roundabout then fork left on the B2188, signposted to Maresfield.

After a few miles the road enters Ashdown Forest in East Sussex, an expanse of heathland with Scots pines. Turn sharp right on the B2026 towards Hartfield. Continue for about a mile and, just beyond the junction on the left with a minor road to Coleman's Hatch, turn left into Gills Lap car park. Gills Lap is one of the highest points of Ashdown Forest. Take the footpath from the car park to a trig point and the Enchanted Place viewpoint. A memorial to A.A. Milne and E.H. Shephard, author and illustrator of the Winnie the Pooh stories, bears the inscription 'And by and by they came to an enchanted place on the very top of the forest called Galleons Leap.'

Ashdown Forest to Westerham

5 Turn left on the B2026. Go through Hartfield. Turn left on the A264, then right, continuing on the B2026 towards Edenbridge. After 2½ miles turn right at Cowden Pound crossroads, signposted to Hever Castle and Penshurst. From Markbeech, follow signs to Hever Castle. The 14th-century moated castle with later Italian gardens is reputedly where Henry VIII wooed Anne Boleyn. It was restored by US newspaper magnate William Waldorf Astor, who bought it in 1903.

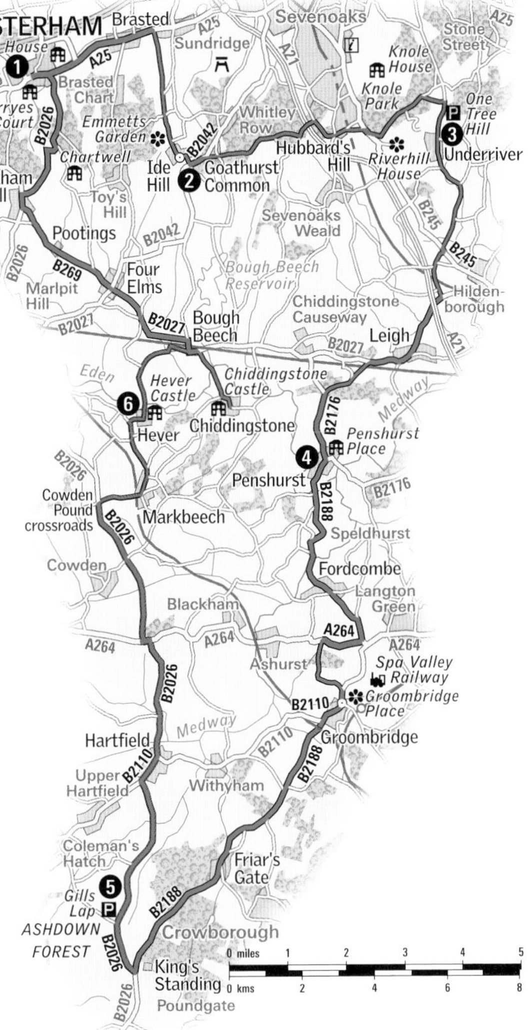

6 Continue on a minor road to a road junction. Go straight on along the B2027 and almost at once turn right, over the River Eden, then left at crossroads to the village of Chiddingstone, which was purchased in its entirety by the National Trust in 1939. The village's long history resonates in its leaning Tudor houses and in its 'chiding stone'. This huge natural sandstone boulder was, according to legend, the place where villagers once scolded chattering women. This fanciful story is false: the village name is a derivation of 'stone of Chidd's people.' Chidd is believed to have been a Saxon tribal leader.

Return to the junction with the B2027 and turn left. At Four Elms go straight on, following the B269 through Pootings to a T-junction opposite the Royal Oak pub at Crockham Hill. Turn right on the B2026 and follow the road as it climbs back to Westerham.

KENT

7 CRANBROOK

TOUR LENGTH 51 miles

Explore Kent's high weald – a beautiful landscape of forest and field on rolling hills. The wealden villages, with their tile-hung, half-timbered and weatherboarded houses, prospered from hop-growing and the old iron industry and retain their historic charm.

Cranbrook to Rolvenden

❶ The River Crane, one of the many small rivers and streams that crisscross the hilly wooded Weald countryside gave its name to Cranbrook. The little market town, with a white working windmill above it, was once the cloth-making centre of Kent; its fine St Dunstan's Church was built from the profits. With the George Hotel on the right, drive along the main street and turn first right, towards Tenterden. Follow signs to Sissinghurst, then turn right in the village on the A262 opposite the church and Bull Inn. After ½ mile, take the lane on the left to Sissinghurst Castle (NT), whose garden was created in the 1930s by the writer Vita Sackville-West.

❷ Return to the A262 and continue to Biddenden, with its medieval and Tudor houses, a tithe barn, green and pond. At a T-junction in the village centre, turn right, following the A262. After ½ mile, where the main road swings left to Tenterden, take the minor road ahead, towards Benenden. After 1¼ miles, turn left at Castleton's Oak pub. At the T-junction turn right on the A28 to Rolvenden Station, on the Kent and East Sussex Railway. Continue to Rolvenden.

Rolvenden to Battle

❸ Carry on along the A28 to a T-junction and turn right on the A268 towards Hawkhurst. At Sandhurst, fork left by the village green along a minor road towards Bodiam. Sandhurst's Church of St Nicholas is 1 mile from the village; in the Middle Ages it was left isolated when the local community moved away after an outbreak of the plague. Turn left at the next T-junction and continue for ¼ mile to 14th-century Bodiam Castle (NT), towering in feudal grandeur above its tranquil moat.

❹ Cross the medieval bridge over the Rother and continue to Staplecross, where the road joins the B2165. At Cripp's Corner, fork right onto the B2089 towards Battle. A mile farther on, on the left, just before a signpost for the A21, there is a car park with nearby picnic tables and a view over trees towards Hastings. It provides access to Forest Enterprise's Footland Wood. Fork left, signposted to Hastings, then turn left on the A21. Just beyond a converted Victorian church, turn right along a minor road to Battle. Turn right up the High Street, then left at a roundabout, and park in the large car park by Budgens to explore the town, the Abbey and the field where the Saxon King Harold lost his life and his country to William the Conquerer in 1066.

Battle to Lamberhurst

❺ Follow the A2100 towards London and Sevenoaks, joining the A21 after 3 miles at John's Cross. Continue to a crossroads at Flimwell. Turn left on the B2087 towards Ticehurst. After 1 mile turn right down Rosemary Lane. At the bottom of the lane, park by the roadside for fine views

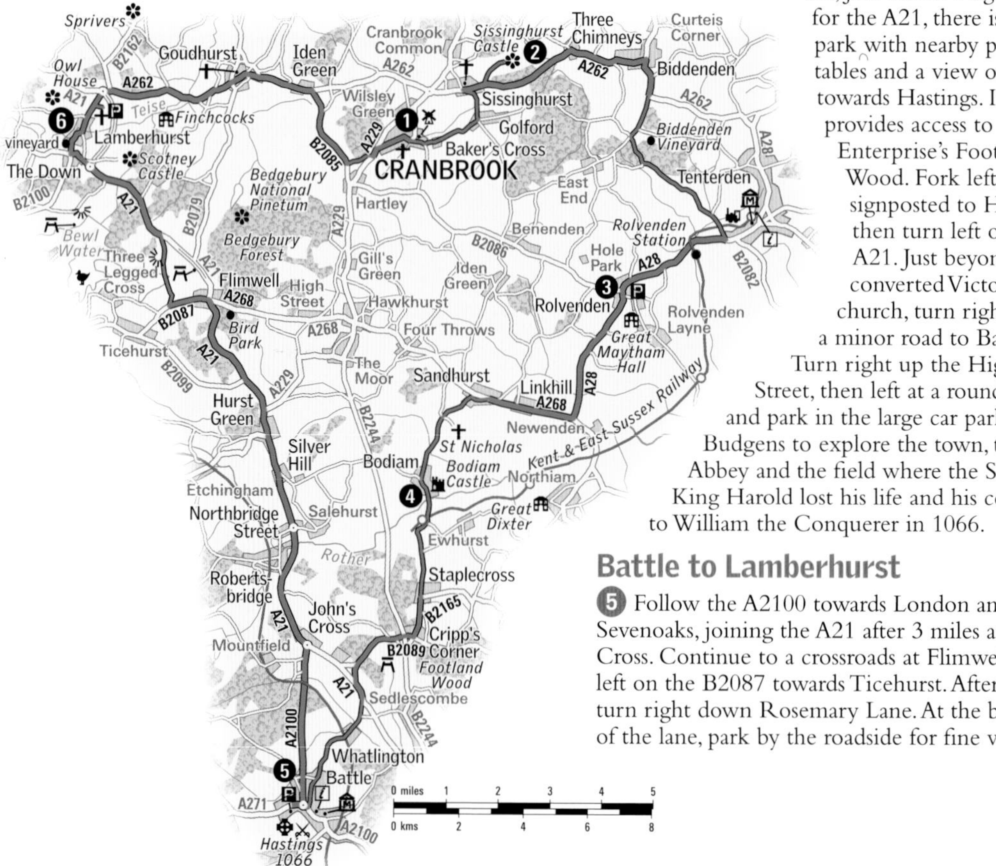

across Bewl Water reservoir, the largest stretch of inland water in south-east England and a prime breeding site for waterfowl.

Continue up Rosemary Lane and turn left on to the A21 to Lamberhurst, which straggles steeply uphill from the River Teise. At a roundabout take the first exit, the B2169, and follow the road to the High Srreet. Once the centre of a flourishing iron industry, Lamberhurst is now better known for its vineyard, off the main road in the older part of the village. Park in the car park beside St Mary's Church – on a hill at the top of the village – to explore or enjoy the view.

Lamberhurst to Cranbrook

6 Return to the B2162. At a roundabout, take the second exit, the A262 to Goudhurst, a hillside village of tile-hung and weatherboarded houses high above the Teise. The church stands on the summit of the hill – the tower is open to visitors in summer months and offers magnificent views. Continue on the A262, forking right after 1½ miles at the Peacock Inn on to the B2085 towards Hawkhurst. After 2 miles, turn left along narrow Turnden Road. At the T-junction turn left again on to the A229 and almost immediately take the first turning right back into Cranbrook.

HORSMONDEN PARISH CHURCH, NEAR GOUDHURST

KENT

8 WYE

TOUR LENGTH 35 miles

Rolling downs, strewn in summer with chalkland flowers, and a bird's eye view of the Channel Tunnel terminal are two features of this journey, in which ancient country lanes contrast with the trappings of 21st-century travel.

Wye to Hythe

1 The market town of Wye lies at the foot of the North Downs on the River Stour. In the 15th century Archbishop Kempe founded a college there which has become a world-famous centre for the agricultural sciences. It was students of Wye College who cut the huge crown in the chalk hillside near the town in 1902. From Wye there are many splendid walks on the Downs above the town and south towards the coast.

Follow signs towards Hastingleigh, then turn right towards Brook. At a sharp bend right, turn left to Brabourne, then continue through farmland and woodland, with a ridge of hills on the left, through the village.

Near Stowting the road doubles up for about a mile as part of the North Downs Way, a 140 mile walker's trail linking Farnham in Surrey with Dover. By the village church, about ¼ mile left off the main road, are the faint remains of an ancient motte-and-bailey castle.

2 Follow the road for 1½ miles to a junction with the B2068. Turn right and follow the signs to Lympne over a roundabout above the M20. At a second roundabout turn right on the A20 and continue ahead into Lympne (pronounced lim).

THE DEVILS KNEADING TROUGH

A NATURAL AMPHITHEATRE ON THE WYE DOWNS

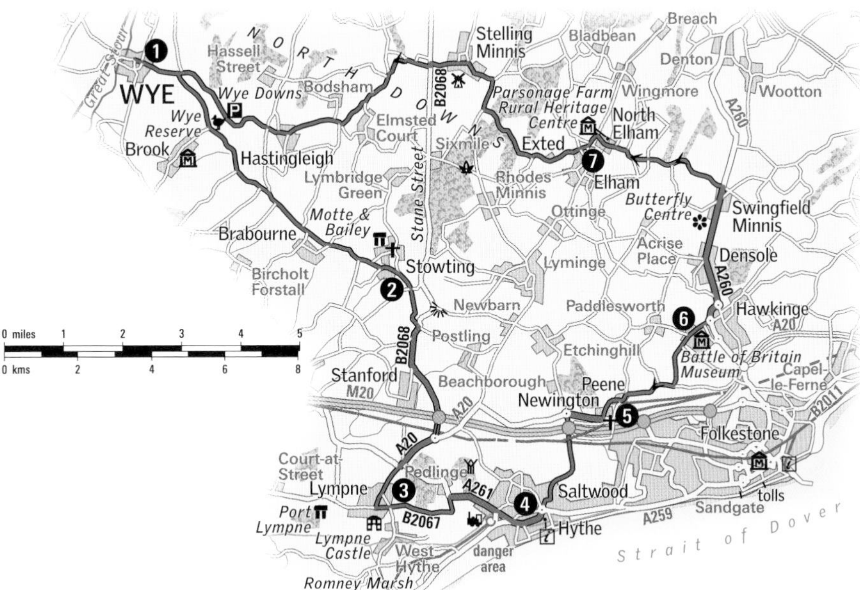

3 Remains of the Roman fort of *Portus Lemanis* can be seen on the hillside near 14th-century Lympne Castle, overlooking Romney Marsh. At the T-junction in the village centre, turn left and follow signs for Hythe, then turn right on to the A261 into the town. Where the road divides, at the bottom of the hill, follow the road left towards town centre and Folkestone, joining Military Road.

Hythe to Elham

4 Take the A259 towards Folkestone to a roundabout, then turn left towards Etchinghill. Follow the road over the M20 to a roundabout and turn right towards the Channel Tunnel. After about ½ mile, just before the large railway bridge overhead, turn left on minor road to Newington.

5 Continue on minor road through Peene, ½ mile away. Beyond Peene the road narrows and climbs sharply to the top of Folkestone Downs, with views of the Channel Tunnel terminal stretching out below and the English Channel in the distance. About a mile out of Peene, turn left on a narrow road towards Hawkinge. Almost immediately right after a T-junction is the Kent Battle of Britain Museum, which houses a collection of Battle of Britain relics in original 1940 wartime buildings. There is also a small display of First World War items.

6 Continue ahead to a roundabout and take the first exit on to the A260, following the road to the scattered village of Swingfield Minnis. The word minnis is thought to be of Saxon derivation, meaning common land used as pasture. The origin of Swingfield – place where pigs are kept – is easier to read from the modern name. Today, there are butterflies, not pigs in the village. McFarlanes Butterfly Centre maintains about 25 species from around the world.

Turn left on a narrow country lane signposted to Elham, which meanders through farming country to the hamlet of North Elham. A gigantic model of a duck announces Parsonage Farm Rural Heritage Centre, for old and rare breeds.

Elham to Wye

7 At a T-junction turn left, then take the second right to Exted; the road, called Park Lane, is not signposted here and is easy to miss. Drive through Exted and, immediately after a sharp bend left, turn right onto a narrow road. At a T-junction turn right, then at the next junction turn left into Stelling Minnis. In the village follow the road left, passing a sign to a smock windmill. The windmill closed in 1970, but has since been restored and is now open to the public on Sunday afternoons in summer.

Continue to a junction with the B2068, the long arrow-straight Roman road known as Stane Street, linking Canterbury and Lympne. Turn left then immediately right on the narrow road signposted to Wye. About 1¼ miles after the old parish of Hastingleigh, high on the Wye Downs is a car park. This has panoramic views and is a good starting point for downland walks.

To return to Wye, turn right from the car park and follow the road for about 2 miles as it descends gently through woodland.

HOGTROUGH HILL, KENT
'Before the Roman came to Rye or out to Severn strode,
The rolling English drunkard made the rolling English road...'
G.K. CHESTERTON

Rambling round the shire

Rustic lanes may seem to meander aimlessly through southeastern England, yet their twists and turns are anything but haphazard.

The writer G.K. Chesterton knew knew what he was talking about when it came to English ale, and he also knew a good deal about the byways of the old country. 'The reeling road ... that rambles round the shire' that he mentions in his wonderful poem 'The Rolling English Road' remains one of the best-loved features of the southeast corner of England. So how did this network of narrow roads and winding lanes come to characterise the region?

The trackways of our prehistoric ancestors kept to the high ground as much as possible, where it was safe, and by and large pursued a long, straight course. On descending – to ford a river, for instance – the trackways made by human and animal feet would begin to bend and snake about. People found it hard to navigate in a straight line once they had abandoned an elevated viewpoint, and the valleys were marshy and thick with trees, impossible to cross without deviating this way or that.

Later, the super-efficient Romans, during their 400-year occupation of Britain, drove straight roads through every type of landscape. These, almost incredibly, formed the country's chief road network for most of the following two millennia, until the advent of the Industrial Revolution forced the British to improve their transport system and to build new, straight, well-engineered roads. Through all that time, though, local roads remained much as they had always been – crooked, wandering lanes and tracks, dusty in summer, miry in winter.

Soft ground

Early fields were small and irregular, and the lanes that threaded between them dodged around the field boundaries. In Cornwall and the Celtic fringe of Britain, this pattern remains widespread, but in the southeast of England, Britain's most heavily populated and developed area, few of these paths have survived in recognisable form. It's geology that plays a big hand hereabouts.

The southeast of England is composed mostly of chalk, greensand (a type of sandstone) and clay. Geologically, it is the softest region in Britain. On the High Weald of Kent, sandstone and clay are surrounded by softer ground. Towns and villages were built on the harder ridges, the winding roads dipping into the valleys and up to the next settlement. In Sussex and Hampshire, the uplands are dominated by soft chalk, so settlements arose in the valley bottoms, built on more stable flint and gravel.

The villages, ancient in form and developed by the Saxons, were gathered round a central green, house or church. They formed a rounded shape rather than spreading out along a road. The roads came to them from anywhere the geology would allow. East Meon in Hampshire, a classic nucleated village in a stream valley at the foot of steep Park Hill, lies like a spider at the hub of a web of six separate roads. These roads straggle down to the village, bending and twisting along with half a dozen footpaths from all quarters of the compass.

Beaten tracks

Kent and Sussex were always more pastoral than arable. They tended to retain grazing land rather than convert to the plough-friendly open field system when it first appeared in the early Middle Ages. A network of byways proliferated as villagers wended their way to and from the pastures to tend their herds and flocks. North Kent was pig territory and some old roads reflect the association, with either 'pig' or 'hog' in their names. On the North Downs, Hogtrough Hill snakes down the steep scarp slope from Knockholt on the way to Brasted, crossing the equally winding Pilgrims Way.

Lanes and tracks tended to follow the line of least resistance. Centuries of travellers – pilgrims, drovers, farmers, itinerant tradesmen as well as local people – found it easier to follow a stream or valley around a dense patch of wildwood than it was to go through it. To avoid going up and over hills, folk followed the contours and looked for natural breaks in the slope. Sunken lanes, once known as hollow ways, cut deeply through banks or ran through natural ravines. Formed by the passing of heels, hooves and wheels – pigs and cattle, sheep and oxen chose the line of least resistance, too – they deepened with use. Some developed along the channels made by flood streams in winter as torrents of water poured through softer clay and chalk, skirting round the harder rock as it went.

Many of these old routes continued in use through the years, their surfaces consolidated as motor vehicles came into general use. However, some in the network never carried enough traffic to justify the expense of modernisation, and these ancient byways still survive as grassy lanes and earthy tracks, often isolated and overgrown, and a haven for wildlife.

Road to nowhere

The tides of history swept away most of Britain's common land, including in the southeast. In the 14th century the Black Death emptied the countryside; 200 years later the Reformation put monastery lands on the market; landowners in the 18th and 19th centuries took what they wanted under the Enclosure Acts. Fields became bigger, boundaries straighter. The main roads were turnpiked, improved, straightened.

Many of the country roads were altered and diverted to follow suit, but by no means all. Old wriggly lanes still follow the geography, still wind and sinuate round vanished woods, through soft chalk banks and along ancient field boundaries. Sometimes they seem to be following a tortuous route for no particular purpose – Grovehurst Lane runs northeast from Horsmonden in Kent, twisting around as it crosses a ridge, winding down the hillside by Mount Easy Farm until it peters out inconclusively in the boggy bottom of the River Teise valley. Some more lines from 'The Rolling English Road' spring to mind: 'A merry road, a mazy road, and such as we did tread, the night we went to Birmingham by way of Beachy Head.' G.K. Chesterton would have loved Grovehurst Lane.

OXFORDSHIRE

The gentle pace of the county's rivers lend their quiet character to the landscape, where charming towns with fine houses and waterside walks offer a host of pleasant touring destinations.

9 THAME

TOUR LENGTH 50 miles

The countryside between the Chilterns and the Cotswolds is one of wide hilltop views, with strawberry-brick and black-timbered buildings scattered among little streams. At its heart is the market town of Thame, with its profusion of historic architecture.

Thame to Brill

1 Much of Thame's history is reflected in the buildings in Church Lane. These include the former grammar school, founded in 1569, the brick-and-timber almshouses next door, St Mary's Church, mainly 13th century but restored in Victorian times, and the prebendal house behind the church, also built in the 13th century.

Take the B4011 to Long Crendon. Turn right along Long Crendon High Street to visit the Courthouse (NT). Probably built in the 14th century, the courthouse was originally used by three lords of the manor, and sessions were held in its upper room. Leave the village by the B4011, taking the next right turn and following signs to the Buckinghamshire village of Brill. On reaching the village, bear right at the first junction, then left at the Sun Inn along Windmill Street. There is a car park beside the windmill, erected sometime in the 1680s for milling wheat and barley. It has recently been restored and is open to the public on the first Sunday of the month in summer.

Brill to Cuddington

2 Drive back along Windmill Street towards the Sun Inn and turn left towards Kingswood. Where the road divides, fork right to Wotton and Kingswood. Turn right at the next T-junction, then left after crossing the railway and bear right at the next junction to Kingswood. Turn right on the A41 at the crossroads, then left to Quainton and the Buckinghamshire Railway Centre, whose station served the main line and the Metropolitan Railway. The centre has a miniature railway and a collection of locomotives and runs steam train rides.

3 Drive on to Quainton. The main features of the village are a tall, red-brick tower windmill and 17th-century almshouses by the Church of Holy Cross and St Mary. At a T-junction, turn right towards Aylesbury, then right at the crossroads and right on the A41 to Waddesdon. Go left at the Five Arrows Hotel and follow the drive to Waddesdon Manor (NT), built by Baron Ferdinand de Rothschild between 1875 and 1883. Much of the 18th-century furniture, porcelain and carpets once graced the Palace of Versailles, and later became a backdrop for the baron's art collection. Return to the A41, turn right towards Aylesbury, then right on a minor road to Winchendon. Continue through Upper Winchendon then turn left towards Nether Winchendon and Cuddington. Follow the road to the right at the church, then turn left and left again to Cuddington, a village regularly used as a location for the TV series *Midsomer Murders*.

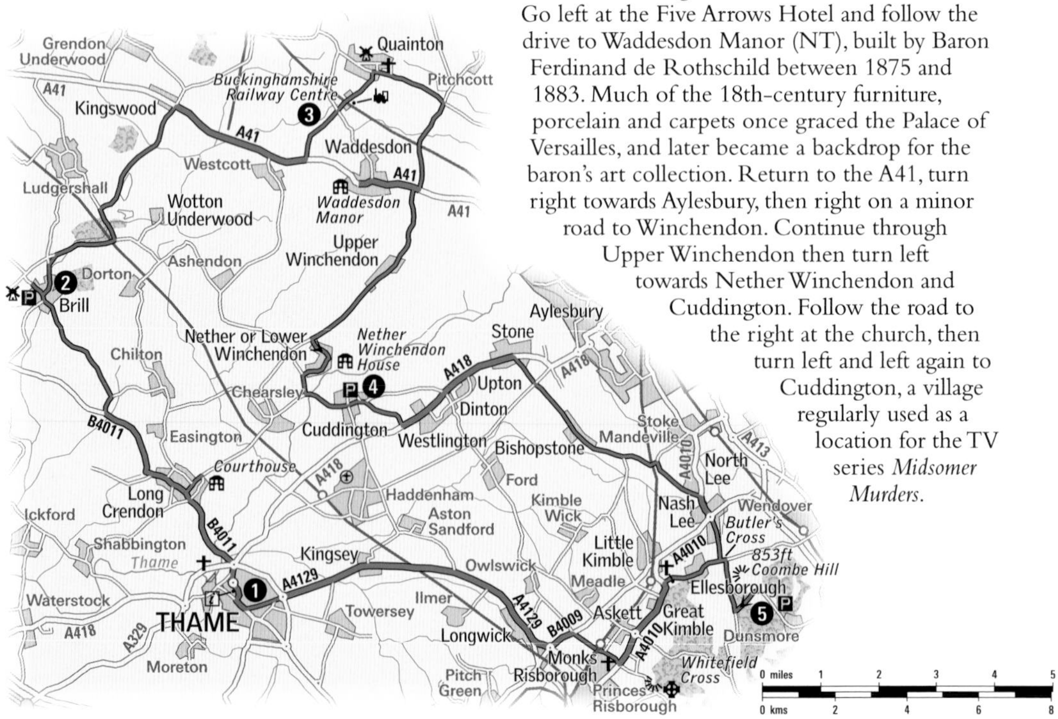

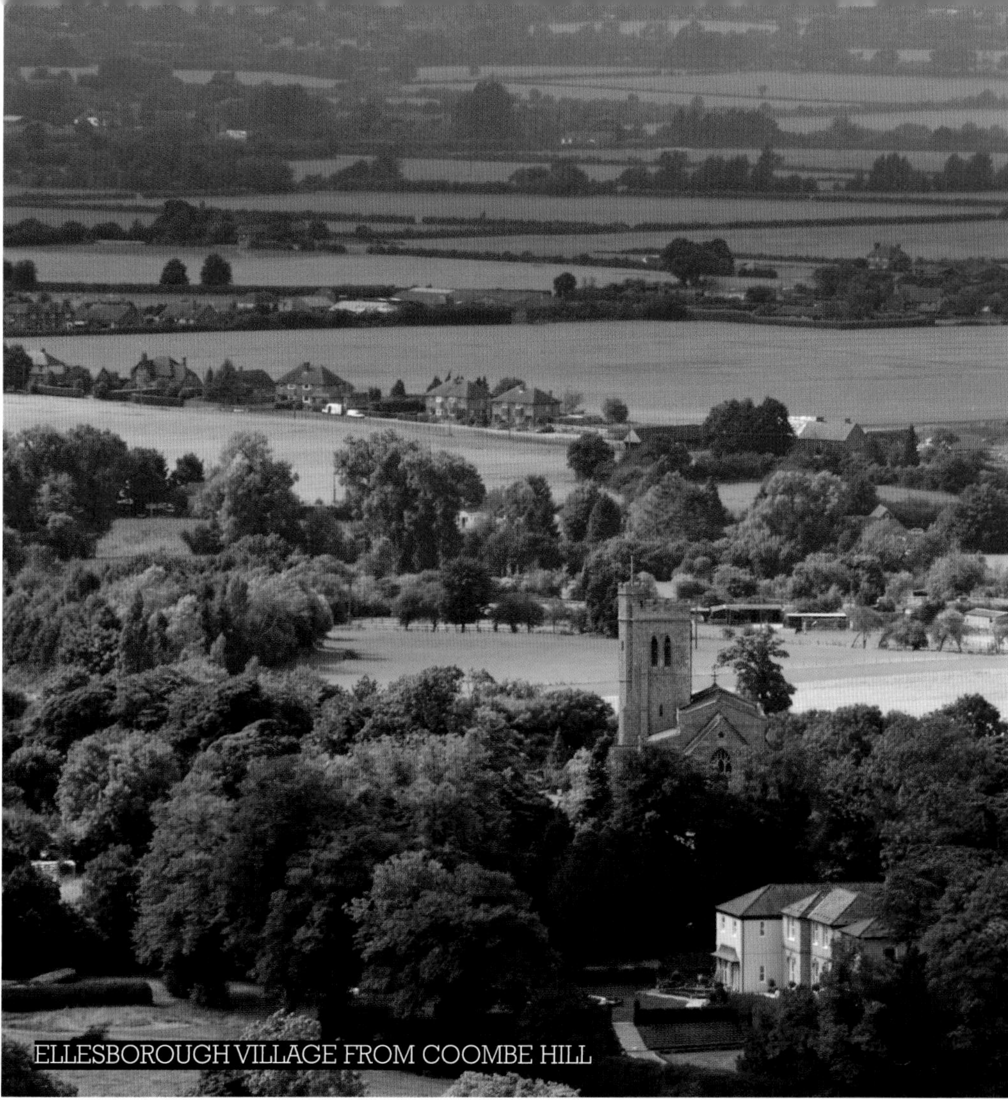
ELLESBOROUGH VILLAGE FROM COOMBE HILL

Turn left into Upper Church Street at The Crown pub. Follow the road past the church and Tyringham Hall, designed by Sir John Soane and under private ownership. Park in Lower Church Street opposite the village green to explore the village on foot. Cuddington is notable for its house and boundary walls made of wychert – local clay mixed with straw and stones – built on a foundation of 'grumpling,' or rocks. The village's annual fete attracts thousands of visitors every year.

Cuddington to Coombe Hill

4 Return to the main road into Cuddington and turn left at the crossroads. Turn right at the next junction, then left at a T-junction on the A418. At Stone, turn right on minor road to Bishopstone. Go straight on over the crossroads, and continue through the village and over a level crossing, turning right at a T-junction on the A4010. At a roundabout, take the first exit and immediately turn right for Butler's Cross and Ellesborough. Continue over the staggered crossroads at Butler's Cross, take the first left to Dunsmore and park at Low Scrubs on the left.

The car park marks the start of a walk to Coombe Hill, at 260m (852ft) the highest viewpoint in the Chilterns. An indicator on the summit points out sights from Chequers to Brill Hill, the Vale of Aylesbury and the Cotswolds beyond Oxford.

Coombe Hill to Thame

5 Return to the crossroads at Butler's Cross and turn left to Little Kimble, whose All Saints Church has some outstanding medieval wall-paintings. Continue to a T-junction beyond the church and turn left on the A4010 to Great Kimble, where in 1637 John Hampden and his parliamentary colleagues refused to pay King Charles I's tax known as Ship Money – starting a rebellion that would eventually lead to the outbreak of Civil War. Continue on the A4010 to Monks Risborough and the 14th-century Church of St Dunstan. Cut into the turf on the hillside opposite the village is the 24m (80ft) high Whiteleaf Cross. The cross is believed to have been carved in the 17th century – possibly to mark a junction of long-distance routes. From Monks Risborough return to Thame on the A4129.

OXFORDSHIRE

10 HENLEY-ON-THAMES

TOUR LENGTH 47 miles

Set off from a Thames boating town, loosely following the river's path until Cookham, when the route rises into the Chiltern Hills. Stop off for riverside walks, or a peek into the gallery of Cookham's Stanley Spencer.

Henley-on-Thames to Stonor

1 The first week in July sees Henley-on-Thames fill with people in blazers, white flannels and summer dresses, ready for the Henley Regatta. The rowing event began in 1839 and remains part of the English social calendar. The finishing post is the five-arched bridge built in 1786, overlooked by the 17th-century Red Lion inn and the flint-and-stone 16th-century tower of St Mary's Church. The town's prosperity was founded on beer as well as on boats, and the Henley Brewery has been brewing on its New Street site since 1826.

Leave Market Place on the Reading road and turn second left on Station Road, then right on Meadow Road to reach a car park. From here, you can stroll along the towpath following the regatta course.

For the drive, take the A4130, signposted to Wallingford. After 1¼ miles, turn right on the B480 to Stonor Park. The house dates from the 12th century and has been owned by the Roman Catholic Stonor family for more than 800 years. They gave sanctuary to the Jesuit Edward Campion, who was executed in 1581. At the first junction after Stonor Park, turn right, signposted to Turville Heath. At the next junction, turn right.

Stonor to Cookham

2 Continue along the Turville Heath road and turn right on a winding lane to a T-junction, with Turville to the left. Turn right and then left to Fingest. Bear left at the next junction through farmland and beech woods. At a junction with the B482 go straight on to the junction with the A40. Turn right to West Wycombe, a village of 17th and 18th-century houses. West Wycombe Park (NT) was rebuilt in the 18th century by Sir Francis Dashwood, the founder of the Dilettanti Society and the Hellfire Club, whose members were known for gambling and carousing. On a hill above the village is St Laurence's Church, altered by Sir Francis Dashwood, and the vast Dashwood Mausoleum built in 1765. Under the hill are caves dug in the 1750s to extract chalk; the caves were later used for Hellfire Club parties.

A TOWN MADE PROSPEROUS BY BOATS AND BEER

HENLEY-ON-THAMES

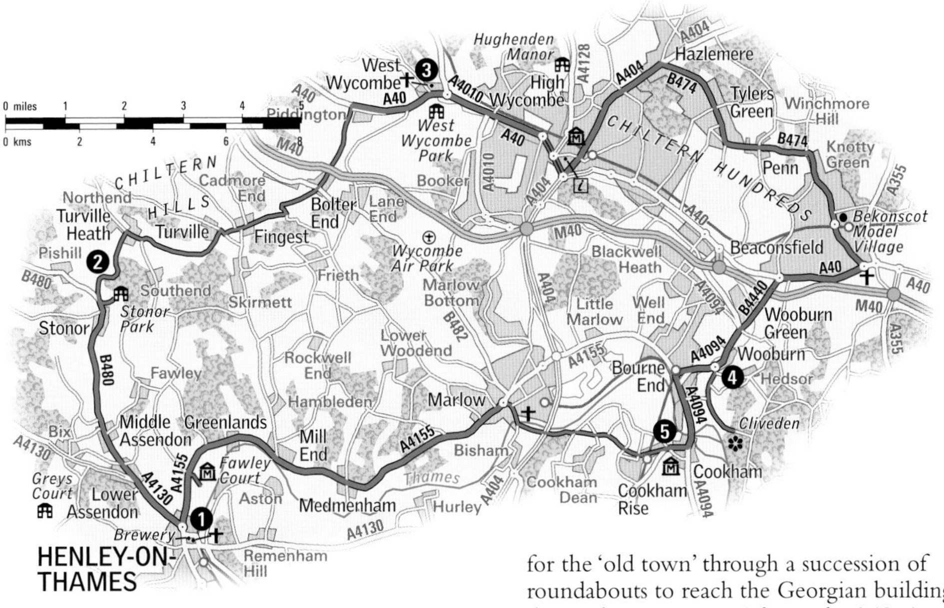

❸ Continue on the A40 into High Wycombe. Follow the A404 Amersham signs through a series of roundabouts to join the A404 towards Amersham. After 2½ miles, turn right on the B474 to Beaconsfield. Bekonscot Model Village, built in 1929, is indicated to the left. Follow signs for the 'old town' through a succession of roundabouts to reach the Georgian buildings of the High Street. Turn right on the A40, signposted to High Wycombe. At a double roundabout turn left on the B4440 towards Bourne End. At Wooburn Green junction, turn left on the A4094.

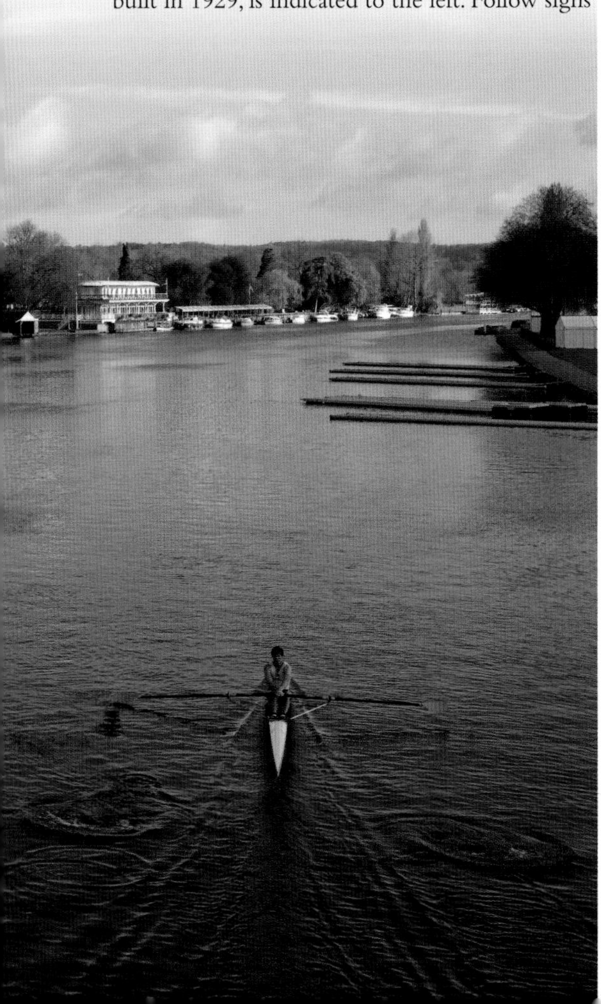

❹ After ¾ mile, take the turning from the roundabout to Cliveden, a 19th-century Italianate house (NT) designed by Sir Charles Barry. It was once the home of Nancy, Lady Astor, the first woman MP to take her seat in the Commons. The house is now a hotel, but some rooms and the gardens (NT) may be visited. Follow the A4094 to Bourne End and turn left to Cookham. Turn first right after the bridge into the High Street. The painter Stanley Spencer spent most of his life in and around Cookham – for him the scene of heavenly visitations. The Stanley Spencer Gallery is situated in the town's former Methodist chapel, open every day in summer and from Thurdsay to Sunday in winter.

Cookham to Henley

❺ Continue past Cookham railway station on a road that, after climbing steadily, winds steeply downhill, passing under the A404 to a T-junction. Turn right and cross a suspension bridge built in the 1830s into Marlow, past the tall spire of the 19th-century All Saints Church. The poet Percy Bysshe Shelley lived at Albion House in West Street with Mary Godwin, later his wife, in 1817-18.

Turn left at a roundabout onto A4155, signposted to Henley. Continue for 6 miles, through riverside villages of Medmenham and Mill End, to a left turn for Fawley Court, built in 1684 by Sir Christopher Wren, with carvings by Grinling Gibbons and grounds by Capability Brown. The mansion is owned by the Marian Fathers, a Polish religious order. Follow A4155 back to Henley.

SURREY

Manicured grounds and estate gardens give way to glorious greensand heaths in this scenic county. Tour idyllic villages with traditional Surrey architecture, and visit pretty churches with memorable histories.

11 SHERE

TOUR LENGTH 23 miles

A gentle drive through the undulating Surrey backwaters close to Dorking, through pretty hamlets and woodland hollow ways on the fringes of the North Downs.

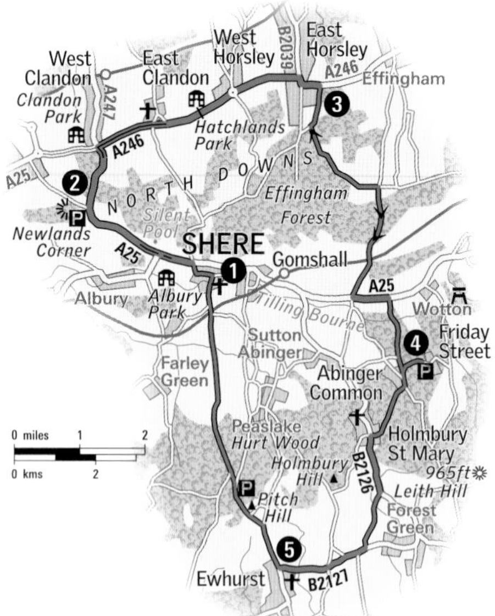

Shere to Newlands Corner

1 At the heart of Shere is a small triangular green, known as The Square, surrounded by houses and cottages varying in style from medieval half-timbered to Victorian. A lych gate leads to the 12th-century St James' Church. On the north wall of its chancel are two openings, behind which was a tiny cell, home to a 14th-century hermit, Christine Carpenter. Through one opening she received Holy Communion, and through the other she could see the altar. The Tilling Bourne river runs through Shere, dividing the flinty chalk of the Downs from the sandstone ridge of Hurt Wood. Both offer varied walking and fine views.

Take the A25 towards Guildford. On the right after ½ mile are the crystal-clear waters of the Silent Pool. Legend says that in 1193 a young woman bathing naked in the pool was disturbed by Prince John (later King John). To preserve her virtue, she retreated into the pool and drowned.

Follow the A25 to Newlands Corner. Turn left into the car park at the top of the hill for a viewpoint and lovely views across the Weald.

Newlands Corner to Friday Street

2 Continue on the A25 to some traffic lights. Turn right on the A246, signposted to Leatherhead. Just north of the junction is Clandon Park, a mansion (NT) designed in the 1730s by the Venetian architect Giacomo Leoni, with gardens by Capability Brown. To the left after ¾ mile is the village of East Clandon, grouped around the Norman church of St Thomas. Close by is Hatchlands Park (NT), built in the 1750s. The lovely grounds include a small garden designed in 1914 by Gertrude Jekyll. Continue on the A246, which zigzags past a Victorian gatehouse at the south end of East Horsley, once the main entrance to Horsley Towers, the home of Earl Lovelace, Lord Byron's son-in-law, who gave the village a Gothic Revival facelift in the 1860s.

3 Turn right onto a minor road, then fork left into Effingham Forest, with trees such as Douglas fir, Lawson cypress and western hemlock. At the next junction, turn right on a narrow road, signposted to Abinger, which rises through woodland and drops down to the A25. Turn left, then right on a road signposted to Abinger Common and Friday Street. After 1¼ miles, opposite Abinger Common, turn sharp left on a very narrow road, signposted to Friday Street. There is a car park on the right, just before the hamlet. Friday Street's half-timbered cottages sit among pine-clad hills facing a pond that once powered the local ironworks.

Friday Street to Shere

4 Return to Abinger Common. Turn right to Holmbury St Mary, in a valley below Holmbury Hill. It was popular with rich Victorians, whose houses in the pine woods on the steep slopes were designed by architects such as Norman Shaw and George Edmund Street. In 1879, Street built St Mary's Church at his own expense.

At a T-junction, turn left on the B2126. After 1 mile, turn right, then right again after about ½ mile onto the B2127 to Ewhurst.

5 At the Bulls Head pub turn right, signposted to Shere. Bear left on the rising road and turn sharp right at the top of Pitch Hill into the car park. There is a path rising from the car park past a sand quarry to the summit of Pitch Hill, which has magnificent views.

To return to Shere, continue north on narrow road, through woodland and farmland.

12 HASLEMERE

TOUR LENGTH 37 miles

Retreat to Surrey's deep green fringes, touring wooded roads that lead to charming villages on the county's sandy hills. Stop off at a country winery; a common famous for its profusion of wildlife; or visit woodland gardens with lakeside planting.

Haslemere to Lurgashall

1 Haslemere was hardly more than a village when the railway arrived in the 1850s, bringing with it eminent Victorians, such as the writers George Eliot and Sir Arthur Conan Doyle. In the town centre, the wide, gently rising High Street boasts some fine 18th-century buildings, notably the Georgian Hotel, and the dignified Town House. Every summer Haslemere hosts the Dolmetsch Music Festival, begun in 1925 by Arnold Dolmetsch, a pioneer in making early instruments such as lutes and harpsichords.

Take the A286 towards Midhurst. At the first major roundabout continue on the A286. After ¼ mile turn left onto Fernden Lane, which skirts the wooded heights of Black Down in the neighbouring county of West Sussex. The poet Lord Tennyson built the French style Gothic Aldworth House in 1869 on the east of the hill, and lived there – enjoying the luxury of piped water – until his death in 1892. The house remains in private ownership. Follow the road as it descends steeply.

2 At the T-junction at the bottom of the hill, turn right on Jobson's Lane towards Lodsworth. The road leads past Lurgashall Winery, where fruit and flower wines, meads and liqueurs are made. After ½ mile, turn left to Lurgashall, a lovely village neatly arranged around a wide triangular green. Park by the green to explore the village. Walkers can follow footpaths from the village on to Black Down for the highest point in Sussex and fabulous views.

Lurgashall to Hambledon

3 With the pub and church across the green on the left and the shop on the right, drive uphill and over the crossroads to the A283. Turn left through Northchapel with its timber-framed houses. After 2½ miles, a left turn at Ramsnest Common leads to Ramster gardens in Surrey, a woodland garden with lakes and ponds, open from early April to the end of June.

Follow the A283 to Chiddingfold, set around an unspoilt nucleus of tile-hung houses. The Crown Inn is said to date from 1285. A small lancet window in St Mary's Church has more than 400 fragments of glowingly coloured medieval glass – a remnant of the days when Chiddingfold had a flourishing stained-glass industry. A church is believed to have stood on the site of St Mary's since AD *c*978; there are now three churchyards with the Old Ground burials closest to the church layered four deep.

4 Continue on the A283 towards Witley. After 1½ miles, just past Wormley village sign, turn right, signposted to Hambledon. To the right, down Vann Lane, is the 16th-century Oakhurst Cottage (NT) – open by appointment. Its interior is preserved as a 19th-century labourer's dwelling. Continue ahead past handsome Victorian and Edwardian red-brick and tile-hung houses on the slopes of low sand hills. Turn right past Hilltop Farm and follow Church Lane to St Peter's Church to explore the lovely village of Hambledon – a Domesday village recorded in 1086 as *Hameledune*. The Greensand Way passes through the parish, taking walkers through woodland and over hills. In the churchyard of St Peter are two enormous yew trees – one hollow with a 9m (30ft) circumference. If you walk round the interior of the yew three times – according to local legend – you will see a witch. ▷

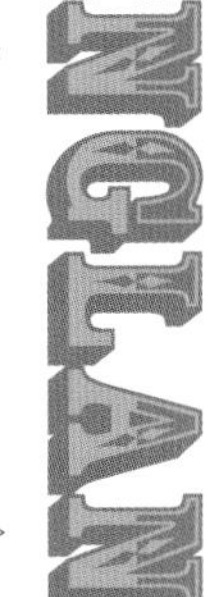

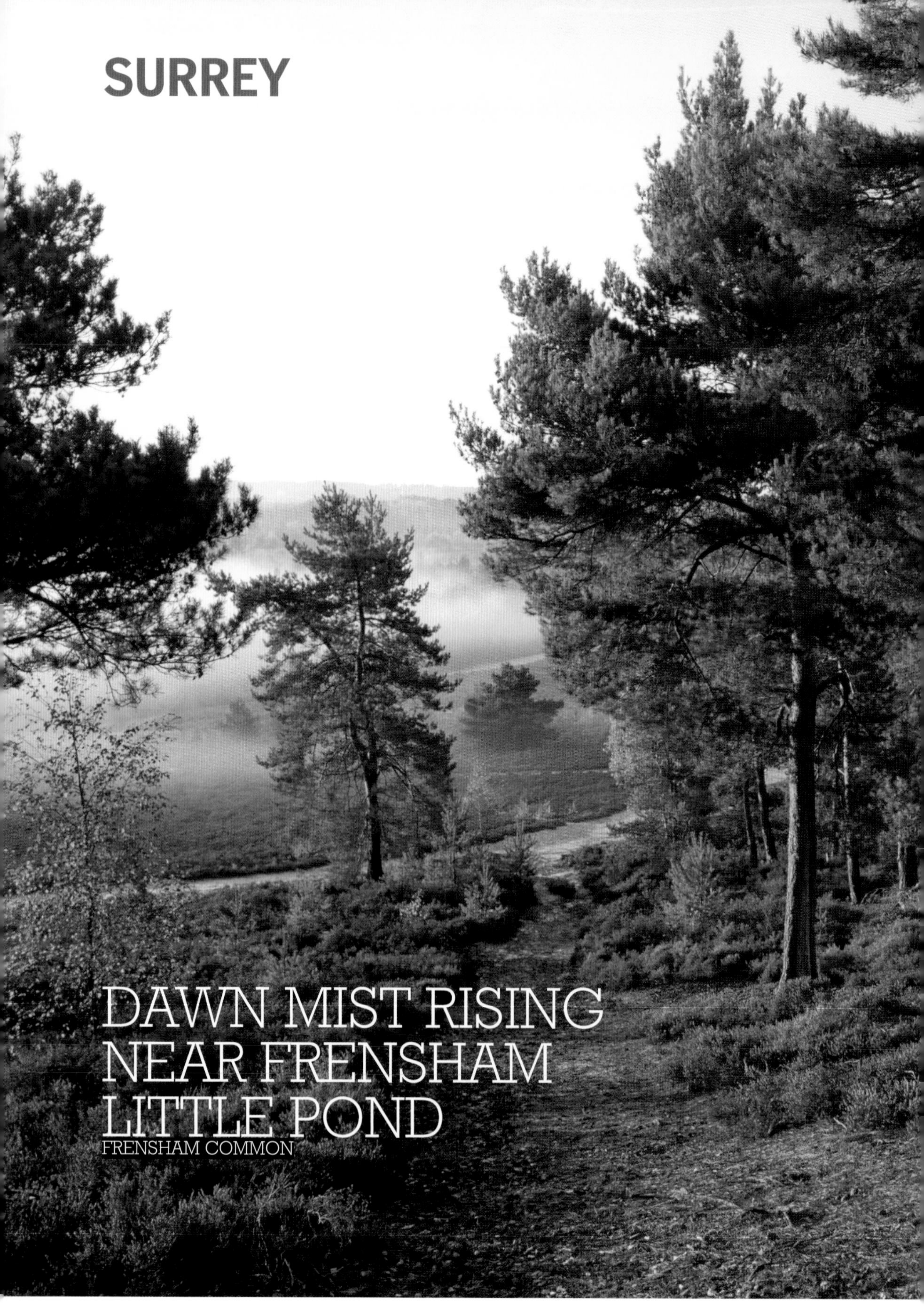

DAWN MIST RISING NEAR FRENSHAM LITTLE POND
FRENSHAM COMMON

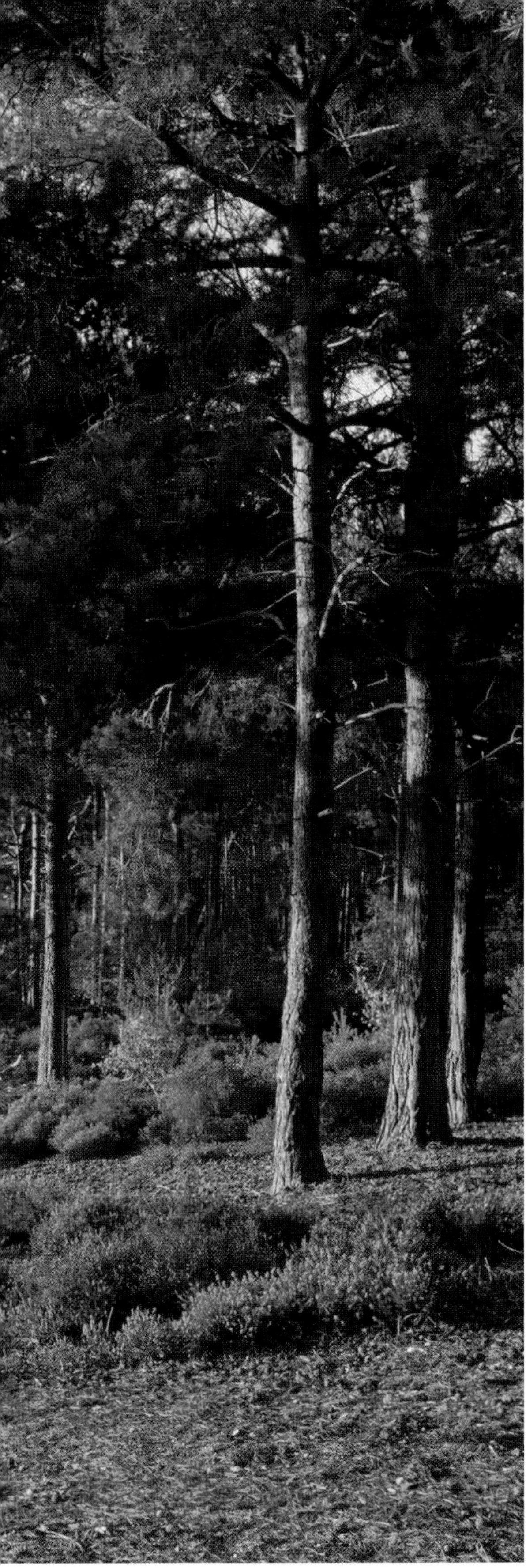

Hambledon to Frensham Common

5 Follow the A283 to Witley. Half-timbered, brick and tile-hung cottages cluster round All Saints Church, with its octagonal spire. The novelist George Eliot lived at The Heights in Witley from 1877 until her death in 1880.

Just before the Star Inn, ½ mile past the church, turn left on Wheeler Lane to the A286. Cross the A286 and follow the lane to the car park for Witley Common, a mixture of largely Scots pine woodland and open heath. It is rich in birdlife, such as goldcrests and crossbills, and butterflies, including the rare silver-studded blue.

6 Continue on the A286 and take the next right along Lea Coach Road to the A3. Turn left and after ½ mile turn right to Thursley. A winding street leads up to St Michael's Church, with its 15th-century timber belfry. The architect Sir Edwin Lutyens (1869-1944) grew up in a house near the green.

At the T-junction turn left towards Churt, then right at the T-junction towards Tilford. At end of Rushmoor village, turn left on lane to Frensham Little Pond (NT). The Great Pond and Little Pond date from the Middle Ages and were created to supply fish for the Bishop of Winchester's court when the court was residing at Farnham Castle. Frensham Common is a Site of Special Scientific Interest, its scrub, ponds and woodland a haven for local wildlife. There is a car park for the common on the left.

Frensham Common to Haslemere

7 Continue to the junction with the A287. Turn left and pass through Churt village, where the statesman David Lloyd George lived from 1925 to 1944. Follow the road through Hindhead. East of Hindhead is the deep bracken and heather-covered valley known as the Devil's Punch Bowl. Gouged into the greensand ridge, it is more than 2 miles long and ½ mile wide. The Devil, according to local lore, was supposed to have scooped the earth from it to fling at one of his foes, but it owes its existence to more earthly forces. Natural springs eroded the soft greensand rock forming a natural amphitheatre: it is the largest spring-formed feature in Britain.

On nearby Gibbet Hill, three men were hanged in 1787 for the murder of a sailor on the London to Portsmouth road. The site of the gibbet is marked by a cross. Continue on A287 and turn left into Haslemere past the railway station.

SUSSEX

Two drives tour the heritage of East and West Sussex, a southern county with a wealth of fascinating places to visit. Viewpoints from the high chalk downland abound, while pretty villages shelter in the valleys.

13 ARUNDEL

TOUR LENGTH 29 miles

Explore the lovely English landscape of the South Downs, starting at the picturesque town of Arundel, taking in a Roman villa, a medieval spired church, deep thatch cottages and a pretty river.

Arundel to Slindon

1 The small West Sussex town of Arundel, set on a hillside above the River Adur, is dominated by the mighty castle of the Dukes of Norfolk, whose battlements and towers loom over the surrounding trees. Settled by the Normans soon after the Conquest, the town has been steadily enlarged and strengthened through the centuries. The vast Roman Catholic cathedral across the road from the castle was built in the 1870s by the 15th Duke of Norfolk.

Leave Arundel on the A284 signposted to London and Dorking. After 2½ miles turn left at a roundabout on the A29 to Slindon. A parking place on the left 1 mile beyond the roundabout, at Fairmile Bottom, is the start of two waymarked woodland walks through a nature reserve.

Continue on the A29 for 2 miles and turn right on minor road to Slindon, a typical downland village, with many of its cottages built largely of flint, the local building material. The National Trust owns much of the village, including the post office and forge, as well as 3,500 acres of heavily wooded downland behind it. Park near the Newburgh Arms for a stroll around the village or a walk further afield.

Slindon to Bignor Hill

2 Continue on the road through Slindon for 1½ miles and turn right at a T-junction to Eartham, another flint-built village. Turn right at a T-junction in the village, continue to the A285 and turn right towards Petworth. This is a fine stretch of switchback road, across open downland backed by woods on either side. Two miles beyond Upwaltham the road leads up steep Duncton Down, where there is a viewpoint car park, and down the other side. Just before the bottom of the hill, turn right on a minor road to Sutton.

3 This zigzag road, linking the A285 and A29, runs along the lower edge of the Downs and is very narrow – mainly single-track with passing places. In Sutton look out for a right fork at the White Horse Inn to Bignor. Go through Bignor, following a sign by a church lych gate for the Roman villa, and passing a medieval yeoman's house on the left. At the next T-junction, turn right then immediately left by a thatched barn up to the car park on Bignor Hill. Ignore a track off to the left halfway up. The lane is narrow, bumpy and steep. From the car park it is a ½ mile walk along the South Downs Way to the hilltop; walkers are rewarded with magnificent views.

Bignor Hill to Amberley

4 Return to a T-junction at the foot of the hill and turn right to the Roman villa and West Burton. Bignor Roman Villa, one of the best-preserved Roman buildings in Britain, was discovered in 1811, when a ploughman unearthed a mosaic pavement. It was built for a powerful landowner, within easy reach of Stane Street, the main Roman road from Chichester to London. The mosaics include representations of gladiators, Medusa, and Ganymede carried off by an eagle.

Continue through West Burton to the A29. Turn right then immediately left down a lane to Bury, which bends right by a signpost to Amberley. To visit Bury, follow the sign for 'church and ferry closed'. Bury, once home to the writer John Galsworthy, nestles at the foot of the Downs. Its main street leads down to the tall-spired medieval Church of St John and a cluster of picturesque old houses beside the Arun. It was once linked by ferry to Amberley, across the river.

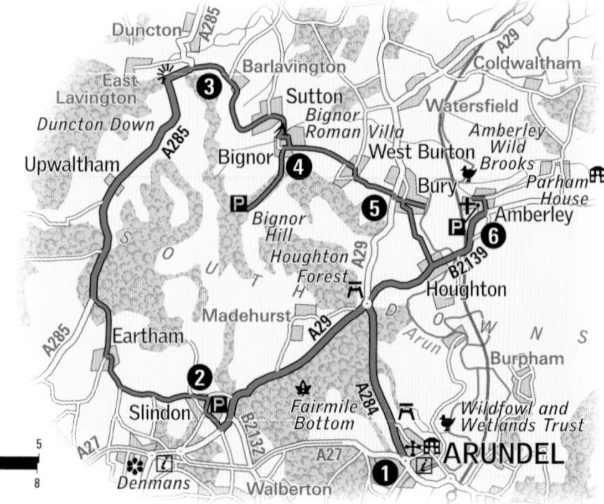

5 Continue to Houghton and turn left on the B2139 towards Storrington. Go under the railway line, and after ½ mile turn left to Amberley, one of West Sussex's prettiest villages, characterised by half-timbered thatched cottages surrounded by flower-filled gardens. Turn left in the village and park near St Michael's Church to explore on foot. The village's museum is dedicated to the southeast's industrial heritage and includes a display on the history of road making. Amberley Wild Brooks, on the floodplain of the River Arun, accessible by foot from the village, is a RSBP nature reserve noted for large numbers of wintering wildfowl, especially wigeon and teal.

Amberley to Arundel

6 From Amberley, return along the B2139 through Houghton to a roundabout. Turn left on the A284 to Arundel. Houghton Forest picnic site by the roundabout is the start of a waymarked walk through oak and beech plantations. The path is pre-Roman: follow the trail past an ancient tumulus to Bignor Hill.

ARUNDEL CASTLE

SUSSEX

14 LEWES

TOUR LENGTH 35 miles

A southern downland drive taking in the chalk clifftops of East Sussex, passing through the seaside town of Seaford, with its impressive coastal views of the Seven Sisters and Cuckmere Haven.

Lewes to East Dean

1 Lewes is a town of vistas, with the abrupt yellow-green slopes of the South Downs forming impressive backdrops to the historic streets. Its medieval, Georgian and Victorian buildings display an unusually diverse range of materials, including brick, knapped flint, plaster, pantiles, timber and stone. The High Street stretches along a sloping ridge from which walled paths and narrow lanes, known in the old Sussex dialect as 'twittens', drop steeply. The South Downs Way passes close by, offering bracing strolls along chalk ridges overlooking the western Weald's patchwork farmland.

Drive west up the High Street past the White Hart hotel on the left. Turn left at the traffic lights near the prison on a road signposted to Rodmell and Piddinghoe, and turn right at a mini-roundabout by the Swan Inn. The novelist Virginia Woolf, who died in 1941, spent her last years at Rodmell, living in a weatherboarded cottage called Monk's House (NT). At Piddinghoe a brick 'bottle kiln' bears witness to the village's 19th-century ceramic industry. St John's Church has a round tower, topped by a gilded weather vane depicting a salmon trout.

2 On the approach to Newhaven bear left on the A259, and follow the A259 by taking the first left off the one-way system towards Eastbourne. Continue to Seaford, and turn right on Marine Parade, signposted to the seafront. At the far end of Marine Parade is the massive bulk of Seaford Head, where a path climbs up to give magnificent views of the Seven Sisters and Cuckmere Haven. Seaford's Martello tower, part of a 19th-century chain of defence against Napoleon, is capped by a cannon and houses a museum of local history.

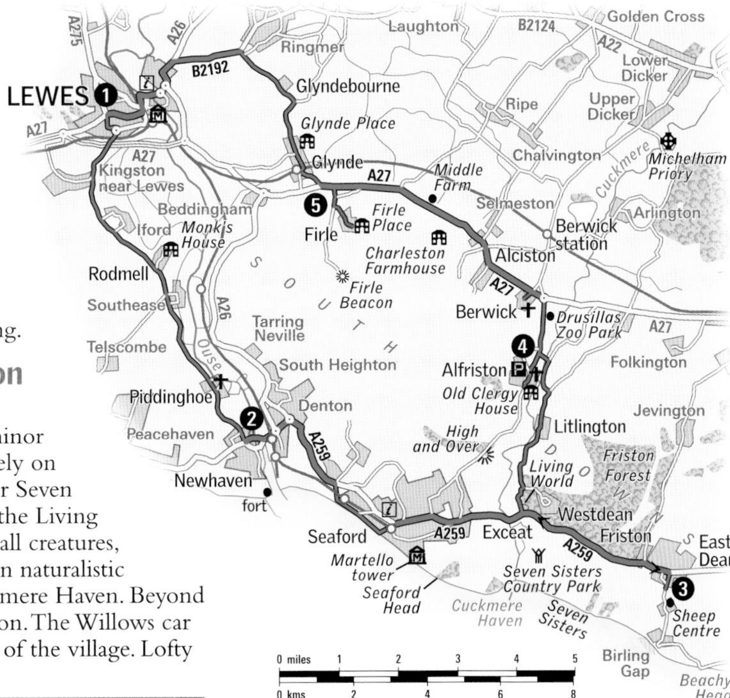

Continue on the A259 towards Eastbourne, crossing the Cuckmere to Exceat, Friston and East Dean. At East Dean turn right at the bottom of the hill towards Birling Gap. Flint-walled cottages overlook a war memorial and flagpole on the village green. Visitors to Seven Sisters Sheep Centre, south of the village, can see milking, shearing and spinning.

East Dean to Alfriston

3 Return on the A259 to Exceat and turn right on a minor road to Litlington. Immediately on the right is a visitor centre for Seven Sisters Country Park, where the Living World exhibition features small creatures, such as snails and scorpions, in naturalistic settings. A trail leads to Cuckmere Haven. Beyond Litlington, turn left to Alfriston. The Willows car park lies at the northern end of the village. Lofty 14th-century St Andrew's Church stands behind the main street. The thatched and half-timbered Alfriston Old Clergy House was the National Trust's first purchase, costing £10 in 1896.

ALFRISTON ON THE SOUTH DOWNS

Alfriston to Firle

4 From Alfriston follow the sign for Berwick station. On the right of the road, next to the English Wine Centre, is Drusillas, a family-run zoo whose features include a meerkat dome.

Turn left at the roundabout onto the A27 to Lewes. The first road on the left leads to Berwick, whose Church of St Michael and All Angels contains works by Duncan Grant, Vanessa Bell and Quentin Bell, the artists who lived at Charleston Farmhouse for a long period from 1916. The A27 leads past Middle Farm, a countryside centre with the largest selection of draught ciders in Britain. Turn left to Firle. Bear left again at the sign for the village and church.

Firle to Lewes

5 Return to the A27 and take the first right to Glynde and Ringmer. Glynde Place has a weatherboarded cupola topping a structure of Caen stone and local flint and chalk. The ancestral home of the Viscounts Hampden, it includes paintings by Zoffany and Rubens. The road leads past Glyndebourne, scene of one of the world's most celebrated opera festivals, held annually from May to August. Turn left on the B2192 to Lewes.

Scunthorpe
A18
M180
A15
A631
A1(M)
Peak District National Park
Castleton
3
A623
Buxton
2
A6
4
Bakewell
A61
M1
A619
Chesterfield
Worksop
A156
A57
A614
A1
Lincoln
A15
Matlock
Mansfield
A617
Newark-on-Trent
12
A46
A17
DERBYSHIRE
82-87
NOTTINGHAMSHIRE
104-105
A53
Leek
A523
Stoke-on-Trent
M6
A50
Stone
Ashbourne
A52
A515
Nottingham
A46
Derby
A52
A50
Grantham
Whitchurch
Oswestry
A49
A53
A41
A5
STAFFORDSHIRE
110-111
Tutbury
15
Stafford
A518
A51
Burton-upon-Trent
A606
A607
A1
Loughborough
Melton Mowbray
Shrewsbury
Telford
Cannock
Lichfield
A38
LEICESTERSHIRE
Stamford
8
Oakham
M54
Tamworth
Leicester
SHROPSHIRE
106-109
Walsall
A5
A444
A47
Wolverhampton
M6Toll
M42
M69
M1
A6
A458
14
Bridgnorth
Nuneaton
Market Harborough
A427
Corby
A49
Birmingham
WARWICKSHIRE
118-119
M6
Kettering
A14
Ludlow
13
Kidderminster
Coventry
A45
NORTHAMPTONSHIRE
A456
A449
Bromsgrove
Rugby
Redditch
A49
WORCESTERSHIRE
M1
A508
A509
A45
Warwick
Leominster
A44
M40
Daventry
Northampton
HEREFORDSHIRE
A46
Stratford-upon-Avon
19
A438
Worcester
A5
A43
Great Malvern
Evesham
A429
Hereford
A438
A465
A49
M50
A44
Tewkesbury
5
Stow-on-the-Wold
7
A417
Ross-on-Wye
Cheltenham
Gloucester
GLOUCESTERSHIRE
88-93
Forest of Dean
6
Painswick
Cotswold Hills
Cirencester
A48
M5
A46
M4

Central England

From the Peak District in the north to the wild expanse of the eastern fens, the tours of central England embrace a landscape that shifts from rugged to gentle, revealing the country's spectacular scenic variety.

CAMBRIDGESHIRE

The county's quiet roads offer far-reaching vistas, its fields and wooded horizons dotted with old church spires and towers. To the north, the Fenland capital of Wisbech makes a superb base for waterside tours.

1 WISBECH

TOUR LENGTH 111 miles

This drive around the haunting flatlands of the Fens takes in some attractive Georgian towns, in Norfolk as well as Cambridgeshire, touching the coast before ending with a detour to the River Nene and The Wash.

Wisbech to Snettisham

1 Wisbech once bordered The Wash, but as a result of centuries of drainage and reclamation, it is now situated 12 miles inland. Despite this, the town still operates as a port. North and South Brink, two fine Georgian streets, face each other across the River Nene, and Peckover House (NT) is pre-eminent among the many handsome buildings. Octavia Hill, the co-founder of the National Trust, was born at 1 South Brink Place, which is now a museum (not NT).

To start the drive, take the B198, signposted to Walsoken and West Walton. At the roundabout turn left on to the A47 for about 8 miles towards King's Lynn, in Norfolk.

2 At the roundabout where the A17 joins from the left, turn right over the Great Ouse, then turn left at the next roundabout and enter King's Lynn through its imposing South Gates. By the 14th century, the town, also then on the coast, was a major port, and its merchant wealth is reflected in the handsome medieval guildhall and 17th-century custom house.

3 Leave King's Lynn on the A1078. After a while, the road joins the A148. Turn left at a roundabout on to the A149, then first left to Castle Rising, where the Norman castle (EH) has a vast 12th-century keep.

4 Continue on the A149 for about 2 miles and turn right towards the royal estate of Sandringham. To the left is a visitor centre with parking. The estate was given to the future Edward VII by Queen Victoria, and he rebuilt the house in neo-Jacobean style in 1870. Many of the rooms, the gardens and a museum in the old stable block can be visited, when the Queen is not in residence.

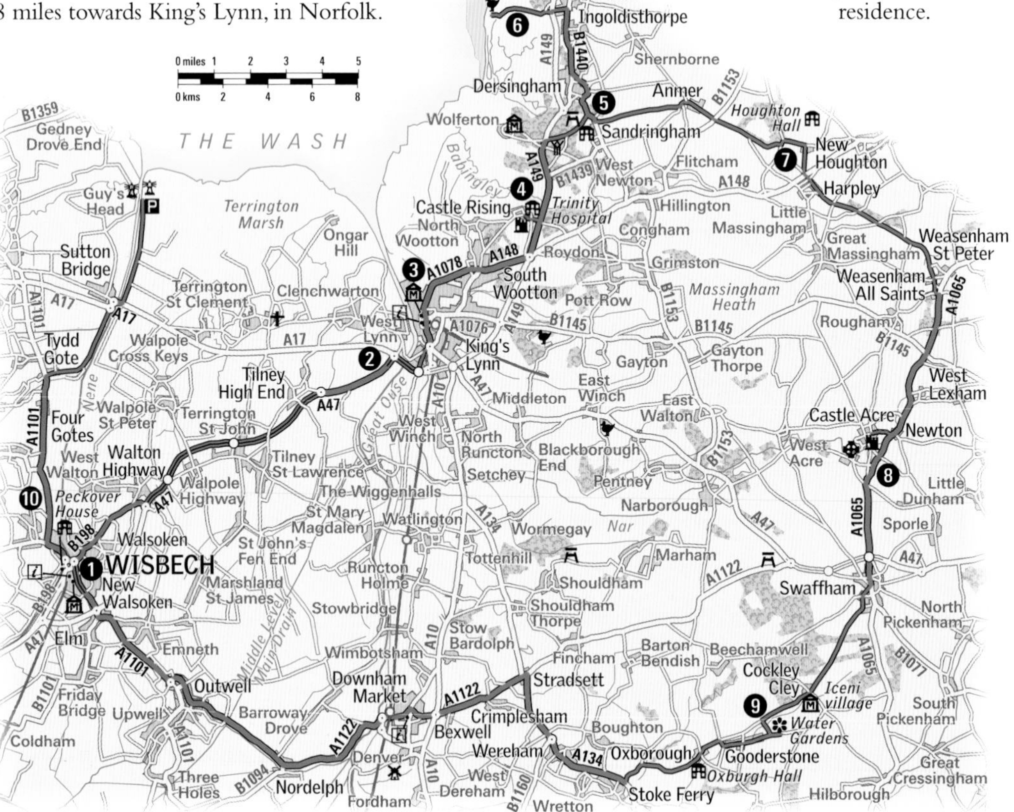

SANDRINGHAM HOUSE

5 Continue beyond the visitor centre to a T-junction beside the ornate Norwich Gates, and turn left on to the B1440 to Dersingham. At the traffic lights, turn right. Continue to Snettisham. Turn left on to Station Road. A sign points to Snettisham Mill. At the T-junction with the A149, turn left then right to Snettisham beach.

Snettisham to Castle Acre

6 Return to the Norwich Gates and turn left, keeping to the B1440. Take the second left turn (unsigned) past Sandringham Stud to the crossroads beyond Anmer. Go straight on, signposted to New Houghton. At a T-junction turn left, then right to New Houghton. Enter the village to reach Houghton Hall, a Palladian house built in the 1720s for Sir Robert Walpole, Britain's first prime minister.

7 Turn right at the gates of Houghton Hall and continue to Harpley. Cross the A148 and go over several unsignposted junctions. Then follow the signs to Weasenham. In the village, go straight over the crossroads. Turn left at a T-junction and immediately right on to the A1065. At Newton, turn right for Castle Acre. A 13th-century bailey gate with two round towers spans the village street and the ruins of the priory (EH) are among the best-preserved monastic sites in England.

Castle Acre to Wisbech

8 Return to the A1065 and turn right to the Georgian town of Swaffham. By the domed market cross, take a minor road signposted to Cockley Cley, where there is a replica of a stockaded village of AD 60.

9 Continue on the minor road – a detour to the left goes to Gooderstone Water Gardens – and turn left to Oxborough and Oxburgh Hall (NT), a 15th-century moated manor house with a gatehouse that towers over its surroundings. Continue to a T-junction with the A134 and turn right. At the junction with the A1122, turn left to the old town of Downham Market. Keep to the A1122 through the town, merging with the A1101 at Outwell. Continue to Wisbech.

Wisbech to The Wash

10 Follow the A1101 through Wisbech. At Tydd Gote, turn right to follow the River Nene to Sutton Bridge. Where two roundabouts adjoin, follow the signs to King's Lynn, cross the Nene and then turn immediately left towards Wingland. Fork right over a cattle grid to a car park. Two lighthouses stand by the River Nene, one on each bank. Originally, the lighthouses were at the very edge of the coast, but the land beyond has since been reclaimed from the sea.

DERBYSHIRE

The hills and dales of Derbyshire's Peak District are a scenic delight and thrilling to drive, while the county's pretty towns and aristocratic country halls offer pleasant interludes to each journey.

2 BUXTON

TOUR LENGTH 44 miles

From Buxton and the nearby Buxton Country Park, this round trip leads across high moors and down dales through some of the most spectacular scenery in the Peak District, interspersed with a towering railway viaduct, a mill town and two reservoirs.

Buxton to Miller's Dale

1 The elegant spa town of Buxton is set in the Derbyshire hills 305m (1,000ft) above sea level. The Slopes, landscaped in the early 19th century, sweep down from the market place, offering magnificent views over The Crescent, which was built in the late 18th century by the 5th Duke of Devonshire. The lavish Edwardian Opera House and the huge dome of the former Devonshire Royal Hospital can also be seen.

To start the drive, take the A6 towards Matlock and Derby, descending between limestone slopes into Ashwood Dale and then Wye Dale. Above the Wye to the left is the old railway track that once linked Buxton with the London to Manchester line. The sinuous road climbs to a designated viewpoint, where parking is available.

2 Less than a mile beyond the viewpoint, take a left turn on to the B6049 for Miller's Dale, just after a single-track road. At the hamlet of Blackwell, go straight over the crossroads. The road dips under an arch of trees and winds sharply down to the river. Turn left for Wormhill and left again into the old station car park at Miller's Dale. The nearby viaduct offers dramatic views of the River Wye, and inside the station the National Park Authority has installed a display about the area.

Miller's Dale to Gradbach

3 Return to the A6, turn right towards Buxton and then left on to the A5270 signposted to Brierlow Bar. At a T-junction turn right on to the A515, then first left to Longnor. Just past a huge quarry works on the left, the peaks stretch out ridge after ridge as far as the eye can see. The road descends steeply to Glutton Bridge over the River Dove, the boundary with Staffordshire. Follow the road into Longnor, which has an imposing Victorian market hall – now a craft centre – which bears a list of market tolls payable in the early 20th century.

4 Retrace the route out of Longnor, and take the first left to Flash. At the T-junction turn left on to the A53 and shortly afterwards take first right turn to Flash. At 462m (1,518ft) above sea level, this is the highest village in Britain. At one time its inhabitants were known for making counterfeit money.

Follow the road down through hills carpeted with bracken, heather and gorse to the River Dane. The left fork goes to the Gradbach Youth Hostel, which is a converted 18th-century flax mill, and a Peak National Park car park. Drystone walls crisscross lush pastures in the surrounding hills, defining ancient field boundaries.

Gradbach to Bollington

5 Return to the road and turn left on a hairpin bend over the River Dane to Allgreave. At a T-junction by the Rose and Crown pub, turn left on to the A54 towards Congleton. After the road crosses Clough Brook, take the first right turn for Wildboarclough, a former mill community where, in the 15th century, England's last wild boar were hunted to extinction.

At a T-junction, with the Stanley Arms on the right, turn left towards Macclesfield, and bear left at the next fork, nearly a mile farther on. At the next T-junction turn left on to the A537, pass the

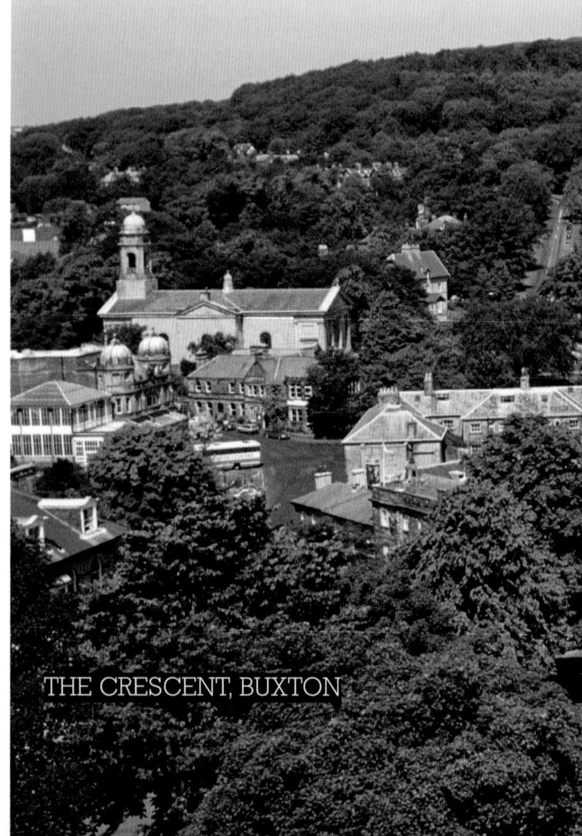

THE CRESCENT, BUXTON

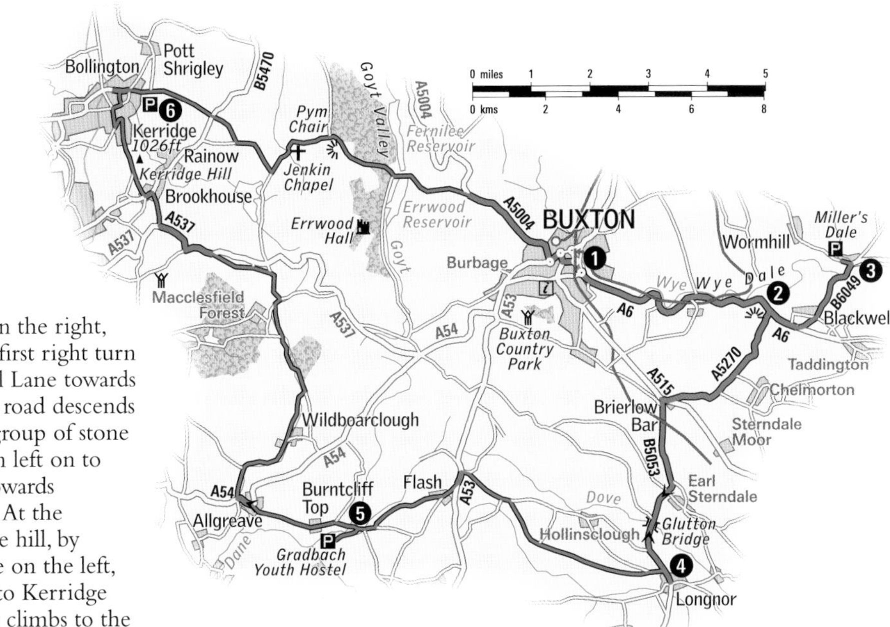

Setter Dog on the right, and take the first right turn into Bull Hill Lane towards Rainow. The road descends steeply to a group of stone cottages. Turn left on to the B5470 towards Macclesfield. At the bottom of the hill, by a stone house on the left, turn right into Kerridge Road, which climbs to the Redway Tavern. Bear left; at the next T-junction turn right into Bollington, a stone-built mill town. In the main street, the turning opposite the Spinners Arms leads to Pool Bank car park.

Bollington to Buxton

6 Follow the signpost to Rainow along the narrow Ingersley Road. After 2 miles, turn right at a T-junction on to the B5470 and then immediately left towards the Goyt Valley. High above is the 18th-century Jenkin Chapel, in a pretty tree-lined churchyard. The road climbs to the viewpoint of Pym Chair, then narrows and drops steeply to the Goyt Valley.

Errwood Reservoir and Fernilee Reservoir to its north have replaced the paint mill, gunpowder factory and farms of 60 years ago, but the ruins of the Victorian mansion Errwood Hall, in the care of the Peak Park Authority, can still be visited.

At Errwood Reservoir and before a gateway, turn left, signposted to Buxton. The road rises on to bare moors. At the T-junction, turn right on to the A5004 to Buxton.

DERBYSHIRE

3 CASTLETON

TOUR LENGTH 47 miles

The starkly beautiful Snake Pass and a 17th-century village feature on a route through dramatic territory, where the White Peak's pale limestone rubs shoulders with the Dark Peak's gritstones and shales.

Castleton to Hathersage

1 Framed by an amphitheatre of cliffs and steep-raked slopes, Castleton is sheltered by a steep escarpment, a natural wall split by the deep ravine of Cave Dale and gouged by Peak Cavern, the yawning mouth of which is 30m (100ft) wide and 18m (60ft) high. The ruins of Peveril Castle (EH) are perched high on the edge of the escarpment overlooking the village.

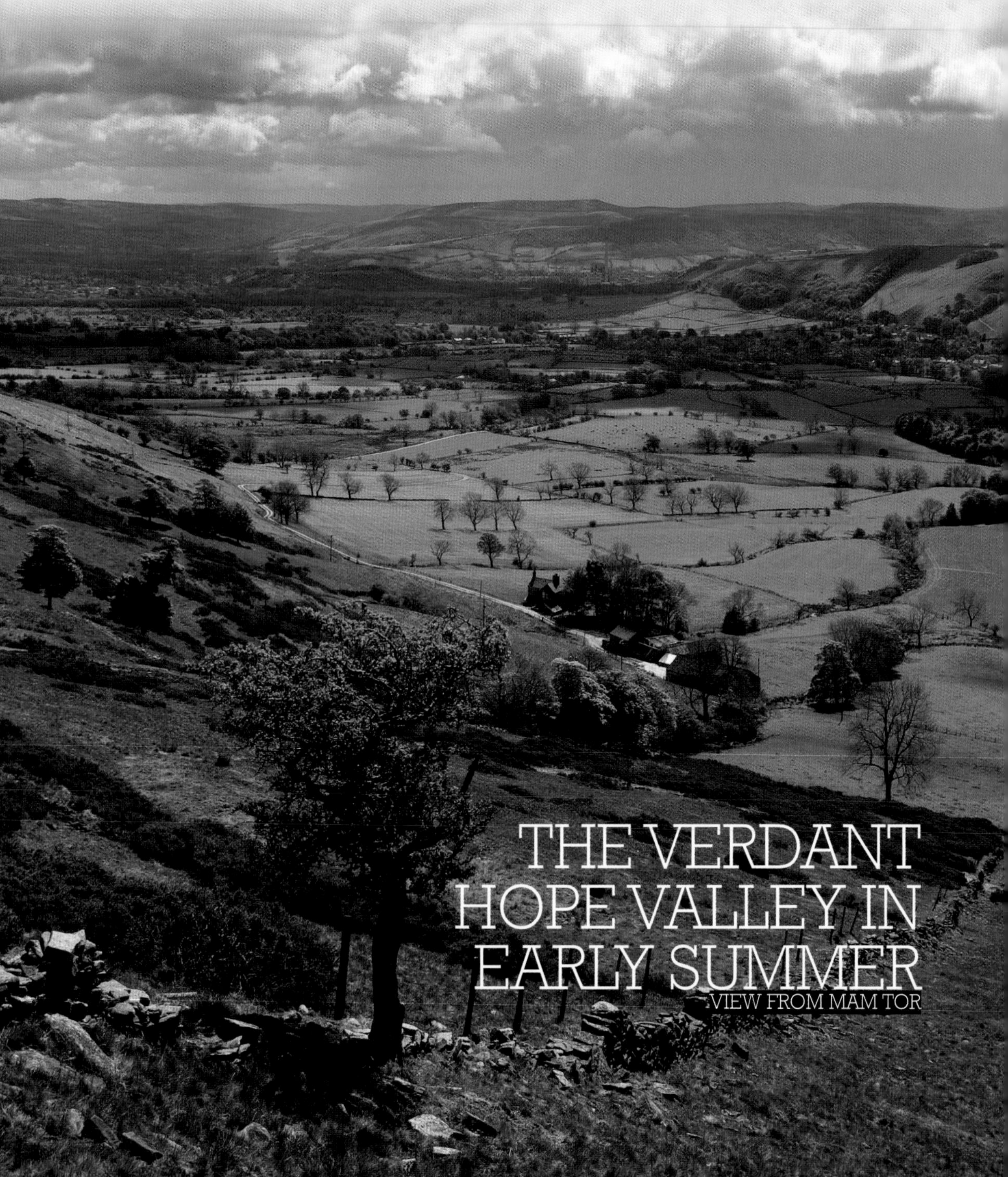

THE VERDANT HOPE VALLEY IN EARLY SUMMER
VIEW FROM MAM TOR

For the first leg of the drive, take the A6187 through Hope to Hathersage, which was once a centre of needle, metal button and wire manufacturing. St Michael's Church is linked with the writer Charlotte Brontë, who took the name of Eyre – a local family commemorated by brasses in the church – for her eponymous heroine in *Jane Eyre* (1847). The churchyard contains what is said to be the grave of Robin Hood's lieutenant, Little John. For the car park, turn right on to the B6001 in the middle of town, then left into Oddfellows Road.

Hathersage to Edale

2 Return to the A6187 and turn left, then almost immediately right on to Jaggers Lane. Take the first right, Coggers Lane, and fork left where the road divides. At the T-junction turn left, signposted to Ladybower.

3 The minor road descends to a junction with the A6013. Turn right on to the A6013, and the Ladybower dam can be seen straight ahead. Continue past the side of the dam to Ladybower Reservoir – the largest artificial lake in Britain when it was opened in 1945. Cross a viaduct to a T-junction and turn left on to the A57. The road goes over another viaduct, with a viewpoint car park a short distance beyond, on the right.

4 Continue on the A57, which follows the tapering finger of water all the way to its tip, then begins to climb the Woodlands Valley, through which the River Ashop flows. This stretch of the drive is called Snake Road, after the coiled serpent design on the coat of arms of the Cavendish family, the dukes of Devonshire. Beyond the head of the valley lies the 503m (1,650ft) high Snake Pass, a desolate stretch of rock and peat. From the top of the pass the road runs downhill to Glossop.

5 On the edge of the town, turn right to Old Glossop – a well-preserved 17th-century village set around a tiny square with a fine church, St Luke's. Return to the A57 and turn right to reach the centre of Glossop. This mill town has a clutch of Victorian civic buildings, including the Market Hall, Norfolk Square and the station.

6 From Glossop, take the A624 towards Chapel-en-le-Frith. The road goes through Hayfield, a centre for hill walking, which is also situated on the Sett Valley Cycleway. At a roundabout just beyond where the A624 goes under the A6, on the edge of Chapel-en-le-Frith, turn left and at the next roundabout turn right on to the A6. Then take the first slip road off the dual carriageway and turn left on a minor road signed for Slackhall. After 1 mile, a left turn at a minor crossroads in Slackhall leads to the Chestnut Centre, an otter haven and owl sanctuary.

7 Return to the crossroads and turn left. The road climbs gently for a few miles to a picnic site and parking place with a view ahead of the ridge between Mam Tor and Lose Hill and, to the right, of a high limestone plateau. Turn left at the picnic place towards Edale. Barber Booth, a hamlet at the head of the vale, is one of five similar farming communities – the Booths – scattered along Edale. All lie on a south-facing slope, slightly above the valley floor. The village of Edale is a starting point for ramblers and the station has a car park.

Edale to Castleton

8 Stay on the valley road past Nether Booth to Edale End, where the River Noe makes a great bend southwards, squeezing through a narrow gap in the hills. The road follows the valley through Townhead Bridge to Hope. At a T-junction in Hope, turn right on to the A6187 to return to Castleton.

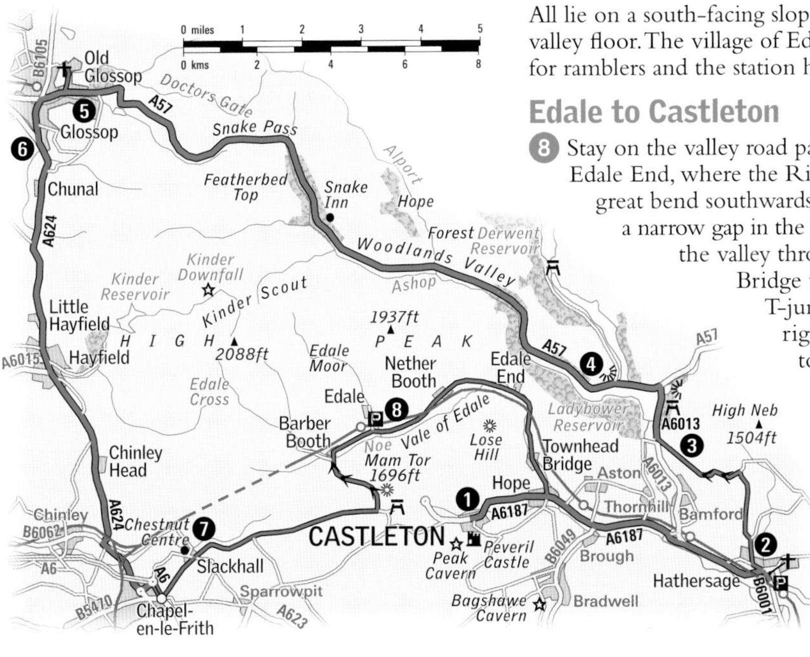

DERBYSHIRE

4 BAKEWELL

TOUR LENGTH 38 miles

Historical grandeur, in the shape of Chatsworth, complements the old stone villages and open landscapes of this short drive, which starts and ends at Bakewell in the heart of the Peak National Park.

Bakewell to Stanton Moor

1 The market town of Bakewell, first settled in Roman times, has some fine old buildings, including the Market Hall, the Old House Museum, the Town Hall and the Rutland Arms Hotel, where Jane Austen is said to have stayed. In *Pride and Prejudice* she disguised Bakewell as 'Lambton'. Around 1860, a chef at the Rutland Arms created Bakewell pudding, a local delicacy still made today. Bakewell's regular Monday market and its August show attract huge crowds.

To start the drive, take the A619 signposted to Sheffield and Chesterfield, crossing a medieval bridge on Baslow Road, and continue up through lightly wooded countryside. Where the A6020 joins from the left, fork right on to the B6048 to Pilsley and Chatsworth. At the entrance to Pilsley, one of three estate villages, is the Chatsworth Farm Shop.

2 At a T-junction beyond the village, turn right on to the B6012, following signs for Chatsworth. Just past a second estate village, Edensor, there is access to Chatsworth Park, where sheep and deer graze on gentle slopes below woodland.

3 Continue on the B6012, crossing the River Derwent by a single-track humpback bridge, and go past Beeley, another estate village. At a T-junction turn right on to the A6 at Rowsley, passing Caudwell's Mill, a flour mill and craft centre off to the left. After 1 mile, turn left on to the B5056 towards Ashbourne and Youlgreave. Ignore the right turn to Youlgreave but turn left uphill through the stone village of Stanton in Peak and continue climbing steeply for 1 mile to Stanton Moor. This heather-clad, gritstone plateau was used extensively as a burial ground in the Bronze Age, and as a place of worship. Remains include stone and ring cairns, stone circles and a massive megalith known as Cork Stone.

Stanton Moor to Beresford Dale

4 Drive on past a quarry works, bearing right into Birchover, and at the next T-junction turn left to rejoin the B5056. Robin Hood's Stride, a dramatic gritstone outcrop crowned by twin tors 21m (70ft) apart, can be seen to the right. At the first crossroads, turn left on to the B5057 for Winster, a former lead-mining centre and market town. The late 17th-century Market House (NT) acts as a tourist information centre.

5 Turn right up West Bank, just past a church. At the T-junction turn left on to the B5056 and immediately right, signposted to Elton and Newhaven. After 3 miles, turn right on to the A5012 and go through Pikehall. Follow the road through moorland crisscrossed with drystone walls. At Newhaven turn right on to the A515 signposted to Buxton and Sterndale Moor.

6 A short detour from the route leads to Beresford Dale – after 1 mile turn left on to the B5054 through Hand Dale to pretty Hartington. Another mile beyond the village, the road on the left leads to Beresford Dale and the tranquil River Dove. This was once a favourite haunt of the poet, writer and ardent fisherman Izaak Walton, who expressed his quiet philosophy and passion for his sport in *The Compleat Angler* (1653). A little way along the river, the ruins of the house built by his friend and fishing companion Charles Cotton may be seen.

Beresford Dale to Bakewell

7 Go back to Hartington and a mile beyond the village, turn left up Long Dale, signposted to Crowdecote and Earl Sterndale.

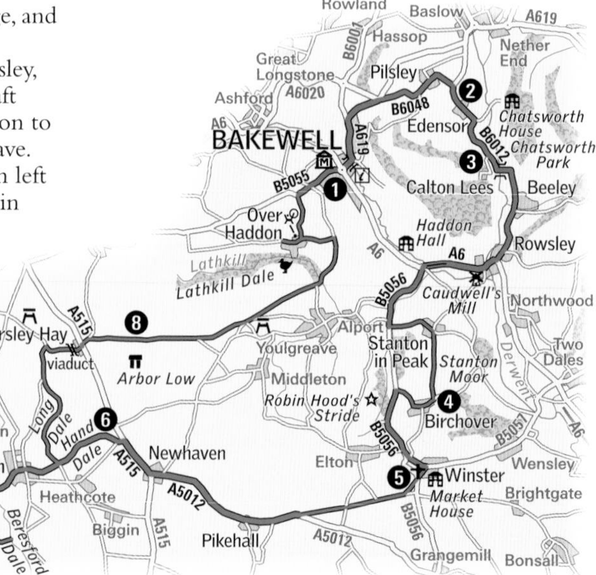

0 miles 1 2 3 4 5

0 kms 2 4 6 8

Continue for 2½ miles, climbing gently between craggy slopes where trees sprout from rocky outcrops in a landscape of isolated calm. Just past a solitary farm, turn right for Parsley Hay. Go under an old railway viaduct, turn left on to the A515 and then right on to a road signposted to Monyash, Youlgreave and Arbor Low (EH). Almost immediately, turn right towards Lathkill Dale and Youlgreave. After ¼ mile, a farm track on the right leads to a small car park for Arbor Low, a henge monument comprising a ditch and bank, and a circle of fallen limestone slabs. It is thought to have been built 4,000 years ago. The track is privately owned and there is a charge for using it, although entrance to the monument is free.

8 Continue on the Youlgreave road. Beyond a stone works, where the main road bears right to Youlgreave, take the road ahead that is signposted to a picnic area. Pass the turning to Youlgreave on the right and the picnic site and continue along the hilltop and down a slope to cross the River Lathkill. A mile beyond the river, turn left opposite a farm driveway,

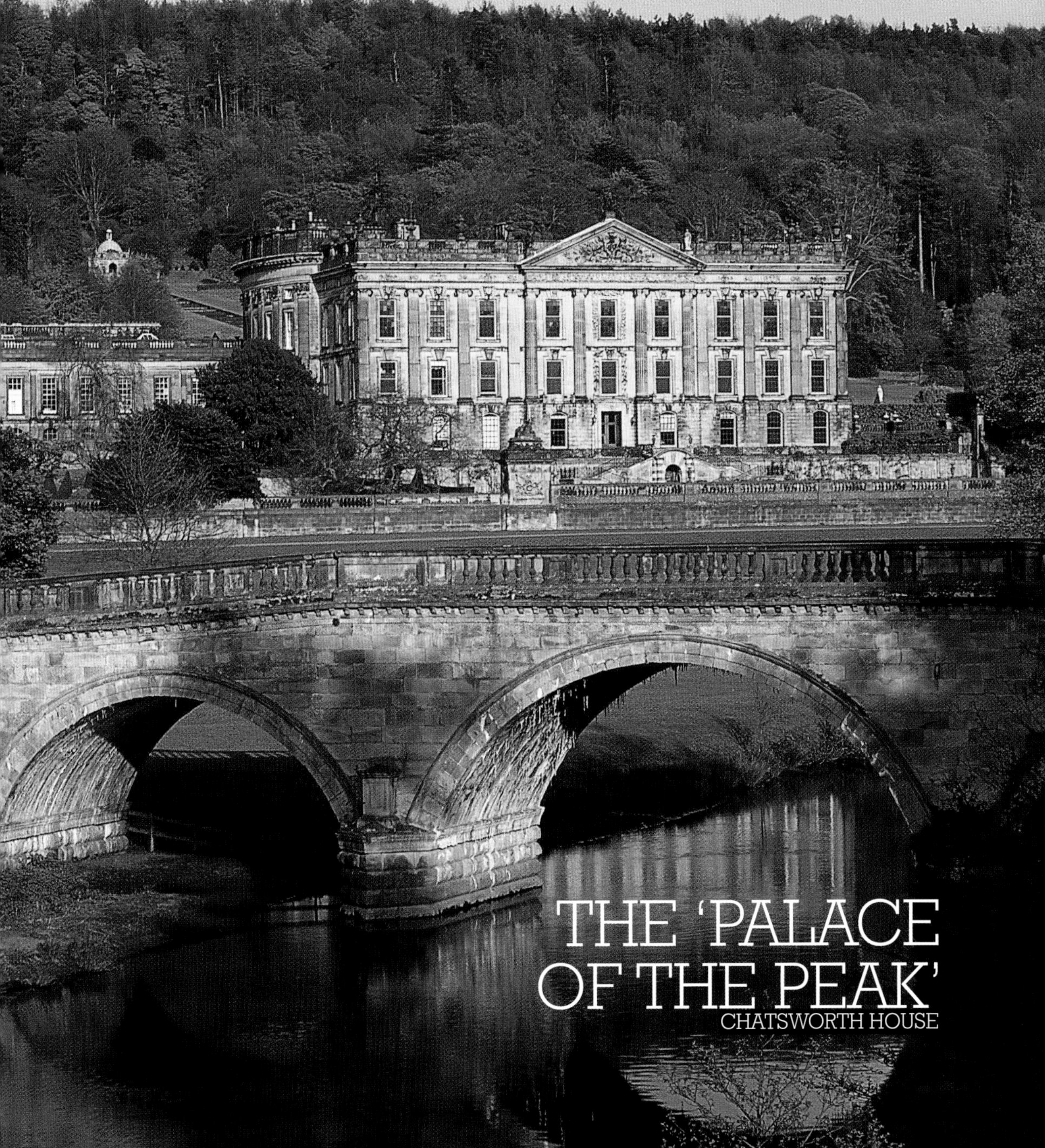

THE 'PALACE OF THE PEAK'
CHATSWORTH HOUSE

GLOUCESTERSHIRE

Extending from the Cotswolds into the lush Severn Valley, Gloucestershire offers matchless scenic tours in all seasons. Enjoy the blossom vales in spring, village flowers in summer and chilly hilltop views in winter.

5 TEWKESBURY

TOUR LENGTH 41 miles

Flanked by the Malvern Hills to the west, Tewkesbury bridges the vales of Evesham and Gloucester to the south. Head out from the town on a circular tour through some of England's loveliest landscapes.

Tewkesbury to Apperley

1 Strategically placed at the confluence of the Avon and Severn rivers, Tewkesbury was chosen in the late 11th century as the site of an imposing abbey. It was saved from destruction at the time of the Dissolution when local people bought it from Henry VIII for £453.

To start the drive, leave Tewkesbury on the A38, following the signs to Worcester. After ½ mile, turn left on to the A438 towards Ledbury, and cross the Severn. After a 2-mile drive along the tranquil Severn valley, turn left to Forthampton.

2 At the crossroads, turn left to Chaceley. After a sharp right bend, carry on to Forthampton Court crossroads and turn right to Chaceley, following the road into the village. Follow signs for Tirley and Ashleworth to a junction with the B4213. Turn left across Haw Bridge and continue for ¾ mile, ignoring the first left turn to Apperley. Drive on for another mile and take an unsigned left turn into the village.

Apperley to Winchcombe

3 Continue on to the B4213 towards Cheltenham, and turn left on to the A38 towards Tewkesbury. After less than a mile, turn right through Tredington. Continue to the outskirts of Bishop's Cleeve and turn right at a roundabout on to the A435. At the next roundabout, continue towards Cheltenham, then turn left at traffic lights to Southam and Cleeve Hill. In Southam, turn left at a T-junction and follow the B4632 towards Winchcombe.

4 As the road climbs up Cleeve Hill, splendid views appear. Over the brow, the road descends gently into Winchcombe. St Peter's church is famed for its collection of gargoyles, believed to be images of local inhabitants.

Winchcombe to Overbury

5 From Winchcombe, take the B4632 towards Toddington. After 2 miles, a right turn on to a narrow track leads to the ruins of Hailes Abbey (EH and NT), which was founded in 1246 by Cistercian monks.

6 Back on the B4632, continue to a roundabout and turn right on to the B4077, and almost immediately right again to visit Toddington Station on the restored Gloucestershire and Warwickshire Railway. From the station, turn left back on to the B4077, go straight on at the roundabout and continue past Toddington. After 3 miles, turn right, opposite a garage, to Alderton.

7 In Alderton, turn left, following signs to Beckford. Cross the A46 into the town, where the silk-printing centre is open to visitors. Continue to Conderton, where there is a hand-painted-silk centre and a pottery, and on to Overbury.

Overbury to Tewkesbury

8 From Overbury, with the cruciform church of St Faith on the right, follow a minor road through Kemerton to Bredon. Take the B4080, passing under the M5, and follow the road back to Tewkesbury.

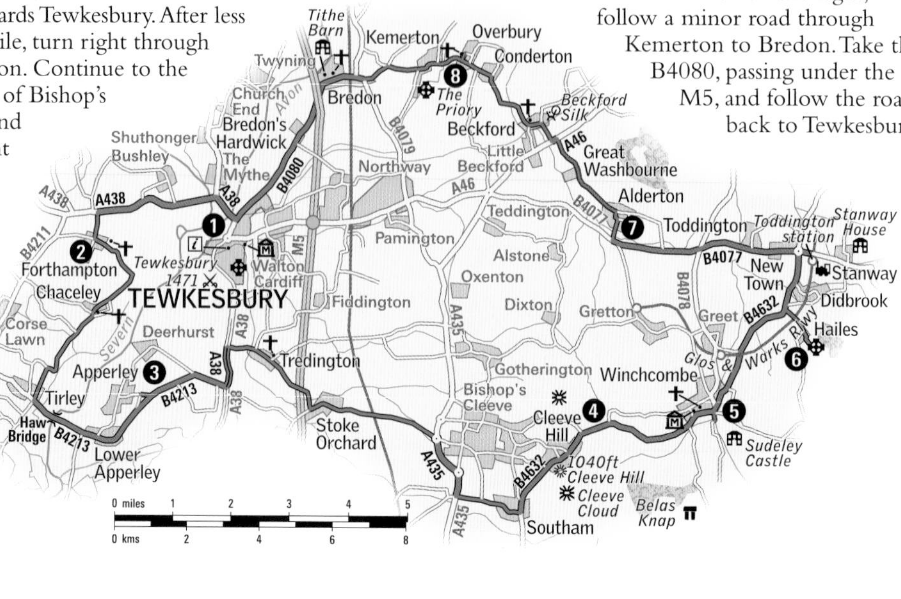

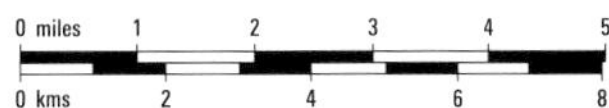

6 PAINSWICK

TOUR LENGTH 46 miles

This is mill territory. The road leads over lush hills and through fertile valleys, crossing woods and heaths, where cultured towns and pretty villages built with wealth from the wool trade continue to operate as craft centres.

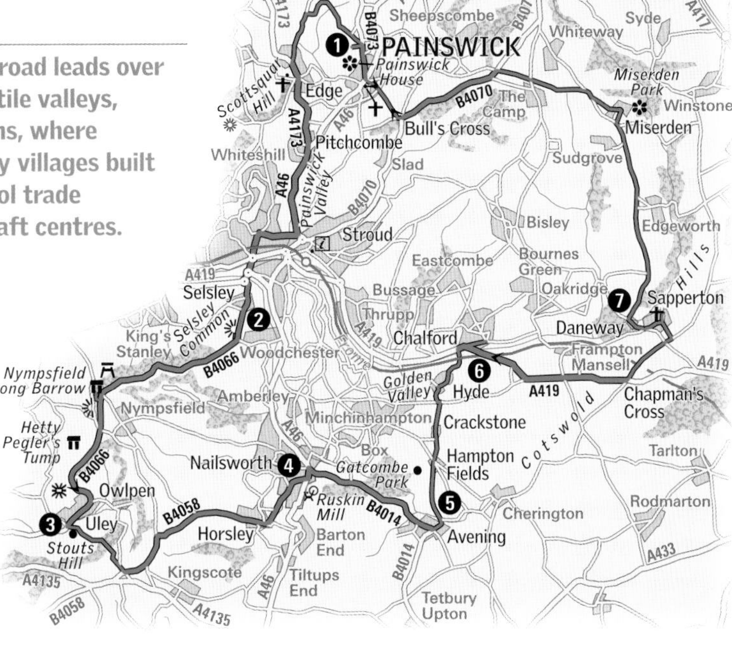

Painswick to Uley

1 Genteel Painswick bears the traces of the industry from which it prospered. The grand houses of its 17th and 18th-century mill owners line steep winding streets, and the Falcon Hotel has England's oldest bowling green. St Mary's Church, which dates from Norman times, dominates the town. In its churchyard, 99 yew trees were planted in the 1790s and it's said that if another is planted, one of the old trees will die.

From Painswick, take the B4073 and after ½ mile bear left to visit the rococo garden in the grounds of Painswick House, built in Palladian style. The gardens are run by the Painswick Rococo Garden Trust, a charity, and are generally open from January to October. Seasonal displays include cyclamen in January and great drifts of snowdrops in February. The sculptural kitchen garden produces food for the garden's restaurant. Check times before visiting.

Return to the B4073, turn left and take the first turning on the left on to a narrow lane. At the T-junction turn left towards Edge. Turn left again on to the A4173 and continue to a T-junction. Turn right on to the A46 along the lovely Painswick Valley. Follow the signs to Dursley around the outskirts of Stroud and, at a major roundabout, take the B4066 towards Uley.

2 The road climbs steeply out of Stroud, with views to the right over the Severn valley. Just after a signpost on the left to the village of Nympsfield, turn right to Nympsfield Long Barrow, a Neolithic burial mound, where there is a car park and a picnic area with fine views. The barrow was excavated in 1862 and 1937. Within were the remains of at least 13 human skeletons together with pottery fragments and objects that included three quartz pebbles and red ochre, a pigment frequently found in burials in Britain and abroad.

Return to the B4066 and turn right. After ½ mile, Hetty Pegler's Tump, another long barrow, once found to contain the remains of 15 skeletons, can be seen on right up a short path. Continue ahead, winding downhill and bending right into Uley, a pretty village popular with ramblers owing to its position near the Cotswold way. Once famous for the Uley Blue cloth the villagers produced in the 18th century, today Uley is better known for its brewery that uses local springwater and hops to produce award-winning ales, including Pigs Ear, Old Spot and Laurie Lee.

In 1976 the remains of a Roman temple were discovered on nearby West Hill. Among the finds was a carved head of Mercury made from Cotswold limestone, now on display in the British Museum. Many curse tablets were uncovered – small sheets of inscribed lead requesting the gods' help in bestowing ill on those who had done the writer a personal injustice.

Uley to Sapperton

3 At the crossroads just beyond the village, turn left up a steep hill, passing a striking Georgian Gothic mansion, Stouts Hill, a timeshare property, on the right. The road continues climbing through woodland. At the next crossroads, turn left on to the B4058, a high road with fine views.

At Horsley, the road begins to descend to Nailsworth, a small town that once supported 17 cloth mills. Six have been converted, including Ruskin Mill, which houses craft workshops and a café.

▷

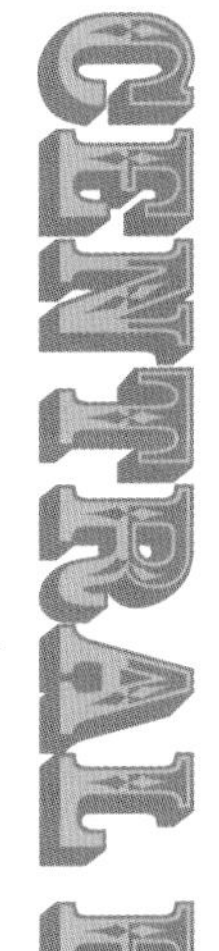

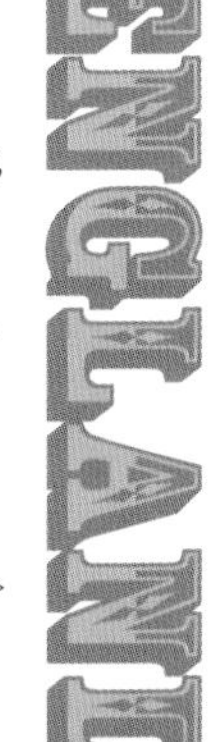

4 In Nailsworth town centre, at the junction with the A46, turn left towards Stroud then downhill and right on to the B4014 to Avening. The road follows the Nailsworth mills valley, past Spring Mill and Longford's Mill, climbing through woodland.

5 In the village of Avening, where the main road bends to the right, turn left on to the road to the left of the Cross Inn, towards Minchinhampton. At a junction in Hampton Fields, fork right, following signs to Minchinhampton Common and Stroud, through Crackstone. At a T-junction, with the Ragged Cot Inn on the right, turn left and immediately right, down Hyde Hill to Hyde. Go under a railway bridge, cross the River Frome and turn right on to the A419 towards Chalford and then left on a minor road to visit the old mill village.

The original village was one of a number of squatter settlements, built to house weavers and cloth workers of the wool and silk industries in the early Middle Ages. It remained a cloth centre for many centuries, producing 'Stroud', a cheap woollen cloth much exported to America. Stroud cloth is still produced today as a speciality cloth at Lodgemore Mills in Stroud, and is used to cover tennis balls and snooker tables.

6 From Chalford return to the A419 and turn left, climbing out of Golden Valley. At Chapman's Cross, turn left and follow the signs to Sapperton. St Kenelm's Church, built on the site of a stone church known to date from the 12th century, is romantically set at the edge of the thickly wooded Frome valley. The present church dates from the 18th century but retains its 14th-century tower. East of the village are several houses built in the Cotswold Arts and Crafts style by architects Sidney Barnsley and Ernest Gimson.

Sapperton to Painswick

7 Continue through Sapperton and at the junction turn right to Daneway. Cross the bridge and follow the road to the right, past the Daneway Inn. Continue for 3 miles, then turn right to Miserden, where some gardens and a nursery are open to the public. Check times with the Miserden Estate Office before visiting. Bear left through the village and follow the signs to Birdlip and Whiteway. Then turn left towards Painswick. Go over the crossroads, turn left towards Stroud on the B4070. At Bull's Cross junction, fork right and after 150m turn right on to a single-track road to Painswick.

PANORAMA OF THE SEVERN VALE NEAR STROUD

FROM COALEY PEAK COUNTRY PARK

GLOUCESTERSHIRE

7 STOW-ON-THE-WOLD

TOUR LENGTH 57 miles

The old town of Stow, a place of quiet charms, sets the scene for this drive through rolling hills and wooded valleys, dotted with honey-coloured villages. At Bourton-on-the-Water five bridges span the clear waters of the River Windrush.

Stow-on-the-Wold to Adlestrop

1 Eight roads converge on the hilltop town of Stow-on-the-Wold. The name means 'meeting place on the hill', reflecting its history as a major Cotswold market town. In 1107, Stow received a Royal Charter authorising a weekly market and a twice-yearly fair for traders in sheep and wool. Today, the trade is in horses, and the Market Square, with its impressive stone buildings and medieval stocks, is still the town's focal point.

Start the drive on the A436 heading in the direction of Chipping Norton. The road descends past stone-walled fields. After 2½ miles, cross a railway bridge and turn left, then right at a T-junction to Adlestrop.

Adlestrop to Bourton-on-the-Water

2 Follow the road through Adlestrop to the A436. Turn left and almost immediately right on to a minor road. At the crossroads turn right and continue through Kingham to a T-junction with the B4450. Turn left and then right through Lyneham to a T-junction with the A361. Turn right to Shipton under Wychwood, where the Shaven Crown inn overlooks the green. Once a guesthouse for Bruern Abbey, 2½ miles to the northwest, the inn was first licensed 600 years ago.

3 Continue to Burford, with its 15th-century almshouses and 16th-century merchants' meeting house, now the Tolsey Museum of local history. Go back over the river and turn left on to the A424. Where the road bends right, keep going forward on a minor road into Great Barrington,

HIGH STREET, BURFORD

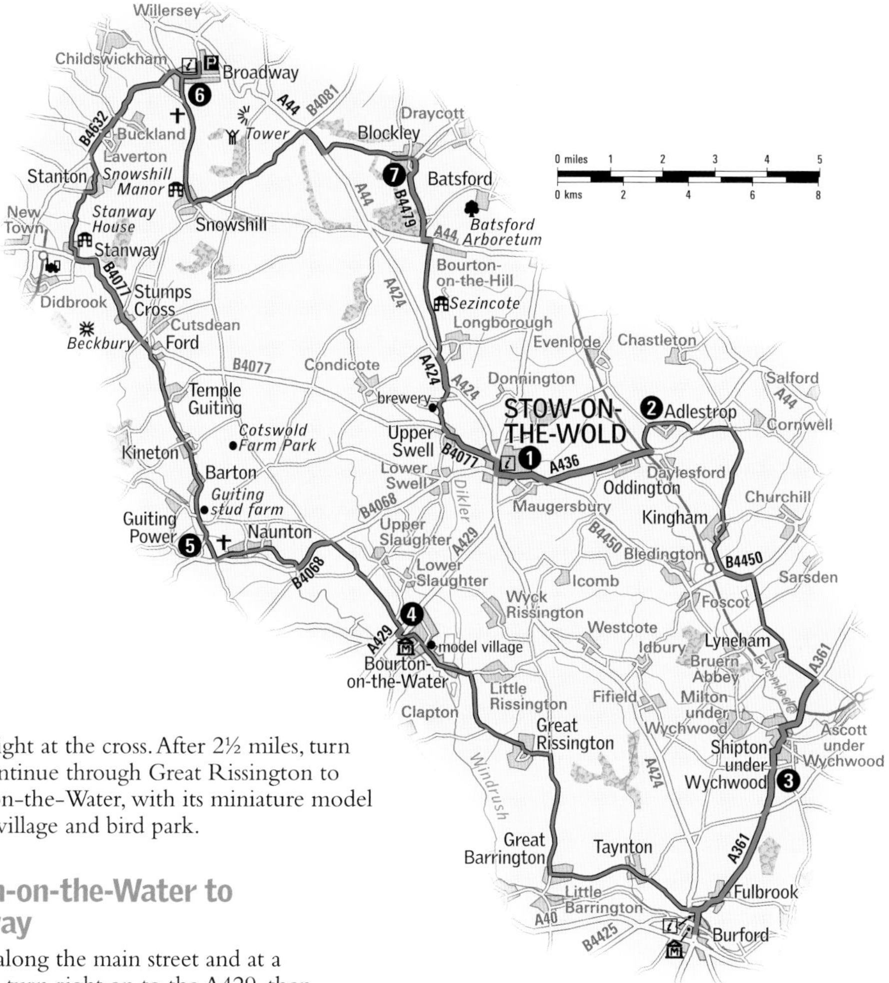

and turn right at the cross. After 2½ miles, turn left and continue through Great Rissington to Bourton-on-the-Water, with its miniature model Cotswold village and bird park.

Bourton-on-the-Water to Broadway

4 Drive along the main street and at a T-junction turn right on to the A429, then immediately left. After 2 miles, turn left at crossroads on B4068. Turn right to visit the long main street of Naunton, strung out along the infant River Windrush. The Saxons called the place *Niwetone* (New Town), and a small Saxon cross is set into the wall of St Andrew's Church.

5 Turn right to rejoin the B4068 and immediately right again. At a T-junction turn right and follow the road for about 4 miles to the B4077. Turn left on to the B4077 and at the bottom of the hill turn right to Stanway, passing the elaborate gatehouse of Jacobean Stanway House. Continue through Stanton, turn right on to the B4632 and follow the road into Broadway. Turn left into Leamington Road for the car park. Among the town's historic buildings is the Lygon Arms, where both Charles II and Cromwell stayed.

Broadway to Stow-on-the-Wold

6 Return to the High Street, turn right and then left on to a minor road to Snowshill Manor, a Tudor house (NT) with an extraordinary collection of curios assembled by the 20th century sugar baron and would-be alchemist Charles Paget Wade. From the NT car park, turn right back on to the minor road, and fork left in Snowshill. Take the next left, continue for 2½ miles and turn right on to the A44. After ½ mile turn left to Blockley, where the main street is terraced into the side of a valley and the shop fronts are made of cast iron.

7 At a T-junction, turn right and immediately left. Turn right on to the B4479, and at the T-junction with the A44, turn left and immediately right, signposted to Longborough, to reach Sezincote, an oriental-style house built in 1810, which was the inspiration for the Brighton Pavilion. The house is open to the public, although children are not welcome without special permission. Check times before visiting.

Continue to the junction with the A424 and turn left towards Stow. After 1 mile turn right, signposted to Donnington trout farm. Donnington brewery is on the right.

At the B4077, turn left through Upper Swell, with its attractive millpond on the left, and continue to Stow.

LINCOLNSHIRE

The county has long attracted tourists to its coastal resorts, but there are many more gems to discover inland. From the fens to the wolds, Lincolnshire boasts lakes, castles, manors, parks and fine landscapes.

8 STAMFORD

TOUR LENGTH 61 miles

Passing through elegant towns, past castles and under a long viaduct, the route skirts another of man's grand designs, Rutland Water. Britain's largest man-made lake has been carefully planned to host anglers and yachtsmen as well as birdwatchers.

Stamford to Exton

1 The Georgian town of Stamford on the River Welland was once a major wool centre. Built of the golden brown local stone, several tall church spires add to its olde worlde charm. Every March a huge fair is held in the town, a tradition that has gone on for hundreds of years.

For the first section of the drive, take the A606 towards Oakham and ½ mile past Empingham, turn left for the Butterfly and Aquatic Centre, overlooking Rutland Water. Open during the summer months, it displays fish, exotic plants, butterflies, insects and reptiles.

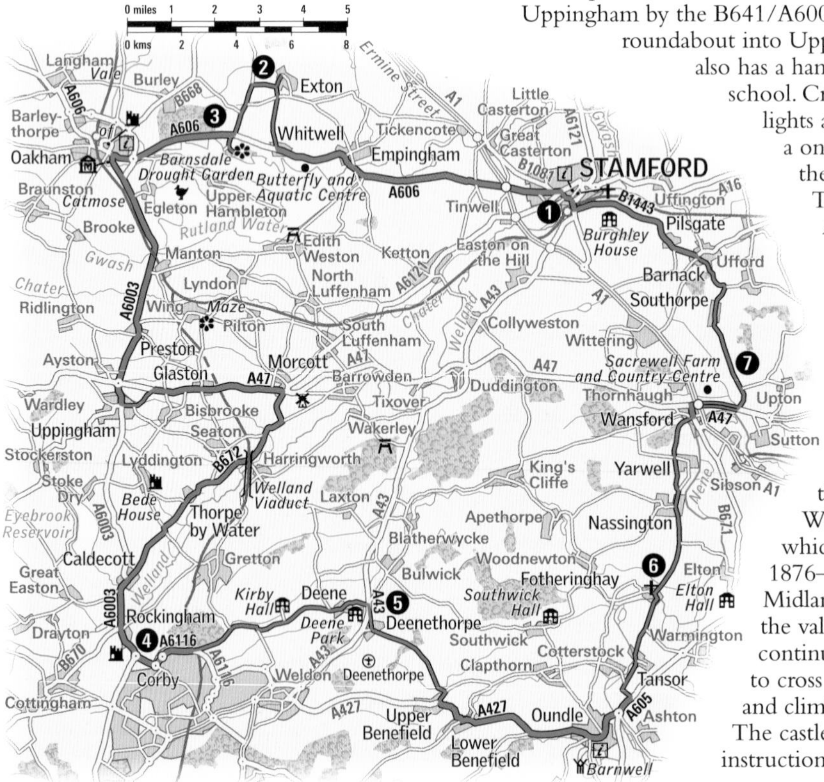

Turn left back on to the A606 to Whitwell, which has a nearby marina and water-sports centre, and then go right uphill to Exton. In the church of St Peter and St Paul is a colossal statue of Viscount Camden, his four wives and 19 children. It is one of the few marble sculptures by Grinling Gibbons, better known for his exquisite wood and stonework at royal palaces and St Paul's Cathedral. Gibbons was paid £1,000 for the work in 1683.

Exton to Rockingham

2 Coming out of the village again, turn right at the T-junction, and at the next T-junction, turn left on to Barnsdale Avenue, passing Barnsdale Plants and Gardens, used by the late Geoff Hamilton in his TV gardening series. Turn right on to the A606, then almost immediately left to a parking place beside Barnsdale Drought Garden and Arboretum, which is stocked with a variety of plants that can survive with very little water.

3 Return to the A606, turn left and continue to Oakham, going straight on at the roundabout on the town's bypass. Oakham is the county town of Rutland, which has a 12th-century castle and an old public school. Leave, southwards, towards Uppingham by the B641/A6003. Go ahead at the roundabout into Uppingham, which also has a handsome public school. Cross over the traffic lights and turn left down a one-way street in the centre. At the T-junction with the A47, turn right for Morcott. At Morcott, turn right towards Caldecott on the B672, which zigzags along the Welland valley, passing beneath the magnificent Welland viaduct, which was built in 1876–8 to carry the Midland Railway over the valley. At Caldecott, continue on the A6003 to cross the River Welland and climb to Rockingham. The castle was built on the instructions of William the

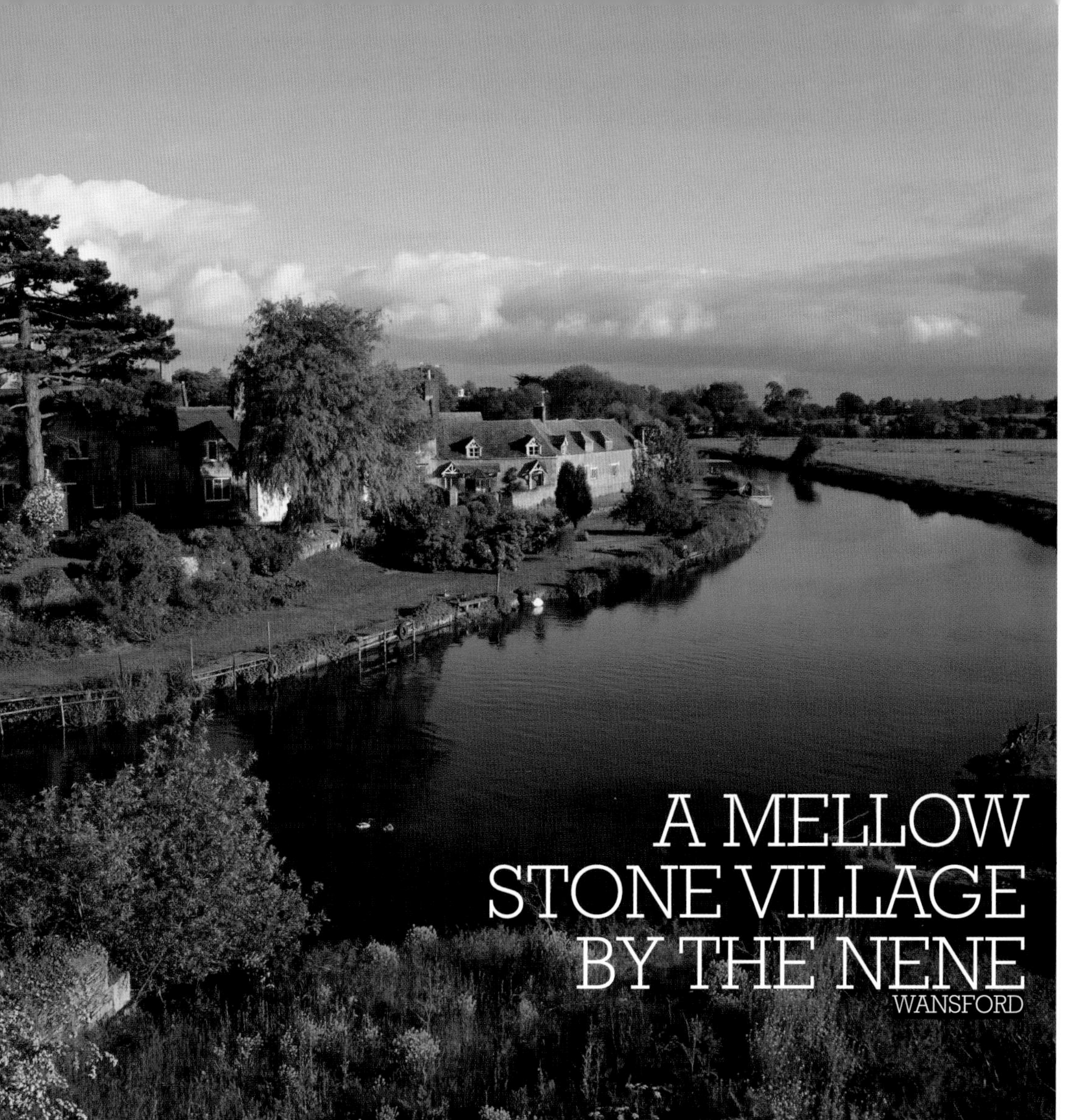

A MELLOW STONE VILLAGE BY THE NENE

WANSFORD

Conqueror and, for the last 450 years, has been occupied by one family and their descendants. The castle is open to the public, but not Saturdays.

Rockingham to Stamford

4 Just beyond Rockingham Castle on the A6003, fork left on to the A6116 and turn left at the first roundabout. Follow the A6116 around the outskirts of Corby and turn left for Deene and Kirby Hall. Keep following the signs for both, taking the second minor road on the left past the driveway to Kirby Hall (EH) on the left. Continue to Deene. The grand house at nearby Deene Park is largely Tudor, and remains in occupation, although both house and gardens are open to the public at certain times. Check before visiting.

5 Turn right on to the A43, then left to Deenethorpe. In the village, turn left towards Benefield. Turn right at the T-junction to Upper Benefield and then left on to the A427 to Oundle, a stone-built Georgian town. Cross the River Nene and turn left at the roundabout on to the A605, then take the first left towards Cotterstock and Tansor. Follow the road and cross a narrow humpbacked bridge into Fotheringhay, where only a grassy mound remains of the castle where Mary, Queen of Scots was executed in 1587.

6 Opposite Fotheringhay's splendid church, turn right down a minor road towards Nassington and the picturesque village of Wansford on the River Nene. At Wansford, turn right and immediately left to reach the A47 at a roundabout. Turn right on to the A47, pass over the A1, and after ¼ mile turn left for Sacrewell Farm and Country Centre for a glimpse of bygone rural life.

7 Return to the A47, turn left and first left again through Southorpe and Barnack. Then turn left on to the B1443, past Burghley and back into Stamford.

LINCOLNSHIRE

9 LOUTH

TOUR LENGTH 57 miles

The rolling chalk hills of the Lincolnshire Wolds have inspired generations of painters and poets, including Turner and Tennyson, and this tour shows why.

Louth to Well

1 An array of Georgian red-brick buildings packed into a quadrangle of streets around a fine medieval church characterise Louth. The slim, hexagonal spire of St James's, soaring to nearly 92m (300ft), caught the eye of painter J.M.W. Turner, while round the corner is the 'old wall covered with wild weeds' that the poet Lord Tennyson remembered from his days in the schoolhouse opposite.

For the first leg of the drive, take the B1200 signposted to Manby. At the roundabout go straight ahead on the A157 then turn right on to a minor road for Little Cawthorpe. Where the main road bends right through the village, turn left on to Buston Lane and carry on through a ford and past a duckpond before rejoining the main road by a church and manor house. Go through Muckton. On the left, long views stretch across the marshes towards the coast. At a T-junction, bear left and follow the signs for Belleau, passing a large brick dovecote on the right. Carry on through Belleau.

2 At the next T-junction turn right to Claythorpe Mill and Wildfowl Gardens, where peacocks, pheasants, cranes and storks wander in the grounds of a white-painted former watermill, dating from 1724. Beyond the mill turn right under an old railway bridge to Aby.

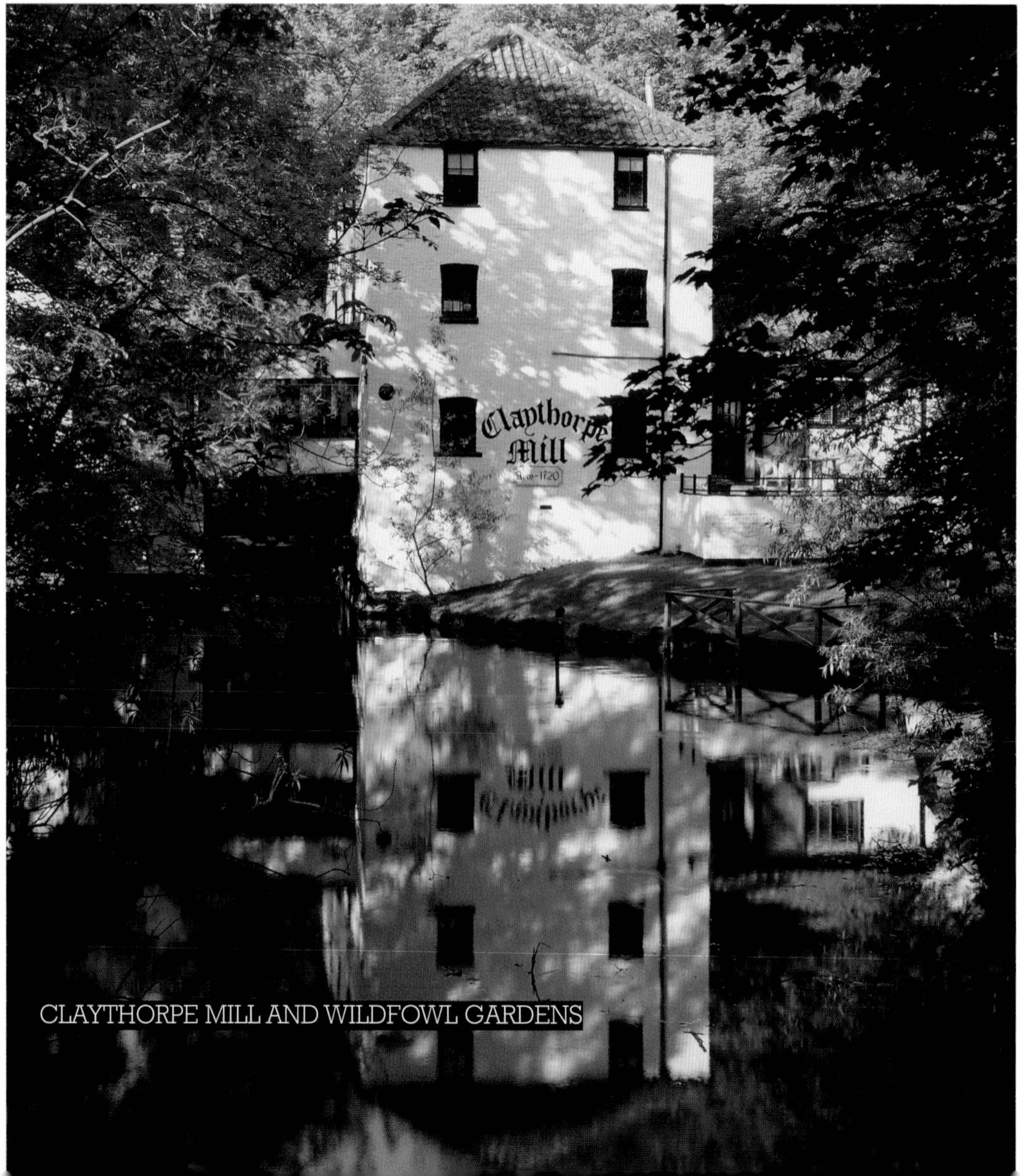

CLAYTHORPE MILL AND WILDFOWL GARDENS

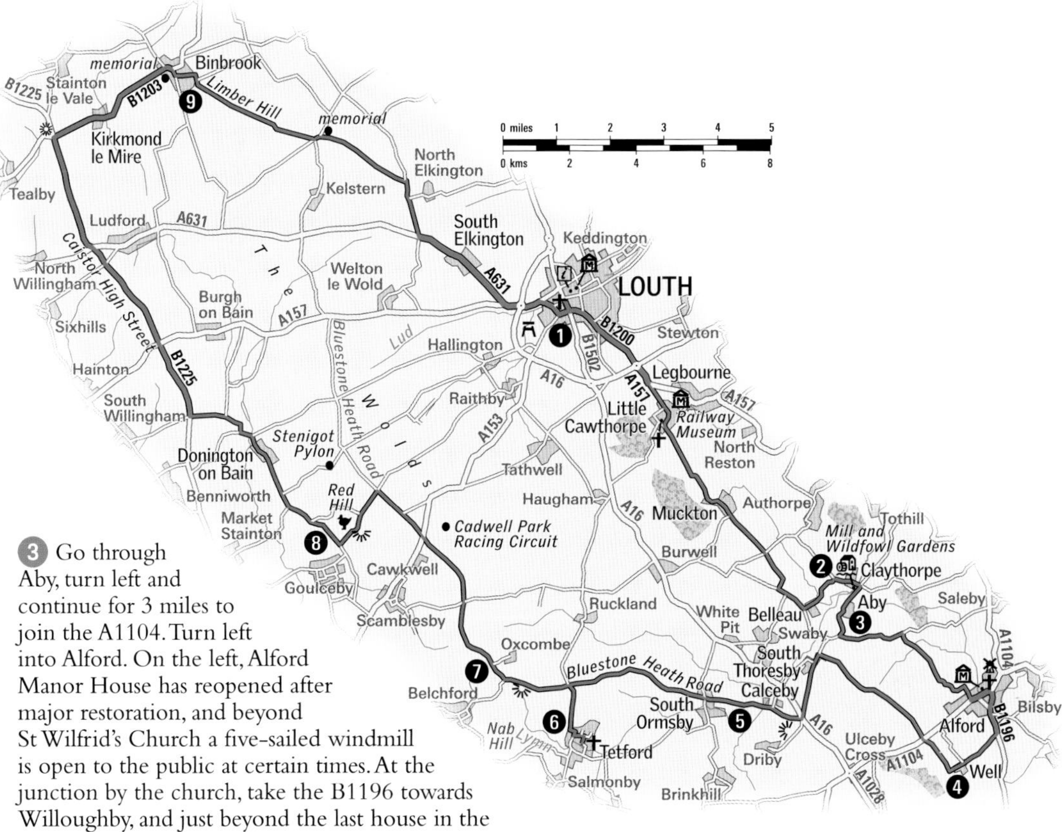

3 Go through Aby, turn left and continue for 3 miles to join the A1104. Turn left into Alford. On the left, Alford Manor House has reopened after major restoration, and beyond St Wilfrid's Church a five-sailed windmill is open to the public at certain times. At the junction by the church, take the B1196 towards Willoughby, and just beyond the last house in the village, turn right to Well.

Well to Tetford

4 Continue along Well High Lane, which bends sharply to the right and soon crosses the A1104. Carry on to South Thoresby. Turn left and cross the A16 taking a minor road signposted to Calceby. This is the start of the Bluestone Heath Road, which follows a prehistoric trackway along the crest of the Wolds. A layby after 350m gives a view across rolling fields dotted by farms and ribboned with dark green hedges.

5 At a crossroads, keep ahead towards Belchford, and at the next crossroads go left downhill to the pretty village of Tetford, where the White Hart Inn was once the haunt of Samuel Johnson. Each May a scarecrow festival is held in Tetford to raise funds for selected charities and for the local church, St Mary's, which dates from the 14th century.

Tetford to Binbrook

6 Return to the Bluestone Heath Road and turn left. After 1 mile, a layby at the Bluestone Heath Road viewpoint gives a panorama of the Wolds. The River Lymn winds through the valley below, and on either side are low arable hills where thousands of sheep once grazed. The name Bluestone Heath is a mystery – 'bluestones' are boulders deposited in the last Ice Age, but none has been found along the old road.

7 Continue along the crest of the Wolds, crossing the A153 and heading towards the Eiffel Tower-like Stenigot Pylon, a relic of an aircraft navigational system used during the Second World War. After 1 mile, turn left downhill, signposted to Stenigot, to the Red Hill Nature Reserve. From the second of two parking spaces there is a clear view of the layer of red chalk in the exposed cliff face.

8 At the foot of the hill, turn right and go through Donington on Bain, bearing left at the next junction, signposted to South Willingham, to the B1225. Turn right, following the course of an old Roman road, Caistor High Street. Ignore side turnings and go across the A157 and A631. At a crossroads about 4 miles after the A631, turn right on to the B1203 to Binbrook, which was an RAF base during the Second World War. RAF Binbrook closed as a base in 1988 but continued to be used as a relief airfield for RAF Scampton until 1995.

Binbrook to Louth

9 In the village, turn right, signposted to Louth, through the square, and go up Limber Hill, through woods then between fields. Beside a left turning towards Ludborough there is a memorial to 625 Sqn RAF. Turn right at the next junction and then left on to the A631 to Louth.

Travelling the Roman way

Among the legacies left by the Romans, roads are probably the most enduring – the first one they built is still carrying vehicles.

Driving north towards Bath on the A37 through the green pastures of Somerset; riding the Cotswold hills on the A429 around Bourton-on-the-Water and Stow-on-the-Wold; following the linear B4455 for 20 miles past Warwick and Coventry; coursing along the A46 for 50 miles towards Lincoln. What could such geographically and scenically diverse roads have in common? Answer: they all form part of one mighty, 230 mile long thoroughfare, the Fosse Way. It was built through the forests and swamps of Iron Age Britain by the Romans immediately after they had arrived as invaders in AD 43.

The Romans, well-organised and determined, were intent on occupying a large island that was rich in minerals and corn, but heavily wooded and poorly provided with infrastructure. So the newcomers just bypassed the rough old British trackways. The Fosse Way was the start of a road-building programme that, within 100 years, produced a 10,000 mile network of well-drained, cleverly engineered, broad and straight roads throughout occupied Britain.

Line of defence

The Fosse Way, or 'Ditch Road', doubled as a defensive frontier in the early years of Roman rule, separating the Roman-occupied and civilised east of Britain from the unsubdued and barbarous west. It ran across the country in a northeasterly direction from Exeter (Isca), passing through Bath (Aquae Sulis), Cirencester

THE FOSSE WAY, GLOUCESTERSHIRE

(Corinium) and Leicester (Ratae Coritanorum) before arriving at Lincoln (Lindum Colonia) – laid out in a straight line for almost its entire length.

Lacking compasses or any modern surveying equipment for direction-finding, the Roman engineers relied on a very basic instrument called the groma – essentially, two plumblines on a cross of wood, one in front of the other. When they were aligned, the surveyor looked past the lead weights to the spot on the horizon that lay in line with them, and aimed for that – simple, but extremely effective. As for who actually built the Fosse Way, in common with all the other Roman roads, it was the hard-working legionary with pick and shovel. The soldiers cleared the ground, dug a trench and filled it with three layers of hardcore – large stones at the bottom, smaller pebbles or fragments of brick on top. They shaped the surface into a convex curve or camber to help water to drain off, sealed it with paving stones and laid stone kerbs along the verges. Every 12 miles (a day's journey by ox-cart) they built a mansione or service station – at Bourton-on-the-Water in Gloucestershire, for example, and at Brough on the River Trent, a day's stage south of Lincoln. The best-equipped of these mansione offered travellers a bath, a meal, a bed for the night, a place to deliver or pick up the post, and a stable for the horses.

Original route

Substantial stretches of the Fosse Way are still in use as major roads, connected by country byways, green lanes and forgotten stretches that lie in hedgerows and under cornfields. A good deal of the original route can be followed by shaping a course from Exeter along the A30 to Honiton, then taking the A35 and minor roads to Axminster; continue from there through the hilly landscape of Dorset and south Somerset via the A358, B3167 and A30, and go across country to the A303 at Ilchester. From there, take the A37 to Bath, and then the A433 over the Cotswolds to Cirencester, where the way crosses Akeman Street, a Roman road coming west from London (Londinium). Take the A429 out of Gloucestershire, and the B4455 across well-wooded Warwickshire to High Cross on the borders of Leicestershire. Here the Way crosses another famous Roman road, Watling Street (A5), heading northwest from London to Chester (Deva). A short stretch of the B4114 takes the route on to Leicester, and from there the A46 heads between the rolling cornfields to Lincoln.

All along the route there are signs of the old road for those with sharp eyes and time to explore – for example, between Shepton Mallet and Nettlebridge in Somerset, or farther north between High Cross and Stoney Bridge on the Warwickshire/Leicestershire border, where the tarmac road diverges and the Roman way continues as a private lane or field track, slipping in unnoticed several miles farther on to blend with the modern highway once more. Lumps and bumps of ditches, and raised trackbeds in the woods give it away.

Hundreds of place-names hold clues to the old route – 'castra', a fortified camp (Cirencester, Chesterton); 'strata', a paved highway (Stratton-on-the-Fosse, Street-on-the-Fosse); and, of course, 'fossa', a ditch (Fossebridge, Stretton-on-Fosse). Every now and then, during construction or repair work, a memento is unearthed – coins and pottery at Brough near Lincoln, a stone-lined Roman well at Bingham in Nottinghamshire, a mosaic of Daphne and Apollo at Dinnington in Somerset – ghostly appeals, across the centuries, not to forget these erstwhile colonial rulers and the remarkable civilisation they brought to these shores 2,000 years ago.

NORFOLK

Take to Norfolk's quiet roads for a tour of the Broads, passing charming coastal resorts and waterside villages. Tidal creeks and wild marshes offer wildlife watchers an abundance of magnificent birds to see.

10 BURNHAM MARKET

TOUR LENGTH 44 miles

Long horizons, small creeks and immense beaches makes a drive around this part of the Norfolk coast a rewarding experience. The route goes through Little Walsingham, where the ancient shrine still thrives, and past villages where Nelson spent his youth.

Burnham Market to Weybourne

1 Georgian flint and red-brick houses and smart shops and cafés line the broad double green in Burnham Market, at one end of which stands a 14th-century church. A curate here was married to Horatia, Lord Nelson's daughter by Lady Hamilton. The six villages known as the Burnhams are where Nelson spent his childhood, and so pubs tend to be named The Hero or The Lord Nelson.

The village is thought to have been a centre for the amber trade; amber, or *brand stein* (burning stone) in German is found near the coastal town of Cromer, washed up from beneath the North Sea. It is believed all the Burnhams had a part in the trade. Others suggest the name comes from the River Burn that flows nearby.

To start the drive, take the B1355 towards Fakenham and turn left on to a minor road to Burnham Thorpe, Nelson's birthplace. His parents are buried in All Saints Church, where the Admiral is commemorated with personal mementoes and fragments of HMS *Victory*. The dramatic ruins of Creake Abbey (EH) stand 1 mile to the south. Fire in the 15th century, then plague in the 16th put an end to the abbey and its community.

2 Continue through Burnham Thorpe towards a long wood, marking the edge of Holkham Park. At the end of the park wall, go straight on at the crossroads. Turn right at the junction with the B1105, then second left down a narrow road to the village of Little Walsingham. In 1061, Richeldis de Faverches, the lady of the manor, was ordered by a vision of the Virgin Mary to build a replica of the Holy Family's house in Nazareth on her own estates. Around this simple shrine grew a great abbey that attracted thousands of pilgrims. At the Reformation, the buildings and the cult were ruthlessly expunged, but the Shrine of Our Lady of Walsingham has been built up again and pilgrims come from all over the world to visit and walk the holy mile.

3 From Little Walsingham, follow signs to Great Walsingham and the small village of Binham. Binham has a fascinating priory church. The architecture is predominantly Norman and the west front of the nave has a huge bricked-up window. The church stands next to the ruins of a Benedictine priory (EH), founded in 1091, of which it was once part.

4 Continue through Langham, turn left on to the B1156 and drive through open country to Blakeney, which was once an important port. Together with neighbouring Cley next the Sea, Blakeney sent 36 ships to fight the Spanish Armada in 1588. Its colourful quay, overlooking the marshes, is often crowded with yachts, and boat trips are advertised across to the lonely, grassy dunes of Blakeney Point (NT). This 3½ mile sand-and-shingle spit, part of Blakeney National Nature Reserve, is home to birds and grey and common seals.

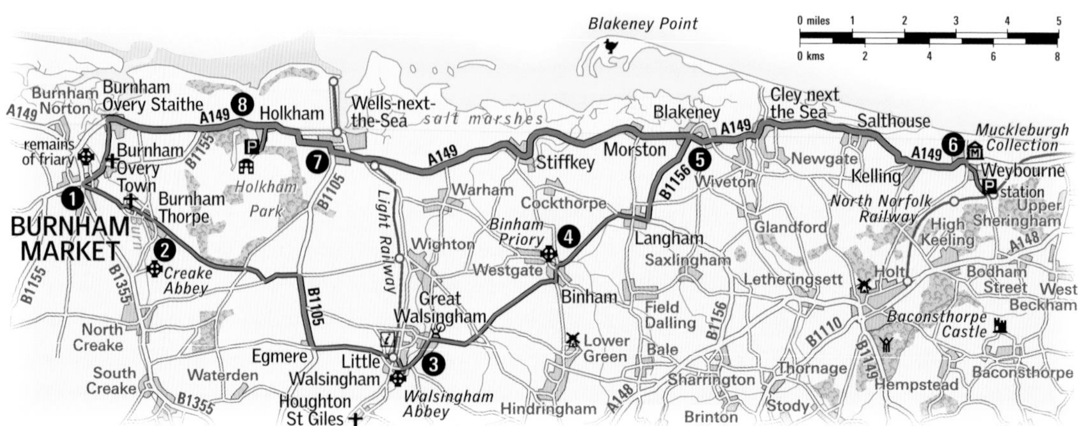

BLAKENEY HARBOUR

5 Turn right along the A149 to Cley next the Sea and Salthouse. The splendour of their churches reflects the fact that half of medieval England's wool was exported through this area. The Cley (pronounced 'cly') marshes are part of a string of bird reserves along the north Norfolk coast. The village is no longer 'next the sea' owing to land reclamation carried out in the 17th century.

Continue to Weybourne, where parking is available at the station – turn right in the village centre, signposted to North Norfolk Railway. This steam train links Weybourne with Sheringham and Holt. Deep waters off Weybourne's pebble beach attract sea anglers, who are often to be found here.

Weybourne to Holkham

6 Return from Weybourne on the A149, passing the Muckleburgh Collection of militaria on the right. This is privately owned and usually open from April to the end of October.

Carry on to Blakeney and Stiffkey, where cockles, known as Stewkey Blues, are still harvested. Beyond is the resort and port of Wells-next-the-Sea, from where a narrow-gauge railway runs to Little Walsingham. Longbow archers practised on the Buttlands green in the 16th century.

7 Continue on the A149 to the Victorian estate village of Holkham. Turn left at the sign for Holkham Hall and Bygones Museum for the village car park, on the right. The privately owned Holkham Hall has been occupied by the Coke family since the 1750s, and this large Palladian Hall and estate is open to the public (check times before visiting). The Bygones Museum is housed in the stable block, alongside a permanent exhibition on the history of farming.

Holkham to Burnham Market

8 Follow the A149 to Burnham Overy Staithe, a charming sailing centre on a tidal creek. Turn left down a narrow road to Burnham Overy Town, which was once a port but has been gradually sealed off from the sea by land reclamation and by Yorkshire sand and shingle being washed down the coast. Follow the B1155 out of Burnham Overy Town across the River Burn. Past the ruins of St Mary's Carmelite friary and back into Burnham Market.

NORFOLK

11 AYLSHAM

TOUR LENGTH 61 miles

Thatched churches and cottages, busy villages and reed-fringed waterways – all under seemingly enormous skies – are features of this drive, which explores the Broads, the network of shallow lakes created from flooded medieval peat diggings.

Aylsham to Potter Heigham

1 The little flint and red-tiled town of Aylsham has been a royal manor since before the Norman Conquest, and St Michael's Church has a chancel screen dating from 1500. The red-brick, mainly Georgian, marketplace, often busy with stalls, is where the 17th-century Black Boys Inn with its fine plasterwork can be found, and an assembly room where Lord Nelson once danced. Leave Aylsham southwards, crossing the railway and heading for the A140. At the roundabout, turn left on to the A140 then after ¼ mile, right on to a minor road following signs for Buxton, now called Buxton-with-Lamas. For Lamas, turn left at the village hall. Follow the road through Lamas to Buxton Mill, a beautiful wooden mill-house, and over the river to the site of an Old Quaker Chapel, where Anna Sewell, who wrote *Black Beauty*, is buried.

2 Return to Buxton village hall and turn left on the Coltishall road. Coltishall lies at the head of navigable waters on the River Bure, and a place where cabin cruisers moor in front of elegant 18th-century houses and antiques shops.

3 Continue on the B1354 to Wroxham, passing a minor road on the left that leads to Wroxham Barns Craft Centre. At a crossroads in Hoveton, turn right on to the A1151 to Wroxham. This busy village offers a brisk introduction to the

BESIDE THE RIVER BURE
COLTISHALL

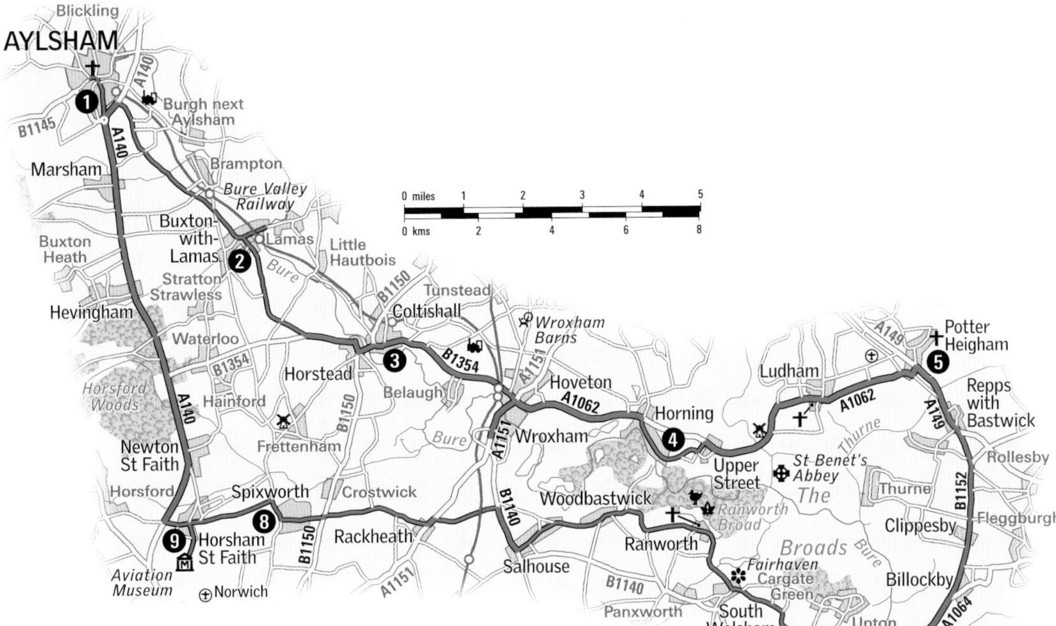

reed-fringed serenity of the Broads. From Wroxham, return to Hoveton crossroads and turn right on to the A1062 towards Horning. Turn right off the main road, following signs to the village. Here, the river is lined with decorous villas, each of which has its own landing stage.

4 The road from the village loops back to the A1062 – turn left at a minor crossroads following signs for Ludham, then turn right back on to the A1062 through Ludham and into Potter Heigham. The town, now a thriving holiday resort and boating centre, has a medieval bridge and a beautiful church, St Nicholas, which is thatched and has a round tower.

Potter Heigham to Reedham

5 At Potter Heigham, turn right on to the A149, following the signpost to Great Yarmouth. At Repps with Bastwick, turn right on to the B1152, signposted to Acle and Norwich, and continue across increasingly fen-like terrain. Carry on as the road merges with the A1064, and cross the bridge over the River Bure into Acle. In the thatched church of St Edmund, a chilling 15th-century inscription tells of the terror that the Black Death brought to Norfolk in 1349.

6 From Acle, follow signs south to Reedham, turning right at a minor junction opposite the thatched church, and driving under a railway bridge. Here, there is a delightful river frontage with two pubs. Pettitt's Crafts and Animal Adventure Park is another attraction. Parking is available at the railway station, from where the train goes to Berney Arms, a remote village in the middle of Halvergate marshes, inaccessible by road. The windmill now houses an exhibition of mill and Broadland life. Ask the driver to stop when getting on the train, because it stops at Berney Arms only on request.

Reedham to Aylsham

7 Return to Acle village centre then follow signs north to Upton, then South Walsham. At the village green turn right to Ranworth, where a nature reserve supports a wide variety of birds, including common terns and great crested grebes. Continue through Woodbastwick, a village of thatched cottages, and at Salhouse turn right on to the B1140 at a T-junction signposted to Wroxham and Coltishall. Take the next left signposted Stonehouse Lane and continue for some 6 miles, crossing the A1151 then the B1150 at staggered junctions to Spixworth.

8 Follow the signs to St Faith's Crematorium and at the crossroads in Horsham St Faith, turn left for the City of Norwich Aviation Museum, where the collection features a massive Vulcan bomber, among many other aircraft.

9 Return to Horsham St Faith and turn left. At the T-junction, turn right and follow the A140 to Aylsham.

NOTTINGHAMSHIRE

The eastern reaches of Nottinghamshire are a verdant mix of forest, farmland and floodplain, characterised by the Trent Valley and the hills around the village of Thurgarton.

12 NEWARK-ON-TRENT

TOUR LENGTH 78 miles

Starting from a former busy staging post on the Great North Road, this tour encompasses the ancient oaks and ferny glades of Sherwood Forest as well as the wooded hills of the Vale of Belvoir with its grand castle.

Newark to Clumber Park

1 Fine buildings, ranging from massively timbered Tudor to elegant Georgian, reflect Newark's commercial success, while St Mary Magdalen is one of England's most beautiful churches. The spire dominates the town. The tides of war have washed around Newark. It stands on the Fosse Way, boundary of the Roman Empire in the 1st century AD; Royalist Newark withstood three Civil War sieges before yielding; and in the 20th century the flat neighbouring country resounded to the drone of aircraft of Bomber Command, taking off and returning from wartime missions.

To start the drive, cross the bridge near the castle and go to the roundabout on the A46. Go straight ahead to join the A616 and continue to the small town of Ollerton, where a working 18th-century watermill stands on the site of one listed in the Domesday Book. Continue on the A616 to a roundabout on the far side of Ollerton and turn right on to the A614 towards Doncaster.

2 The straight road enters the Dukeries – an area where England's aristocrats carved estates out of Sherwood Forest in the 18th century and built grand stately houses. Follow the road past the entrance to the largest of them, Thoresby Hall, now a hotel and spa. Three miles farther on, turn left at Apleyhead Lodge, the main entrance to Clumber Park (NT), the northernmost part of Sherwood Forest. Continue along an avenue of lime trees – the longest in Europe, nearly 3 miles – and through a paypoint. Fork left after the paypoint, and then turn left at a crossroads for the car park. In the park, there is a walled kitchen garden, a chapel and a lake.

Clumber Park to Woolsthorpe

3 Return to the main drive, turn left and continue through the estate to a T-junction with the B6034. Turn left and follow the road to a T-junction with the A616, just beyond a minor crossroads. Turn left through Budby, and after 1 mile, turn right on to the B6034 towards Edwinstowe. The road enters another remnant of Sherwood's once vast oak and birch forest. A car park is on the right.

4 Follow the B6034 through Edwinstowe, going straight ahead at the crossroads with the A6075 in the village.

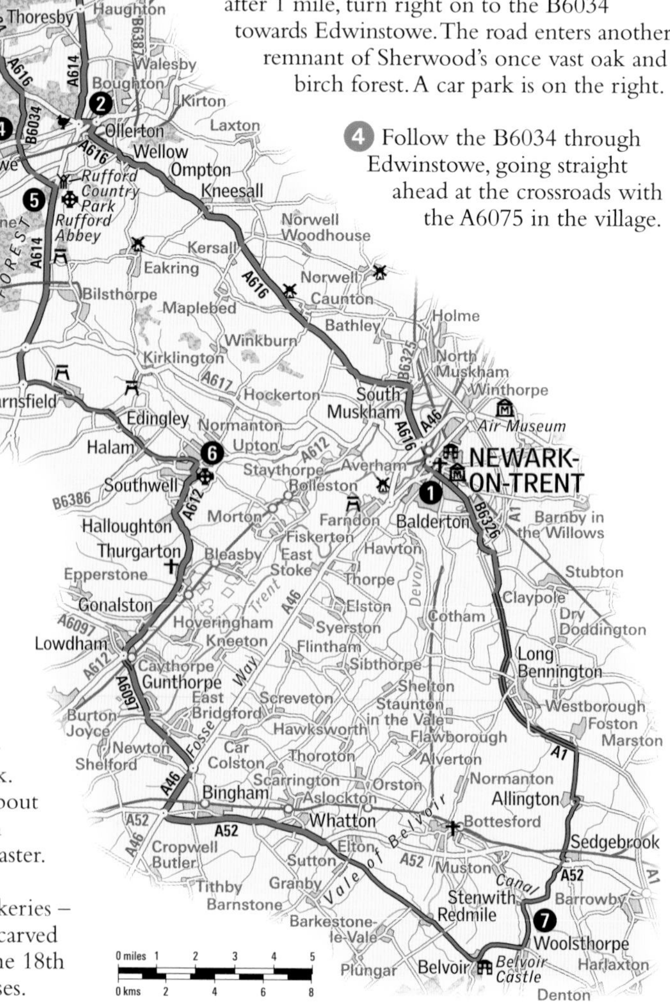

Continue to a T-junction with the A614 and turn right. The entrance to Rufford Abbey (EH), where a country park and craft centre has been created around a restored 12th-century Cistercian abbey, lies almost immediately on the left.

5 Continue for about 4½ miles to the second roundabout, and just after passing the White Post Farm Centre, turn left at the roundabout on to a minor road to Farnsfield, Edingley, Halam and Southwell, where the minster is one of the greatest ecclesiastical gems in England.

6 From the crossroads in the centre of Southwell, take the A612 towards Nottingham. Continue through the village of Thurgarton, where the church of St Peter is all that remains of a 12th-century priory that once rivalled Southwell Minster in size. At the roundabout in Lowdham, turn left on to the A6097 and cross the River Trent, continuing to the junction with the A46. Turn right and at the roundabout, reached after about 1¼ miles, take the second left on to the A52. Follow the road for 4 miles, then turn right by the Haven Inn, towards Redmile and Belvoir Castle. The road makes a beeline for the turrets of the castle, which is famous for its rococo interiors, French tapestries and picture collection. The home of the Duke and Duchess of Rutland, Belvoir Castle is open to the public, but check times before visiting. Fork left by the castle car park to Woolsthorpe.

Woolsthorpe to Newark

7 At the crossroads on the edge of Woolsthorpe, turn left and drive straight on for 1 mile to the hamlet of Stenwith, where the road divides. Fork right, following the road over Grantham Canal. Go straight ahead at the crossroads on the A52 to a minor T-junction, which is very close, on edge of Sedgebrook village. Turn left and continue through Allington, following the signposts for Newark, to reach the A1, the Great North Road. Turn left along a section of dual carriageway for 4 miles, then turn right on to the B6326 to return to Newark.

IMPOSING RUINS RISE FROM THE RIVER TRENT

NEWARK CASTLE

SHROPSHIRE

Magnificent relics of early industry, mighty fortified castles and medieval towns are some of the highlights of this western county, once at the forefront of the Industrial Revolution.

13 LUDLOW

TOUR LENGTH 70 miles

A trip around the border territory between England and Wales takes in some brooding castles that once defended the Marches. The route also passes the Stiperstones, a series of jagged tors in the Shropshire hills.

Ludlow to Croft Castle

1 The well-preserved medieval town of Ludlow lies close to the Welsh border in southern Shropshire. Overlooked by the ruins of a massive 11th-century sandstone castle, Ludlow has more than 500 listed buildings, including the 16th-century Castle Lodge and the Feathers Hotel, a half-timbered building with intricate carving.

To leave the town, take the B4361 and after 1 mile fork right to Richards Castle, where the Norman church of St Bartholomew has a detached 14th-century bell tower.

2 Continue on the B4361, then follow the B4362 round a right-hand bend to Bircher, and 1½ miles beyond it, turn right for Croft Castle (NT). This castellated manor has one of Herefordshire's finest walled gardens and vineyards.

Croft Castle to Stiperstones

3 Returning to the B4362, turn right towards Mortimer's Cross, where the future Edward IV won a major victory against the Lancastrians during the Wars of the Roses. Pass the 18th-century Lucton Mill, usually called Mortimer's Cross Water Mill (EH), a partly working water-powered corn mill, and turn right through the village on to the A4110 to Aymestry. Continue up a wooded valley to Wigmore. Medieval Wigmore Castle (EH) was once home to the powerful and rebellious Mortimer family, and the conserved ruins dominate the hill top.

4 Go through Adforton on the A4110, which is joined by the A4113 just before Leintwardine. Beyond Leintwardine, fork left on to the B4385, signposted to Craven Arms. After 1½ miles, turn left at a sharp right-hand bend and continue to Hoptonheath. At Hoptonheath station, follow the signs for Clun and Bishop's Castle. After 3 miles, turn left on to the B4368 to Clun through Clunton, with a wide valley to the left. At Clun, the ruins of an 11th-century border castle (EH) rise raggedly from its earthworks above the valleys of the Clun and the Unk.

5 Follow the A488 towards Shrewsbury and after 5½ miles turn left on to the B4385 to Bishop's Castle. The museum, the medieval House on Crutches, stands opposite the Town Hall at the top of a steep main street, lined with timber-framed, stone-built and red-brick houses.

6 Bear right to rejoin the A488, which runs through Lydham before climbing to an open plateau with hills to left and right. At White Grit, turn left and follow the signs for the Bronze Age stone circle of Mitchell's Fold, erected between 2000-1200 BC.

THE LAWLEY AND CAER CARADOC FROM THE SLOPES OF LONG MYND

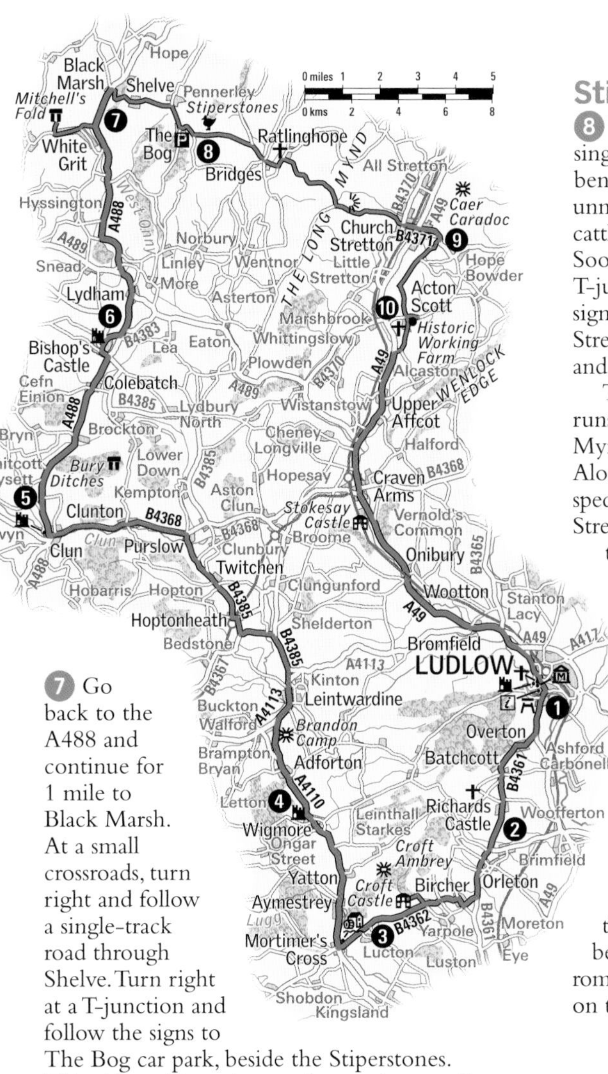

7 Go back to the A488 and continue for 1 mile to Black Marsh. At a small crossroads, turn right and follow a single-track road through Shelve. Turn right at a T-junction and follow the signs to The Bog car park, beside the Stiperstones. This ridge of jagged quartzite tors is one of Shropshire's best-known landmarks.

Stiperstones to Church Stretton

8 Turn right out of the car park up the twisting single-track road and bear right around a hairpin bend towards Bridges. After ½ mile, take a left unmarked fork, and follow the road across several cattle grids and 2 miles of open countryside. Soon after the road drops sharply, it comes to a T-junction. Turn left and then immediately right, signposted to Ratlinghope Church and Church Stretton. Pass a youth hostel on the right, bear left and then turn right towards Church Stretton.

The road climbs between beech trees and then runs over dramatic moorland, part of the Long Mynd ridge. At a small T-junction, turn left. Along the road are a series of parking places giving spectacular views over the hills to Church Stretton and beyond to Wenlock Edge. Follow the road down into Church Stretton.

Church Stretton to Ludlow

9 Carry on through Church Stretton on the B4371, over a railway bridge, and cross the A49 at traffic lights, going up Sandford Avenue. After ½ mile, turn right up a steep road that winds for 2½ miles to a crossroads. Turn left for Acton Scott Historic Working Farm, which is open in summer.

10 Return to the crossroads, turn left and follow the lane past Acton Scott church to the A49. Turn left on to the A49 and a mile beyond Craven Arms, turn right to visit romantic Stokesay Castle (EH). Return to Ludlow on the A49.

SHROPSHIRE

14 BRIDGNORTH

TOUR LENGTH 55 miles

Set amid glorious countryside, the region's industrial past is evident in this tour, which includes a working watermill, a fine-china museum and the famous iron bridge that spans the Severn Gorge.

Bridgnorth to Bewdley

1 Bridgnorth is divided in two. Low Town, once a port, lines the Severn's banks; High Town, on a plateau above, grew up around a Norman castle. All that remains of the castle – the keep on the town's southern edge – leans more steeply than the Tower of Pisa. The town's two parts are linked by seven sets of ancient steps, by a steep old cartway, and by Britain's oldest cliff railway, opened in 1892.

First, take the B4555 signposted to Highley, which leads past Daniel's Mill. Powered by a cast-iron waterwheel 11.5m (38ft) in diameter, the restored 18th-century mill makes and sells wholemeal flour.

2 Continue on the B4555 through Chelmarsh and Woodhill to Highley, an ancient mining village once owned by Lady Godiva. Highley is also a stop on the Severn Valley Railway. Old steam engines and carriages still run along the 16 mile route from Bridgnorth to Kidderminster.

Carry on for 2½ miles to a T-junction and turn left on to the B4363. At Kinlet, turn left again on to the B4194. Continue through Wyre Forest to Bewdley.

Bewdley to Kingsford

3 From Bewdley, follow the B4190 towards Kidderminster, crossing Thomas Telford's three-arched bridge over the Severn. The road leads past the West Midland Safari Park.

4 Continue on the B4190 for 3 miles. At the roundabout in Wolverley, turn left on to the B4189. After 1 mile, turn right, following signs for Kingsford Country Park. Turn left at a T-junction in Kingsford on Kingsford Lane towards Kinver. After ¾ mile, turn right into a car park. A gate at the far end gives access to Vale's Rock, a cave dwelling dug from sandstone centuries ago. Outer rooms were added in brick, and the place was inhabited until the early 1960s.

Kingsford to Ironbridge

5 Continue to Kinver, turning right into the village. The high street is lined with timber-framed buildings. Turn left at the next junction, following signs for Enville, and fork left at the junction with A458. Turn right in Enville, signposted to Swindon, and fork right up Blundies Lane. Take the left fork, in the direction of Swindon, and the next left, signposted 'Airport'. Go straight over at the crossroads and continue to Halfpenny Green, where vineyards, established in 1983, are open to the public. There is also a craft centre and a tea room. The airport was originally used by the RAF but is now a base for a flying school.

6 With the Royal Oak pub on the right, continue straight ahead over the crossroads to Upper Aston. At Upper Aston, go

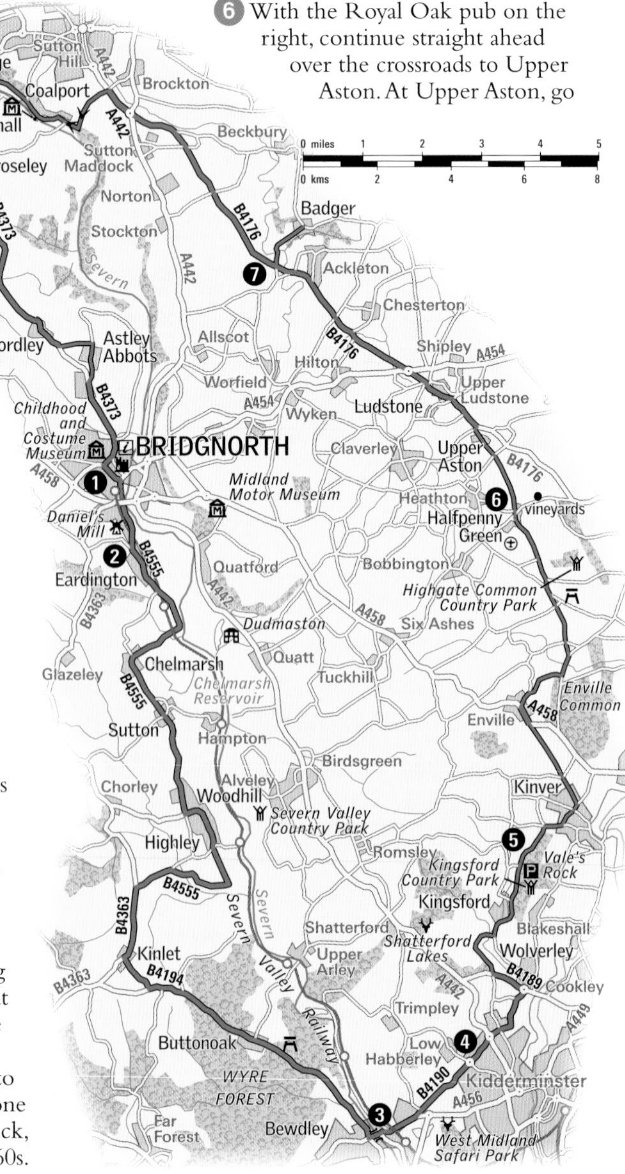

THE IRON BRIDGE, BUILT IN 1779

over the crossroads and almost at once turn left on to the B4176 towards Telford. Continue for 4½ miles, crossing the A454 at a roundabout midway, and turn right on to a narrow road to Badger, a picturesque village of duckponds, timber and thatch.

7 Return to the B4176 and continue towards Telford. At a major roundabout on the A442, go straight ahead, and after ¾ mile turn left to Coalport. Continue downhill and, just before reaching the river, turn right into the town, made famous the world over for its Coalport China, a make of porcelain. Uncover its history and development in the town's China Museum.

Go left for Ironbridge, following the north bank of the Severn, and left again to cross the bridge. Follow the signs for the long-stay car park beside the iron bridge. Built by Abraham Darby III in 1779, the bridge spans 36.5m (120ft) and was the world's first bridge to be made of iron. Over the bridge and alongside the river to the left is a visitor centre.

Ironbridge to Bridgnorth

8 Turn right out of the car park and immediately bear left uphill towards Benthall. Turn left at the T-junction on to the B4375 into Broseley, on the edge of the Severn Gorge. The town's industrial past is evident in the fine cast-iron tombs in the graveyard of All Saints Church, and its history of pipe manufacturing is recalled at a clay pipe museum. Set on hilly woodland, the town's buildings nestle in the trees, displaying three centuries of architectural style. The first iron boat was built here, as was the world's first flanged wheel railway. The irregularly planned cottages, known as jitties, have been restored in recent years.

9 Fork right in Broseley town centre, following the signs to Bridgnorth. Just outside Broseley, join the B4373. Continue through the hamlet of Nordley and turn left for Astley Abbotts, which has some fine old houses, including timber-framed Severn Hall, and views over the Severn Valley. Return to the B4373 and continue to Bridgnorth.

STAFFORDSHIRE

The scenic journey through Staffordshire starts on the county's eastern fringe, where old village traditions hold fast. The drive traverses Areas of Outstanding Natural Beauty, skirting several architectural gems.

15 TUTBURY

TOUR LENGTH 63 miles

Vast fertile farmlands and patches of once-great forests, a theme park and a nature reserve feature on this drive. The route goes through market towns and passes stately mansions and a ruined abbey.

Tutbury to Alton

1 Castle ruins dating from the 14th century brood over Tutbury. Mary, Queen of Scots, was imprisoned there in 1569, and at intervals until 1585. The ornate west front of the Norman church of St Mary the Virgin faces the castle. The town's prosperity, emphasised by Georgian townhouses, was based on silk and cotton milling.

From the High Street follow the road downhill to a roundabout. Go ahead on the A511 Hatton road. After a railway line, turn second left to Scropton and go on to the junction with the A515. Turn right then left to Sudbury and 17th-century Sudbury Hall (NT), which has sumptuous interiors and a Museum of Childhood.

2 At the junction with the A50, follow signs underneath the A50, via two roundabouts on to the A515. Take the first left towards Somersal Herbert. At a junction, with a chapel on the right, turn left and continue to Somersal Herbert. Just before a left turn for Doveridge, take an unsigned right turn past a farm. At a T-junction turn left to Marston Montgomery. At the next junction, turn left and cross the River Dove to Rocester – Rosseter in George Eliot's 1859 novel, *Adam Bede*.

3 Continue to a junction and turn right towards Ashbourne. At the next junction, with a JCB factory on the left, turn right then immediately left at a roundabout on to the B5031 Cheadle road. At a second roundabout, after crossing the River Churnet, go ahead to

SHUGBOROUGH HALL ACROSS THE RIVER SOW

Denstone, then at a T-junction turn left on to the B5032. Just after a sign for Alton Towers, turn sharp right into Alton, passing the early 19th-century circular village lock-up on the left. Alton's Gothic, fairytale castle of gables and towers was built in 1847-52 by the architect A.W. Pugin.

Alton to Milford Common

4 Go downhill through the village and cross the River Churnet. Pass disused Alton Station, which is now owned by the Landmark Trust, on the left and mock-Tudor Alton Lodge on the right, and continue uphill. On the right are the gardens of Alton Park, laid out in the early 19th century by the 15th Earl of Shrewsbury. The 16th Earl, aided by Pugin, built Alton Towers palace – now partly ruined amid the Alton Towers theme park. Follow the road towards Farley. After passing a white clock-towered building on the right, turn sharp left towards Farley. Continue to a T-junction and turn left through Oakamoor, over the River Churnet, and then follow the climbing road. After 1 mile, turn right between gate pillars to visit the Hawksmoor Nature Reserve.

5 Back on the Cheadle road, go round a sharp left bend. Then immediately before the road bends sharp right, take the unsignposted lane on the left. At the next junction, turn right on to the B5032, then left towards Freehay. After 1 mile, turn left towards Great Gate. After a steep descent, turn right on to a lane. After ¼ mile, bear left towards Croxden. Cross a ford and go through Great Gate. Just beyond a farm, turn right to Croxden and the peaceful 13th-century ruins of Croxden Abbey (EH).

6 Continue to a T-junction and turn right. Just before the Hollington village sign, turn sharp left and follow the lane to Stramshall. Turn left at the junction, passing the Hare and Hounds pub. At the next junction, turn right on to the B5030 and continue to the horse racing town of Uttoxeter.

7 Follow the A518 signs towards Stafford. Beyond Uttoxeter, at Blount's Green, turn left on to the B5013. Before Abbots Bromley, turn right on to the B5013 towards Rugeley over the vast waters of Blithfield Reservoir, opened in 1952. After 2 miles, at a sharp left-hand bend, turn right towards Stafford. Continue to the junction in Bishton and turn left, then left again over the River Trent to a roundabout. Turn right on to the A513 to Milford. Shugborough Hall (NT), on the right just before the village, is complete with mansion house, servants' quarters, model farm and walled garden. A little way farther on, Milford Common has a designated car park – turn left at the roundabout opposite the Barley Mow pub.

Milford Common to Tutbury

8 Go back over Blithfield Reservoir. Turn right on to the B5014 to Abbots Bromley, where every September the Horn Dance is performed, an old medieval tradition. The green is flanked by the half-timbered Goat's Head Inn, the 17th-century Butter Cross and Georgian houses.

9 Beyond Abbots Bromley, turn left on to the B5234 towards Burton. After Newborough, ignore a left turn to Tutbury and continue over the A515 through Needwood Forest. This is now little more than clumps of woodland but it once covered much of Staffordshire. At the Needwood roundabout take the second turn on the left to Tutbury.

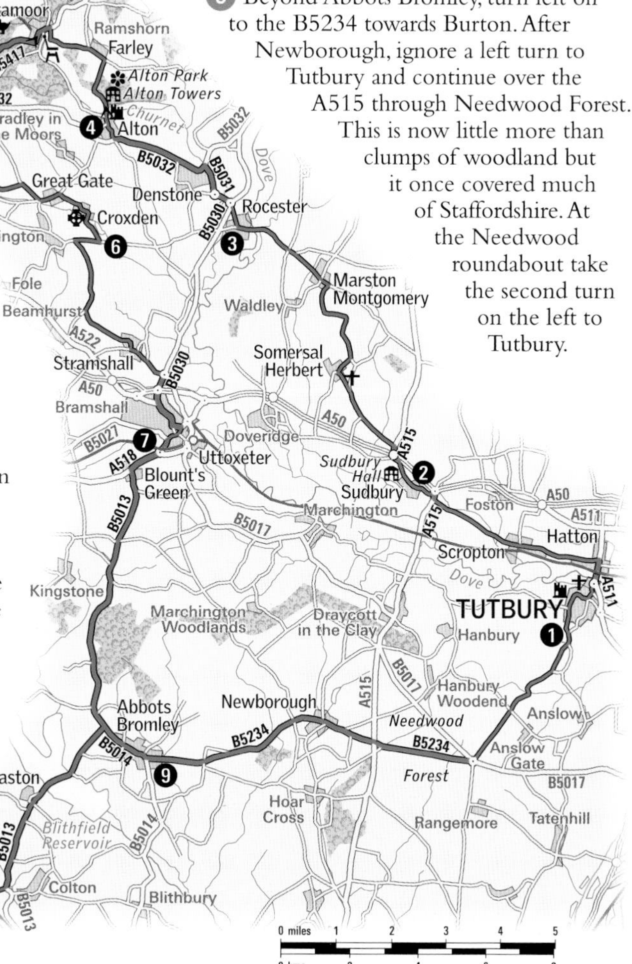

SUFFOLK

At the time of the Norman Conquest, Suffolk was one of the most densely populated parts of England. Today, it is a largely rural county, pleasant roads linking quiet villages and old medieval towns.

16 BURY ST EDMUNDS

TOUR LENGTH 58 miles

The legacy of the wool industry and its generated wealth pervades the Suffolk landscape in the shape of grand medieval churches and half-timbered merchants' houses. An extension to the drive takes in West Stow Country Park.

Bury St Edmunds to Long Melford

❶ Buildings of old stone, a monastic past and a riverside setting at the confluence of the Lark and the Linnet give Bury St Edmunds the air of an ancient university town. It took its name from the shrine of St Edmund, once housed in the great Benedictine abbey around which the town grew up in early Norman times. Fine 16th-century and Georgian buildings bear witness to the town's prosperous centuries as a cloth-making centre.

Follow the A134 towards Sudbury. Just before Sicklesmere, turn left and follow the signs to Bradfield St George, which has an attractive flint-and-stone church. Just before the village, the road bears right, signposted to Felsham. In Maypole Green, turn right on to a narrow road signposted to Bradfield St Clare, skirting the village.

At the next T-junction, turn left towards Cockfield and go through Great Green, down the left side of its large triangular green, and follow the signs for Felsham. Fork right towards Thorpe Morieux, then turn right on to a lane to Thorpe Green, where dense hedgerows open out to give broad views across flat, wooded country with rows of trees planted as windbreaks.

❷ Continue to a T-junction in Thorpe Morieux and turn right and right again at Church Corner, past the triangular village sign. After a short way take a left turn over a bridge, following signs to Preston. Follow the road round, and at a T-junction, turn left to Preston St Mary. The village church has fine stained-glass windows and, beside the church, Preston Hall, an Elizabethan timber-framed private house, has tall, ornate chimneys.

❸ Return to the T-junction and take the road to Lavenham, notable for its beautiful half-timbered medieval buildings, including the Guildhall (NT). Take the B1071, past Lavenham's magnificent church of St Peter and St Paul – the tower is the tallest in Suffolk – then turn right at a garage and follow the signs to Long Melford, where half-timbered and Georgian houses stretch out along the High Street. Turn right on to the A134 and immediately left on to Hall Street. Holy Trinity Church stands at the upper end of the slanting green. The church was completed in 1484 and owes its splendour to the wealth of the cloth merchants. Melford Hall (NT) on the A134 is a well-preserved Elizabethan mansion.

Long Melford to Cavendish

❹ Take the B1064 to Foxearth over the county border in Essex. The village once boasted a fine church spire, its square walled tower built on an older structure in 1862. The spire was destroyed in 1948 when it was struck by lightning during a violent storm and the damaged parts blown into a neighbouring field. The spire was never re-erected; today only the tower remains. Continue on the B1064 to Pentlow, a village

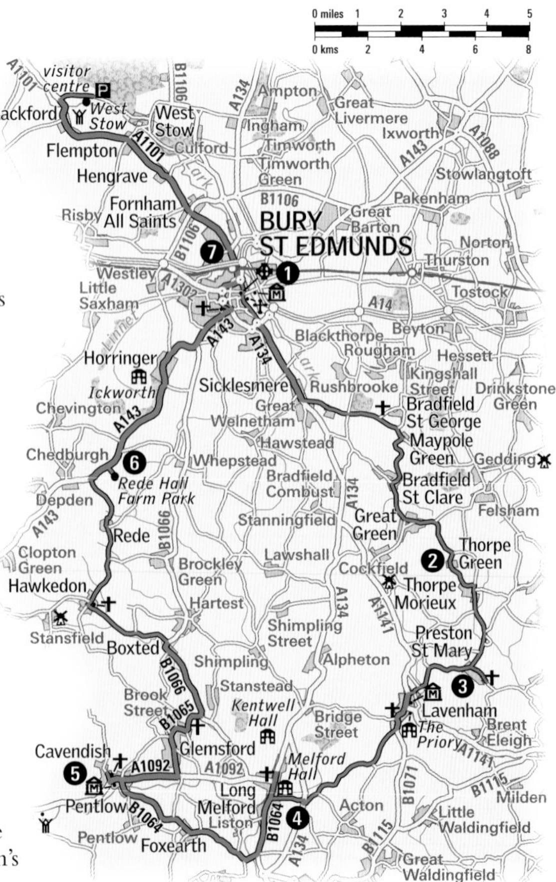

HYDE PARK CORNER, CAVENDISH

curiously divided into two sections 1 mile apart. Cross the River Stour, and turn left on to the A1092 to Cavendish. The 14th-century St Mary's Church overlooks thatched almshouses that stand by the village green. Unusually, the church has a chimney – a priest's room in the tower was built with a fireplace.

Cavendish to Bury

5 Leave Cavendish on the A1092 towards Long Melford, and turn left on to the B1065 to Glemsford. At the T-junction beyond St Mary's Church and the timber-framed Monks Hall, which is privately owned, turn left on to the B1066 towards Bury St Edmunds.

Go through Boxted, then turn left on to a minor road to the hamlet of Hawkedon, which has an old hall, colour-washed houses and a tall church, St Mary's, standing in the centre of the broad village green. Between the church and the war memorial, turn right to the village of Rede and continue on the same road, following signs for Chedburgh. Turn right on to the A143 and after about ⅓ mile turn right for Rede Hall Farm Park to see agricultural life as it was in the early 20th century and Suffolk Punch horses at work.

6 Continue on the A143 for 2 ½ miles to Horringer. Behind the green, Ickworth House (NT) is set in parkland. The mansion has a huge rotunda and houses good collections of furniture, paintings, porcelain, silver and sculpture. Continue on the A143 to return to Bury St Edmunds.

Bury to West Stow

7 From Bury, take the A1101 and follow the signs for West Stow Country Park and Anglo-Saxon village, going through Fornham All Saints, Hengrave and Flempton, villages with many Grade II thatched cottages. Hengrave's round-towered church has Saxon origins. It stands in the grounds of the privately owned Hengrave Hall, a 16th-century manor.

Continue through Lackford to West Stow Country Park and Anglo Saxon Village, where there is a car park and visitor centre. The site has been occupied since the last Ice Age; evidence for hunter gatherers, Neolithic and Iron Age peoples, Roman settlers and Saxon tribes has been found on the site, which today features a series of reconstructed Saxon dwellings made from wood, thatch, wattle and clay.

SUFFOLK

17 HADLEIGH

TOUR LENGTH 54 miles

Sleepy medieval villages dotted with thatched cottages, the Orwell and Stour estuaries cutting deep inland and peaceful nature reserves make this an idyllic trip, taking in the mills, churches and waterways of Constable country.

Hadleigh to Shotley Gate

1 Hugging the right bank of the River Brett, a tributary of the Stour, Hadleigh was a wealthy centre of the medieval wool trade. Its magnificent 14th and 15th-century buildings include St Mary's Church; the half-timbered Guildhall with a splendid crown post roof; and the six-storeyed and turreted Deanery Tower.

Take the A1071 towards Ipswich, passing Wolves Wood RSPB reserve on the left, after 1¼ miles. This wet woodland of oak, hazel, ash and willow attracts woodpeckers, nightingales, tawny owls and kestrels among other birds, and supports orchids and ferns. Just beyond Hintlesham, turn right on to a narrow road signposted to Washbrook. After ½ mile, turn right to Washbrook church.

2 At the T-junction turn left to Copdock. At the next T-junction, turn left and immediately right, signposted to Wherstead. Follow the road past Belstead to the A137 and turn left. Just before the roundabout, turn right towards Wherstead. Follow the lane to the B1456 and the River Orwell, where the great arch of the Orwell Bridge straddles the river on gigantic legs. It is the longest single span of pre-stressed concrete in England.

3 Turn right on to the B1456 to Woolverstone and then Chelmondiston. Turn left at the sign for Pin Mill, which was once a smuggling haven and a centre for building Thames barges. The Butt and Oyster pub down by the harbour dates from the 16th century. Follow the B1456 to Shotley Gate, where the Orwell and Stour meet the sea.

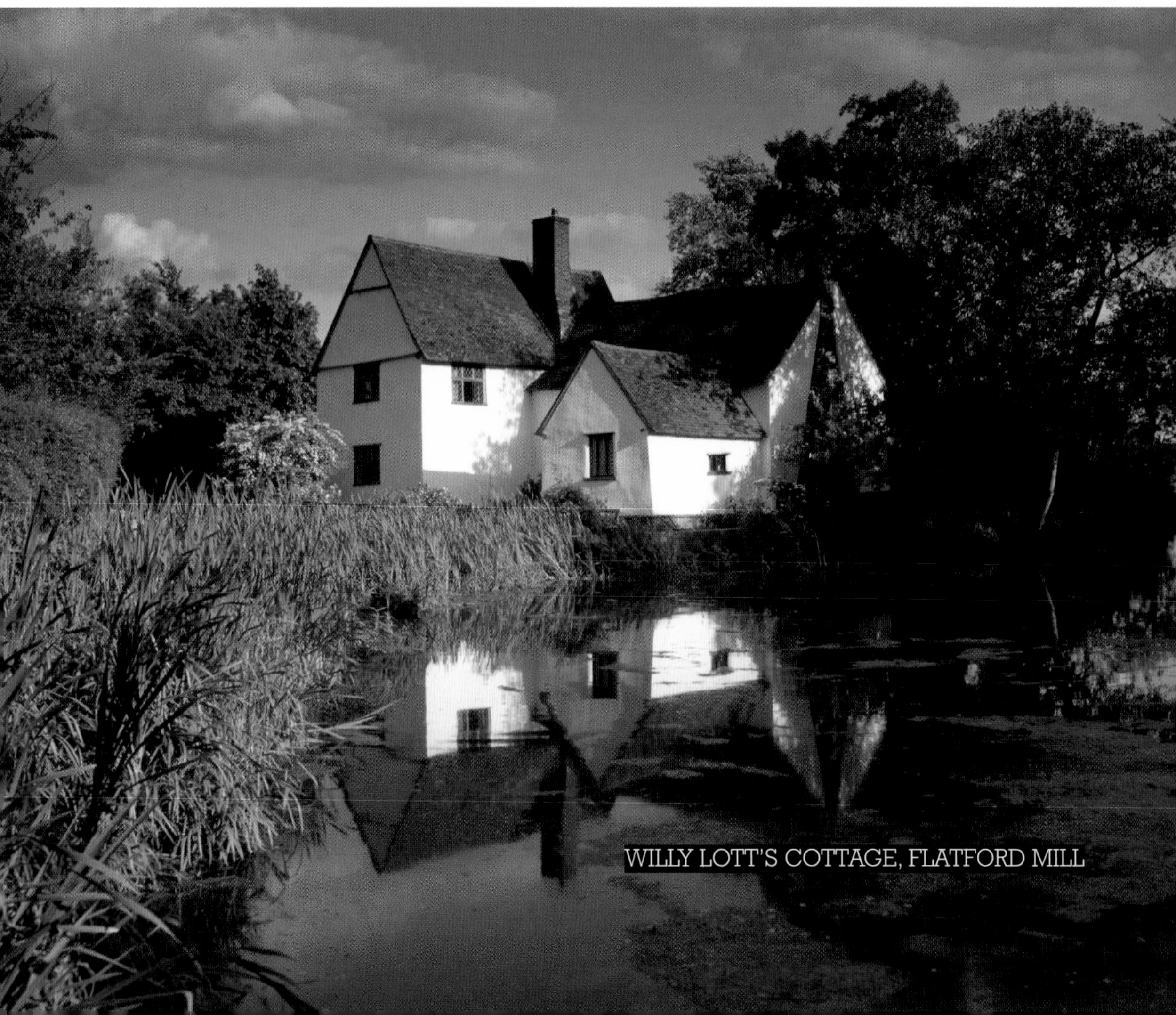

WILLY LOTT'S COTTAGE, FLATFORD MILL

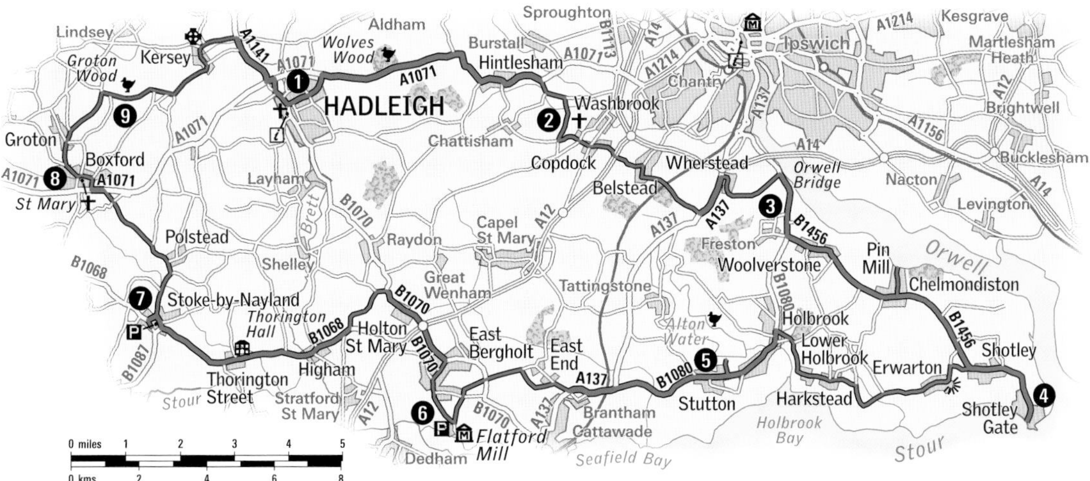

Shotley Gate to Flatford Mill

4 Follow the B1456 back to Shotley. Just beyond the village, turn left, signposted to Erwarton, passing Erwarton Hall. The privately owned house was built in Tudor times but its elegant gables and mullioned windows are upstaged by its bizarre gatehouse, which was added in 1600.

Follow the road through Harkstead and Lower Holbrook to the junction with the B1080 at Holbrook. Turn left, and just beyond Holbrook – which is dominated by the neo-Gothic Royal Hospital School – turn right for Alton Water, the largest reservoir in Suffolk, which specialises in sailing and birdwatching.

5 Continue through Stutton, joining the A137 towards Brantham. Just before the road bends sharp left into Brantham, turn right, signposted to East Bergholt. Turn left at the T-junction and go straight on at the next two junctions, following signs for Flatford, into Flatford Road. A large car park is situated north of Flatford Mill (NT). The mill, Valley Farm and Willy Lott's house are leased to the Field Studies Council and are used for a series of arts-based courses, but Bridge Cottage is open and has an exhibition dedicated to the painter John Constable, who spent his youth in the Stour valley.

Flatford Mill to Stoke-by-Nayland

6 Turn left out of the car park and left again into East Bergholt, where Constable was born in 1776. The bells of the massive early Tudor church of St Mary are sited at ground level in a unique 16th-century timber bell cage.

Take the B1070 to Holton St Mary. Beyond the village, turn first left and follow the signs to Higham. In the village, bear right to stay on the B1068. On the right, after 1¼ miles, Thorington Hall (NT), built about 1600, is open by appointment only, although it usually has an open day in September. Follow the road to the pretty village of Stoke-by-Nayland. For the car park, go ahead at the crossroads, bear left round the village and take the first left, School Lane. The church tower is 36.5m (120ft) tall and was often painted by Constable. It soars over the 16th-century, half-timbered Guildhall.

Stoke-by-Nayland to Hadleigh

7 Turn right out of the car park. Take the first right, and then turn left at the next junction to Polstead. Keep the village pond to the right, and follow the signs to Boxford. At the junction with the A1071 turn left and then right into the village of Boxford, which has many medieval half-timbered houses. The 14th-century wooden porch of St Mary's Church is reputed to be the oldest in England.

8 Turn right opposite St Mary's and follow the road into Groton. Beyond the church, take the first right, signposted to Kersey Tey. After 1 mile turn right and pass Groton Wood nature reserve, where woodland plants such as woodruff, early purple orchid and violet hellborine thrive.

9 Continue to Kersey, where the medieval timber-framed houses lining the main street date from the village's heyday as a wool centre – it even gave its name to a woollen fabric. The main feature of the town is the 15th-century tower of the church of St Mary and the ford or water splash, a tributary of the River Brett which flows through the town.

Ford the river and north of Kersey turn right. At the junction with the A1141 turn right, and where the road meets the A1071, turn left then immediately right to Hadleigh.

SUFFOLK

18 ALDEBURGH

TOUR LENGTH 66 miles

Something of Benjamin Britten's inspiration may be sensed on this splendid airy drive round the region. The route diverts through old towns and villages but never strays far from the seaside, whether cheery resort, flat shore or marshy lagoon.

Aldeburgh to Thorpeness

1 Squeezed between the River Alde and the sea, Aldeburgh consists mainly of two long, parallel streets with colour-washed 19th-century houses. The red-brick Moot Hall, a Tudor building used for meetings, once stood in the middle of town. Now the waves lap and draw at the hissing shingle just metres away, as Aldeburgh slowly loses its fight against the encroaching sea. The sea's drama echoes in the music of Benjamin Britten, who lived in Aldeburgh and brought it lasting fame by establishing an annual festival. He is buried in the churchyard beside his collaborator, Peter Pears.

Leave Aldeburgh along the coast road to Thorpeness, passing watery pastures on the left, and wide, shingle beaches on the right. Thorpeness is an endearingly eccentric seaside resort, constructed around the Meare, a huge boating lake dug in 1910. Country club, golf club and holiday housing followed. Parking is available opposite the Meare.

Thorpeness to Dunwich Heath

2 Follow the B1353 to Aldringham and turn right on to the B1122 to Leiston, where a sign points to Sizewell Beach. The beach offers amazing views of the most modern of Britain's nuclear power stations. The old ironworks in Leiston is now a museum. Continue on the B1122, and after 1 mile look out for a small left turn to Leiston Abbey. The extensive ruins of the 14th-century abbey (EH) are attached to a Tudor house. The house, together with a restored tithe barn and Guesten Hall in the grounds, now provide the setting for the Pro Corda school of chamber music.

3 Continue through Theberton and at the next junction turn right on to the B1125 to Westleton. At the end of the village, turn right across the heath towards Dunwich. A right-hand turn, signposted, leads to Minsmere RSPB Reserve. To see the Coastguard Cottages (NT), carry on past the turn to Minsmere and take the next right, signposted to Dunwich Heath, and continue to the end of the road. A walk past the cottages leads on to some of the last wild heathland in East Anglia.

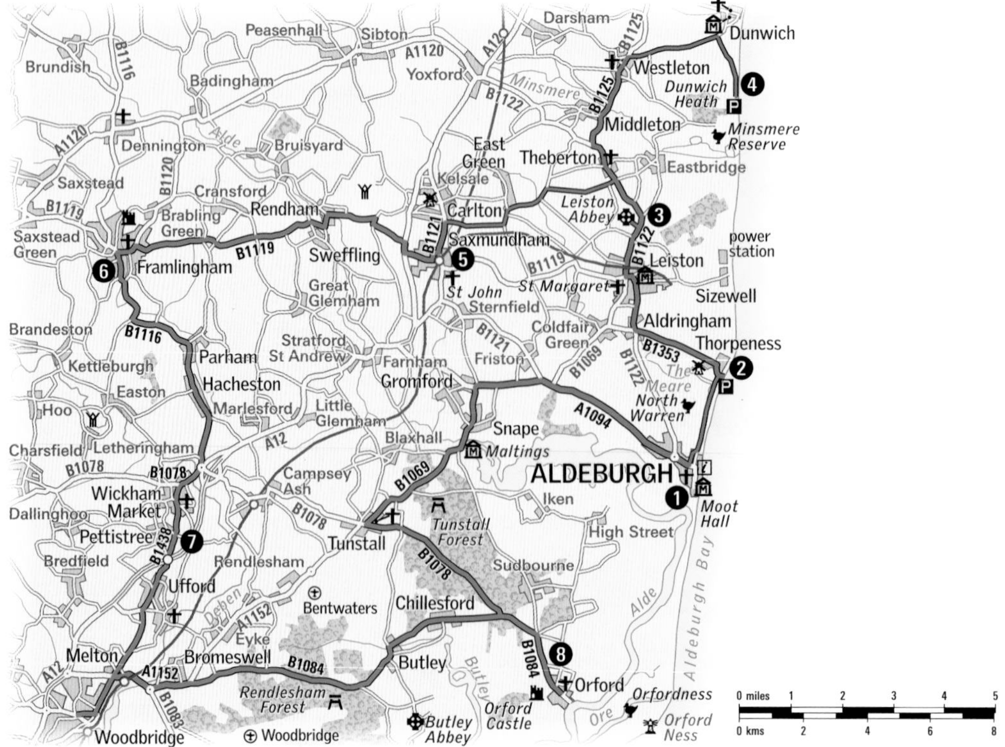

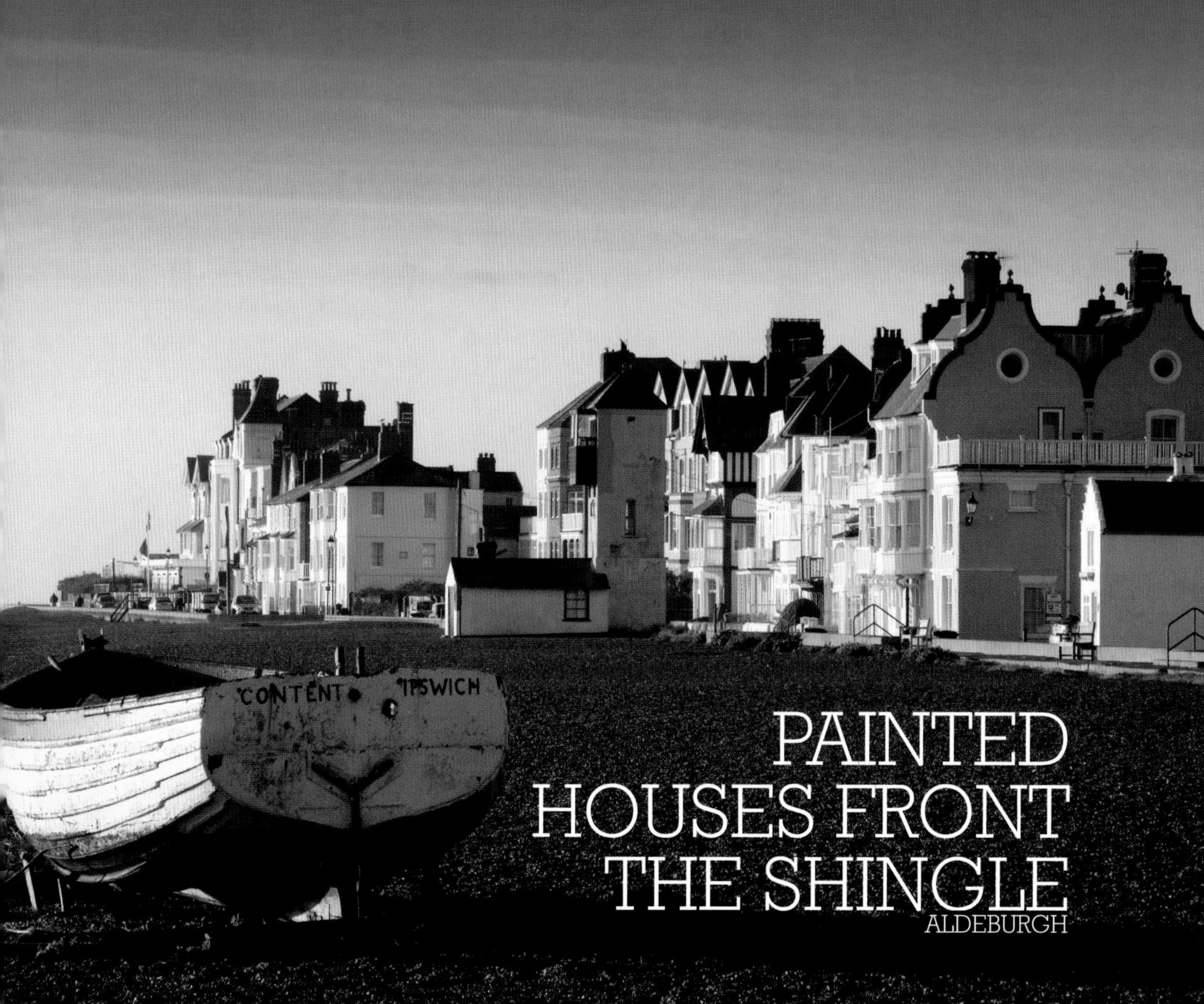

PAINTED HOUSES FRONT THE SHINGLE

ALDEBURGH

Dunwich Heath to Orford

4 Return through Theberton, and just past the village, turn right on to a minor road towards Kelsale and Saxmundham. Turn left on to the B1121 to Saxmundham, where St John's Church has an inclining chancel, a Suffolk feature said to represent the angle of Christ's head on the cross.

5 Take the B1119 to Framlingham, where in 1553 Mary Tudor's retinue sheltered at the Swan Inn before she rode to London to oust Lady Jane Grey from the throne. Above the town stand the walls of 12th-century Framlingham Castle (EH). Later a poorhouse was built within the walls, which was still in use in 1839.

6 Follow the B1116 towards Wickham Market. After 5 miles, turn right at a roundabout on to the B1078 to Wickham Market. Georgian buildings flank the market place, which is known as the Hill.

7 Continue on the B1438 to Woodbridge, where boats have been built since the 14th century. A walkway beside the River Deben leads to an 18th-century tide mill. Return to the traffic lights at the junction with the A1152 and turn right. At the roundabout, continue on the A1152 for 1 mile before turning right onto the B1084. Follow this to Orford.

Orford to Aldeburgh

8 Two notable medieval buildings – Orford Castle (EH) and St Bartholomew's Church – stand at opposite ends of the square. The quay, once the focus of an important medieval seaport, is now a haven for pleasure craft.

Leave Orford on the B1084, fork right on to the B1078 to Tunstall and turn right on to the B1069, signposted to Snape. Just before the town, look out for the Maltings – a group of 19th-century buildings on the banks of the river Ore. In 1965, they were taken over by Benjamin Britten as a home for the Aldeburgh Festival, and the huge barley-drying kiln was converted into a concert hall. It continues to develop as a musical centre, with shops and cafés for visitors.

At Snape crossroads, turn right on to the A1094 to return to Aldeburgh.

WARWICKSHIRE

This quiet county's southwest reaches span river valleys and the Cotswold hills, its winding roads tracing a pattern already long established at the time of Shakespeare's birth at Stratford.

19 STRATFORD-UPON-AVON

TOUR LENGTH 57 miles

A rural landscape shaped by the calmly flowing Avon is the backdrop for this drive. Villages, mansions, churches and monuments reflect almost every period of English history.

Stratford to Radway

1 Streets of medieval houses, Tudor-beamed teashops and the Bard's family properties remain at the heart of this busy market town, while on the banks of the River Avon, the Royal Shakespeare Company puts on a full programme of plays in its splendid venues.

To start the drive, take the B4086 beside the river and go through Tiddington, bearing right at Alveston war memorial to Wellesbourne. The road passes Charlecote Park (NT) on the left. The house was rebuilt in 1558 by Sir Thomas Lucy.

2 Continue through Wellesbourne and follow the signs to Kineton, staying on the B4086 as it climbs through woodland. About ½ mile beyond the junction with B4455 is the entrance to Compton Verney, a restored 18th-century house and art gallery, which is open to the public.

3 Past a windmill, the road descends into Kineton, where the Earl of Essex and his Roundhead army spent the night before the Battle of Edgehill, the first major battle of the Civil War. Turn right at a T-junction towards Banbury, on the B4086 past a small pillar commemorating the battle. About a mile beyond it, turn right and then right again at a T-junction into the pretty village of Radway. From here it's possible to walk up Edgehill to an octagonal tower, now the Castle Inn, said to mark the spot where Charles I raised his colours before the battle.

Radway to Ilmington

4 Return through the village, bearing right to the B4086. Turn left and, after about 200m, turn right to Northend. At a T-junction, turn left on to the B4100 and follow the signs to Northend and Fenny Compton, turning right after ¼ mile to cross over the M40 where the 14th-century beacon tower looms ahead in Burton Dassett Hills Country Park. Turn left through Northend and continue for Fenny Compton.

5 Follow the signs for Burton Dassett through Fenny Compton, continue down to Avon Dassett and recross the M40. At the junction beyond it, turn left towards Warmington on the B4100, following the road as it climbs, skirting Warmington. Continue over high ground and turn right to Horley.

6 In Horley, turn right to Hornton and continue to a T-junction. Turn right on to the A422 towards Stratford. On the left, after ½ mile, is the entrance to 17th-century Upton House (NT), which is presented as it was in its 1930s heyday when it was owned by the 2nd Lord Bearsted. The house contains a remarkable collection of art and has superb terraced gardens.

7 Follow the A422 as it winds steeply down the Edge Hill escarpment. Turn left to Tysoe and go through Middle Tysoe and Upper Tysoe, following signs to Brailes and Compton Wynyates. About ¾ mile beyond Upper Tysoe, where the road bends right, follow the sign to

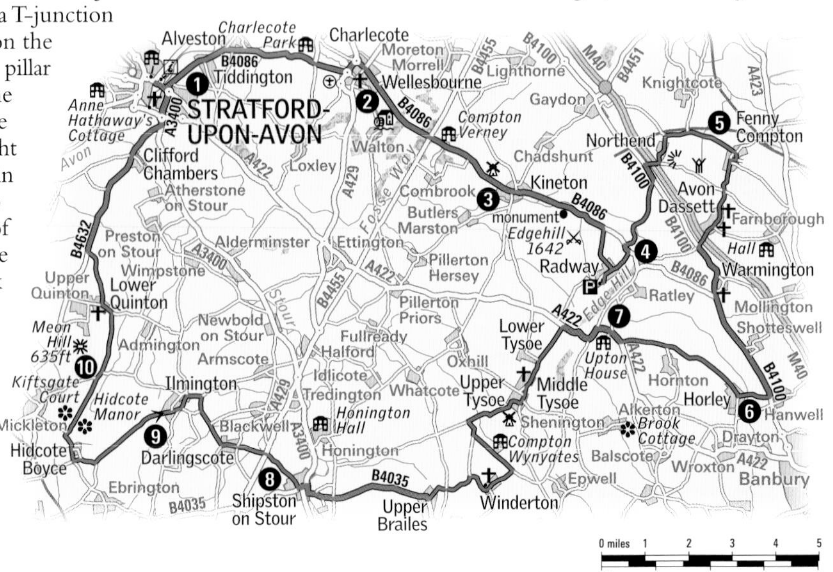

Compton Wynyates, a superb brick-and-stone Tudor house, privately owned and not open to the public. Continue along the narrow road and turn right through Winderton, then left at a T-junction to Brailes. At the T-junction after Upper Brailes, turn right on to the B4035 and cross the river into the old market town of Shipston-on-Stour.

8 Following the signs to Chipping Campden, turn right at a T-junction on the A3400 then left on to the B4035. Almost immediately, turn right to Ilmington and cross the A429. Follow the road through Darlingscote and turn left into Ilmington. This unspoilt village of stone-built cottages lies just within Cotswold country. It has a restored manor house and gardens, which are usually open to the public once or twice a year, and a 400-year-old inn, the Howard Arms. St Mary's Church, reached by a footpath between cottages, was extensively renovated in the 19th century, although parts of it date from much earlier.

Ilmington to Stratford

9 Leave Ilmington following the signs to Hidcote Manor Garden, past Nebsworth radio masts. Turn right at the junction signposted Hidcote Manor Garden, left after ¼ mile and then right at the crossroads. Past Hidcote House, turn right to Hidcote Manor Garden (NT), which has an eclectic collection of shrubs, trees and plants. Opposite is Kiftsgate Court Garden, where the rare plants have been collected by three generations of women gardeners. The gardens, privately owned, are open to the public.

10 From Kiftsgate, continue downhill. As the road bends right, turn left towards Stratford and Quinton past Meon Hill. At a T-junction, turn left into Lower Quinton, and just before the College Arms pub, bear right along a single-track road. At the next T-junction, turn right on to the B4632. Go past Clifford Chambers to a T-junction and turn left on to the A3400 back to Stratford.

COMPTON WYNYATES

Northern England

The landscape of the north has long been an inspiration to artists, poets and writers. Today, it retains its place as one of Britain's best loved touring regions, its mountain roads and valley drives offering magnificent vistas of the fells, lakes and dales.

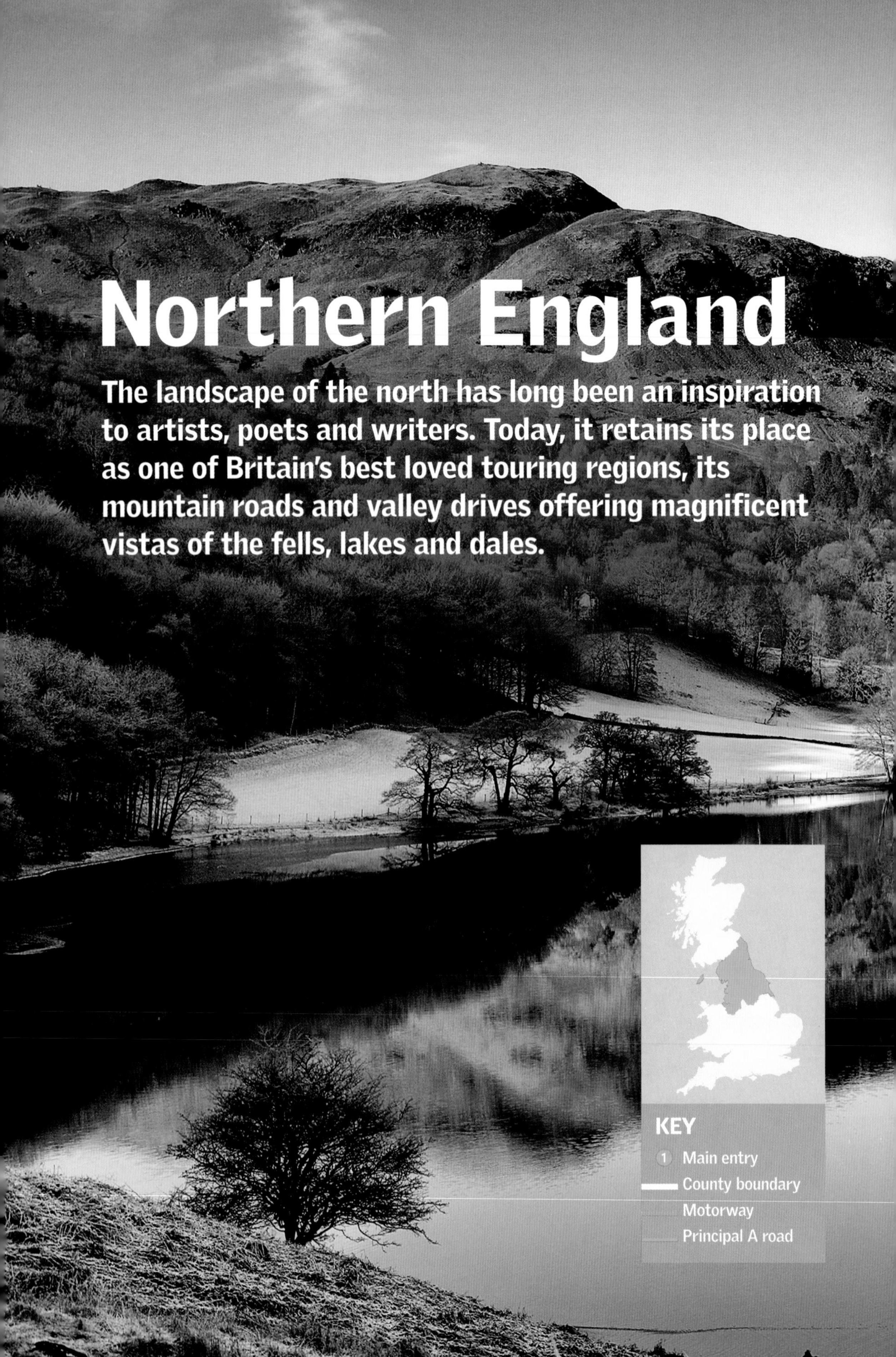

Berwick-upon-Tweed
Bamburgh
Alnwick
Northumberland National Park
Otterburn
Morpeth
NORTHUMBERLAND 134-137
Newcastle-upon-Tyne
Hexham
Gateshead
Sunderland
Carlisle
Consett
Alston
Durham
CUMBRIA 122-131
The Pennines
DURHAM
Hartlepool
Workington
Penrith
Bishop Auckland
Keswick
Whitehaven
Barnard Castle
Middlesbrough
Brough
Darlington
Lake District National Park
Ambleside
Whitby
North York Moors National Park
Windermere
Richmond
Kirkby Lonsdale
Hawes
Reeth
Kendal
Broughton in Furness
Thirsk
Helmsley
Scarborough
Pickering
Yorkshire Dales National Park
Barrow-in-Furness
Ripon
YORKSHIRE 138-151
Bridlington
Grassington
Lancaster
Settle
Harrogate
York
LANCASHIRE Liverpool and Manchester
Clitheroe
Blackpool
Hebden Bridge
Leeds
Selby
Beverley
Kingston-upon-Hull
Preston
Burnley
Bradford
Blackburn
Halifax
Wakefield
Southport
Huddersfield
Bury
Rochdale
Wigan
Bolton
Doncaster
Oldham
St Helens
Salford
Manchester
Rotherham
Liverpool
Warrington
Stockport
Birkenhead
Sheffield
Runcorn
Wilmslow
Ellesmere Port
Macclesfield
Chester
CHESHIRE and The Wirral
Crewe
Ramsey
Douglas
Castletown
ISLE OF MAN 152-153
1
2
3
4
5
6
7
8
9
10
11
12
13
14
15

CUMBRIA

The magnificent mountains, still lakes and deep valleys of rural Cumbria have inspired writers and artists throughout the ages. Historic towns, preserved railways and Roman remains provide additional attractions.

1 BROUGHTON IN FURNESS

TOUR LENGTH 52 miles

Branching off from Coniston Water's forested shore, the road crosses craggy fells and winds through spectacular high passes. The views on the way back to the elegant old market town are glorious.

Broughton in Furness to Coniston

1 Painted Georgian houses face the central square of Broughton in Furness, close to where the River Duddon joins the sea. The town was once a centre for wool and cattle sales. Markets are no longer held here, but the slabs on which fish were placed for sale can still be seen, as can the old town stocks, where miscreants were once punished. The market charter, which was granted in the reign of Elizabeth I, is read out each August 1, when councillors throw pennies to children from the obelisk built to commemorate the golden jubilee of George III in 1810.

Take the road signposted to Coniston, soon joining the A593. At Torver, turn right on to the A5084 and continue to Water Yeat, with the southern end of Coniston Water on the left. In the village, turn left towards Nibthwaite, then at a T-junction with the lakeside road turn left again.

It was on Coniston Water in 1959 that Donald Campbell piloted his boat 'Bluebird' to a world water-speed record of 260.35mph, and where he crashed to his death while attempting to reach 300mph in 1967.

2 Continue beside the lake – with views across the water to the 803m (2,635ft) summit of The Old Man of Coniston – to Brantwood, home of writer and social reformer John Ruskin from 1872 until his death in 1900. The house and garden, run by an independent charity, are open to the public from March to November. Check times before visiting.

3 About 3 miles after Brantwood, fork right to join the B5285 to Hawkshead, where William Wordsworth attended the village grammar school. The school is now a small museum containing a desk with the future poet's name carved on it.

4 From Hawkshead, return on the B5285 towards Coniston. At Hawkshead Hill, fork right and follow the signs for Tarn Hows, a popular

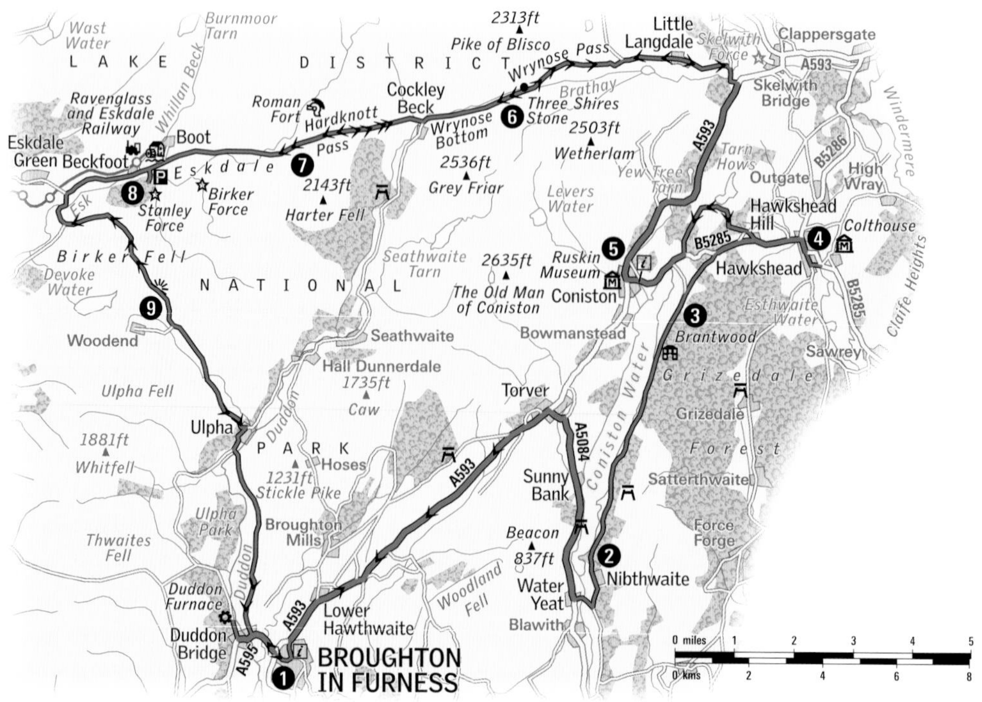

LITTLE LANGDALE

beauty spot created in the 19th century by joining two tarns, or small lakes. Beatrix Potter, who owned the tarn and its surroundings, sold Tarn Hows to the National Trust in the early part of the 20th century and left the rest of the estate to the Trust in her will. Accessible paths through the woods and around the tarn provide sheltered walks. Continue to Coniston, where there is a National Park information centre.

Coniston to Eskdale

5 From Coniston, turn right on to the A593 towards Ambleside. After 3½ miles turn left on to a narrow road signposted to Wrynose, soon forking left steeply uphill to the hamlet of Little Langdale before climbing Wrynose Pass. At the top of the pass, the Three Shires Stone marks what was, until 1974, the meeting point of the counties of Westmorland, Cumberland and Lancashire.

6 Continue for about 2 miles as the road descends steeply, then levels along Wrynose Bottom to a junction by a bridge and a lone house at Cockley Beck. Turn right to Hardknott Pass. The narrow road is one of only five in Britain with a gradient of 1 in 3 and, beyond the summit, offers views across Eskdale and the Irish Sea to the Isle of Man, 50 miles away. Just beyond the summit are the ruins of Mediobogdum (NT/EH), dating from the 2nd century AD and now known as Hardknott Roman Fort. Visible remains include the bathhouse, parade ground and granary.

7 The road now descends into Eskdale. Just beyond Dalegarth station, the eastern terminus of the narrow-gauge Ravenglass and Eskdale Railway, turn left on to the road signposted to Dalegarth Falls. From the small car park next to Trough House Bridge it is a short walk to St Catherine's church, which dates from the 12th century although it was largely rebuilt in the 1880s.

Eskdale to Broughton in Furness

8 Return to the main road, turning left towards Eskdale Green. After 1½ miles turn left towards Broughton, climbing on to Birker Fell. At the top of the road, the views east and north encompass the soaring pointed form of Bow Fell, with Crinkle Crags to its right. Other prominent peaks include Harter Fell and Illgill Head.

9 Continue for about 6 miles to the junction with the A595. Turn right over Duddon Bridge, then right again on to the road signposted to Corney. About 100m beyond is the 18th-century Duddon Furnace, a relic of the iron industry in the care of the Lake District National Park. Return to the A595 and turn left to Broughton.

2 KIRKBY LONSDALE

TOUR LENGTH 64 miles

The treeless slopes of the Yorkshire Dales contrast with wooded countryside out towards the coast. This round trip through vast, flat-topped, limestone hills and deep valleys ends with a gentler drive past a nature reserve and on to Morecambe Bay.

Kirkby Lonsdale to Dent

1 Set above the River Lune is the busy market town of Kirkby Lonsdale, where its bridge – the Devil's Bridge – dates from the 13th century. It is now famous for its Sunday gatherings of bikers from all over the north of England. The town is the meeting point of Cumbria, Lancashire and Yorkshire and this drive takes in all three counties.

Start from the centre of town, facing the Royal Hotel in the market square, and turn left down Main Street. At a T-junction, turn left towards Skipton and Ingleton along the A65. Cross the river then immediately turn left on to the A683 towards Sedbergh. Go through Casterton and after about ½ mile turn right on a minor road to Barbon, an attractive village guarding the approach to the high hills.

2 Continue on a minor road towards Dent. After 3 miles, the road enters the treeless Barbondale pass, running along Barbon Beck at the bottom of a steep-sided valley. A cattle grid marks the entrance to the Yorkshire Dales National Park, flanked by high Calf Top on the left and Crag Hill on the right. After a steep descent, turn right at a T-junction and follow signposts to the picturesque village of Dent.

Dent to Clapham

3 Follow the main street to the church, then turn left, crossing the River Dee and continuing along its north bank. Meadows and barns line the

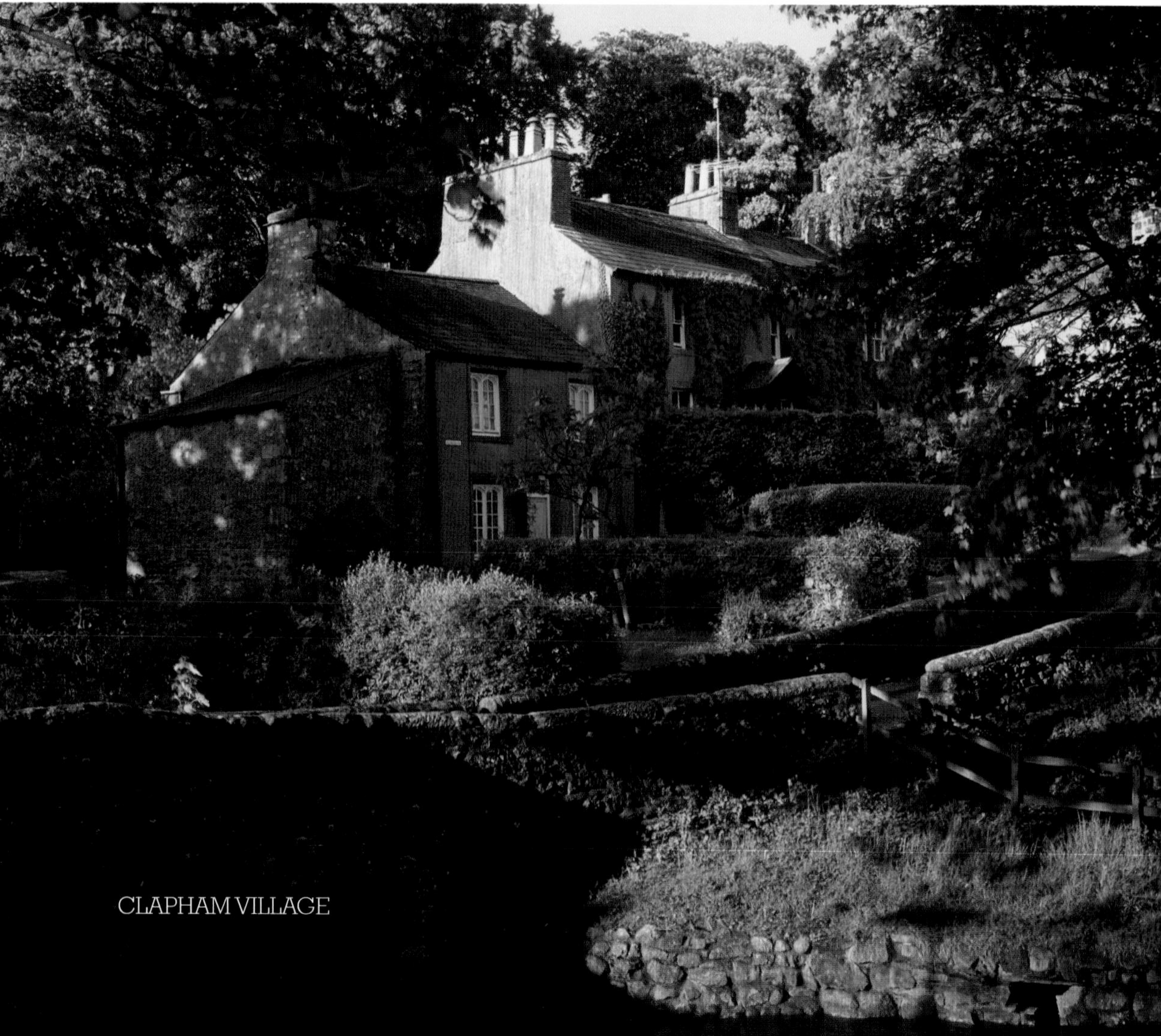

CLAPHAM VILLAGE

valley, and there are good views of Crag Hill to the right. The road crosses the river twice more and climbs to meet the Dent Head Viaduct, on the Settle to Carlisle railway line, which was opened in 1876. To the south, the line enters the Blea Moor Tunnel. Over a mile long, the tunnel was dug mostly by hand. Several men were drowned in the cuttings during a terrible rainstorm in 1870.

4 Continue on the road, which climbs through the high moorland of north Yorkshire, then drops to the junction with the B6255. Turn right towards Ingleton. The road widens, and the views are expansive and austere. Ahead in the distance is the summit of Ingleborough.

After 3½ miles, just beyond a side road on the left to Horton in Ribblesdale, is the Ribblehead Viaduct, also on the Settle to Carlisle railway line. A footpath opposite the turn-off to Horton skirts the railway, giving a view from the side of all 24 of the viaduct's arches.

5 Continue on the B6255 under the railway line. The road soon enters an eroded limestone landscape, following the shoulder of the valley, with the River Dee winding below, passing White Scar Cave, one of many caves and caverns eaten into the rock. The underground tunnels and waterfalls, and galleries of stalactites and stalagmites, are easily accessible.

6 About 1½ miles beyond White Scar Cave, turn left on a minor road to Clapham. Continue through gently rolling pasture for about 4 miles, following the edge of the National Park. At a T-junction turn left into Clapham, where there is a National Park Centre.

Clapham to Kirkby Lonsdale

7 Turn left out of the car park, then turn right at a T-junction. Cross the bridge over Clapham Beck and after about ¼ mile turn right on to the A65. Continue along the road to Kirkby Lonsdale.

Kirkby Lonsdale to Silverdale

8 For an extension of the drive to the attractive old village of Silverdale, in Lancashire, face the Royal Hotel, away from the monument in Market Square, and turn left down main street. At the junction with the A65, turn left again and immediately right to Whittington on the B6254. Turn right on to a winding minor road signposted to Hutton Roof and carry on along this, ignoring side roads. After about 5 miles, the road drops through woodland and past the parkland of Dalton Hall (once farm buildings and now a business centre) to a junction with the A6070.

9 Turn left then immediately right, signposted to Yealand Redmayne, following the road over the M6 and Lancaster Canal to the junction with the A6. Go straight across the A6, then follow the signs to Silverdale. After a few miles, the road passes, on the left, the reedbeds of Leighton Moss RSPB nature reserve, which is open all year. The reedbeds, the most extensive in northwest England, attract breeding bitterns, marsh harriers and bearded tits as well as hundreds of butterflies.

At a T-junction by a golf course, turn left to Silverdale, which is situated in a designated Area of Outstanding Natural Beauty and lies within easy reach of Morecambe Bay. From Jenny Brown's Point on the headland, look across the bay to Humphrey Head where, according to legend, the last wolf in England was killed. The Victorian novelist Mrs Elizabeth Gaskell regularly stayed in Silverdale and the Gaskell Memorial Hall was erected in her memory. Return to Kirkby Lonsdale by the same route.

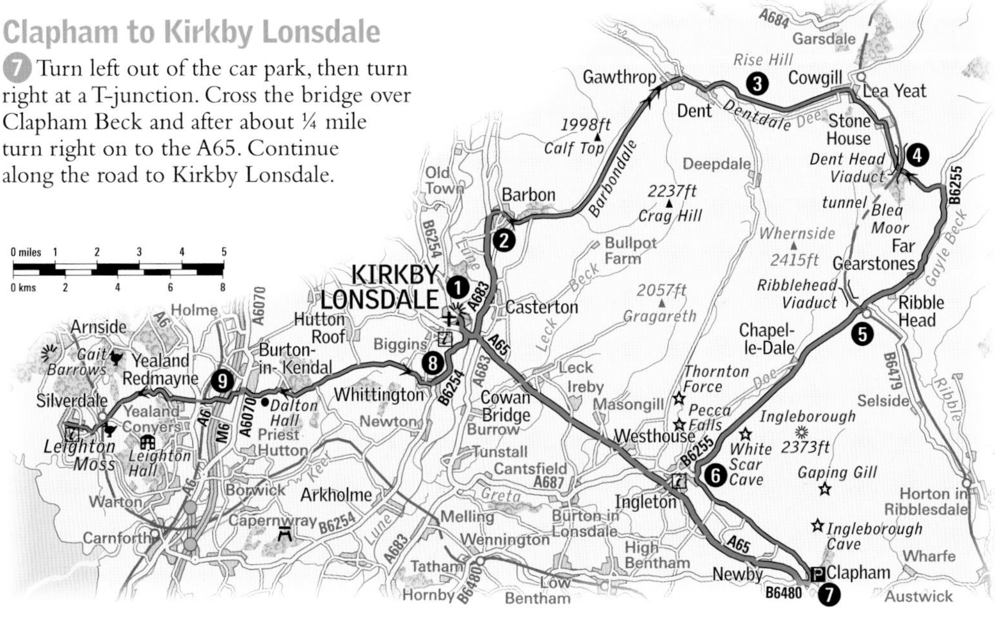

CUMBRIA

3 AMBLESIDE

TOUR LENGTH 45 miles

The wild, untamed beauty of the Lake District is evident as the road passes through countryside that captivated Wordsworth, with its cloud-topped hills and swift-flowing streams.

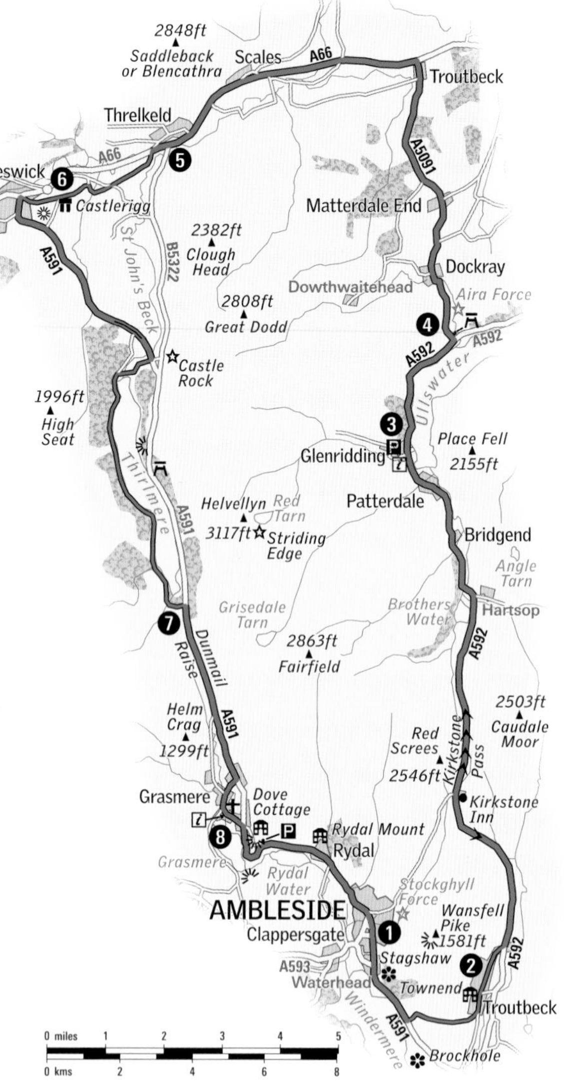

Ambleside to Glenridding

1 The little town of Ambleside lies at the heart of the Lake District. William Wordsworth, the region's best-known son, lived nearby and frequently walked to the town. The same journey today would cause him few surprises, despite the number of visitors. More than 150 years later, Ambleside is still a town divided into two parts – grey stone Victorian villas looking down the length of Lake Windermere and older cottages huddling on the slopes around Stock Ghyll, a swift-flowing beck that was once lined with working mills.

From Ambleside, take the A591 towards the town of Windermere for about 2 miles, then turn left on a minor road to Townend, a wealthy yeoman's house (NT). The house was occupied by the same family from 1626 to 1943, remaining largely unaltered during all that time.

2 Continue through Troutbeck to the junction with the A592 and turn left. The road climbs to the Kirkstone Pass, which, at 457m (1,500ft), is the highest in the Lake District. Beyond the top of the pass, the road drops past Brothers Water, reputedly named after two brothers who drowned there.

Continue through Patterdale to Glenridding on the shore of Ullswater. A left turn in the village leads to the National Park information centre, where there is a car park.

Glenridding to Grasmere

3 Return to the A592 and turn left. Less than 2 miles along the road, immediately beyond the junction with the A5091, turn left into the car park for Aira Force, a spectacular waterfall surrounded by woodland, which lies close to the place that inspired Wordsworth's famous poem 'I Wandered Lonely as a Cloud'.

4 Return to the junction and turn right on to the A5091 and continue to the T-junction in Troutbeck – the second place of the same name on this drive's route. Turn left on to the A66 towards Keswick, passing below the overhanging, rocky brow of Blencathra, also known as Saddleback, an 868m (2,848ft) high summit at the centre of radiating ridges.

5 Continue past Threlkeld on the A66 then, immediately beyond the junction with the B5322, turn left, following the signs to 3,500-year-old Castlerigg Stone Circle, overlooking the fells west of Derwent Water.

6 Carry on along the minor road to the junction with the A5271 on the edge of Keswick and turn left, then almost immediately turn left again on to the A591, signposted to Windermere. About 5 miles from Keswick, at the end of a section of dual carriageway, take a right turning signposted as 'public road around lake'. Drive across the Thirlmere dam to a junction, and turn left on to the lakeshore drive.

Thirlmere is an artificial reservoir created in 1879 by enlarging two natural lakes. Its construction was controversial, causing a national outcry led by John Ruskin and William Morris.

7 At the head of the lake, turn right on to the A591 and drive over Dunmail Raise, before descending into the Vale of Grasmere, with Helm Crag (known variously as 'The Lion and the Lamb', 'The Old Woman Playing the Organ' or 'The Howitzer') high on the right. Turn right on to the B5287 into Grasmere village, described by Wordsworth as 'the loveliest spot that man hath ever found'. The poet and his wife both lie buried in the churchyard.

Grasmere to Ambleside

8 Just outside Grasmere, where the B5287 rejoins the A591, stands Dove Cottage, where Wordsworth spent several years as a young writer. The house, now a museum and art gallery, is open all year. Check times before visiting.

Continue on the A591 for about a mile to the head of Rydal Water. White Moss Common car park is next to the main road, and the A591 carries on to Ambleside.

KIRKSTONE PASS

CUMBRIA

4 KESWICK

TOUR LENGTH 39 miles

Rugged fells rear up into sheer rockfaces on this route. The still water of quiet Buttermere mirrors their austere beauty while, farther round the circuit, the hills blend into rolling pastures.

Keswick to Grange

1 Once a thriving mining centre, Keswick is a town of narrow streets and sober, grey stone buildings. It was discovered by Victorian artists and writers, including Samuel Taylor Coleridge, whose enthusiasm for the area attracted visitors from all over the world. Set at the north end of Derwent Water, and sheltered by Skiddaw mountain, Keswick is an ideal base for exploring the northern Lake District.

Take the B5289 towards Borrowdale. A right turn at a roundabout on the edge of Keswick leads to Derwent Water, where launches can be taken across the lake and rowing boats hired.

2 Follow the B5289 for about 2 miles, then turn left on to a narrow road signposted to Watendlath. The road winds along the foot of Castlerigg Fell to a car park at Surprise View, one of the few easily accessible spots giving a view over the whole lake.

3 Return to the B5289 and turn left, with views of Derwent Water to the right. After 2½ miles turn right on to a narrow road signposted to Grange and Newlands. Cross the bridge into the farming village of Grange, which dates from medieval times, when the valley was owned by the monks of Furness Abbey.

Grange to Buttermere

4 Go back to the B5289 and continue through Borrowdale. Ahead and to the right is Castle Crag, clothed in larch and oak trees. The road follows the River Derwent for some 5 miles then, at the little settlement of Seatoller, starts twisting and climbing steeply to the high open fells and Honister Pass. At the highest point, 356m (1,168ft) above sea level, a car park on the left acts as a viewpoint from which to survey the bleak, windswept pass and desolate fells.

5 The road descends, with scree and boulder-covered slopes to right and left, crisscrossing Gatesgarthdale Beck to Gatesgarth at the head of Buttermere. Continue for 1½ miles, with the lake on the left, to Buttermere village.

BORROWDALE VALLEY

Buttermere to Keswick

6 Follow the B5289 past Crummock Water. The road narrows in places, and at Hause Point it is etched into the cragside above the shore. Good views of the lake and the high fells are to be had from roadside parking spots.

7 After another 2 miles the road passes two mountains, Grasmoor and Whiteside. To the left, the pastures roll away towards the Cumbrian coast, and hedges replace drystone walls. At a junction follow the B5289 right, signposted to Cockermouth and Keswick. At Low Lorton the road skirts the River Cocker as it twists through the gentle valley.

8 About ½ mile past Low Lorton, bear left at a junction, keeping to the B5292 and ignoring a right turn to Keswick. Continue to Cockermouth, where William Wordsworth was born. His family home, Wordsworth House (NT), is open to visitors.

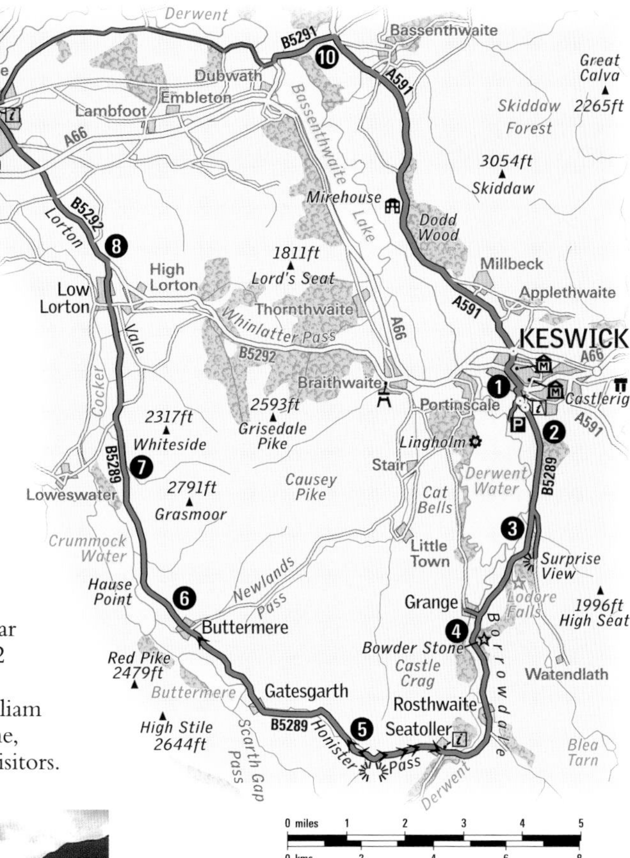

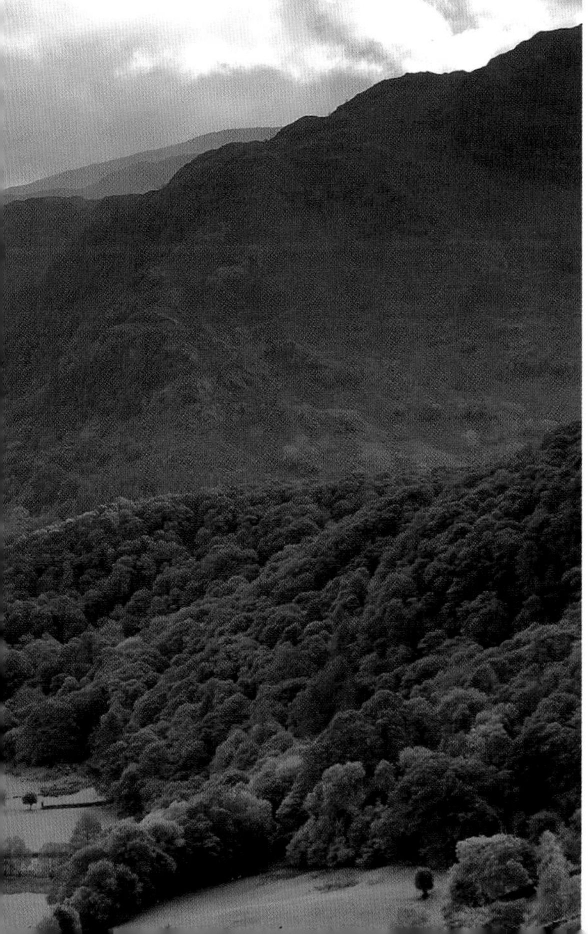

9 At a T-junction in the town centre, turn right on to the wide Main Street and follow signs for Embleton. Go past Market Place and continue for ½ mile. After passing a high wall on the left, turn left on to a road signposted to Hospital and Isel. Follow the quiet country lane for some 5 miles, Skiddaw dominating the view. At a T-junction turn left and take the next left over a bridge. Roadside parking spots give views of Bassenthwaite Lake, with Skiddaw towering above it.

10 At the T-junction, turn right on to the A591 signposted to Bassenthwaite and Keswick. About 3½ miles farther on, at the foot of Skiddaw, Dodd Wood has attractive woodland walks. Across the road, the sheltered gardens and lakeside walks at Mirehouse are open most days. The house itself, built in the 17th century and owned by the same family since 1688, is open at selected times only. Check before visiting. Mirehouse is a member of the Historic Houses Association.

Continue on the A591 to a roundabout. Take the second exit, signposted to Keswick and Borrowdale, and at the T-junction turn left to Keswick town centre.

CUMBRIA

5 ALSTON

TOUR LENGTH 94 miles

Remote villages and bare hillsides show traces of lead mining, and well-preserved Roman sites record a much earlier occupation. This high moorland route strays into Northumberland and Durham.

Alston to Vindolanda

1 The River Tyne is still a mountain stream as it flows through isolated Alston, England's highest town at 274m (900ft) above sea level. Follow the A686 towards Penrith and turn right at the war memorial on to the A689. At Knarsdale, turn right on to a lane towards Haltwhistle. The road climbs, allowing views across the moors to the hills above the Solway Firth.

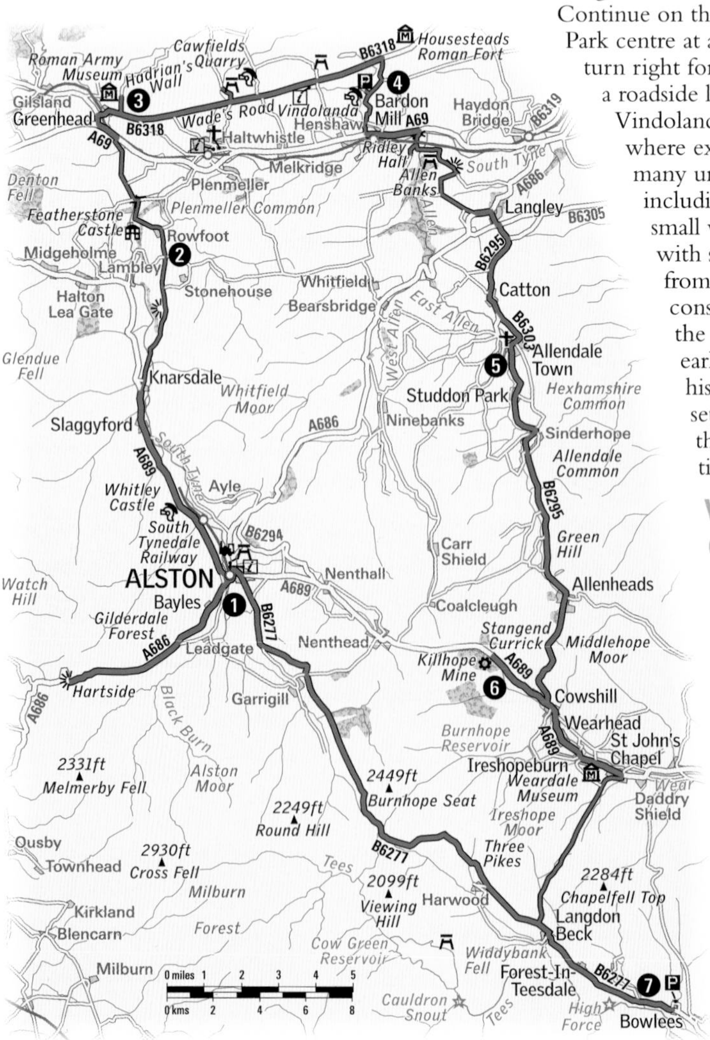

2 Go straight on at the crossroads and take the next left to Featherstone Park. Featherstone Castle, which can be rented for holidays, dates from the 14th century, although the battlements and towers were added in the 1820s by the first Lord Wallace, a former mayor of Newcastle.

Continue ahead, turning left across a bridge, then bear right, staying on the same road and climbing from the valley. At the junction, turn left on to the A69, then after ½ mile turn right for Greenhead. Turn right again at the T-junction on to the B6318 to visit the Roman Army Museum, which has videos, models and artefacts re-creating life as a soldier in the Roman Empire.

3 Back on the B6318, a left turn 3 miles farther on leads to Cawfields Quarry, where a milecastle stands above a lakeside picnic area. Milecastles – small forts that acted as gatehouses – were constructed at intervals of 1 Roman mile along the length of Hadrian's Wall.

Continue on the B6318 past the National Park centre at a crossroads, and after 2 miles, turn right for Bardon Mill. Turn right after a roadside limekiln, then right again to Vindolanda, a Roman army settlement where excavations are ongoing and many unique finds have been made, including the Vindolanda Tablets: small wooden 'postcards' covered with spidery writing. These date from the year before the construction of Hadrian's Wall in the 1st century AD, and form the earliest written archive in British history. A reconstruction of the settlement is also on show, and there is a small car park. Check times before visiting.

Vindolanda to Bowlees

4 Continue to Bardon Mill and turn left on to the A69. After 1 mile turn right for Ridley Hall, now a conference centre. Across the river, go under a railway bridge and turn left towards Langley. At Allen Banks there are walks through the gardens of Ridley Hall.

Carry on, turning right at the junction with a farm road, and climbing uphill with views over Haydon Bridge. Turn right towards Langley, and then bear left for Haydon Bridge. Turn left on to the A686, then right on to the B6295.

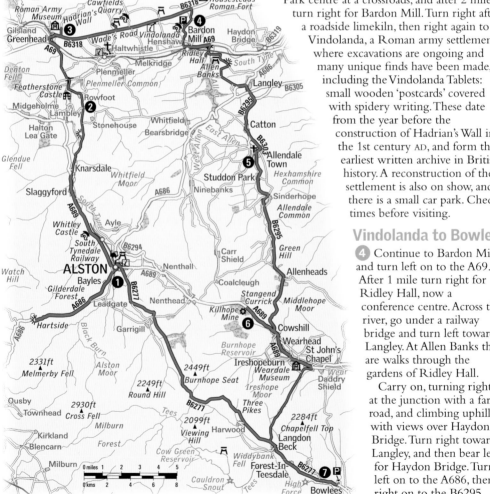

Continue over the staggered crossroads and take the B6303 to Allendale Town. According to a sundial in the churchyard, the town is at the geographical centre of Britain.

5 Rejoin the B6295 to Allenheads, once a prosperous lead-mining centre, commemorated by a village trail. At Cowshill, turn sharp right on to the A689 to visit Killhope Mine. Renovated mine buildings and a giant water wheel are the attractions, along with the old tunnels, running deep into the hillside. Check opening times before visiting.

6 Return on the A689 through Cowshill to St John's Chapel, then turn right over moorland towards Langdon Beck. At the T-junction, turn left on the B6277 through Langdon Beck, continuing for 4 miles to Bowlees visitor centre, which is housed in a Methodist chapel. A short walk from the car park leads through a wooded gorge to Gibson's Cave, where ferns and primroses grow from the rock face to create a natural hanging garden. A waterfall splashes down from overhanging rocks, curtaining a shallow cave behind. Legend has it that the cave is named after an outlaw, who used it as a hideaway.

Bowlees to Hartside

7 From Bowlees, take the B6277 back to Alston. For a postcript to the drive, take the A686 towards Penrith, following the winding road to the top of Hartside Pass – a route much loved by cyclists and bikers. The bleak landscape is dotted with the odd lone cottage, and from the top there are awe-inspiring views across the Vale of Eden to the Lake District, and across the Scottish border. Return by the same road.

ISOLATED COTTAGES DOT THE LANDSCAPE
HARTSIDE PASS

Motorway magic

As the M6 bends and curves its way up bleak hill and down shadowy dale, it offers panoramic views of a vast landscape.

Motorways are curious beasts. Ever since the first stretch in Britain came into use – the Preston bypass, opened by Prime Minister Harold Macmillan in 1958, and now part of the M6 – they have been bywords for prosaic functionality, ploughing brutally through the landscape with little craft or sensitivity invested in their design. What you see is what you get – a river of traffic on a bed of concrete. Yet motorways hold mystery. Who would believe, pulling up at the cashier's booth on the M6 Toll, that they are paying to drive over someone's dreams? Yet that's exactly the case. Millions of unread books containing untold trillions of words, shredded into minute pellets of a fibrous substance called bitumen modifier, were used to bind the surface and cut down the noise of the new toll road. As for design – the M6, as it enters its most beautiful stretch 150 miles farther north in Cumbria, shows how landscape and road, against all expectations, can actually complement one another.

The M6 was not only the first motorway in Britain; it is also the busiest, and the longest, running some 230 miles from its junction with the M1 southeast of Birmingham to the Scottish border near Carlisle, where it merges with the A74(M). Entering Cumbria from Lancashire, it makes some serious height, climbing 1,000ft in 30 miles, from Carnforth at sea level to Shap in the Pennine hills. Transition curves are built into the roadway, smooth sinuations that introduce a driver gently rather than abruptly into a bend. These curves offer variety to combat the danger of falling asleep at the wheel from the sheer boredom of looking at a straight line of road unrolling ahead. They are at their subtlest and most pleasing in the section of this hilly country most vulnerable to ugly engineering – the high-sided gorge of the Lune Valley.

Imposing hills

The River Lune springs in the Cumbrian hills above Ravenstonedale, and reaches the lowlands of coastal Lancashire by way of a cleft it has carved for itself in the fells. The uplands on the west of the Lune gorge are impressive enough in the looming shapes of Greyrigg Forest and Roundthwaite Common, but it is the landscape to the east that claims all eyes as the traffic heads through the deep valley on the M6. Here rise the Howgill Fells, billowing hills with graceful folds and curves like the limbs of a Henry Moore sculpture of a reclining nude.

All this high ground forms an east-west barrier, with the Lune gorge offering the only practical route from south to north. Thoroughfares of one kind or another have threaded the valley since prehistoric times, from farm tracks to a Roman road and a Georgian era turnpike highway. In the mid 19th century came the west coast mainline of the London & North Western Railway (later the London, Midland & Scottish Railway). The Lune gorge became a favourite location for railway photographers. They would position themselves on the western slopes above the valley to capture a classic shot – a crimson steam locomotive of the LMS, smoke blowing back in a plume, pounding through the gorge with a rake of ten or eleven coaches, all backed by the vast green bulge of the Howgill Fells.

Isolated landmarks

In terms of countryside, big is beautiful, especially when offset against something tiny, and particularly if that object speaks of man's smallness within an enormous landscape. There are no steam locomotives in the Lune gorge today; instead, it is the isolated farmhouses that point up the grandeur of the surrounding hills to drivers on the M6. Entering the valley from the south, a glance to the right shows Beck House and Whins, tiny shapes at the foot of the rounded fell of Whin's End. They stand above Howgill Lane, the route of the former Roman road. Occasionally, diminutive figures are visible far above – walkers on the steep track from Beck House up to Black Force waterfall, a climb of some 800ft. Farther into the gorge, Low Carlingill Farm is beautifully set on a green saddle of ground below the deep cleft of Carlin Gill, backed by the curved flanks of Blease Fell and Uldale Head.

The village of Tebay stands at the northern end of the Lune gorge. From here for about 10 miles north towards Penrith the opposing carriageways of the M6 are divided, over two separate sections, by very broad central reservations. This is the highest section of the M6, and the harsh Pennine winters often bring fog and snow to the motorway. The wide separation between the carriageways means that while one may be blocked, there's always the chance that the other is clear. It has also created an anomalous situation – the stranding of a local road in the middle of a motorway. It's possible to drive north from near Scout Green up the central reservation for the best part of two miles, with cars and lorries whizzing north to the left and south to the right. It's a bit like being a mouse trapped between two hungry cats, but at least there is wonderful scenery all the way by way of compensation.

In its most beautiful stretch, the M6 shows how landscape and road can actually complement one another

M6 IN CUMBRIA

NORTHUMBERLAND

An aura of peace surrounds the famed island of Lindisfarne, established many centuries ago as a centre of religion and learning. Inland, the Cheviot Hills impose their own splendour on the sparsely populated county.

6 BERWICK-UPON-TWEED

TOUR LENGTH 72 miles

Remains of old conflicts crowd the borders of England and Scotland, while at Holy Island, off the wild and empty coast, hundreds of migrant birds flock around the ruins left by early missionaries.

Berwick-upon-Tweed to Norham

1 A border town that changed hands no fewer than 14 times before finally falling to England in 1482, Berwick-upon-Tweed retains massive bastions and walls encircling its compact centre.

Take the A698 towards Coldstream. Turn right on to the A1 towards Edinburgh, cross the Tweed into Scotland and turn left on to the B6461 to Paxton. Paxton House, a Palladian mansion the grounds of which slope to the riverbank, was designed by the Adam brothers in 1757. It is open to the public, but check times before visiting.

Continue past Fishwick, then turn left on to a minor road to the hamlet of Ladykirk, where the church was built by James IV of Scotland in gratitude for his salvation after he nearly drowned in the Tweed in 1497. Go through Ladykirk and turn left to Norham, crossing back into England.

Norham to Kirknewton

2 From the village green, continue for ½ mile and turn right on to a lane that goes over a disused railway and past the old station, which now houses a Railway Museum (tours by arrangement). Cross the A698 and at a T-junction, turn left and immediately right. Carry on, joining the B6354 to Etal. The village street leads to the ruins of Etal Castle, a fortified 14th-century tower house (EH).

3 Continue to Ford, passing Heatherslaw Mill, which is a working water-driven cornmill. The village hall at Ford has 19th-century murals by Lady Waterford, featuring her tenants as characters from the Bible.

LINDISFARNE CASTLE, HOLY ISLAND

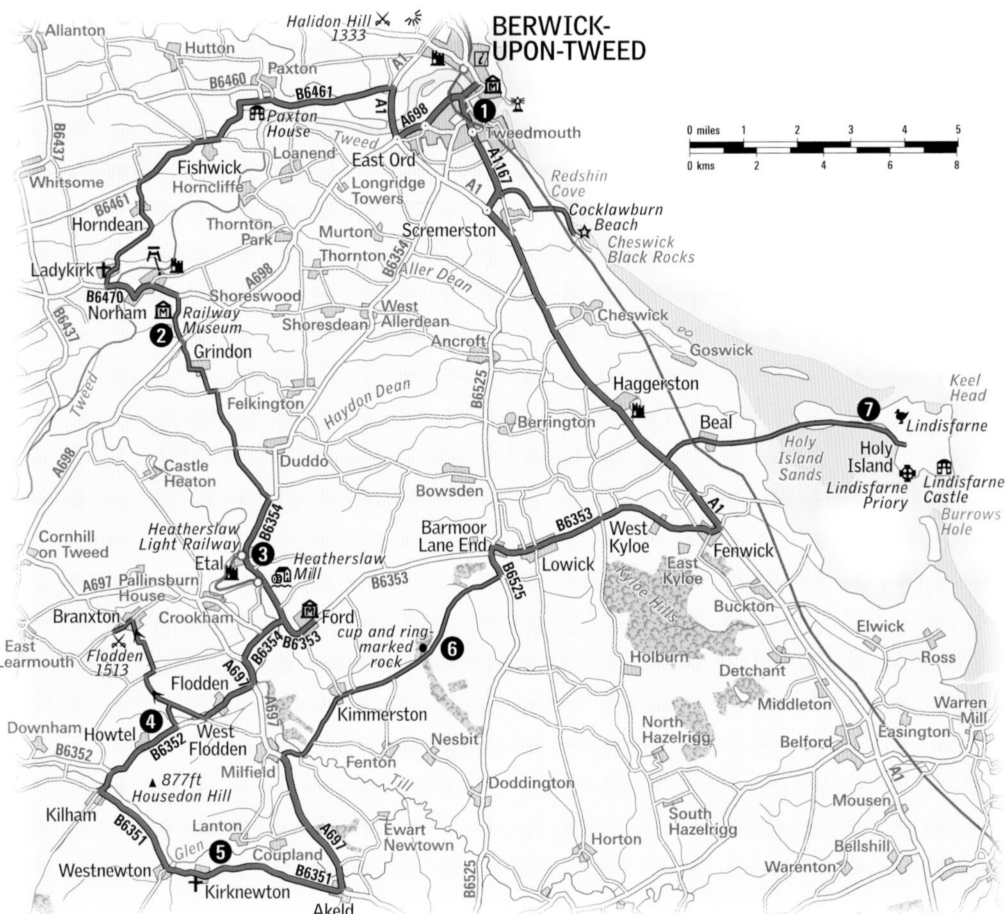

Return towards Etal for ½ mile, then turn left over the bridge towards Wooler. At a T-junction turn left on to the A697, then after ½ mile turn right, signposted to Howtel. At West Flodden, a minor road to the right leads to Flodden Field, where James IV's army was defeated by the English in 1513.

4 Back on the main road, which winds up to the Cheviots, follow the signs to Kirknewton, where St Gregory's Church has a curious stone carving of the Adoration of the Magi, dating from the 10th or 11th century. The Magi are depicted wearing kilts.

Kirknewton to Holy Island

5 Continue on the road to Akeld, then turn left on to the A697. After 3 miles, turn right on to a minor road to the village of Kimmerston. About 2 miles past Kimmerston, on the edge of a wood opposite a lane to Fenton House, is a large flat stone with 'cup and ring' patterns, thought to have been inscribed by Bronze Age Britons around 1500 BC.

6 Continue for 2 miles, turn left at the crossroads then turn right on to the B6353, through Lowick, with views over Holy Island. Turn left on to the A1 towards Berwick, and after 1½ miles turn right to Holy Island, also known as Lindisfarne. The causeway to the island is under water twice a day, at high tide. Once an important centre of Christianity and learning, the island has a ruined castle (NT) and priory, and is a birdwatcher's heaven of sand dunes, mudflats and saltmarsh.

Holy Island to Berwick-upon-Tweed

7 Return to the A1 and turn right, passing the gaunt stone tower of Haggerston Castle, part of an Edwardian mansion that stood for just 15 years. The site, incorporating several lakes, is now a holiday park. Carry on to a roundabout and take the A1167 towards Berwick. Turn right for Scremerston and promptly left to Cocklawburn Beach, noted for its rock formations and for the wild flowers growing on the lime-rich soil near the ruins of old kilns. Return to the A1167 and turn right to Berwick.

NORTHUMBERLAND

7 ALNWICK

TOUR LENGTH 77 miles

Across the Cheviot moorland and through the river valleys of the Northumberland National Park, this route avoids major roads as much as possible. It touches the stark and rocky shore north of Alnmouth Bay before heading back inland to Alnwick.

Alnwick to Alwinton

1 Since the early 14th century, Alnwick Castle has been the base of the Percy family, later Dukes of Northumberland. Surrounded by Hulne Park, the castle still dominates the cobbled streets and magnificent old buildings of Alnwick.

Leave the town on the B6341 signposted to Rothbury. Continue for 5 miles, then turn right to Edlingham. The castle (EH), now ruined, was once a manor house, fortified during the border wars of the 14th century.

2 Return to the B6341, turn right towards Rothbury and cross the A697. After 2 miles of moorland, the road winds through a valley wooded with exotic trees, part of the Cragside estate (NT). Cragside is a Victorian mansion, designed by Norman Shaw for the industrialist Sir William Armstrong. It was the first house in the world to be lit by hydroelectricity. The extensive grounds include woodlands and lakes, and the largest sandstone rock garden in Europe.

3 Continue on the B6341 through Rothbury, then follow the road along the valley. Two miles beyond Thropton, fork right on a minor road to Sharperton. Cross the bridge outside Sharperton and take the first minor road on the left to Holystone to visit the Lady's Well (NT).

By the side of the well is the 'holy stone', an altar that is reputed to be where Paulinus, a 6th-century monk, baptised a huge number of people whom he had newly converted to Christianity. A well-known 17th-century pub in Holystone, the Salmon Inn, has now reverted to use as a private dwelling.

Alwinton to Chillingham

4 Return to the road to Alwinton, crossing the river 1 mile beyond Harbottle, and then turn left across the bridge into the village of Alwinton. Walks from here give access to breathtaking views across wild moorland scenery.

Go back over the bridge and turn left. At Netherton, bear right towards Thropton, then turn immediately left to Whittingham to visit a fine medieval church, which has evidence suggesting that early Christians worshipped on the site, and a derelict 14th-century tower behind the village green.

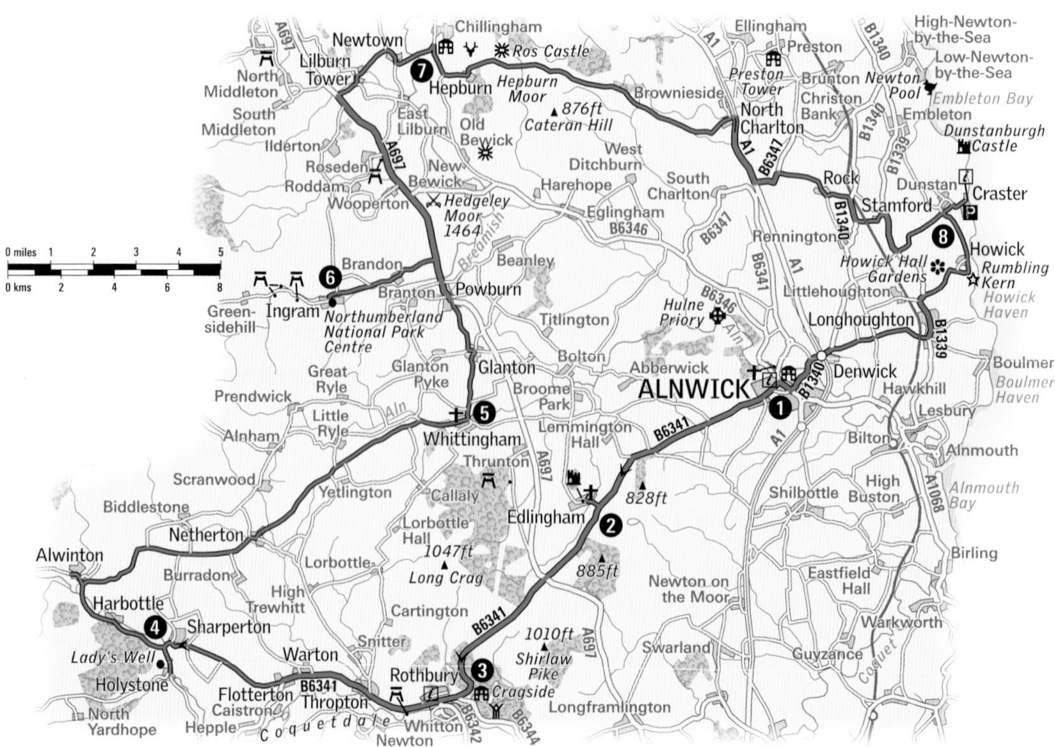

5 Turn left in Whittingham to Glanton, and left again at a T-junction in Glanton. Then bear right for Powburn. Across the valley to the right, a pele (defensive) tower can be seen on the skyline next to a farmhouse. In Powburn join the A697 towards Wooler. A mile outside Powburn, turn left and follow the signs to the Northumberland National Park Centre at Ingram, which is open in summer, to find out more about the area.

6 Return to the A697 and continue towards Wooler. After 4 miles, turn right opposite the Station House restaurant to Chillingham. Bear left over a bridge, then turn right and follow the signs to Chillingham Castle, which is open during summer, except on Saturdays.

Chillingham to Craster

7 At the T-junction facing the castle, turn right for Eglingham. After ½ mile turn left on a minor road to Hepburn. Continue across Hepburn Moor to North Charlton, turn right on to the A1 towards Alnwick, then left to Rock on the B6347. After a sharp bend, turn right and continue through Rock. Turn left along a lane towards Craster. Turn right at the next T-junction, then left, signposted to Stamford. Cross the railway, and then turn right towards Longhoughton. After 1 mile turn left towards Craster. At the crossroads 1 mile farther on, go straight ahead to Craster through an arch built as a grand approach to the Craster Tower estate. Turn right at the T-junction and follow the lane towards the village. Turn right into the old quarry car park by the information centre. The quarry is now a small nature reserve. The coast at Craster is stark and rocky, backed by a coastal path. The harbour, built by the Craster family, commemorates a soldier son who was killed in the 1904 British Tibetan Expedition.

Craster to Alnwick

8 From Craster return to the crossroads at the ornamental archway. Turn left for Howick and Longhoughton. Ignoring the next turn to Howick, follow the road sharply right to visit the gardens at Howick Hall. The gardens are open during summer. The house, which is not open to the public, was home to Charles Grey, 2nd Earl Grey, the prime minister who passed the Reform Act of 1832.

A mile beyond Howick Hall, the road joins the B1339 to Longhoughton. Pass through Longhoughton and, at the southern end of the village, bear right off the main road. Pass under a railway bridge, and continue to the B1340. Turn left and return to Alnwick, passing over the A1.

CRASTER

YORKSHIRE

Windswept fells, tranquil dales, dramatic coasts, leafy woodlands, atmospheric ruins, picturesque villages, the rocky peaks and moors of Brontë country and relics of an industrial past – Yorkshire has it all.

8 REETH

TOUR LENGTH 79 miles

Drystone walls and winding roads stretch west and south through airy dales and hillside pastures to the farming country around Wensleydale. The route takes in a long spur through historic Middleham to the fertile Nidderdale valley.

Reeth to Bainbridge

1 Reeth is a small, bustling town at the junction of Swaledale and Arkengarthdale, with tearooms, inns and craft workshops set around a wide green. The nearby Swaledale Folk Museum shows how hill farming and lead mining shaped life in the northern dales. Leave Reeth heading west on the B6270, signposted to Gunnerside, following the road along the dale through Healaugh and Low Row. The working smithy in Gunnerside was established in 1795, and incoporates a museum.

2 Continue on the B6270 to Muker, once a lead-mining community. Close to the Farmers Arms is a tearoom and National Park information point. A mile beyond Muker, with Kisdon Hill on the right, turn sharp left on a minor road to Hawes. The road climbs steeply and after about 2 miles a walled layby on the right gives access to a grassy platform for a view of the Butter Tubs. Farmers once lowered butter into these vertical limestone potholes to cool it on their way to market.

3 From the Butter Tubs, continue to the top of the pass, with the valley of Cliff Beck on the left. The road begins to descend, with the summit of Lovely Seat to the left and Great Shunner Fell, on the Pennine Way, to the right.

ASKRIGG

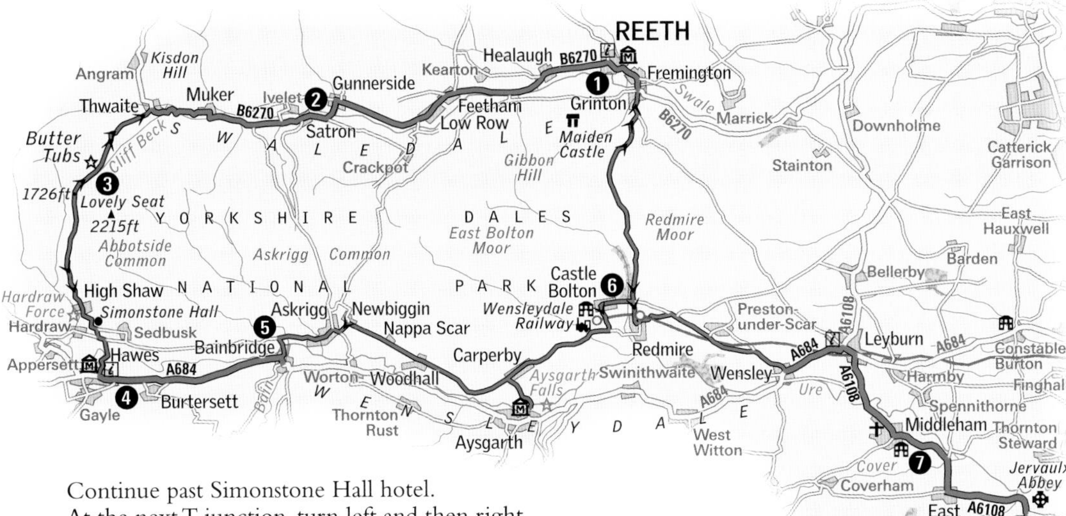

Continue past Simonstone Hall hotel. At the next T-junction, turn left and then right to Hawes, where the old railway station houses a National Park information centre and the Dales Countryside Museum.

4 Leave Hawes on the A684, signposted to Aysgarth and Leyburn, and continue to the quaint, grey stone village of Bainbridge, where the old stocks still stand on the huge, open village green. The River Bain, the shortest river in England, flows through the village, which once housed local foresters. A horn was sounded to guide the men safely home through what was then dense woodland, and this is now on show in the local hotel, the Rose & Crown. On nearby Brough Hill are the remains of a Roman fort and minor settlement, Virosidum.

Bainbridge to Castle Bolton

5 Leave Bainbridge on the minor road signposted to Askrigg, which has a medieval market cross, a fountain and an iron ring set in a stone slab for bull-baiting. Nearby is Cringley House, featured as Skelldale House in the televised James Herriot stories. From Askrigg continue towards Carperby and turn right to visit Aysgarth Falls on the River Ure.

Return to the junction and turn right through Carperby. About 2 miles beyond, turn left on the road signposted to Castle Bolton, a prison for Mary, Queen of Scots, in the winter of 1567, and a Royalist stronghold during the Civil War. The castle is open to the public in summer – check times before visiting.

Castle Bolton to Lofthouse

6 From Castle Bolton continue through the village and turn right at the T-junction to Redmire, where an ancient oak grows on the green. Beyond the green, turn left towards Leyburn. Bear right to a T-junction with the A684 at Wensley. Turn left to Leyburn and right on to the A6108. Turn right again to Middleham. One of Middleham's two marketplaces has a swine cross bearing traces of the white boar symbol of the town's famous son, Richard of Gloucester, who later became Richard III. His castle lies out of sight across the road.

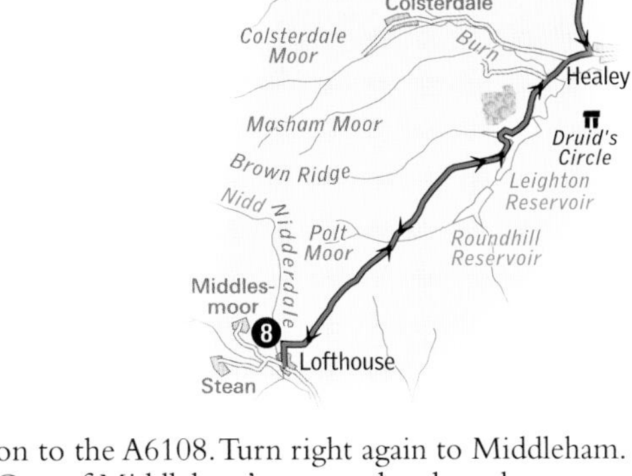

7 From Middleham take the A6108 through East Witton and continue for 2 miles to Jervaulx Abbey, where the Cistercian monks created Wensleydale cheese. Continue on the A6108, then turn right on a minor road, heading to Ellingstring. At the crossroads in Ellingstring turn right. Continue to a T-junction at Healey, turn right and follow the road over moorland for about 6 miles to the picturesque village of Lofthouse, from where relatively easy walking is available in Nidderdale.

Lofthouse to Reeth

8 Return by the same route to Redmire. Continue to follow the road to Grinton, ignoring the turning to Castle Bolton on the left. Cross the Swale into Fremington and turn left to arrive back in Reeth.

YORKSHIRE

9 HELMSLEY

TOUR LENGTH 54 miles

Along the western extreme of the North York Moors, monastic ruins and villages clustered on upland edges give way to river valleys, where green fields and wooded slopes create a softer landscape.

Helmsley to Rievaulx

1 The ruined battlements of Helmsley's castle stand guard over the lively market town, which is a gateway to the Cleveland Hills and North York Moors. Old coaching inns face the impressive square, and houses with red-pantiled roofs line the back streets. From the town, take the B1257 towards Rievaulx Abbey.

The first minor road on the left, about 1 mile out of the town, leads to Rievaulx Terrace, where two 18th-century temples stand on a lawn overlooking the austere but glorious abbey ruins. The turning to Rievaulx Abbey (EH) itself is the next left off the B1257. The abbey was founded in 1132 by the Cistercian order and greatly enlarged in the 13th century. Follow the lane downhill to the abbey car park.

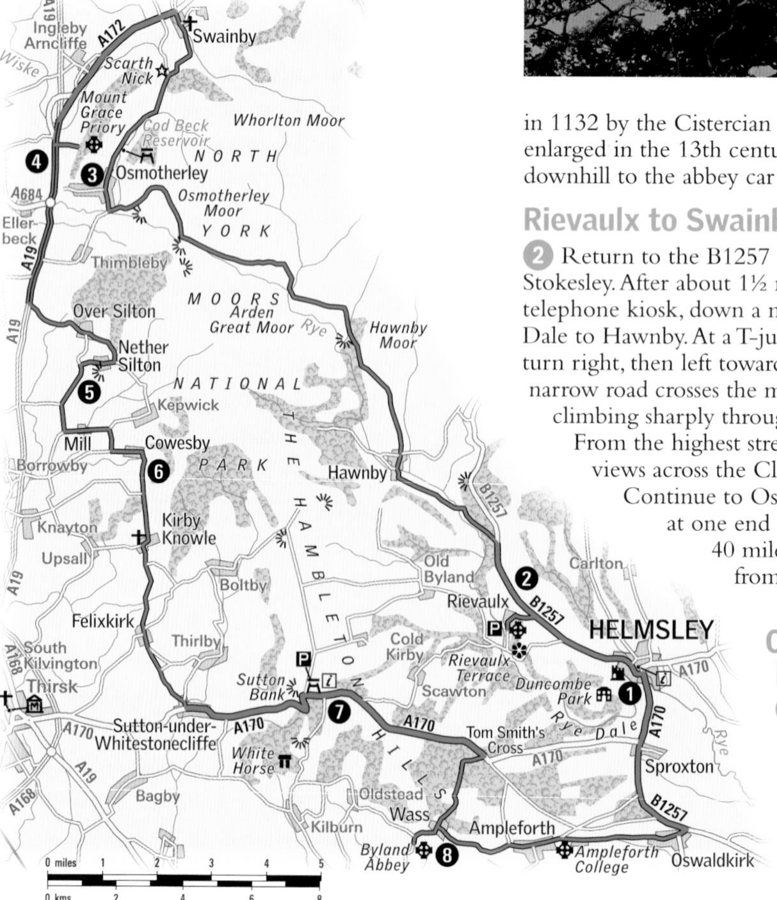

Rievaulx to Swainby

2 Return to the B1257 and turn left towards Stokesley. After about 1½ miles, fork left by a telephone kiosk, down a minor road along Rye Dale to Hawnby. At a T-junction in the village turn right, then left towards Osmotherley. The narrow road crosses the moors, dipping and climbing sharply through some deep valleys. From the highest stretches there are distant views across the Cleveland Plain.

Continue to Osmotherley, which lies at one end of an established 40 mile hike across the moors from Ravenscar.

Osmotherly to Nether Silton

3 From Osmotherley market cross – where John Wesley, who founded Methodism, preached – follow the signs to Swainby. Drive through

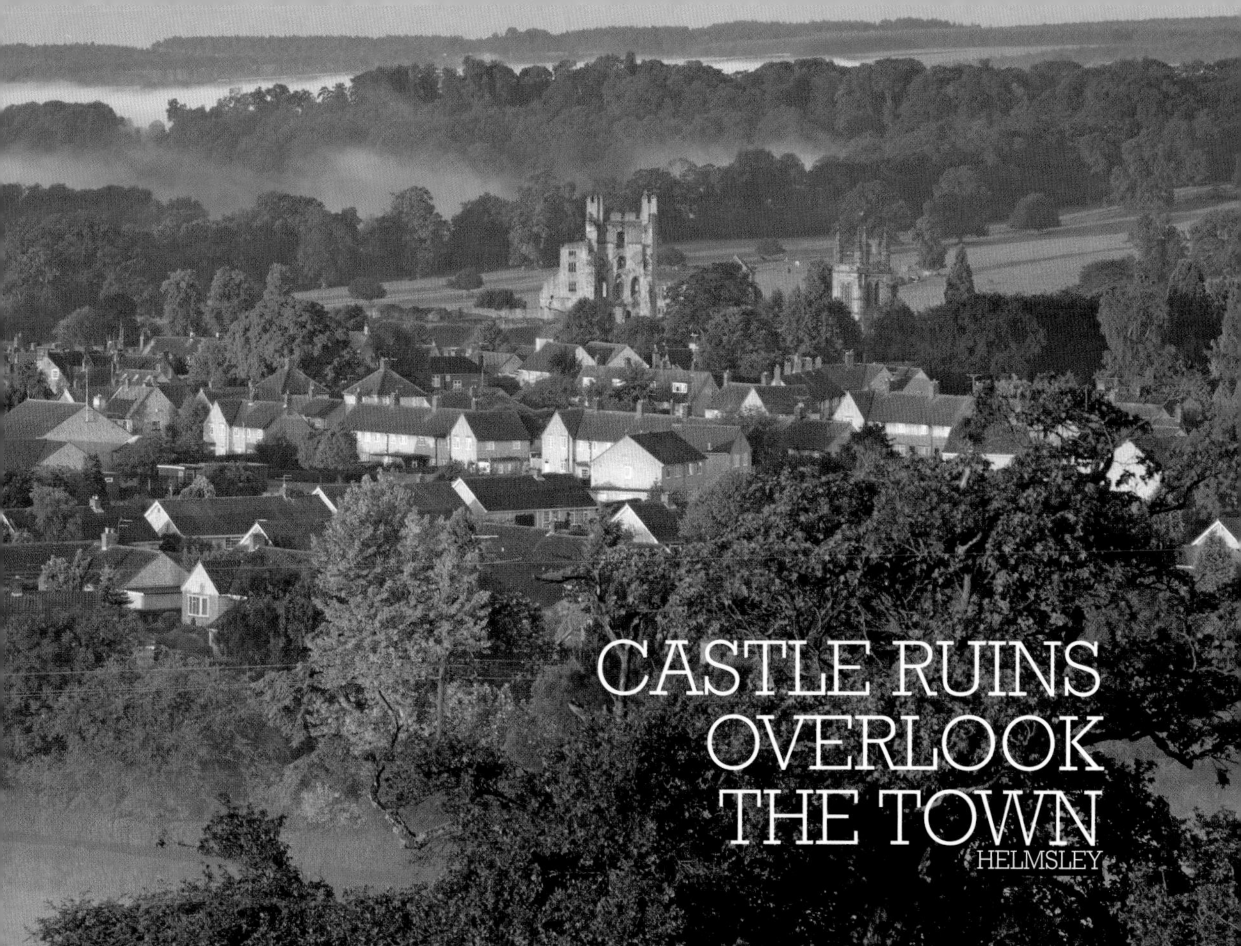

Swainby to the T-junction with the A172 and turn left towards Thirsk. Soon the A172 joins the A19. Carry on for about ½ mile, then turn left to Mount Grace Priory (EH), which is a well-preserved Carthusian charterhouse where one of the old monastic cells has been restored and furnished.

4 Rejoin the A19 towards Thirsk. After passing the junction with the A684, take the second minor road on the left to Over Silton, and then follow the signs to Nether Silton, a sleepy hamlet on the slopes of the Hambleton Hills.

Nether Silton to Sutton Bank

5 From Nether Silton continue for a short distance on the minor road towards Borrowby. Where the road divides immediately after passing under power lines, fork left. At the next junction turn left again, signposted to Kepwick, then take the first right to the village of Cowesby, which, with its stately manor and air of comfortable serenity, seems a world away from the wild and uncultivated moor above.

6 From Cowesby continue to Kirby Knowle, turning left to Felixkirk just beyond the church. On the edge of Felixkirk, turn right towards Thirsk then almost immediately left to reach Sutton-under-Whitestonecliffe and a T-junction. Turn left on to the A170. The road climbs steeply up Sutton Bank, through a hairpin bend. From the car park on the left at the top of the hill, there are spectacular views. A footpath from the hairpin bend, on the right going down, gives access to the Cleveland Way. This route is believed to be the second oldest of Britain's long-distance footpaths (the oldest is central England's Icknield Way) and it stretches over the North York Moors from Helmsley to Saltburn-by-the-Sea and on along the coast to Scarborough.

Sutton Bank to Helmsley

7 Rejoin the A170 towards Helmsley. After 3 miles, at some road intersections known as Tom Smith's Cross, turn right on a minor road then immediately right again. Follow the road through Wass to Byland Abbey (EH), the remains of a large Cistercian monastery founded in the late 12th century.

8 Return to Wass and turn right to Ampleforth, where a much more recent abbey, founded by refugees from Napoleonic France, is now the centrepiece of an independent school. Continue to Oswaldkirk and turn left on to the B1257 to a T-junction with the A170 in Sproxton. Turn right to return to Helmsley.

YORKSHIRE

10 PICKERING

TOUR LENGTH **54 miles**

Above all, this drive commands wonderful views. The route heads for the coast via Dalby's Forest Drive, open fells and leafy clifftops, passing through peaceful rural villages on the way.

Pickering to Lockton

1 Streets of old houses lead to the market place in Pickering, an unspoilt town on the edge of the North York Moors which, according to legend, was founded by Peredurus, king of the Britons in 270 BC. Much later, in the 14th century, Richard II was imprisoned in Pickering Castle (EH). Some of this history is touched on in the museum. The church of St Peter and St Paul in the town centre contains magnificent medieval frescoes.

Leave Pickering on the A169 signposted to Whitby. The road climbs towards higher country with wide views across hills and forests, and enters the North York Moors National Park. About 5 miles out of the town, turn left on a minor road to visit the rural village of Lockton, a settlement of ancient origins.

Lockton to Hackness

2 Return to the A169, turn left and drive on for 2½ miles to a viewpoint car park, which overlooks the Hole of Horcum. This huge natural amphitheatre – 90m (300ft) deep and more than ½ mile across – is the result of glacial ice floes, although legend has it that it was created by a giant, scooping up earth to throw at his wife. It lies to the left of the road.

3 Drive back towards Pickering, past the turning for Lockton, to a junction with a minor road by the Fox and Rabbit pub. Turn left, signposted to Thornton-le-Dale and Dalby Forest, then take the first turning left, nearly 2 miles farther on, signposted to Dalby Forest Drive. Follow the drive, a toll road, to Low Dalby, where an information centre has displays and booklets about the woodlands.

4 Continue through a dramatic landscape of pinewoods and steep valleys to Low Staindale. There, a short walk along a footpath on the other side of the river leads to the Bridestones, a group of strikingly eroded sandstone outcrops. The 122ha (300 acre) nature reserve surrounding the outcrops contains rare species of plants and animals, including the spectacular Emperor Moth.

A HUGE NATURAL AMPHITHEATRE
HOLE OF HORCUM, NORTH YORK MOORS

5 Carry on along Forest Drive for another 3 miles, past Staindale Lake, to a track on the left leading to Crosscliff viewpoint. A short trail gives access to fine moorland vistas over Langdale Forest and Blakey Topping, a conical hill formed in the Ice Age.

6 Rejoin Forest Drive and continue to the toll gate, which marks its end. Beyond lies the hamlet of Langdale End on the River Derwent. Follow the road over the bridge and at the turning to Forge Valley keep left, continuing into Hackness. St Peter's church contains part of a magnificently carved Saxon cross from the 7th-century monastery that once graced the village. There has been a church on this site for more than a 1,000 years.

Hackness to Cloughton

7 Turn left opposite the church up the lane towards Silpho, where a UFO allegedly fell to earth in the 1950s. Continue through Silpho and at the T-junction 1 mile beyond the village turn left. The road follows a high ridge through a forest, with distant views towards the Whitby coast, before descending to Harwood Dale. The village's setting in a broad, low-lying vale of streams and lush green fields belies its proximity to the moor.

8 Where the road divides 3 miles farther on, fork left to Burniston and at a T-junction turn left on to the A171. In Cloughton, fork right, on to a minor road to Ravenscar, then immediately right into Newlands Lane. The village developed during the 19th century as a result of quarrying for building stone and limestone. The disused Scarborough to Whitby railway line passes through Cloughton, where the old station has been converted into a hotel. The railway track is now a pedestrian and cycle path, commanding wonderful views down to the coast.

Cloughton to Pickering

9 Rejoin the A171, turning left. Continue through Scalby, on the outskirts of Scarborough, then turn right on to a minor road to Throxenby, just beyond a bridge over a canalised stretch of the River Derwent. The road divides below a steep bank; turn right and continue through Raincliffe Woods, where there are magnificent views over the Derwent Valley.

10 At the next T-junction, turn left along Forge Valley to reach another T-junction. Turn right on to the A170. Gallows Hill Farm, to the right of the road ½ mile before the village of Brompton, was the family home of William Wordsworth's wife, Mary Hutchinson, and contains exhibits explaining the poet's connections with the area, as well as an art gallery, shop and tearooms. Wordsworth had known Mary since childhood – they went to school together – and the couple were married in Brompton church in 1802. Just three people attended the service, Mary's brothers Thomas and John and her sister Joanna.

11 Stay on the A170, through Thornton-le-Dale, with its lovely streamside cottages, all the way back to Pickering.

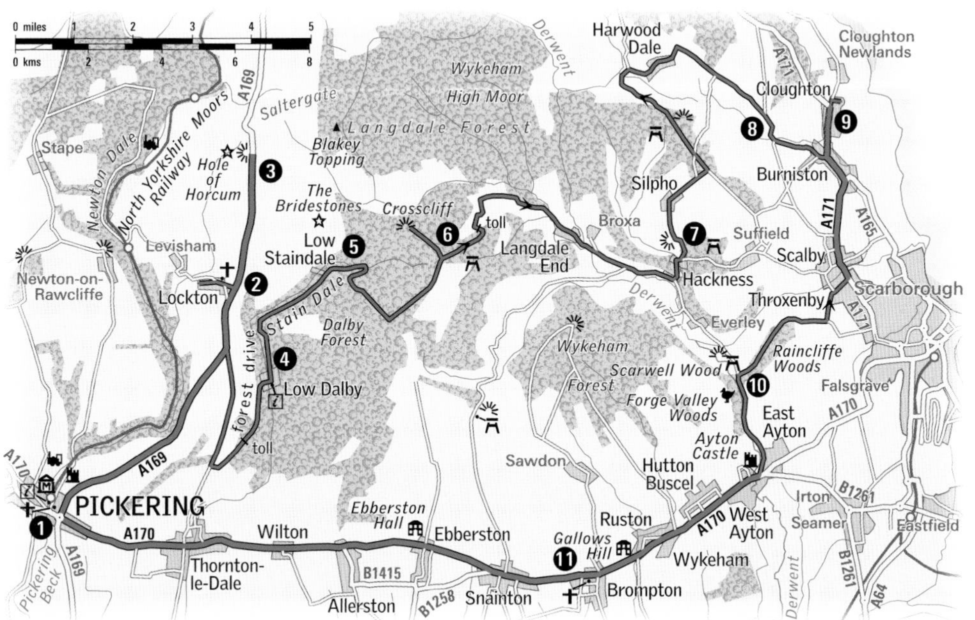

YORKSHIRE

11 WHITBY

TOUR LENGTH **70 miles**

From the sea, the road soon turns inland, crossing bleak moors before wending its way through the sheltered depths of Eskdale. Back on high ground, it passes open village greens where sheep often graze.

Whitby to Hinderwell

1 Captain Cook was apprenticed to Whitby shipwright John Walker and later chose converted Whitby 'cats' or colliers – *Endeavour, Resolution, Adventure* – for his great voyages of discovery. High above the lively harbour and steep cobbled streets a statue of the great South Seas explorer looks out to sea, sharing the clifftops with the ruins of a 13th-century abbey and the sailors' church of St Mary.

Take the A174 to the small resort of Sandsend, which is sandwiched between a long expanse of beach and dense Mulgrave Woods.

2 Continue inland on the A174, and turn right at Ellerby. Follow a steep minor road downhill to Runswick Bay, where a landslip in 1664 swept an entire village into the sea. Now, houses built against the cliffs seem to tempt fate.

3 Return to the A174 and turn right to Hinderwell, where the churchyard contains a well dedicated to St Hilda, who founded the abbey at Whitby. The plain shrine of weathered stone sheltering a small pool was restored in 1912.

Hinderwell to Great Ayton

4 From Hinderwell, continue on the A174 to Dalehouse, ½ mile from Staithes, and turn left on to a minor road signposted to Roxby. In the village is an old blacksmith's forge with a front shaped like a horseshoe. Continue uphill beyond Roxby to the T-junction with the A171 and turn right to Guisborough.

5 Follow the road through three roundabouts, bypassing Guisborough. At the fourth roundabout turn left on to the A173 to Great Ayton, a large village with fine Georgian houses grouped around High Green. Above on the left is the cliff-rimmed and curiously named Roseberry Topping, an iconic feature of the North York Moors.

Great Ayton to Grosmont

6 Immediately beyond the bridge across the River Leven in the village centre, fork left on to a minor road signposted to Easby. Turn left at the first T-junction to reach Easby, then fork left on a minor road, which leads under a railway. Take the first turning left and follow the road along the fertile upper valley of the Leven, through Kildale, to Commondale, a little village clinging to the moorland edge. Continue uphill to a remote T-junction on top of the moors and turn right towards Castleton and Danby, passing between ancient stones and Bronze Age barrows.

7 In Castleton, turn left and follow the road over the River Esk to Danby, where the Moors Centre, housed in an elegant old shooting lodge, provides information on the North York Moors National Park.

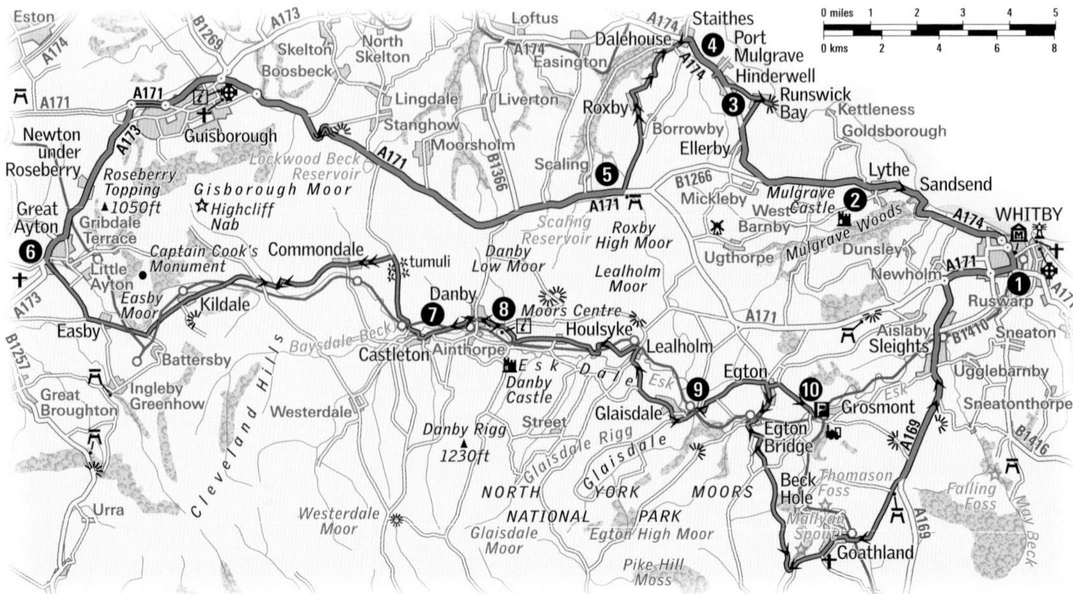

WHITBY

8 Turn right and immediately left in the centre of Danby, and follow the twisty road down Eskdale to a T-junction in Lealholm. Turn right and cross a bridge over the river, then follow a narrow road signposted to Glaisdale, a village with a quaint little station and stone bridge over the river – Beggar's Bridge.

9 Continue past the station to Egton. At a junction in the village, turn right then immediately left towards Grosmont. Turn left into a car park lying between the bridge over the Esk and the centre of Grosmont. This is the northern terminus of the restored steam railway that runs across the moors to Pickering, under the auspices of the North York Moors Historical Railway Trust.

Grosmont to Whitby

10 Return to the centre of Egton and turn left to Egton Bridge, a stone-built village deep in the Esk valley. Cross the bridge, turn left and follow the principal lane uphill, then down and across the narrow valley of the West Beck to Goathland, an atmospheric moorland village, with houses scattered across open common land. A path opposite the church leads down to Mallyan Spout, a waterfall that plunges some 20m (70ft) into a rocky gorge.

From Goathland follow the signs to Whitby, climbing back to the open moor. Turn left at the junction with the A169. Follow the road and turn right on to the A171 to return to the town centre.

12 BEVERLEY

TOUR LENGTH 78 miles

This trip explores the Yorkshire Wolds, a range of low chalk hills, taking in pretty villages with fine churches and historic inns, and a working 19th-century mill. The route continues past a large freshwater lake to the rapidly eroding coastline.

Beverley to Welton

1 The North Bar, the only survivor of Beverley's five medieval gateways, guards the northern entrance to this well-preserved town of narrow streets and market squares. The skyline is dominated by two masterpieces of Gothic church architecture, St Mary's Church and the exuberant Beverley Minster, which was built in the 13th century around the tomb of St John of Beverley.

Start the drive from Wednesday Market, following the signs for the M62. At a pair of mini-roundabouts, turn right on to the B1230 to Walkington, crossing open pastureland and passing between two windmills without sails.

2 Cross the A1079 into Walkington, where the grass verges and 18th and 19th-century brick-built whitewashed cottages are typical of Wolds villages. Turn left to Little Weighton, then at a T-junction turn left to Skidby, which was a busy rope and net-making centre in the 19th century.

3 Follow the signs to Skidby Mill – built in 1821 and still working. Carry on, bearing right at a junction by a road bridge. After about 2½ miles, turn left on to the road to Kirk Ella, then right to Melton. At Melton traffic lights, turn right to Welton. At the Green Dragon in 1739, so legend has it, the highwayman Dick Turpin was finally arrested and sent for trial at York Assizes.

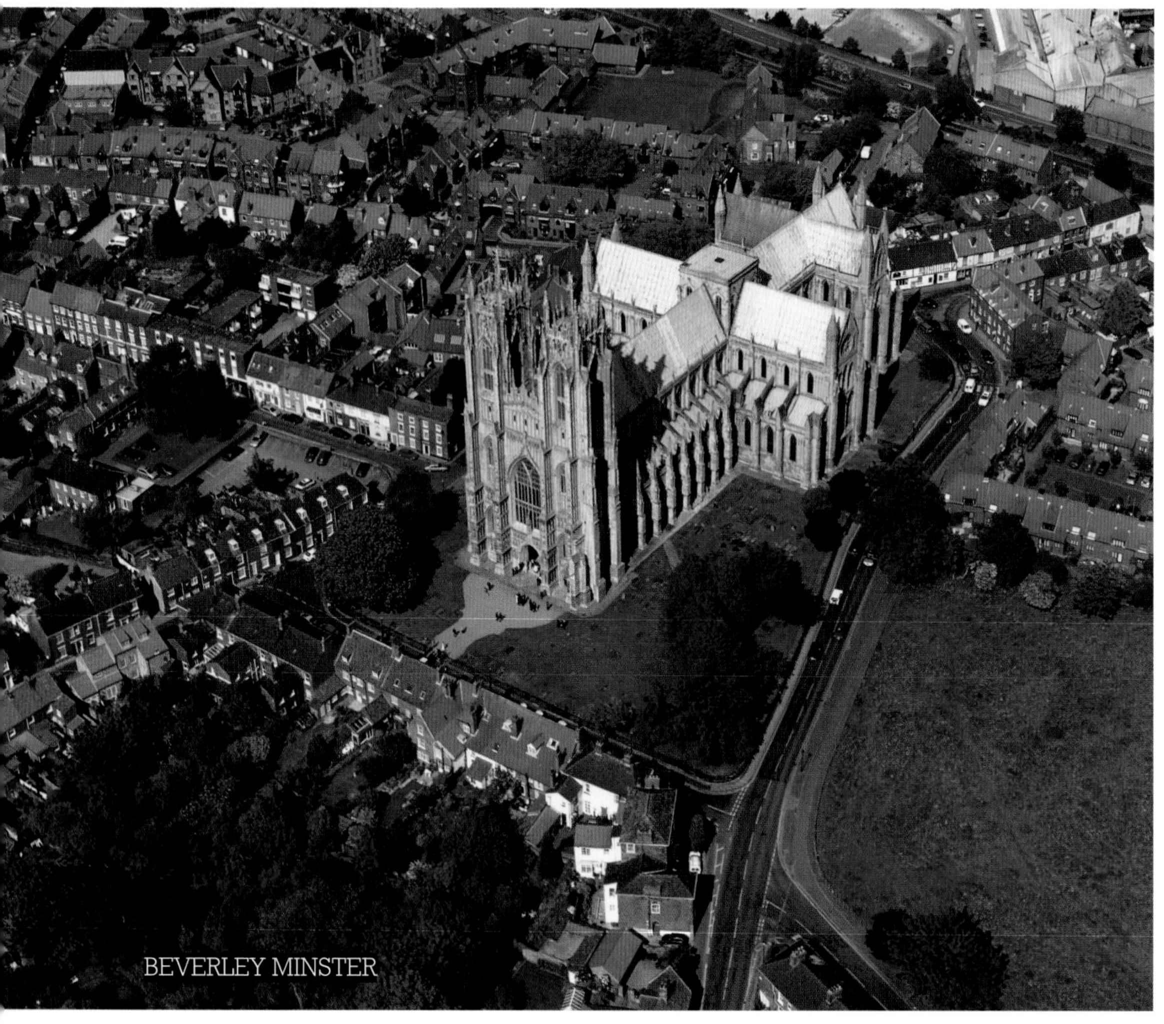

BEVERLEY MINSTER

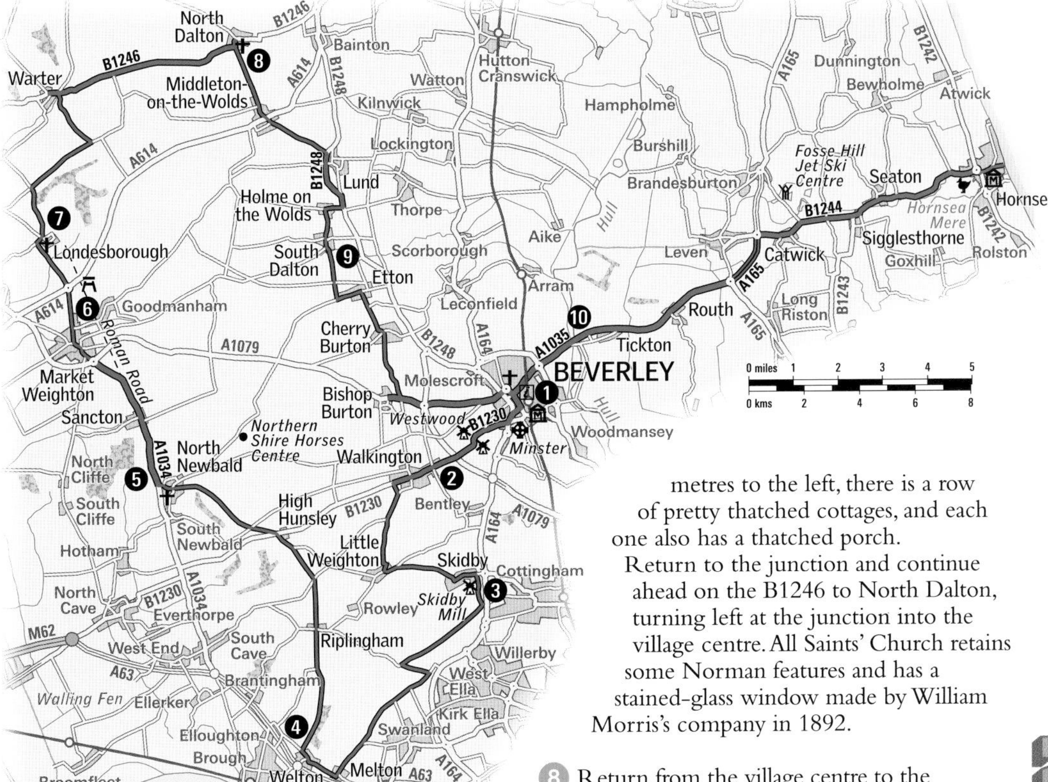

Welton to Market Weighton

4 Follow the signs for Beverley and Newbald. The road cuts through an unpopulated stretch of rolling Wolds scenery to North Newbald, where a fine Norman church has four elaborately carved doorways.

5 From the village green follow the signs to Market Weighton, now a quiet backwater compared with its heyday in the 18th and 19th centuries when it was an important market town, as reflected by the Londesborough Arms Hotel, a listed building that was erected in about 1700.

Market Weighton to Beverley

6 Continue along Londesborough Road to Londesborough, a village of 18th and 19th-century estate cottages. All Saints' Church in the village has three sundials etched in the stone by the south door. The oldest, over the door, dates from the 11th century.

7 Bear left towards Warter, then at the next crossroads turn right. Continue for about 2 miles, with wide views on each side, then turn left, again towards Warter and the B1246. In Warter, at the junction with the B1246, a few hundred metres to the left, there is a row of pretty thatched cottages, and each one also has a thatched porch. Return to the junction and continue ahead on the B1246 to North Dalton, turning left at the junction into the village centre. All Saints' Church retains some Norman features and has a stained-glass window made by William Morris's company in 1892.

8 Return from the village centre to the junction and go south to Middleton, then continue ahead on the road signposted to Beverley. At the junction with the B1248 turn right and then take the second road right, following it round a sharp left bend to South Dalton, an estate village with a diversity of architectural styles.

9 Follow the signs to Etton, then turn right through Cherry Burton to Bishop Burton, where John Wesley, the founder of Methodism, preached from the village green in the 18th century. From Bishop Burton follow the signs to Beverley.

Beverley to Hornsea

10 For an extension of the drive to the coast, take the A1035 out of Beverley towards Hornsea, crossing the canalised River Hull, where leisure craft may be moored. The road leads through the vast flat expanses of the Holderness region. Turn right on to the B1244. After about a mile, a minor road left leads to the Fossehill Camping and Caravanning Park and Jet Ski Centre, set in disused gravel pits. Continue on the B1244, passing Hornsea Mere, Yorkshire's largest freshwater lake, part of which is an RSPB reserve. Carry on into Hornsea, one of the few beach resorts on this fast-eroding stretch of coast, and head for the seafront. Return to Beverley by the same route.

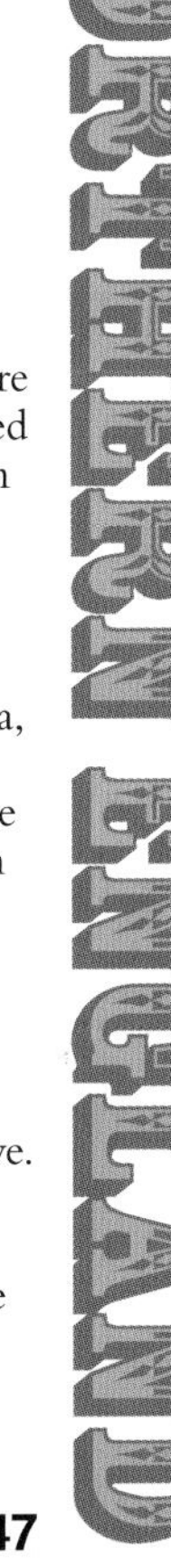

YORKSHIRE

13 GRASSINGTON

TOUR LENGTH **57 miles**

Set in the heart of the Dales, this trip starts amid rich farming country, and continues through dramatic limestone terrain. On the way, it passes a stately home, a medieval castle and a curious squatter's cottage.

Grassington to Skipton

1 Once a site of the lead-mining industry, Grassington is now a quiet country village, and its focal point is a cobbled market square. People have settled here since the earliest times. Traces of Iron Age villages and medieval field systems can be seen on the hillside terraces. On Grassington Moor, disused mines still form visible scars, and two old workers' cottages house the Upper Wharfedale Folk Museum, which has exhibitions of local domestic and working life.

To start the drive, take the B6265, climbing to Hebden, then turn right to Burnsall. Cross the bridge and continue along the river.

At the road junction in Hartlington turn right, then right again to cross the bridge, and carry on to Burnsall, turning left on to the B6160. There is a car park next to the village green. In Burnsall, the church of St Wilfrid has an unusual lych gate and a Norman font.

2 Continue on the B6160 for 3 miles to the roadside remains of Barden Tower, which are freely accessible during daylight hours. The tower, once a 15th-century hunting lodge, originally belonged to the earls of Cumberland. On the death of the 3rd Earl in 1605, his estate was bequeathed to his brother rather than his only child. Lady Anne Clifford spent her life fighting for her inheritance and finally regained it in the mid 17th century. She renovated the estate's buildings, including Barden Tower, where she lived until her death in 1676.

3 Follow the B6160 for another 3 miles to Bolton Abbey, passing Strid Wood, which includes 75 miles of footpaths. Barden Tower and Strid Wood are both part of the Bolton Abbey Estate, which is owned by the Duke of Devonshire. Bolton Abbey is open to the public. Check times before visiting. Also part of the estate, the ruins of a priory stand by the river, next to the restored 13th-century church of St Mary and St Cuthbert.

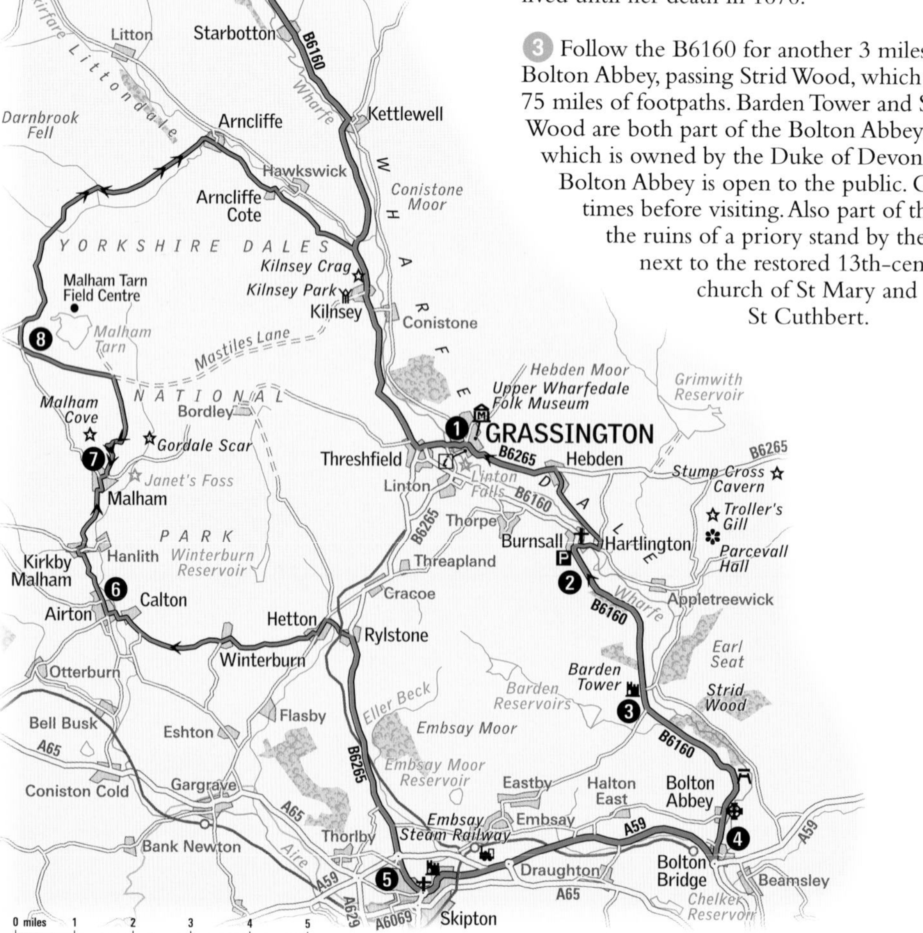

4 Continue on the B6160 and take the third exit at the roundabout, the A59 to Skipton. Continue straight on at the next roundabout, then fork left. Stop in the car park behind the town hall in the main street to visit its medieval castle.

Skipton to Malham

5 Leave Skipton on the B6265, crossing the northern bypass (A65) at a roundabout, and follow the B6265 for 5 miles to Rylstone. Turn left to Hetton and, at the next junction, turn left again. After the Angel Inn, fork right to Winterburn. Bear left through the village, turning right to Calton over a humpback bridge along a narrow road. Bear left into Airton. The road drops steeply over a bridge to a renovated mill. In the middle of the village green is an unusual 17th-century squatters' cottage. When it was built, a law gave the freehold of a property as far as a stone's throw from the front door to anyone who built a home and had smoke rising from its chimney in under 24 hours. Since Airton was once a Quaker village – the meeting house still stands – it has no pub.

6 Turn right beyond Airton village green, then right again at Kirkby Malham, towards Malham. A National Park visitor centre is located on the left as the road enters the village. From here, a ½ mile walk along a gravel track, part of the Pennine Way, leads to Malham Cove, a spectacular amphitheatre of sheer limestone cliff.

Malham to Buckden

7 Continue through Malham, then fork right over the bridge and turn left up a steep road to Malham Tarn. Turn left at the crossroads with a lane, and follow the road through dramatic open moorland. After ½ mile, look out for a footpath on the right, and park on the grass verge beside the road. The footpath leads to Malham Tarn, ½ mile away. This isolated mountain lake, accessible only on foot, is an important breeding place for birds. Nearby Tarn House is a field study centre, offering a variety of courses in natural history and geography.

8 Carry on up the road and at the crossroads turn right, continuing along the narrow road for 5 miles to Arncliffe. Turn right over the bridge, go through Arncliffe and after 3 miles turn left on to the B6160 to Kettlewell, going over the bridge and bearing left. The riverside road leads through Starbotton to the small village of Buckden. A stroll around the village and its environs will give a taste of the superb walking available in the heart of the Yorkshire Dales.

Buckden to Grassington

9 Return to Kettlewell and stay on the main road to Kilnsey Crag. Nearby Kilnsey Park and Trout Farm offers trout fishing and a children's adventure centre. Follow the road to a crossroads at Threshfield and turn left to Grassington.

KILNSEY CRAG

YORKSHIRE

14 HEBDEN BRIDGE

TOUR LENGTH 43 miles

Looming mills characterise the area around Hebden Bridge in the South Pennines, where centuries of textile history have left their mark. The road winds precipitously across moors dotted with stone packhorse bridges.

Hebden Bridge to Haworth

1 Terraces of long-windowed weavers' cottages bear testimony to the trade that flourished in Hebden Bridge from the Middle Ages onwards. The town takes its name from the fine packhorse bridge that still spans the river. Now a lively cultural centre, Hebden Bridge's many attractions include horse-drawn boat trips along the Rochdale Canal.

To start the drive, take the A6033 signposted to Haworth and Keighley, climbing steeply out of the valley past Nutclough Mill, where one of the first workers' cooperatives was established. Just beyond an octagonal former toll house on the left, take the left turn signposted to Midgehole and Hardcastle Crags. Continue for about 1 mile above Hebden Water on the left. Over a bridge there is a National Trust car park, from where a fairly tough walk leads up to Hardcastle Crags.

2 Return to the A6033 and turn sharp left towards Haworth, up through Pecket Well and past the dishes and aerials at Bradford University's base for the world's first robotic telescope. A slim, modern, white windmill is seen ahead as the road descends to Oxenhope, and the terminus of the Keighley and Worth Valley Railway, which operates steam trains.

3 Continue to Haworth, turn left at the first crossroads and at a T-junction turn left on to Bridgehouse Lane over the river and railway. Bear right up Rawdon Road, leading to North Street. Following the signs for the Brontë Parsonage Museum, turn left opposite West Lane Methodist Church.

HEBDEN BRIDGE

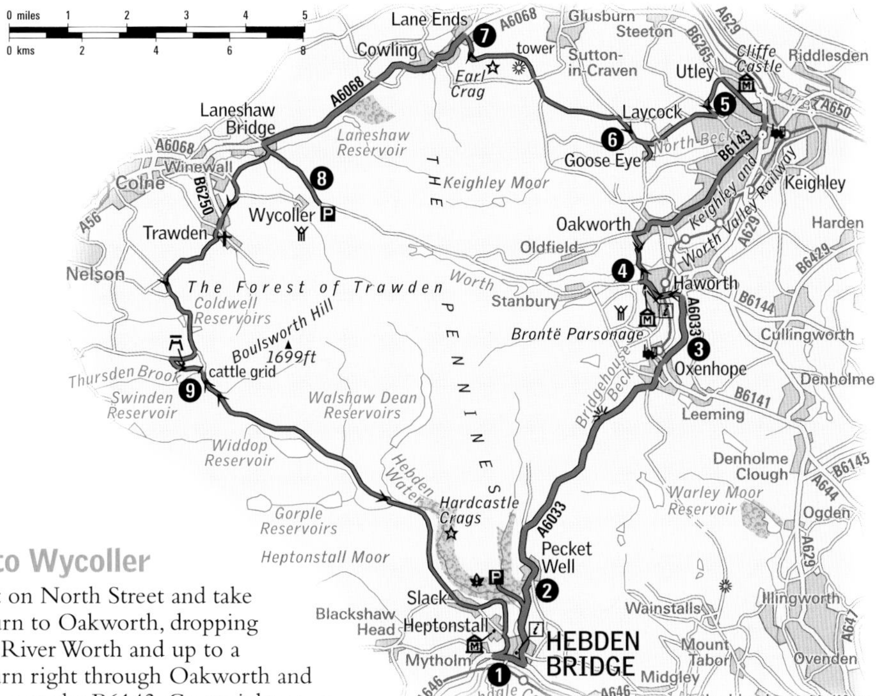

Haworth to Wycoller

4 Turn right on North Street and take the first left turn to Oakworth, dropping steeply to the River Worth and up to a T-junction. Turn right through Oakworth and out to Keighley on the B6143. Go straight on at a major roundabout following the signs for the A629 towards Skipton. After a library at traffic lights, take the fourth turn on the left up Spring Gardens Lane to Cliffe Castle, an ornate museum and art gallery, with aviaries and gardens.

5 Continue uphill and turn left into countryside on Shann Lane. At a T-junction turn left down Black Hill Lane. Take the second turning on the right through the Dales village of Laycock. Just beyond, take a sharp left turn down a precipitous hill to Goose Eye, a tiny old mill village on North Beck.

6 Return uphill, turn left and take the second road on the left. After 2½ miles, the dramatic rock formations of Earl Crag and a tower folly appear. For fine views, park on the left and climb to Lund's Tower and Wainman's Pinnacle.

7 Continue down the road to Lane Ends and turn left along the A6068. At Laneshaw Bridge, take the left turn for Wycoller Country Park, in Lancashire. After 1½ miles, turn right into the car park. Nearby are the ruins of 16th-century Wycoller Hall and a clapper bridge, as well as an information centre. Wycoller was once a thriving community based on weaving but with the advent of power looms came industrialisation and Wycoller's prosperity dwindled. The village was virtually abandoned about 100 years ago. Wycoller is within walking distance of Haworth, and Wycoller Hall is thought to be the original Ferndean Manor, from Charlotte Brontë's *Jane Eyre*. The ruins are also said to be haunted by a spectral horseman and hounds.

Wycoller to Hebden Bridge

8 Drive back towards Laneshaw Bridge and just before a bridge turn left, signposted to Wycoller. Continue uphill and turn left at a T-junction towards Wycoller Country Park. Ignore the next turning on the left to the country park, and continue down to Trawden. At a T-junction, turn left up the main street. Just before St Mary's Church bear right and then turn immediately left towards Hebden Bridge. After 1 mile turn left at a crossroads for Hebden Bridge, descending to Lower and Upper Coldwell reservoirs and back up to the moors. Just past a Second World War pillbox, ignore a left turn to Hebden Bridge and continue towards Burnley. After ⅓ mile, park on the left at a picnic spot for fantastic views over the Thursden Valley.

9 Continue on the road and take the first left turn down to Thursden Brook and cross a cattle grid on to the Hebden Bridge road, winding steeply uphill with a perilous drop to the left. Widdop Reservoir appears and the road descends to skirt its glistening water, then twists uphill past Hardcastle Crags before winding down to the A646. Turn right and left via a turning circle into Hebden Bridge.

ISLE OF MAN

Steeped in history and surrounded by myth and legend, this scenic island in the Irish Sea also has working reminders of a more recent past, with its electric railway and enormous water wheel.

15 DOUGLAS

TOUR LENGTH 73 miles

Starting in the island's capital, the road follows the coast south, where narrow glens dip down to the sea. The round trip continues past medieval castles, Snaefell and a churchyard with distinctive Manx crosses.

Douglas to Port Erin

1 The seaside town of Douglas, spread along 2 miles of coastline, became the capital of the Isle of Man in 1869. It still has a Victorian air, which survives in three of its transport systems – the Isle of Man Steam Railway, the horse-drawn tramway of the 1870s and the Manx Electric Railway, opened in 1893. In late May and early June the peace of the island is broken by the roar of motorcycles when the TT races are run, starting and finishing in the capital.

Leave Douglas on the A1 towards Peel, turning left immediately before the railway station. Cross the river, and at the mini-roundabout turn right on to the A6. Where the road forks, bear left on to the A25.

2 After 1 mile, turn left on to the A37 before the bridge to Port Soderick, a rocky cove with clifftop walks. Continue on the A37, turn right on to the B23 and left on to the A25. At the T-junction turn left on to the A5 to Ballasalla.

Turn left at a mini-roundabout in Ballasalla, pass Ronaldsway airport and go straight on at both roundabouts into Castletown, where the fortress, Castle Rushen, dates from the 12th century. The town also has a maritime museum and an old grammar school museum.

3 Passing the castle on the right, turn left at Smelt's Memorial, and follow the road to the right. The memorial was built in 1832 in honour of a governor, Cornelius Smelt, although public subscription did not provide enough money to build a statue. At the T-junction, turn left on to the A5. At the end of Bay ny Carrickey, turn right and continue on the A5 to Port Erin, going straight on at the roundabout. In the town, turn left just after the pedestrian crossing on Strand Road. Follow the road to the left along the seafront and park at the far end by the lifeboat station. The hills and cliffs around the bay once provided refuges and hideaways for smugglers.

BRADDA HEAD FROM THE BEACH

PORT ERIN

Port Erin to Peel

4 Drive back along the seafront, turn left on to the A32 and follow the road uphill to the right past Bradda Glen. At the T-junction, turn left, and at a mini-roundabout, turn left again on to the A36, climbing through moorland. At the crossroads, turn left on to the A27 to Peel. At Peel, turn left along Station Road and go straight ahead at the traffic lights, behind the House of Manannan heritage centre. Bear right across the bridge and follow the road to the right along the quay. Park at Fenella Beach car park in front of the ruins of Peel Castle. Inside the castle's 14th-century red sandstone walls are the remains of a 13th-century cathedral.

Peel to Ramsey

5 Return past the heritage centre to Station Road. Take the road signposted 'All Routes' to Douglas, and then the second turning left and left again at the mini-roundabout. Turn right on to Tynwald Road to St John's, where the Manx parliament, the Tynwald, meets annually.

6 At the traffic lights, turn left to Ramsey. After 4 miles, just before a Methodist church, turn right on to the B10 towards Snaefell, which at 620m (2,036ft) is the highest peak on the island. Where the road divides, fork left, and at the T-junction turn left on to the A18. On the left is Bungalow Station, on the Snaefell Mountain Railway.

The road descends to Ramsey, the second largest town on the island. It has a working harbour and a beach, and is a terminus of the Manx Electric Railway, connecting Douglas and Laxey.

Ramsey to Douglas

7 Leave Ramsey on the A2 signposted to Laxey. Cross the railway and take the first left on to the A15 to Maughold, where the churchyard contains a collection of Manx crosses.

8 The road winds along, crossing the railway and swinging towards the coast. Turn left on a minor road to Cornaa and the nature trails at Ballaglass Glen. Continue across a ford and turn right at a T-junction. At the next T-junction, turn left, then left again on to the A2 Douglas road. After 1 mile, the road bends to the left, past Dhoon Glen Halt, a stop on the Manx Electric Railway.

9 Continue on the main road, going straight on at the crossroads to Laxey. Immediately after crossing the railway, turn right into Mines Road – the road crosses the railway again – to visit the Laxey water wheel and mining museum.

10 Return to the A2 and continue towards Douglas. About 1½ miles beyond Baldrine, turn left on to the A11 for Groudle Glen and the start of the Groudle Glen narrow-gauge steam railway. Continue ahead on the A11 back to Douglas.

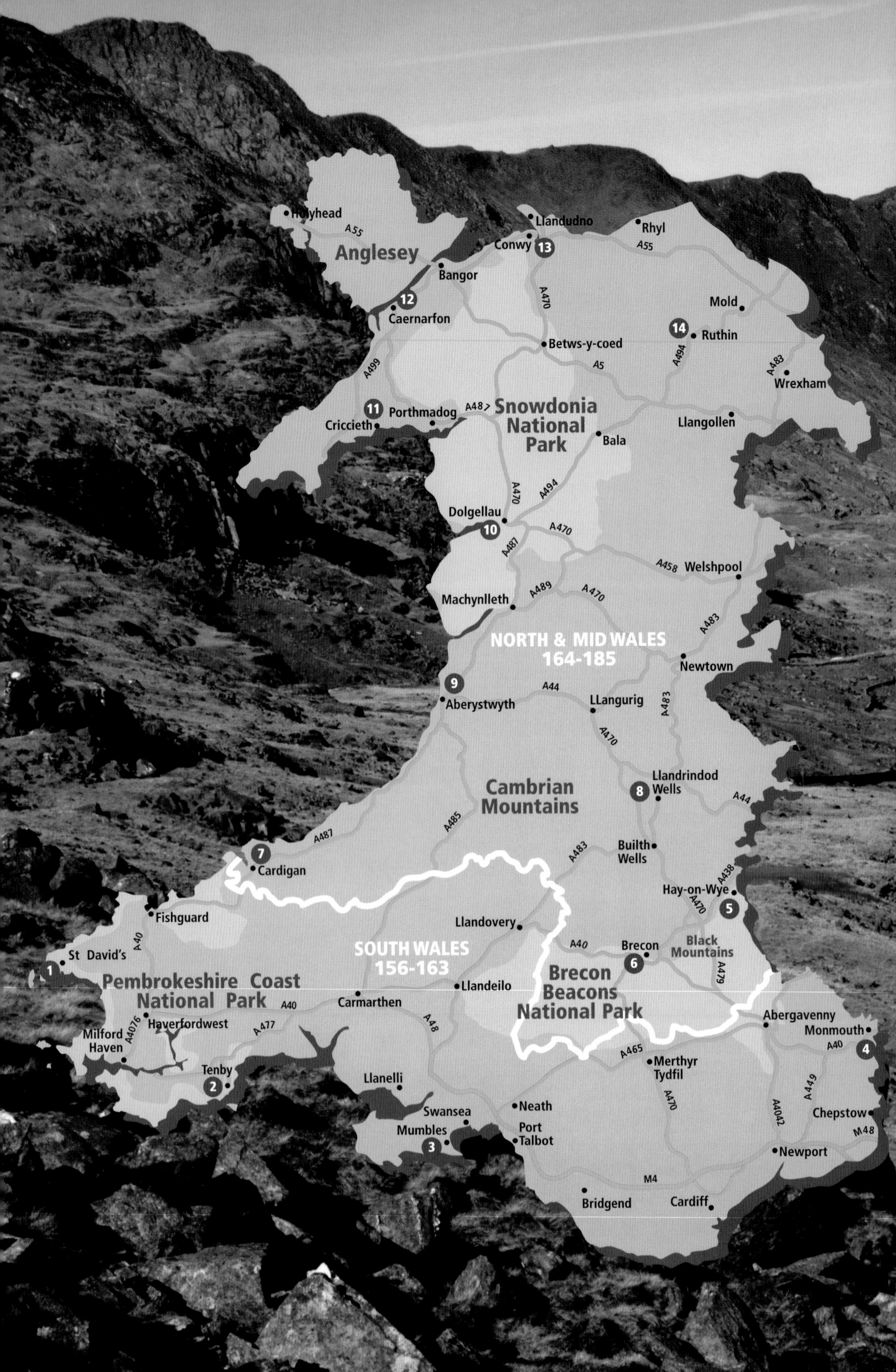

Holyhead
A55
Anglesey
Bangor
Llandudno
Conwy
13
Rhyl
A55
12
Caernarfon
A470
Mold
14
Ruthin
Betws-y-coed
A5
A494
A483
Wrexham
A499
11
Porthmadog
A487
Snowdonia
National
Park
Criccieth
Llangollen
Bala
A470
A494
Dolgellau
10
A470
A487
A458
Welshpool
Machynlleth
A489
A470
A483
NORTH & MID WALES
164-185
Newtown
9
Aberystwyth
A44
LLangurig
A483
A470
Llandrindod
Wells
8
Cambrian
Mountains
A44
A485
A487
7
Cardigan
A483
Builth
Wells
A438
Hay-on-Wye
A470
5
Fishguard
Llandovery
A40
St David's
1
SOUTH WALES
156-163
A40
Brecon
6
Black
Mountains
A479
Pembrokeshire Coast
National Park
Brecon
Beacons
National Park
Llandeilo
Carmarthen
A40
A4076
Haverfordwest
A477
A48
Milford
Haven
Abergavenny
Monmouth
A40
4
A465
Merthyr
Tydfil
Tenby
2
Llanelli
A470
A4042
A449
Chepstow
Swansea
Neath
Mumbles
3
Port
Talbot
M48
Newport
M4
Bridgend
Cardiff

Wales

Nature and heritage vie for supremacy in Wales, as pretty towns and villages give way to rich farmland, and wild tracts lead on to the coast. High in the mountains, drivers need steely nerves, as roads make precipitous descents though beautiful landscapes.

SOUTH WALES

As well as the forests and lakes that grace the famed green valleys, wild rocky coasts and long sandy bays are among the natural attractions of these southern Welsh shores, where signs of Norman occupation abound.

1 ST DAVID'S

TOUR LENGTH 53 miles

A multitude of little coves, natural harbours and dramatic headlands break up the stark coastline of this far corner of Wales. The route leads to historic Fishguard, from where ferries cross the Irish Sea, and returns through narrow valleys and open country.

St David's to Goodwick

1 Suntanned surfers chasing the great, creamy Atlantic rollers that sweep into Whitesands Bay, and seasoned ramblers walking the Pembrokeshire Coast Path, lend a relaxed veneer to St David's, its narrow streets filled with cafés and art galleries. However, nothing disguises the underlying character of this ancient outpost of Christianity, hemmed in on three sides by a ruggedly beautiful and dangerous coast. In the 6th century, the patron saint of Wales founded a cathedral here, but it took 600 years and many Viking raids before the Normans brought security to this remote corner of their kingdom. The cathedral that they started building in 1183, and the ruins of the Bishop's Palace, dominate Britain's smallest city to this day.

Take the A487 from the centre of St David's towards Fishguard. Just beyond the city turn left on to the B4583 towards Whitesands Bay, then almost immediately branch right at a sharp left-hand bend on to a minor road.

Continue to Llanrhian, 5 miles distant, and turn left at the village crossroads to reach Porthgain, a cluster of houses at the head of a deep-cut harbour, from which stone, quarried on the headlands, used to be shipped.

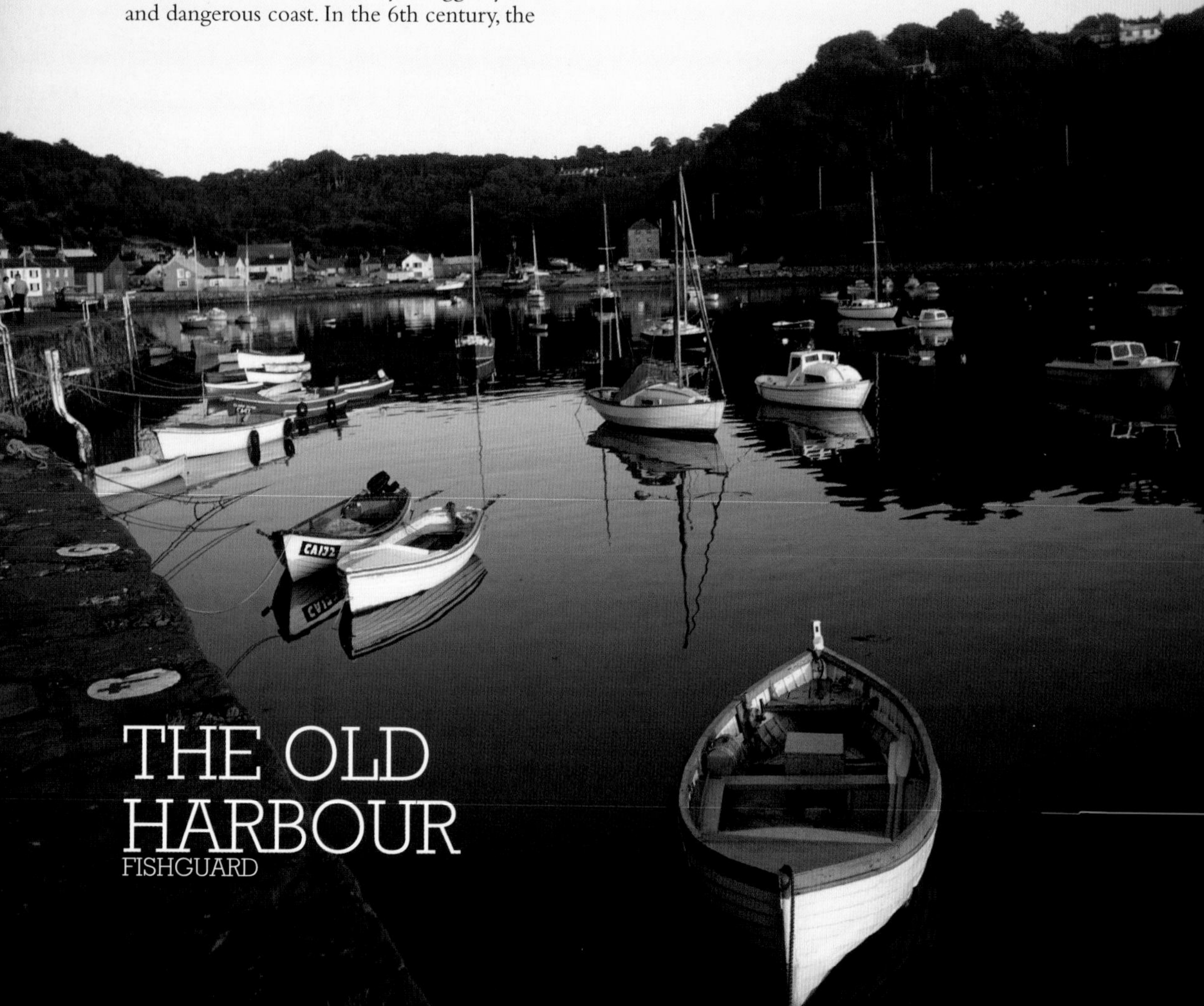

THE OLD HARBOUR
FISHGUARD

2 Return to Llanrhian crossroads and turn left to Trefin, passing the little cove at Aber Draw. Turn left then immediately right in Trefin, towards Abercastle. The first minor road on the left leads to a footpath to Carreg Sampson, an imposing ancient burial chamber with huge stones, from where there are views out over the Irish Sea.

3 At a fork ½ mile beyond Abercastle bear right to reach a minor crossroads. Turn left towards Aber Mawr. The road drops to a T-junction in a narrow valley; turn sharp left, uphill. At the first crossroads turn left to reach the scattered hamlet of Tregwynt, where there is an old, still-working woollen mill.

4 Return to the crossroads, turn left, then turn left again at the next crossroads to St Nicholas. Carry straight on through the hamlet to a crossroads by a telephone box, 1 mile farther on. Turn right, then take the second road on the left, between the rocky summits of Garn Fawr and Garn Fechan, to a junction. Turn left to Strumble Head and its lighthouse. This is a good place to watch for porpoise, seals and sea birds.

5 Return to the junction and turn left towards Goodwick. At the next T-junction turn left, signposted to Fishguard, and continue through Goodwick towards the ferry terminal. To get to the car park, turn right by the Rose and Crown pub at the end of the High Street, cross a railway bridge, and then turn left at the roundabout.

Goodwick to Wolf's Castle

6 Continue on the A40 to Fishguard, where the old part of the town is set prettily around the harbour and there is a charming waterfront. In 1797, the commander of a French invasion force – the last to land on the British mainland – signed surrender terms in the Royal Oak Inn, in the market square.

From the roundabout in the centre of Fishguard, take the A487, signposted to Cardigan, then immediately turn right on to the B4313 towards Maenclochog. The road drops into the wooded Cwm Gwaun, a steep-sided valley with a picnic place on the banks of the river a short distance beyond Llanychaer.

7 Continue along the B4313 to a sharp left-hand bend, then branch right on to a minor road to Puncheston. Around ½ mile beyond Puncheston the road divides. Take the left fork and go straight on at a minor crossroads, then take the first turning on the right to the town of Wolf's Castle. The mound where once a motte and bailey stood are all that remains of the castle. There is a parking place just beyond the bridge carrying the A40.

Wolf's Castle to St David's

8 Join the A40 and turn right towards Haverfordwest, then immediately turn right again on to a minor road leading to a T-junction with the B4330 at Hayscastle Cross. Turn right, then immediately left by the Cross Inn. Go straight over a crossroads and take the second left, at the bottom of Brandy Brook valley. Continue straight on, past Brawdy airfield, to Penycwm. Turn right on to the A487, through Solva, where the creek is usually full of yachts, to return to St David's.

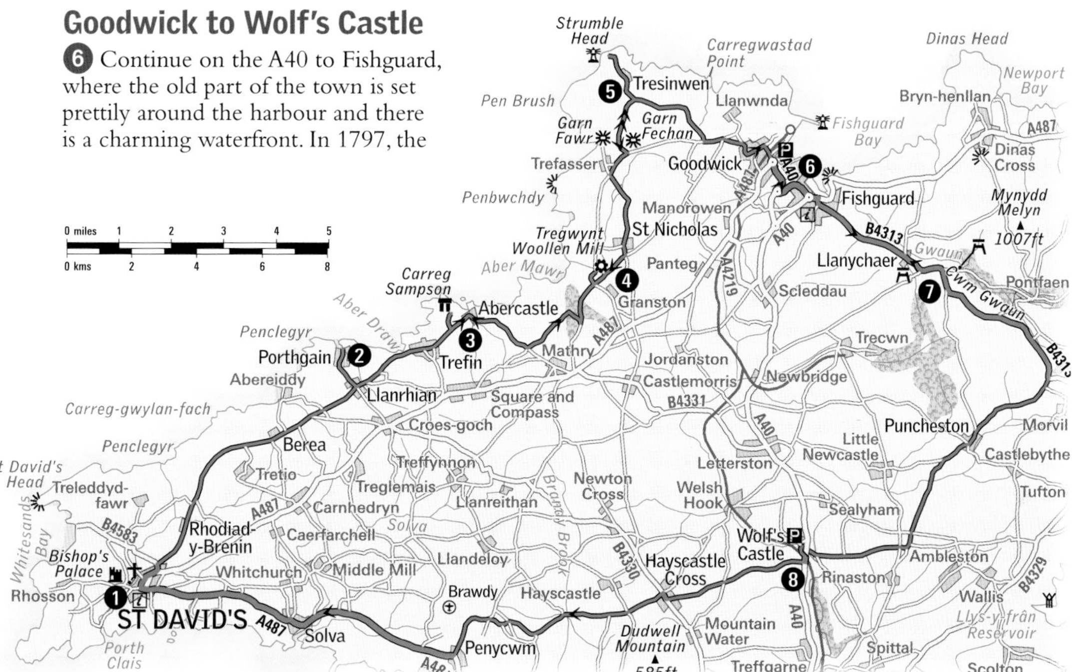

SOUTH WALES

2 TENBY

TOUR LENGTH 55 miles

This route around the beautiful Pembroke peninsula passes Norman castles and churches, and takes in several detours to superb sandy bays as well as one to a tiny chapel perched a little way down the steep cliffs of St Govan's Head.

Tenby to Angle

❶ Tenby was one of the most successful of the Plantagenet 'plantations' – fortified towns where English people were urged to settle under the protection of the Norman kings' crossbowmen – and from which the neighbouring Welsh were excluded. Four centuries later the Elizabethan travel writer William Camden still found Tenby and the Pembroke peninsula to be 'England beyond Wales', a label that stuck. In the early 19th century the vogue for bathing in the sea brought crowds of prosperous visitors to the town. Their legacy can still be seen in the Georgian and Regency terraces behind North Beach – elegant reminders of Tenby's long history as a fashionable seaside resort.

Leave the centre of Tenby on the A4218. The road goes under a railway bridge and bends right past the station. Continue straight ahead at the roundabout, then immediately turn left and follow Heywood Lane to a T-junction on the B4318. Turn right towards Sageston, 3½ miles distant.

❷ Just before Sageston turn left at the roundabout on to the A477, towards Pembroke Dock. 1 mile farther on, at the next roundabout, turn right on to the A4075 to visit the village of Carew, where there is a restored mill, powered by the tide, and the ruins of a Norman castle.

Return to the roundabout on the A477 and turn right. After 1¼ miles, branch left on to the A4075 to Pembroke, which has one of the best-preserved Norman castles in Britain. Run by a charitable trust, it is open all year. Check times before visiting.

❸ Follow the one-way system through Pembroke and take the B4320. Carry straight on past Hundleton. A mile past the junction with the B4319 to Castlemartin, turn right on to a minor road to Angle, where there is a car park behind St Mary's Church. In the churchyard there is a 15th-century fisherman's chapel in which there are murals of sea scenes. Angle is located on Angle Bay, and a short walk westwards leads to the beautiful beach of West Angle Bay with views through saw-toothed rocks to Thorn Island and St Ann's Head in the distance.

Angle to Stackpole Quay

❹ Return to the B4319 junction and turn right towards Castlemartin. The road follows the edge of Freshwater West, a fine surfing bay backed by a huge area of sand dunes. Turn right at the roundabout in Castlemartin, then, provided the road is not closed because of firing on the artillery range, turn right on a minor road to Elegug Stacks, a dramatic formation of limestone cliffs, standing in the sea.

❺ Rejoin the B4319 and turn right. After 2 miles turn right on to a minor road to Bosherston. At the far end of the village the road divides. Fork right and drive to the end of the road, where the tiny 11th-century St Govan's Chapel is tucked away in a cranny in the cliffs. Stone steps lead down to it.

❻ Rejoin the B4319 and turn right, past the Norman church of St Petrox. The high tower was once used as a lookout against raiders. Take the minor road on the right, ½ mile beyond the

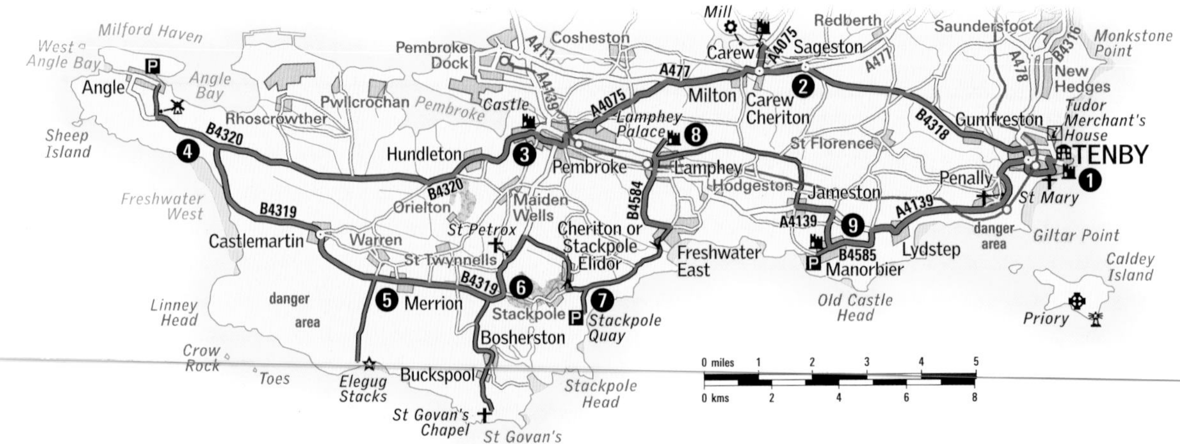

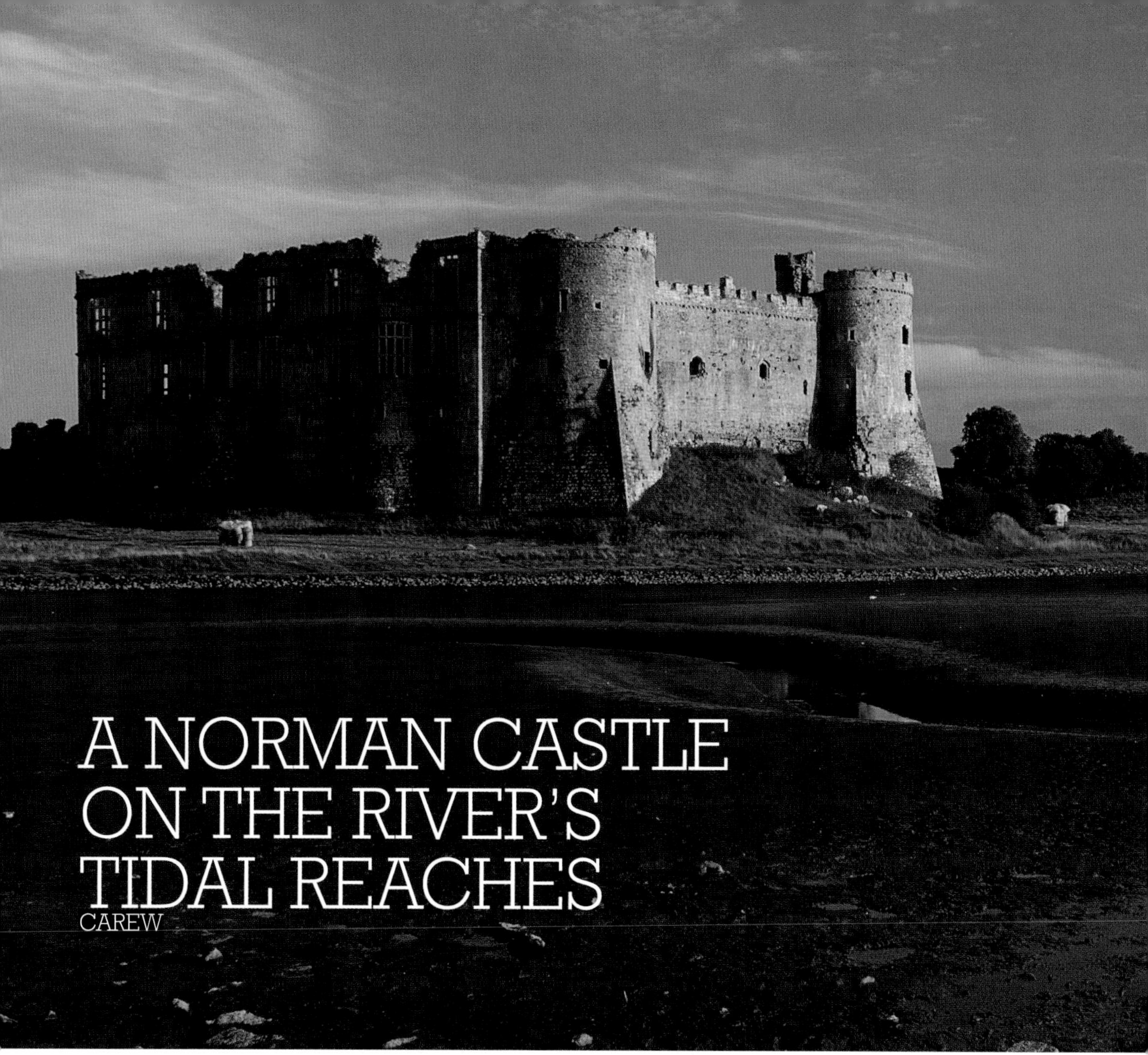
A NORMAN CASTLE ON THE RIVER'S TIDAL REACHES
CAREW

church, to a T-junction. Turn right, through the hamlet of Cheriton or Stackpole Elidor, then drive uphill to a T-junction. Turn left and take the first minor road on the right to Stackpole Quay.

From the bottom left-hand corner of the car park, a path leads above the harbour and along the top of the cliffs to Barafundle Bay, a great sweep of sand bracketed between headlands and backed by dunes. Through an arch in a stone wall, a long flight of shallow steps leads down to the sea shore.

Stackpole Quay to Manorbier

7 Drive back up the access road to Stackpole Quay and turn right at the T-junction to the crossroads in Freshwater East. Turn left at the crossroads on the B4584 to Lamphey.

Go straight ahead at the crossroads just beyond the village church to reach Lamphey Bishop's Palace (Cadw), a ruined country retreat which was originally built for the bishops of St David's and became the property of the earls of Essex in the 16th century.

8 Return to the crossroads and turn left on to a minor road. Carry on for 2½ miles and then turn right to Jameston. In the village turn left on to the A4139 for ½ mile. At the junction with the B4545 turn right to reach Manorbier. In the village centre, turn right on to the beach road, at the end of which is a car park. Overlooking the unspoilt beach stands Manorbier Castle, where the medieval scholar Gerald of Wales was born in 1146. The castle and garden is open to the public every day during summer, but check times before visiting.

Manorbier to Tenby

9 Return to the village centre in Manorbier and turn right on to the B4585. The road climbs to a T-junction on the A4139. Turn right and continue to the village of Lydstep, which contains a small medieval ecclesiastical palace financed by Bishop Gower – the 'building bishop' responsible for the palace in St David's. As the road rounds Giltar Point, Tenby can be seen beyond the wide sandy sweep of South Beach.

SOUTH WALES

3 MUMBLES

TOUR LENGTH 54 miles

From a jolly seaside town to the fabulous sands of Rhossili beach and back via a medieval fortified manor, this drive provides an inviting glimpse of the lovely Gower peninsula.

Mumbles to Oxwich

1 Mumbles has two dominant landmarks – the lighthouse guarding the end of rocky Mumbles Head, and the ruins of Oystermouth Castle, built by the Normans. Houses line the hillside above the seafront and the Victorian pier, with its steel latticework, stretches out into the bay. The town owes its development as Swansea's seaside resort to the Swansea and Mumbles Railway, which used horse-drawn carriages when it opened in 1807.

With the sea on the left, take Mumbles Road, going through a deep cutting past the pier to Mumbles Head. Turn right on Plunch Road, winding through houses to the end, continuing ahead on a narrow, wooded, single-track lane in front of a house.

2 Turn left at the junction on to the B4593 to Caswell Bay. On the left is the Bishop's Wood Countryside Centre, the starting point for woodland walks. Opening times are subject to change. Continue through Caswell on a minor road, climbing through woodland. At a T-junction turn left, then follow the road round to the right through Bishopston to another T-junction. Turn left on to the B4436 towards Port-Eynon. The road winds through more woodland and the village of Kittle. Turn right in Pennard, signposted to Parkmill and South Gower.

3 Follow the road to the junction with the A4118. Turn left to Parkmill. At the far end of the village is the Gower Heritage Centre, based around a 12th-century working watermill, with craft workshops and an animal farm. A lane leads from the village to Parc le Breos burial chamber, dating from around 3500 BC, and Cathole Cave, where bones and tools from around 12,000 BC have been found.

4 Continue on the A4118 through Penmaen and take the second left turn at the mock-castellated entrance to privately owned Penrice Castle, to which there is no public access. The road crosses part of Oxwich National Nature Reserve, with freshwater marshland to the right and saltmarsh and dunes to the left. Follow the road down to a car park on the left at the edge of Oxwich Bay. On a headland nearby stand the remains of Oxwich Castle (Cadw), once a magnificent 16th-century fortified mansion.

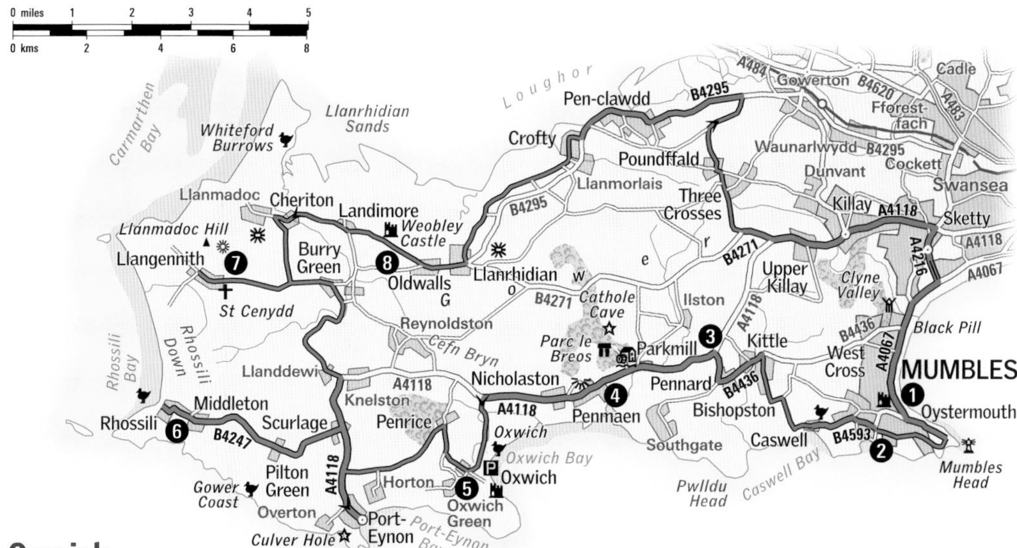

Oxwich to Rhossili

5 Turn right at the crossroads in Oxwich, and then follow a sharp right bend, signposted to Horton, to a T-junction. Turn left, ignore the next left to Horton and continue to the A4118. Turn left to Port-Eynon, where the ruins of a salthouse, once used for smuggling, stand by the sea.

Return on the A4118 to Scurlage, turn left on to the B4247 and follow the road to Rhossili village, which is situated near the end of a stretch of sand more than 3 miles long. In the village, the Norman church of St Mary's has a memorial to Petty Officer Edgar Evans, a native of Rhossili, who died in 1912 on Captain Scott's failed Antarctic expedition.

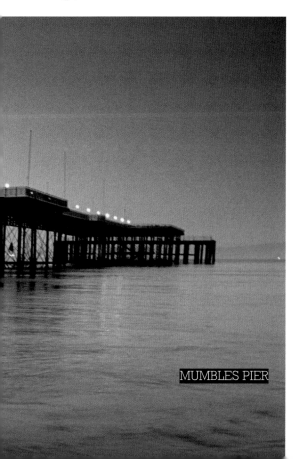
MUMBLES PIER

Rhossili to Mumbles

6 Return to Scurlage and turn left on to the A4118, then left to Burry Green. At the T-junction, turn left to Llangennith, where the Norman church of St Cenydd's is the biggest parish church on the Gower peninsula. It has a huge 13th-century stone tower.

7 Drive back to Burry Green and take the first left towards Llanmadoc. At the T-junction by the Britannia Inn, turn right through Cheriton. Beyond a staggered crossroads on the left stands Weobley Castle (Cadw), the ruins of a fortified manor dating from the 13th century.

8 Continue through Oldwalls, then turn left to Llanrhidian, joining a single-track lane along the coast. The lane is liable to flooding at high tide – to avoid it, join the B4295 at Llanrhidian. At the other end of the lane, continue through Crofty, bearing right at the top of the hill to the B4295. Turn left and continue beyond Penclawdd for 1½ miles, then turn right by a telephone box towards Three Crosses, continuing uphill to the Poundffald Inn. Turn right after the pub on Tirmynydd Road. At the T-junction, turn left on to the B4271, then left on to the A4118. At a roundabout, turn right to Sketty, continue across two more roundabouts then turn right on Sketty Park Road. Turn left at the next roundabout, then right on to the A4067. The road passes Clyne Valley Country Park, an area of mixed deciduous woodland, including oak and alder and containing marsh marigolds and rhododendrons. Continue on the A4067 to Mumbles.

SOUTH WALES

4 MONMOUTH

TOUR LENGTH 42 miles

The River Wye forms an historic boundary between England and Wales, and this exploration of its scenic valley strays across the border to the limestone gorge of Symonds Yat and to the Forest of Dean, where a restored steam railway runs again.

Monmouth to the Forest of Dean

❶ The Normans built a castle at the place where the Monnow joins the Wye as early as 1071, and Monmouth was soon enclosed within defensive walls. The 13th century gated stone bridge over the Monnow in this peaceful market town is the only one of its kind in Britain, and one of only three similar bridges in Europe. The castle was the birthplace of Henry V, whose statue looks down on that of C.S. Rolls, co-founder (with Henry Royce) of Rolls-Royce.

Leave Monmouth on the road signposted to Ross-on-Wye. At the roundabout, turn left on to the A40. After 4 miles take the exit signposted for the A4137, then follow signs back over the A40 to join the B4229 for Goodrich.

❷ Continue on the B4229 and follow the signs to Goodrich Castle (EH). Begun in the 12th century, the castle still towers above the river valley. Its massive red sandstone walls are ringed by a moat cut into the solid rock.

Return to the B4229 and follow the signs towards Whitchurch. After 1 mile turn left on the road signposted to Symonds Yat East. Fork left on to a narrow road to Yat Rock. From the edge of 122m (400ft) limestone cliffs there are superb views of the gorge of the Wye.

❸ Continue to a T-junction in Berry Hill and turn right then immediately left. Carry on to Broadwell, crossing the A4136 and B4028. At the junction with the B4226, turn left towards Cinderford, soon entering Gloucestershire's Forest of Dean. Just beyond the crossroads with the B4234, turn right for Cannop Ponds, a local beauty spot with picturesque walks and wildlife.

Forest of Dean to Tintern Parva

❹ Return to the B4226 and turn right. At Speech House Hotel turn right towards Parkend, passing an arboretum on the left, and continue past New Fancy viewpoint, a landscaped former mining site. At the T-junction turn right to Parkend, then left on to the B4234 towards Lydney. Parkend is the northern terminus of the Dean Forest Steam Railway, which runs from Lydney. There is a museum and shop at Norchard station, which also has a car park.

❺ At Lydney follow the signs for Chepstow, passing Lydney Park gardens, open in May and June for the rhododendron season. At a roundabout join the A48. Continue to Aylburton, then turn right on to a winding minor road to St Briavels with its castle (EH); the castle is now a youth hostel, but its courtyard can be visited in summer.

❻ Take the B4228 towards Chepstow and continue for 1½ miles to the crossroads, then turn right on to a narrow road to Brockweir, on the Wye. This small village used to be a thriving boat-building centre. Cross the bridge and turn left

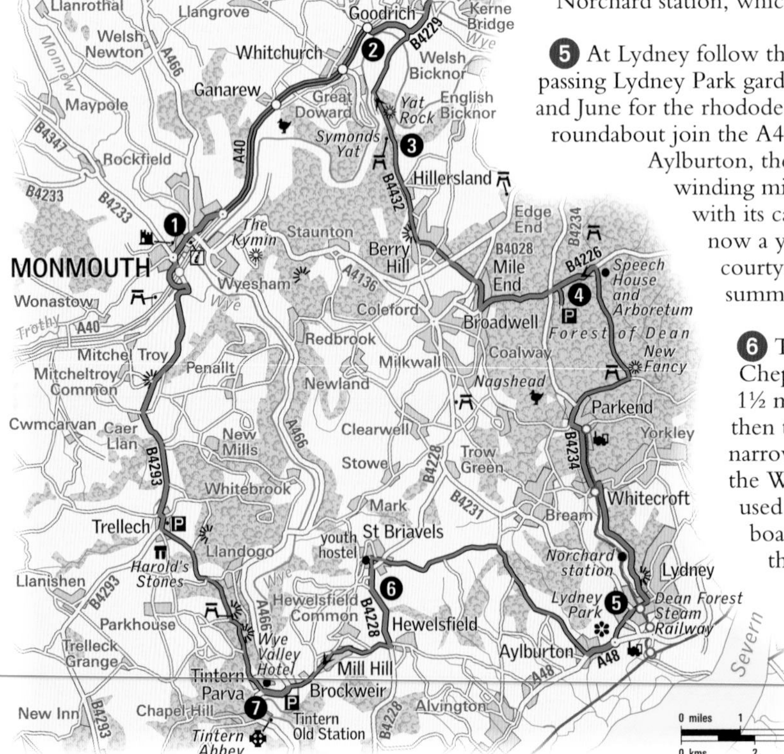

on to the A466, then park at Tintern Old Station, on the left. The station has been restored and is now a family activity centre with a miniature railway (check opening times beforehand), café and picnic site. The signal box sometimes hosts art exhibitions.

Tintern Parva to Monmouth

7 Continue on the A466 to the Wye Valley Hotel then turn right on to the road signposted to Catbrook and climb a wooded hill for 1½ miles to a T-junction at a picnic site. Turn left towards Trellech. At the entrance to the village, turn left at the junction on the B4293. After about 100m, Harold's Stones appear in a field on the left. These three leaning monoliths are made of a volcanic rock known as pudding stone and are thought to have been erected in the Bronze Age. They certainly long pre-date the English King Harold.

Return to Trellech and park in the car park next to the Methodist chapel. A short distance away, in the churchyard of St Nicholas's, a stone altar and preaching cross are thought to be Saxon, and there is a beautiful sundial.

Carry on along the B4293 to Monmouth. On the left, broad views open up, stretching far into South Wales.

THE GORGE OF THE WYE

YAT ROCK

NORTH & MID WALES

In this awesomely mountainous country – dominated by the national parks of Snowdonia, Pembrokeshire and the Brecon Beacons – reservoirs, mining museums and ingenious bridges are all tributes to human inventiveness.

5 HAY-ON-WYE

TOUR LENGTH 70 miles

Along narrow roads on the periphery of the Black Mountains, this route sets off for the atmospheric Llanthony Priory, painted by Turner. Passing three strategic Norman castles, it heads back to the literary town via Abbey Dore in the Golden Valley.

Hay-on-Wye to Llanthony

1 Overlooked by a hilltop Norman castle, the border town of Hay-on-Wye is world famous for its secondhand bookshops, and in May it hosts a Festival of Literature. Offa's Dyke Path passes through Hay, leading south up the escarpment of the Black Mountains – so named because, viewed from the town, they are always in shadow.

From Castle Street, with the Cinema Bookshop on the left, turn left signposted to Capel-y-ffin. From here, the roads become increasingly narrow, with passing places. Carry on for 2⅓ miles. Fork right on an unsignposted road, which leads over a cattle grid on to sheep-grazed hills. Keep left on the higher road to Gospel Pass for a breathtaking view over the upper Wye valley. A path to the left leads to the top of the 677m (2,220ft) high Hay Bluff, giving views of the Brecon Beacons and Malvern Hills.

2 Continue to Capel-y-ffin, where in 1870 the self-styled Father Ignatius founded a monastery. The order closed after his death in 1908 but the monastery, beside a ruined church, is still inhabited.

Three miles farther on, turn left to the 12th-century Llanthony Priory (Cadw). J.M.W. Turner's painting of the ruins hangs in London's Tate Gallery. The nearby church is thought to be on the site of St David's monastic cell.

Llanthony to Skenfrith

3 Farther south along the valley road, Cwmyoy church can be seen on the left; subsidence caused its tower to lean sharply. At the small village of Llanvihangel Crucorney, turn right at the

LLANTHONY PRIORY

T-junction past Wales's oldest hostelry, The Skirrid. The building is Elizabethan, but its history goes back much farther. In 1110, John Crowther was tried here for sheep stealing, and was sentenced to be hanged from a beam. The inn is reputedly haunted, and attracts many curious visitors keen to see, or experience, its ghostly incumbents. The oak beams are made from ships' timbers, and the panelling in the dining room is said to come from a British man o' war from the time of Sir Francis Drake.

4 Follow the A465 towards Abergavenny, and at the dual carriageway turn left on to the B4521, signposted to Skenfrith. Continue for 5½ miles and then turn right for White Castle (Cadw), the finest of the 'Welsh Three' – a trio of castles, including Skenfrith and Grosmont, built by the Normans to control South Wales. The moated remains date from the 12th century.

5 Return to the B4521. Turn right and follow the winding road to Skenfrith, a village of sandstone cottages dominated by the curtain wall of the castle of 1228–32, which screens a circular keep (Cadw). There is also a watermill in the village. Capped by a timber belfry, St Bridget's Church contains tombs of the Morgan family.

Skenfrith to Hay

6 Go back towards Abergavenny and, after just under a mile, turn right on to the B4347 to Grosmont, which is situated above the Monnow river. Opposite the post office, a path leads to the castle (Cadw).

7 Continue to Pontrilas and bear left across the A465 into Ewyas Harold. Follow the road round right and left bends to Abbey Dore in the Golden Valley. The church is all that remains of a Cistercian abbey founded in 1147. Its interior is adorned by a 17th-century carved oak screen and ceiling. A short walk away, Court Gardens, straddling the River Dore, include herbaceous borders and a rockery. Check times before visiting.

8 Return to Ewyas Harold. Turn right and follow a minor road to Longtown. For a detour to the Black Hill, in Herefordshire, which commands spectacular views, turn right by the Crown Inn, signposted to Craswall, then right again. Just beyond the ruins of the Norman castle fork left, following brown signs through Llanveynoe to the Black Hill picnic site.

9 Drive back to Longtown and turn left to Michaelchurch Escley, then follow the signs for Cusop and Hay.

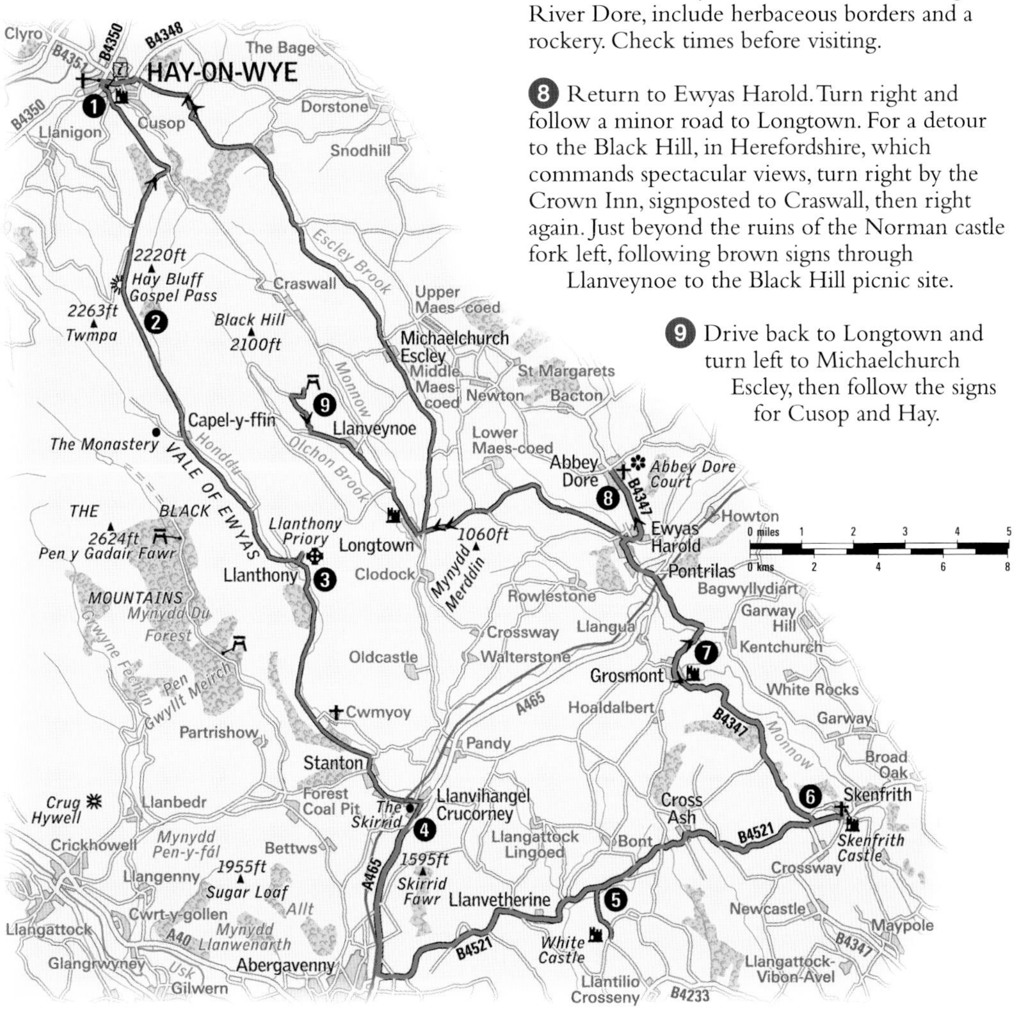

NORTH & MID WALES

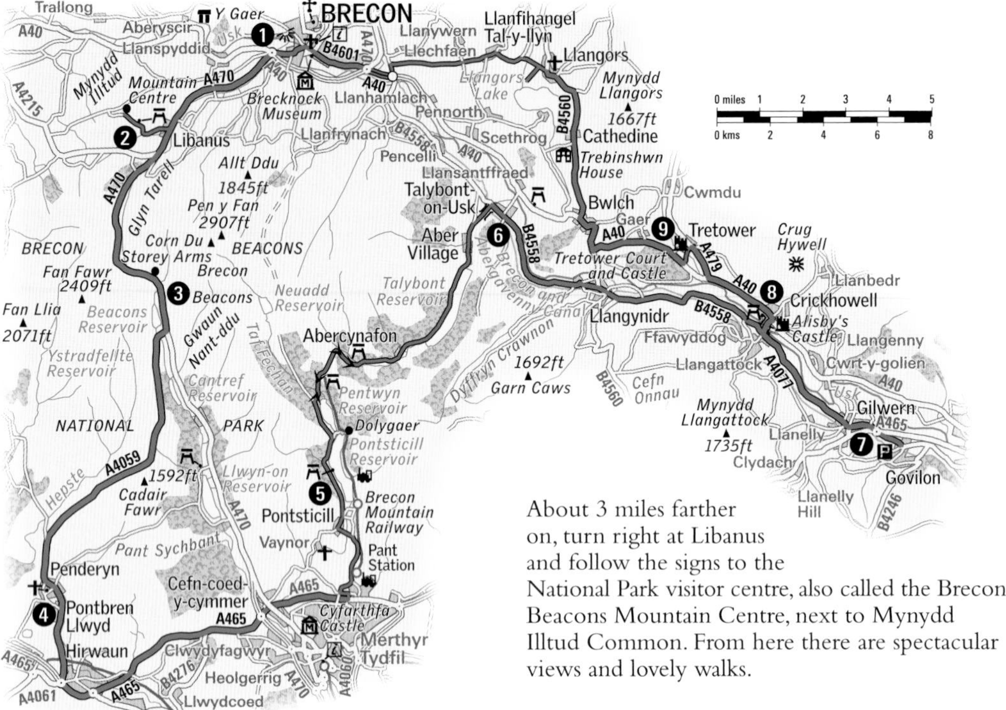

6 BRECON

TOUR LENGTH 81 miles

The Brecon Beacons National Park provides a spectacular backdrop to this trip. The hilly road winds high among escarpments, passing a station for the Brecon Mountain Railway, and skirting several reservoirs.

Brecon to Mynydd Illtud Common

❶ Brecon lies in a mountain valley at the confluence of the Usk and Honddu rivers. In its tight knot of narrow streets, many of the medieval town houses were refronted in Georgian times. The 13th-century cathedral was originally a Norman Benedictine priory, founded in 1093. Inside is a rare 'cresset stone' with 30 cup-like hollows for candles. The cathedral was restored in 1874–5 – its story is told at the heritage centre. In the South Wales Borderers Museum, memorabilia from the battle of Rourke's Drift (1879) is on display. Brecon is busy on Tuesdays and Fridays, market days, and in August thousands converge on the town for an annual jazz festival.

From the Brecknock Museum and Art Gallery, near the medieval church of St Mary in the heart of the town, follow the signs for Cardiff on the B4601. At the roundabout take the A470 towards Merthyr Tydfil.

About 3 miles farther on, turn right at Libanus and follow the signs to the National Park visitor centre, also called the Brecon Beacons Mountain Centre, next to Mynydd Illtud Common. From here there are spectacular views and lovely walks.

Mynydd Illtud Common to Penderyn

❷ Return to the A470 and continue towards Merthyr Tydfil. Beyond the summit of Corn Ddu on the left rises Pen y Fan, the highest point in England and Wales south of Snowdonia. The view extends north to the peaks of Cadair Idris and Plynlimon in the Cambrian Mountains, and south to Dunkery Beacon in Somerset.

❸ Beyond the Beacons Reservoir turn right on to the A4059. After 7 miles, take the first turning on the right into Penderyn. A steep lane leads to St Cynog's church, which has a medieval tower.

Penderyn to Govilon

❹ Continue south on the A4059 to Hirwaun, then turn left at a major roundabout on to the A465, the Heads of the Valleys road, towards Merthyr Tydfil. Follow the A465, going straight across at two more roundabouts, the second being the junction with A470. Take the second exit left after a further 2 miles, following signs for the Brecon Mountain Railway at Pant station. Steam-hauled narrow-gauge trains make a 7-mile return trip to the north end of the Pontsticill (Taf Fechan) Reservoir at Dolygaer, calling at Pontsticill station on the return leg. From Pant station, continue north into Cwm Taf Fechan, then take the first left, a narrow road climbing to Pontsticill village. Turn right at the T-junction on to a minor road for Talybont-on-Usk.

5 Continue along the shores of Pontsticill and Pentwyn Reservoirs, where there are picnic sites and signposted forest walks. Built from 1928 to 1932 to supply Newport, Talybont Reservoir attracts great numbers of wildfowl to its southern shore and is a Site of Special Scientific Interest (SSSI), as well as being a feast for the eyes. Its dam is crossed by the Taff Trail, a route for cyclists and walkers between Brecon and Cardiff.

6 At the entrance to Talybont village, bear right across the Brecon and Abergavenny Canal swing bridge, then turn right on to the B4558. Some 8 miles farther, at the turning to Crickhowell, continue on the A4077 through Gilwern. Go straight on at the roundabout, crossing the A465, to park at the Lion Inn in Govilon, an old village in the beautiful valley of the River Usk.

Govilon to Brecon

7 Return through Gilwern and turn right to Crickhowell, crossing a bridge over the Usk. Erected in 1706 to replace an earlier structure, Crickhowell bridge is unusual in having 13 arches on one side and 12 on the other. In a park near the High Street stand the ruins of Alisby's Castle. Also known as Crickhowell Castle, it was built in 1272 by Sir Grimbald Pauncefoot, whose effigy can be seen in the parish church.

8 From Crickhowell bridge, turn left on the A40. Turn right on the A479 to Tretower, then turn left to Tretower Court – a fortified late-medieval manor house – and Castle (both Cadw). Sheep graze around the circular keep of 1240, still standing at its original height. Both court and castle are the subject of renovation – check if they are open before visiting.

9 Return to the A40 on the minor road passing Tretower Court, turn right and continue towards Brecon. Drive through Bwlch, then turn right on to the B4560 to Llangors. Turn left after the church towards Llanfihangel Tal-y-llyn, then take the left turn soon afterwards to Llangors Lake, the largest natural lake in South Wales.

Return along the access road, turn left away from Llangors, left again through Llanfihangel Tal-y-llyn and continue for 2½ miles. Turn left at the next T-junction to join the A40 to Brecon.

A TRANQUIL HAVEN IN GOOD WALKING COUNTRY
TALYBONT RESERVOIR

NORTH & MID WALES

7 CARDIGAN

TOUR LENGTH 59 miles

Deep wooded valleys separate bare uplands crowned with signs of prehistoric settlement as the road heads into the Pembrokeshire National Park. A detour to the sea takes in a sandy bay carved out of high cliffs.

Cardigan to Newport

❶ During the Middle Ages ships sailed upriver to Cardigan and anchored in the lee of the castle, which is now in ruins. That was before the River Teifi silted up and the town looked to the land for its livelihood, fostering a busy market in and around the central Guildhall – a multi-arched, Gothic building constructed in a time of prosperity in the 19th century. In front of it, a Russian field gun from the Crimean War is a reminder that the 7th Earl of Cardigan was in command at the time of the ill-fated Charge of the Light Brigade (1854).

Leave Cardigan by the 17th-century bridge over the River Teifi and keep straight on to a roundabout on the edge of town. Turn right on to the A478, towards Tenby.

In the hamlet of Pen-y-bryn turn left at a minor crossroads to Cilgerran. The first left turn, just before entering the village, leads to a wildlife centre with viewing hides overlooking the marshy tidal flats of the Teifi.

Continue past Cilgerran Castle (NT), an ancient fortress with twin towers, to the hamlet of Pontrhydyceirt. Turn left by the telephone kiosk in the hamlet, then left at the next T-junction to Llechryd, where the road crosses the Teifi. At the T-junction with the A484 immediately beyond the bridge, turn right, signposted to Newcastle Emlyn.

❷ The road shadows the meanders of the Teifi and, at the village of Cenarth, recrosses the river beside waterfalls and a 17th-century mill that houses the National Coracle Centre, including a large collection of these ancient boats from many countries.

❸ Just beyond the bridge turn right on to the B4332 and continue for 5½ miles. Where the road forks beyond Boncath, go left to a T-junction with the A478 and turn left. Take the first minor road on the right after the village of Crymych, towards Maenclochog, and continue to a T-junction in the middle of the hamlet of

CENARTH FALLS

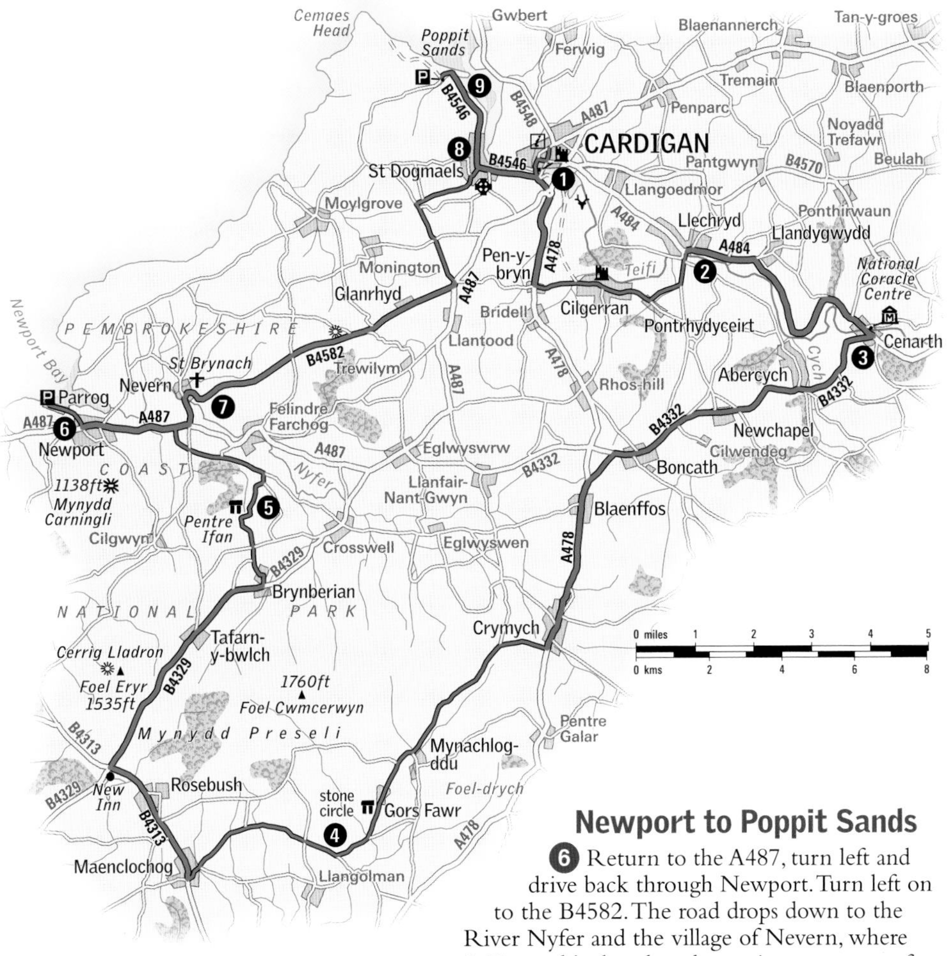

Mynachlog-ddu. Turn right and follow the road into the foothills of the Preseli mountains, passing Bronze Age standing stones and a stone circle at Gors Fawr, which translates as 'great wasteland'.

❹ Turn right at the next T-junction and continue for 3 miles to Maenclochog. In the centre of the village turn right on to the B4313 to the New Inn crossroads, then turn right on to the B4329, which climbs to the high, broad plateau of the Preseli mountains. In the hamlet of Brynberian turn left on to a minor road, which leads over a crossroads to the parking place, ½ mile farther on, for Pentre Ifan burial chamber – a fine megalithic tomb with a 17 tonne capping stone.

❺ The road winds downhill to a T-junction. Turn left to another T-junction, then turn left again on to the A487 to Newport. Take a minor road on the right, just beyond the town centre, to Parrog where there is a beachfront car park. When the tide is low, platforms of rock, festooned with seaweed and cratered with pools, edge exposed sandbanks.

Newport to Poppit Sands

❻ Return to the A487, turn left and drive back through Newport. Turn left on to the B4582. The road drops down to the River Nyfer and the village of Nevern, where St Brynach's churchyard contains an avenue of ancient yews and a 10th-century Celtic cross.

❼ The road climbs steeply out of the valley to a junction with the A487, which is 5 miles farther on. Turn left, then immediately left again, on to a minor road signposted to Moylgrove. Continue over a crossroads and take the second minor road on the right to the quiet village of St Dogmaels, which nestles around dramatic abbey ruins (Cadw). There is also a working watermill.

❽ Turn left in the village, on to the B4546 towards Poppit Sands. Follow the road, which runs beside the Teifi estuary, to the beach car park. The roadside banks are filled with wild flowers in spring and summer, and there are views across the estuary to Cardigan Island.

Poppit Sands to Cardigan

❾ Return to St Dogmaels and continue on the B4546. The road stays close to the side of the estuary – a magnet for waders and other seabirds. Soon the walls of Cardigan Castle and the arches of the town's old bridge come into sight.

8 LLANDRINDOD WELLS

TOUR LENGTH 82 miles

This route through the rolling hills of mid Wales takes in spectacular waterfalls, pretty villages and tranquil churches, as well as the remote moors, reservoirs and impressive dams of the Elan Valley.

Llandrindod Wells to the Elan Valley

1 The age of bath chairs and taking the waters is strongly evoked in Llandrindod Wells, where hotels face neat parks, and Victorian wrought-iron canopies and gabled and turreted villas have been carefully preserved. Visitors can sample the iron-impregnated waters from a spring beneath a tiny ravine in Rock Park. In late August the townspeople dress in period costume for the Victorian Festival. A museum tells the story of the spa, while the National Cycle Exhibition includes such machines as an 1879 Quadrant tandem.

To start the drive, leave Llandrindod Wells on the A4081. After 4 miles turn right at a T-junction on to the A470 to Rhayader. The name is from the Welsh *rhaeadr,* meaning waterfall, and refers to the cascade of the Wye tumbling below Rhayader bridge. The tiny town has craft shops, and a farm trail and a red kite-feeding site at Gigrin Farm.

2 At Rhayader's town clock turn left on to the B4518 signposted to the Elan Valley. For the visitor centre, after about 3 miles fork left in Elan Village (signposted), which was built in around 1909 for the reservoir workers. A nature trail starts from there.

3 From the visitor centre, return to the B4518 and turn left into the Elan Valley, where the reservoirs with huge dams, built to supply water to Birmingham, are an unmissable feature. Follow the road past Caban Coch and Carreg-ddu reservoirs on the left, and continue with Penygarreg and Craig Goch reservoirs on the right. At a T-junction just beyond Craig Goch, turn right. Views from the top of the hill encompass a wind farm and the distant heights of Plynlimon and Cadair Idris mountains.

The Elan Valley to Kington

4 Carry on along the road, turning left at the T-junction with the B4518, to Rhayader. At the crossroads go straight along the A44, signposted to Leominster, and continue to Llandegley. Discovery of a chalybeate spring made the village a popular watering place in the 18th and early 19th centuries. A road on the left leads to The Pales, the oldest Quaker meeting house in Wales.

5 Continue on the A44 passing Radnor Forest on the left. About 6 miles beyond Llandegley, a track from a car park on the left leads to the aptly named Water-break-its-neck, a waterfall plunging into a sheer-sided ravine.

6 Continue for about 1 mile, then fork left into the village of New Radnor, where there are traces of old town ramparts near the church. In the village centre turn right, passing a Gothic memorial to Sir George Cornewall Lewis, a 19th-century Liberal prime minister. Where the road meets the A44, turn left and continue through Walton to Kington, an attractive Herefordshire town with an imposing clock tower.

Kington to Glascwm

7 Return to Walton, and turn left to Old Radnor, where St Stephen's Church has the oldest organ case in Britain.

Follow the road downhill, turning left near the quarry at Dolyhir, then right on to the B4594 to small farming village of Gladestry. Just beyond Gladestry turn right, then left to the village of Colva. In 1870, the curate and diarist Francis Kilvert wrote of the clear echo that can be heard 50m west of the belfry wall of the village church.

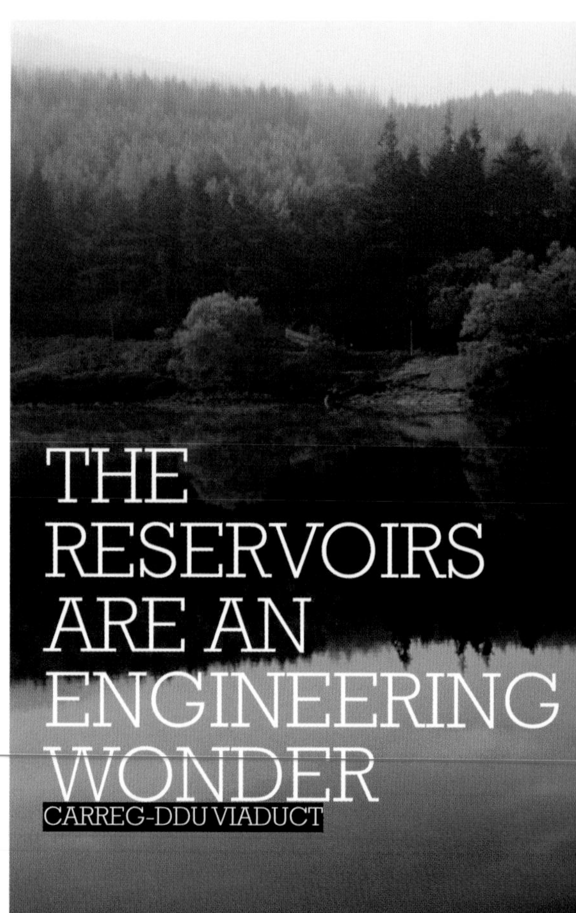

THE RESERVOIRS ARE AN ENGINEERING WONDER

CARREG-DDU VIADUCT

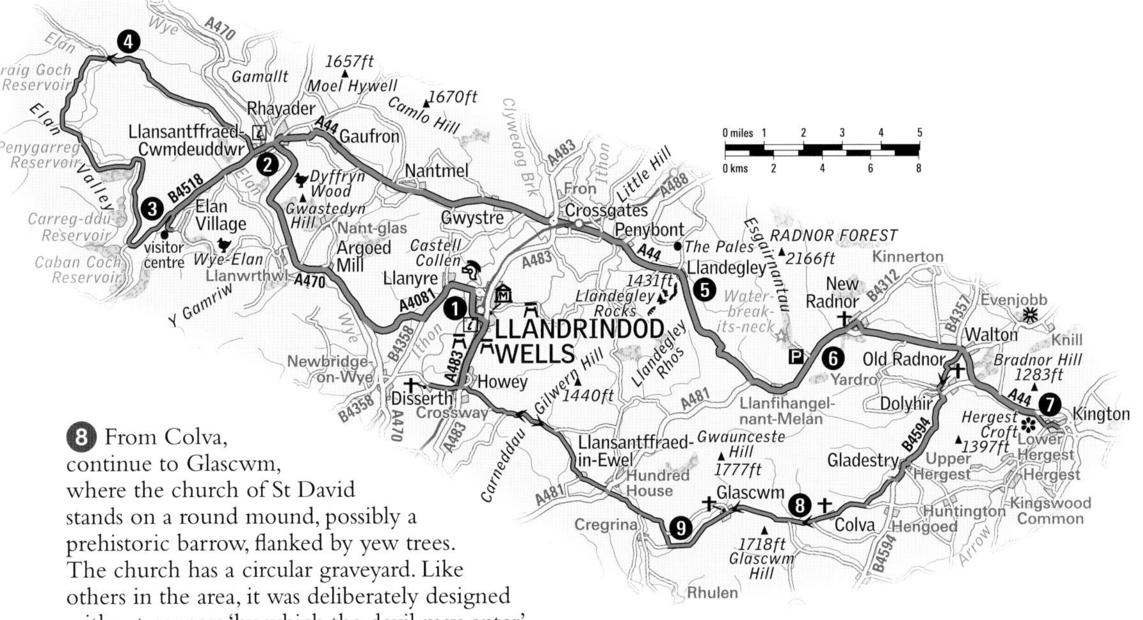

8 From Colva, continue to Glascwm, where the church of St David stands on a round mound, possibly a prehistoric barrow, flanked by yew trees. The church has a circular graveyard. Like others in the area, it was deliberately designed without corners 'by which the devil may enter'.

Glascwm to Llandrindod Wells

9 About 2 miles beyond Glascwm turn right on to a minor road signposted to Hundred House, and continue to the crossroads with the A481. Go straight on, via Llansantffraed-in-Elwel and high ground to the south of Gillwern Hill, to a T-junction with the A483. Turn left and immediately right to Disserth, where the little church, with its thick walls and 16th-century roof, has hardly been touched by time. Return to the A483 and turn left to Llandrindod Wells.

NORTH & MID WALES

9 ABERYSTWYTH

TOUR LENGTH 60 miles

Cliffs, coastal flats, dunes and saltmarshes stretch to the north, while the wooded valleys, gorges and waterfalls of the rugged Cambrian Mountains form a diverse landscape inland. Lakes and reservoirs attract wildfowl as well as harbouring power stations.

Aberystwyth to Ynyslas

1 At first sight, Aberystwyth is a Victorian seaside resort, with a grand promenade, beaches, a pier and donkey rides. Yet the town – home to the University of Wales, the National Library of Wales, the Ceredigion Museum and an arts centre – is primarily a centre of learning and culture. On its south side, the ruins of Edward I's castle stand at the mouth of the River Rheidol. On the north side, a Victorian cliff railway scales Constitution Hill.

Leave Aberystwyth on the A487 towards Machynlleth. Turn left on to the B4572, winding through Clarach and over hills to descend steeply into Borth, where an Animalarium houses a collection of small mammals, birds and reptiles. Three miles of golden sands stretch north.

2 At the junction with the B4353 turn left for Ynyslas and Tre'r-ddol along the seafront, passing Cors Fochno, or Borth bog, on the right. Keep straight on through Ynyslas, following an unsignposted road for 1 mile, to reach Ynyslas Nature Reserve. There is a car park by the beach.

Ynyslas to Furnace

3 Return to the B4353 and turn left, following the road to its junction with the A487, on the edge of Tre'r-ddol. Turn left on to the A487, climbing along the edge of the Cambrian Mountains. Continue for nearly 3 miles to Furnace, where the 18th-century Dyfi Furnace is powered by a water wheel, driven by the River Einion.

4 A short distance farther up the A487, turn left on to a small road to the Ynys-hir Nature Reserve. Waymarked trails lead through 405ha (1,000 acres) of woodland to freshwater pools and saltmarshes, home to wildfowl and woodland birds.

Furnace to Vale of Rheidol

5 From Furnace, take the A487 to Tal-y-bont and turn left on a minor road. Follow signs to Bont-goch and Nant-y-moch reservoir. After ¼ mile, fork left towards Nant-y-moch. The road leads on to heathland and passes a steep drop on the left.

ABERYSTWYTH

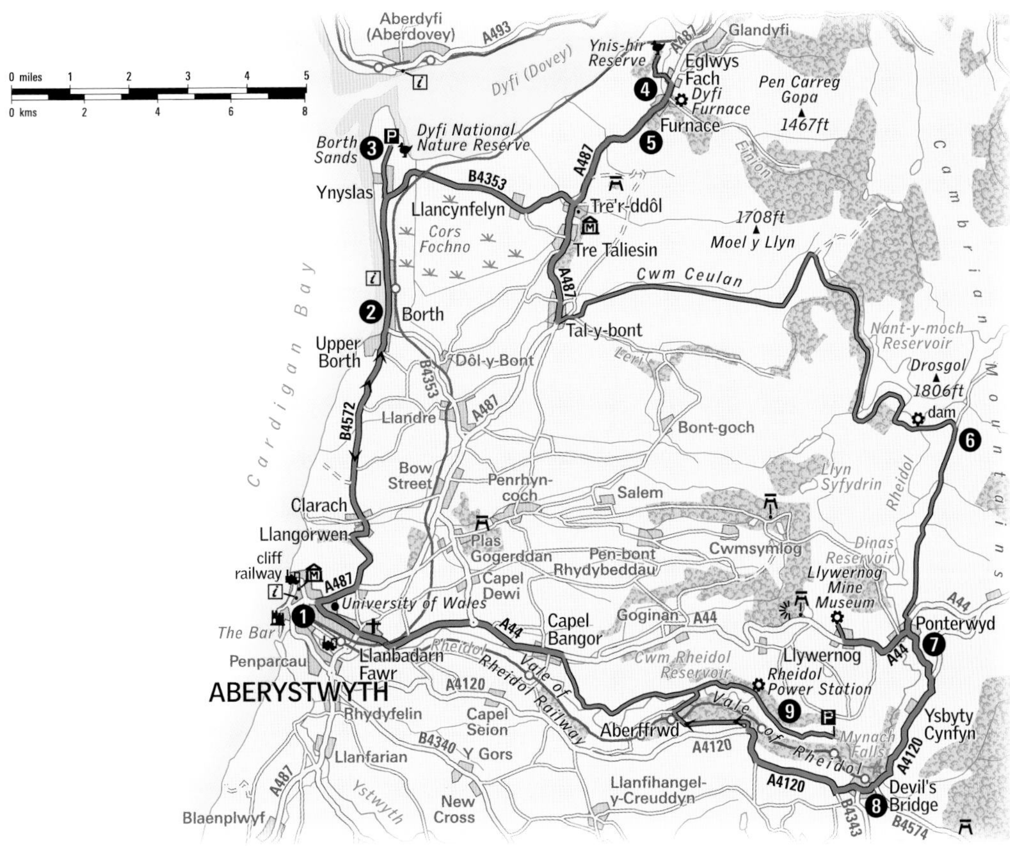

After another 3 miles, the road winds through a forestry plantation before Nant-y-moch reservoir comes into view. The lake is part of the largest hydroelectric scheme operating in England and Wales. Skirt the edge of the reservoir through wild, open country and go over the dam across the River Rheidol.

6 At a T-junction, turn right, passing to the left of Dinas Reservoir. In Ponterwyd turn left, then right at the T-junction on to the A44 and continue for about 1 mile. Turn right to Llywernog Mine Museum. As well as the museum, there is a narrow-gauge tramway, heritage trail and a panning area.

7 Return to Ponterwyd and turn right on to the A4120 to Devil's Bridge. This is where the River Mynach drops 90m (300ft) into the River Rheidol. The resulting Mynach Falls plunge beneath three bridges, built one on top of the other in the 12th, 18th and 20th centuries.

The village is named after the legendary origins of the oldest bridge. The story goes that this was built by the Devil so that a local woman could cross the gorge to retrieve her cow (how the cow got to the other side is not mentioned). His condition was that the soul of the first living creature to cross the bridge would be his. The woman threw some food across for a dog to chase and so the Devil was thwarted, and had to be content with a canine rather than a human prize.

8 Continue on the A4120 for 2 miles and turn right, descending to Aberffrwd. After crossing the Vale of Rheidol Railway, which runs through outstanding scenery between Aberystwyth and Devil's Bridge, turn sharp right towards Capel Bangor and left across the River Rheidol. The Cwm Rheidol Reservoir is on the right.

Turn right on the other side of the bridge, passing Rheidol Power Station, which is open for guided tours in summer. Some beautiful, although fairly hard, walks start from the end of the road past the power station, along a steep-sided wooded valley.

Vale of Rheidol to Aberystwyth

9 Return past the power station and go on to Capel Bangor. At the T-junction, turn left on to the A44 to Aberystwyth. In Llanbadarn, take a right turn to visit Padarn's church – the site of the oldest bishopric in Wales, which was founded in the 6th century.

A drive in the clouds

A trip through Hellfire Pass is an experience never to be forgotten, magnificent and exciting, but not for the faint-hearted.

Anyone with a weak stomach or a poor head for heights should not attempt to drive Bwlch y Groes – or even think about cycling it unless super-fit. This famous and fearsome mountain route, the highest public road in Wales, runs south from Llanuwchllyn, near the southern end of Bala Lake, to Dinas Mawddwy on the A470 Machynlleth-Dolgellau road. In fair weather it takes well under an hour to drive it, but allow half a day to get full value out of the stunning views. The whole 12 mile stretch across the mountains is popularly known as Bwlch y Groes, but strictly speaking the name – the 'Pass of the Cross' – refers to the pass at the summit, where the road tops out at 545m (1,788ft) between the flat-topped hump of Waun Drawsfan to the east and the boggy moor of Clipiau Duon, the black crags, to the west.

Some say that Bwlch y Groes was beaten out as a pilgrim path by penitents travelling through the mountains; others believe that the road was built by the Romans to service a signal tower at the summit. It was certainly used as a drove road in times past; and it always presented a challenge

The road steepens and mighty views extend over the moors and hills.
BWLCH Y GROES

to travellers, the combination of fierce gradients and unpredictable weather earning it the grim nickname of 'Hellfire Pass'.

Gentle start

From Llanuwchllyn, the road is single track, with the hog-backed bulk of Aran Benllyn and Aran Fawddwy soon coming to dominate the view to the right. These fine mountains stand like a wall across the narrow valley of the Afon Twrch, which drops away to the right. The ascent itself climbs fairly gently at first, then steepens, rising about 213m (700ft) in 2 miles before reaching the wooden crucifix that marks the summit. Mighty views extend over the moors and hills to Cadair Idris and the long snaking cleft of the Dyfi Valley.

Bwlch y Groes is a place with a strange, sometimes eerie atmosphere, particularly when mists of low cloud swirl across. Odd tales have clung to the pass since time out of mind. At an Eisteddfod held at Dinas Mawddwy, down at the southern foot of the road, on August 2, 1855, full credence was given to the countless local stories of the fairies or fair folk, who were known to frequent the hills and moors around Bwlch y Groes: 'The side of Aran Fawddwy is a great place for the fair family: they are ever at it playing their games on the hillsides about this spot. It is said that they are numberless likewise about Bwlch y Groes. Once a boy crossed over near the approach of night, one summer eve, from the Gadfa to Mawddwy, and on his return he saw near Aber Rhiwlech a swarm of the little family dancing away full pelt. The boy began to run, with two of the maidens in pursuit of him, entreating him to stay; but Robin, for that was his name, kept running, and the two elves failed altogether to catch him, otherwise he would have been taken a prisoner of love. There are plenty of their dancing-rings to be seen on the hillsides between Aber Rhiwlech and Bwlch y Groes.'

Steep descent

The Afon Dyfi springs from the mountain lake of Creiglyn Dyfi, under the crags of Aran Fawddwy 3 miles to the west, and the real thrill of Bwlch y Groes comes as the road starts down the far side to meet the infant river. The southward slope is truly scary, a tarmac ribbon in the hillside that plunges away at gradients up to 1 in 4, dropping well over 1,000ft in not much more than a mile. Care is needed to negotiate the slopes and bends, and the sheep nonchalantly chewing the cud in the middle of the road, so imagine how tough it must have been for car manufacturers' test drivers in the 1920s, who would drive new models up this tremendous hill to prove their capabilities – for example, a prototype of the Rover 14/45, brought out in 1924, made 50 consecutive ascents of Bwlch y Groes in 12 hours. As for the ultra-competitive cyclists who took part in the round-Britain Milk Races of the 1970s and 1980s, picture their pain as they sweated up this purgatorial treadmill of a road. Now renamed the Tour of Britain, the cycle race has followed other routes in recent years, but Bwlch y Groes remains one of the ultimate tests of a determined amateur two-wheeler.

The road levels out through the farming hamlet of Llanymawddwy to hug the right bank of the river all the way down to Dinas Mawddwy, deep among the trees in the bottom of the Dyfi Valley. From here, proper heroes turn round and go all the way back up again, just to show they can. Mere mortals make for Malwydd and a restorative snifter in the Brigands Inn.

NORTH & MID WALES

10 DOLGELLAU

TOUR LENGTH 45 miles

The Snowdonia National Park is a realm of rock, torrent and tide, and this route amply demonstrates the timeless appeal of such a magnificent landscape, dominated by the precipitous slopes of Cadair Idris.

Dolgellau to Llanfihangel

1 Built of hard, grey dolerite and slate, Dolgellau glistens almost black in the rain, and shines like gunmetal in the sun. But the town's sober suit is immaculately cut and has considerable style – more than 200 of its buildings are listed as being of historic or architectural interest. Many of these lie in a maze of narrow lanes off Eldon Square, where old shopfronts and mills beside the tumbling River Aran testify to Dolgellau's history as a centre of the woollen industry.

Follow the one-way system through Dolgellau to the T-junction in front of Clifton House Hotel and turn left. Continue to a T-junction and turn right on to the A470 towards Machynlleth.

After 2 miles turn left on to the B4416 towards Brithdir and park in a layby on the left, a short distance beyond a one-way bridge. Walk back along the road, towards the bridge, and turn right on to a signposted path. A little way down the path, the awe-inspiring sight of the Afon Clywedog, thundering down a deep wooded gorge, comes into view.

2 Return to the A470 and turn left. At Cross Foxes Inn turn right on to the A487, which leads to the head of a mountain pass. A layby on the right near the top of the pass is the only place to stop and admire the view.

At the bottom of the pass turn right on to the B4405 then immediately right again, into Dol Idris car park and picnic site. A short stroll along a waymarked track leads to a beautiful woodland torrent at the base of Cadair Idris – mountain chair of a mythical giant.

3 Continue on the B4405 along the side of Tal-y-llyn, where St Mary's Church, at the far end of the lake, contains a memorial to Jenny Jones, who followed her husband to the battle of Waterloo and treated his wounds.

Drive on to Abergynolwyn and turn right towards Llanegryn. The road runs through a short narrow pass before reaching a T-junction by a telephone kiosk. Turn right, passing Castell y Bere, the ruins of a 12th-century Welsh castle, hidden among trees. A little farther on, the road comes to Llanfihangel-y-pennant church, St Michael's. Opposite is a car park and from there, hilly tracks and paths lead around the head of the Dysynni Valley.

Llanfihangel to Penmaenpool

4 Return to the T-junction by the telephone kiosk and drive straight on towards Llanegryn. Craig yr Aderyn (Birds' Rock) is unmistakable ahead – a dizzyingly high inland cliff surrounded by wheeling cormorants.

5 Turn right on a road that cuts across the valley below Craig yr Aderyn, to Llanegryn. At a T-junction beyond the village turn right on to the A493 towards Dolgellau. The road meets the coast, where a steep lane on the left, immediately beyond a layby and postbox, leads to the ancient church of St Celynin. The walls are decorated with fragments of a medieval fresco.

6 The fields on either side of the coast road are crisscrossed with stone walls, coloured pale grey with lichen. Beyond Llwyngwril the road climbs over a headland to reveal the great sweep of Cardigan Bay, then drops to the coast at Friog before swinging inland to follow the Mawddach valley. At Penmaenpool, where the road reaches the side of the estuary, turn sharp left towards a toll bridge, then immediately right into a car park. The surrounding land is a nature reserve run by the RSPB.

Penmaenpool to Fiddler's Elbow

7 Stay on the A493 and at the T-junction with the A470 turn left. Cross the bridge over the Mawddach. Turn left at a roundabout on to the A496 towards Barmouth. Continue for ¾ mile beyond a side road to Penmaenpool toll bridge, then turn right into Fiddler's Elbow layby and picnic place. A steep footpath leads to RSPB managed woodland and heathland, a haven for butterflies as well as birds, and carpeted with bluebells in spring.

Fiddler's Elbow to Dolgellau

8 Drive back to the A470, turning right, for Dolgellau, at the roundabout. Take the first minor road on the left to the ruins of 12th-century Cymer Abbey (Cadw) and old Mawddach bridge (closed to traffic). Return to the A470, turn left. Take the first road on the left back to Dolgellau.

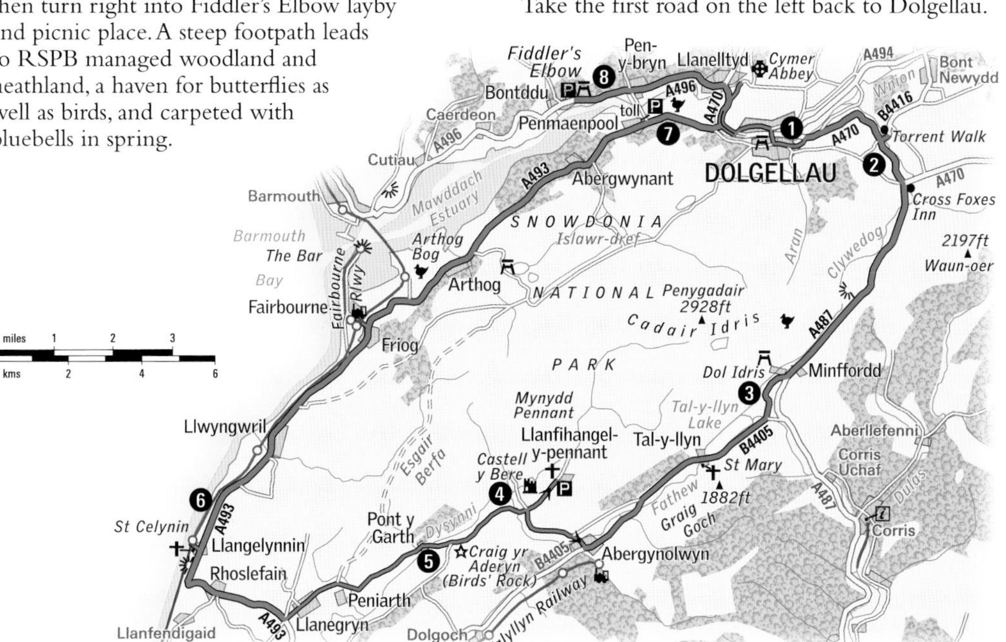

CADAIR IDRIS

NORTH & MID WALES

11 CRICCIETH

TOUR LENGTH 68 miles

This route along the sandy fringes of the Lleyn Peninsula passes a gathering place for pilgrims, a once prosperous fishing village and an old well at one time thought to have restorative powers.

Criccieth to Pwllheli

1 A quiet seaside town, Criccieth lies under the sturdy walls of its castle (Cadw), begun in 1230 by Llewellyn the Great and passed between Welsh princes and English kings over the next 200 years. Wide beaches – part sand, part pebble – attracted Victorian developers, who turned the town into a popular resort.

To start the drive, take the A497 towards Pwllheli, and after 1 mile turn right to Llanystumdwy, where David Lloyd George, British prime minister from 1916 to 1922, spent his early years. A museum and memorial are open to the public.

2 Go through Llanystumdwy, crossing a stone bridge over the River Dwyfor, to the junction with the A497 and turn right. About ½ mile past a holiday camp on the left, turn right to Penarth Fawr (Cadw), a 15th-century hall-house with one huge room open to the rafters.

Continue on the A497 to the resort, port and market town of Pwllheli, which has beaches on both sides of its natural, almost land-locked, harbour.

Pwllheli to Porth Dinllaen

3 At a roundabout on the far side of Pwllheli, take the first exit on to the A499. At Llanbedrog, which is dominated by the headland of Mynydd Tir-y-Cwmwd, turn right on to the B4413. About ½ mile beyond Mynytho, turn left towards Rhiw on a road that winds steeply downhill towards the sea. At a T-junction turn left over a causeway towards Rhiw and continue to a bay, known from its many shipwrecks as Hell's Mouth.

As the road twists and turns round a hill, turn right on a narrow road to Plas-yn-Rhiw (NT), a medieval, Tudor and Georgian farmhouse. Its gardens, laid out in the 1820s, cling to the hillside, with views over Hell's Mouth.

4 Return to the main road and turn right to the ancient hamlet of Aberdaron. From the 5th or 6th centuries, pilgrims have waited here for boats to carry them over to Bardsey Island, off the tip of the peninsula.

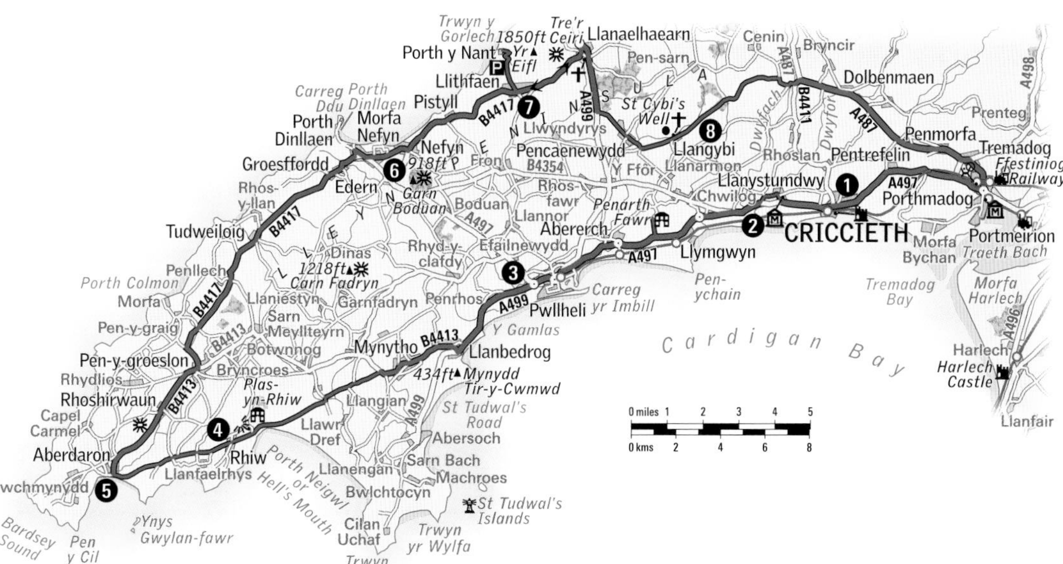

❺ Cross the bridge and turn right over the next bridge on to the B4413. At Pen-y-groeslon, turn left on to the B4417 towards Nefyn. After ¾ mile, the road bends sharp right over moorland. On the outskirts of Morfa Nefyn, turn left towards Porth Dinllaen. In this once busy port, a few houses face the sea across a quiet sandy beach.

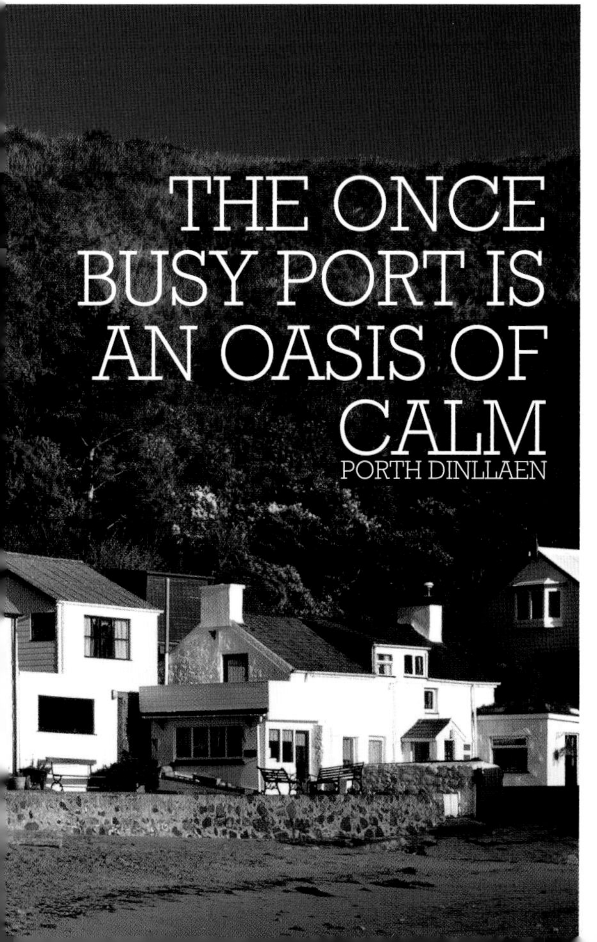

Porth Dinllaen to Llithfaen

❻ Continue on the B4417, turning left in Nefyn, beside hills scarred with quarry faces once worked for granite. At Llithfaen, turn left at the crossroads on to a minor road, marked Gendlaeth. After ½ mile the road reaches a car park. A steep hill on the left leads down the side of a ravine to Porth y Nant, an old quarry village, now a Welsh language centre, set in a spectacular site.

Llithfaen to Criccieth

❼ Return to Llithfaen and turn left on to the B4417. Turn right at Llanaelhaearn village on to the A499 towards Pwllheli. After 2 miles, turn left on to a minor road, signposted to St Cybi's Well. Go straight over the crossroads at Pencaenewydd and at the next crossroads turn left.

After 1 mile, turn left on to the Bryncir road in Llangybi to find the parish church on the left. A path leads from the churchyard to St Cybi's Well, located in an ancient roofless building with beehive vaulting. The well was once thought to cure blindness, lameness, warts and all manner of other ailments.

❽ Continue through Llangybi. After 3½ miles, turn right at a T-junction, then left and left again on to the B4411. At the junction with the A487 turn right and follow the road through Tremadog, the birthplace in 1888 of T.E. Lawrence – Lawrence of Arabia. Continue to the resort of Porthmadog, passing the Welsh Highland Railway. Drive on beyond the roundabout to the Harbour Station, the start of the narrow-gauge Ffestiniog Railway. This opened in 1836 to bring slate from the Blaenau Ffestiniog quarries to Porthmadog for export. Return to the roundabout, take the A497 and follow it to Criccieth.

NORTH & MID WALES

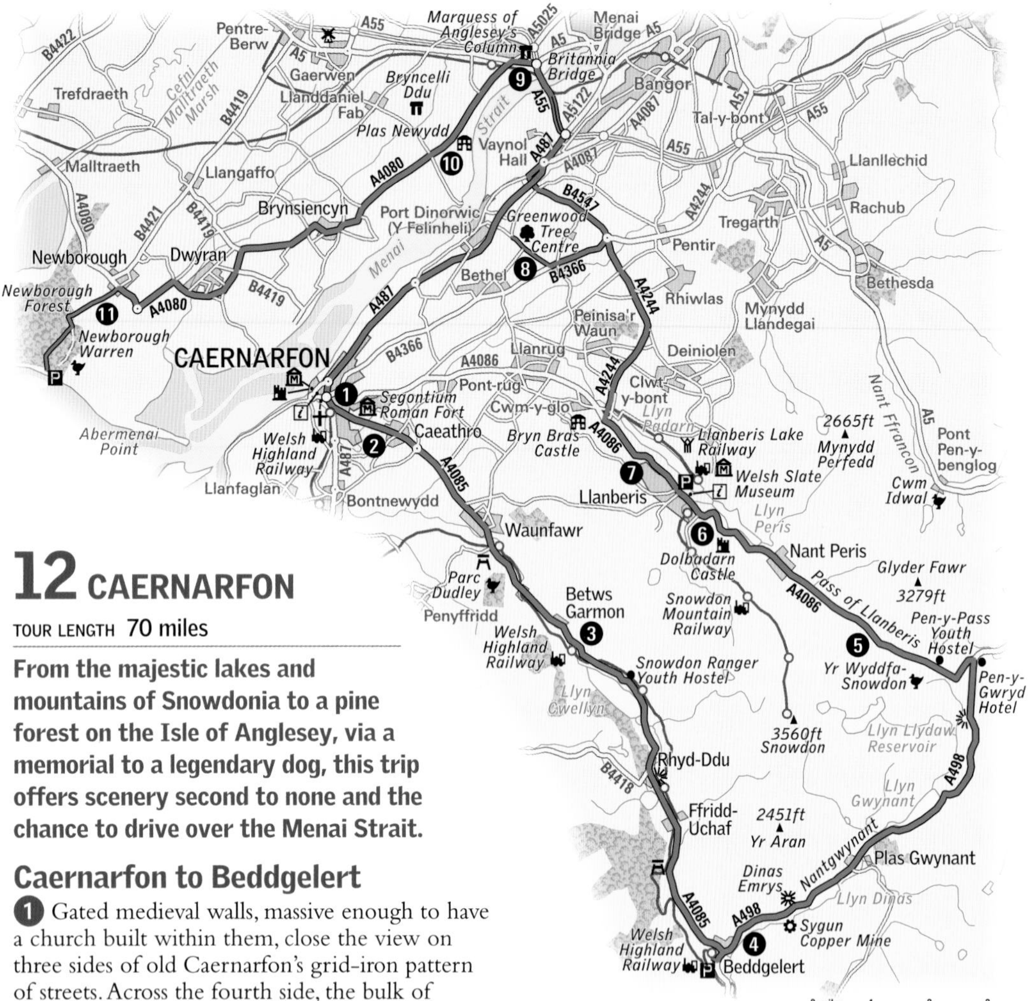

12 CAERNARFON

TOUR LENGTH 70 miles

From the majestic lakes and mountains of Snowdonia to a pine forest on the Isle of Anglesey, via a memorial to a legendary dog, this trip offers scenery second to none and the chance to drive over the Menai Strait.

Caernarfon to Beddgelert

❶ Gated medieval walls, massive enough to have a church built within them, close the view on three sides of old Caernarfon's grid-iron pattern of streets. Across the fourth side, the bulk of Edward I's castle towers above a broad quay from which a century ago ships carried off slate to roof the houses of Britain's burgeoning cities. The story of the town's heyday is told in a maritime museum beside the Victoria Dock.

Take the A487 towards Porthmadog, then turn left on to the A4085 to Beddgelert. After 1 mile, there is roadside parking for Segontium, the remains of one of Rome's main garrisons in Wales (closed on Mondays).

❷ The route now follows the old Roman road, dipping down to give a view of the mountains ahead. Just past Waunfawr, a picnic site on the right is the entry to Parc Dudley Nature Reserve, with a waymarked woodland walk.

❸ Beyond Betws Garmon the road runs beside Llyn Cwellyn, the conifers on the far slopes mirrored in its placid waters. The Snowdon Ranger Youth Hostel marks the start of a popular walk to Snowdon's summit. At Rhyd-Ddu, the start of another summit path, a layby gives a fine view of Snowdon. At Beddgelert turn right across the bridge, signposted to Porthmadog, and follow signs to a car park opposite the Royal Goat Hotel. A lane beside the bridge leads to Gelert's Grave, a memorial erected in the 18th century to mark the alleged burial place of a dog famed in Welsh legend.

Beddgelert to Llanberis

❹ Cross the bridge and turn right on to the A498 towards Capel Curig. After 1½ miles, a right turn leads to Sygun Copper Mine, where visitors are led through a honeycomb of old copper workings. The road passes the wooded mound of Dinas Emrys, and runs beside the blue waters of Llyn Dinas. It then follows the eastern shore of Llyn Gwynant before climbing steeply to give spectacular views across the Gwynant valley. Continue to the Pen-y-Gwryd Hotel, where the team who first conquered Everest in 1953 stayed during their training. Turn left on to the A4086 up to Pen-y-Pass Youth Hostel, where sheep wander among parked cars and walkers set out on the Miner's Track or Pig Track up Snowdon.

5 The road snakes down through the dramatic Pass of Llanberis between high shoulders of rock, raised by ancient volcanoes and shaped by glaciers. A calmer view opens up as the road skirts Llyn Peris, and as it nears the lake there is parking space for riverside walks.

6 Continue to Llanberis, passing the Snowdon Mountain Railway and staying on the A4086 to the public car park on the right next to the car park for the 'Electric Mountain' centre. The National Slate Museum can be reached by crossing the bridge over the river that joins Llyn Peris and Llyn Padarn.

Llanberis to Britannia Bridge

7 Continue on the A4086, then turn right on to the A4244 towards Bangor. At the next roundabout, a left turn on to the B4366 leads to the Greenwood Tree Centre, a 'hands-on' exploration of the world of trees and wood.

8 Return to the roundabout, turn left and follow the B4547 under a road bridge, then right to another roundabout. Take the first exit here on to the A487, and at the next roundabout take the A5 signposted to 'Holyhead, Britannia Bridge'. The Britannia road bridge runs on top of Robert Stephenson's railway bridge of 1850, which was burnt out in 1970 but restored two years later. Thomas Telford's elegant Menai suspension bridge of 1826 can be seen to the right.

Britannia Bridge to Newborough Forest

9 Just beyond the bridge turn left on to the A4080. The Marquess of Anglesey's Column rears above trees on the right. A platform at the top of 115 spiral steps offers a panoramic view across the Menai Strait to the Snowdonia peaks. The column commemorates the 1st Marquess of Anglesey, cavalry leader at the Battle of Waterloo, whose estate of Plas Newydd (NT) is reached 1½ miles farther on. The house is encircled by gardens and woodland, sweeping down to the Menai Strait.

10 Continue on the A4080 to the crossroads in Newborough, and turn left to Llanddwyn Beach. A gap in the dunes at the seaward end of the car park leads on to the sandy beach. On the right is the long, low hump of Llanddwyn Island and behind the dunes stand the Corsican pines of Newborough Forest, created in the 1950s on 283ha (700 acres) of dunes. The beach gets more shingly towards Llanddwyn, and has a variety of seashells.

Newborough Forest to Caernarfon

11 Return on the A4080 by the outward route to Britannia Bridge. Cross the bridge and turn right on to the A487 back to Caernarfon.

LLYN GWYNANT

NORTH & MID WALES

13 CONWY

TOUR LENGTH 48 miles

Starting off from the old town, this route goes through a restored Victorian spa and mill village on its way up to a mountain lake set among densely wooded hills. It wanders back through the Vale of Conwy, via beautiful Bodnant Gardens and a cheerful seaside town.

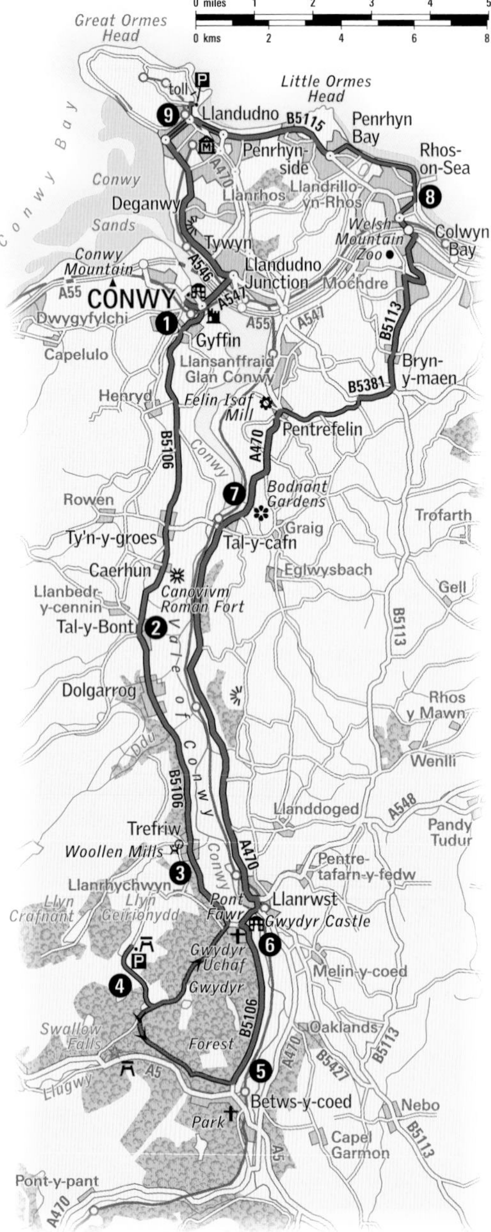

Conwy to Llyn Geirionydd

❶ Edward I's 13th-century fortress (Cadw), seemingly impregnable with its eight huge round towers, dominates Conwy. Contained by fortified walls to the west, and the River Conwy to the east, the ancient town has 200 listed buildings, including the 14th-century Aberconwy House and the Elizabethan Plas Mawr. Three bridges span the river – Telford's delicate suspension bridge, Stephenson's tubular railway bridge and the 1950s road bridge.

To start the drive, follow the one-way system and take the B5106, passing the castle on the left, towards Trefriw.

After 5 miles, at Caerhun, a lane on the left leads to the 13th-century St Mary's Church, which stands on the site of a Roman fort, Canovium, overlooking the wide Vale of Conwy. St Mary's has an unusual double bell cote, but just one bell.

❷ Continue through Tal-y-Bont and Dolgarrog. Shortly before Trefriw, on the right, are the wells that made the village a popular Victorian spa, now restored. In the village, woollen mills produce traditional Welsh bedspreads and tweeds, continuing an industry started centuries ago.

❸ Follow the B5106 for another 1½ miles, and just before Llanrwst turn right, signposted to Betws-y-coed, and immediately right again on to a narrow lane, signposted to Llanrhychwyn. Follow the lane up forested slopes, ignoring the right turn to Llanrhychwyn. After 2 miles, turn right, signposted to Llyn Geirionydd, a large lake, which comes into view on the left. There is a car park on the right.

The placid lake is bordered with Forestry Commission plantations. The trees come down almost to the water's edge but there is a path along the side of the lake.

Llyn Geirionydd to Llandudno

❹ Return to the T-junction, turn right, and after ¼ mile turn left on to a very steep downhill lane. After an S-bend, the lane leads through tall Douglas fir trees beside the River Llugwy. Continue into Betws-y-coed, a Victorian village at the confluence of the Conwy and Llugwy rivers, with historic bridges and waterfalls.

❺ Turn left on to the B5106, following the signs to Llanrwst. After 3 miles, the road passes close to Gwydyr Uchaf on the left. This is a small 17th-century chapel, famed for its painted roof. Gwydr Castle, a fortified medieval manor house, built round a courtyard, is on the right. The house is open to the public at certain times during the summer. Check before visiting.

LLANDUDNO

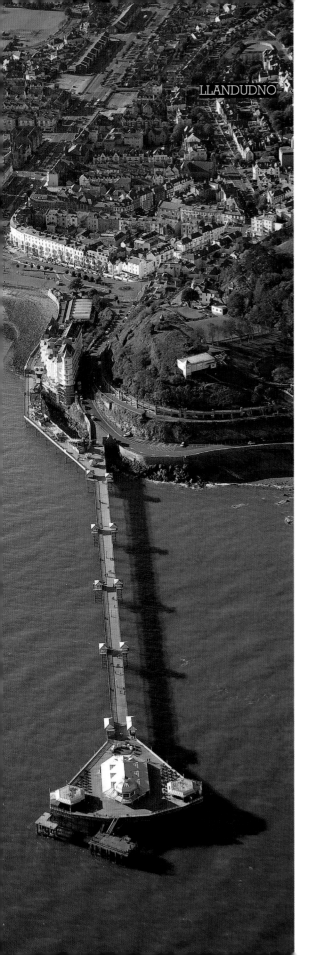

6 Continue to a T-junction and turn right, crossing the 17th-century Pont Fawr bridge into Llanrwst. Turn left immediately over the bridge and follow the A470, signposted to Llandudno, downriver. After about 6 miles, on the right, as the estuary widens, lie Bodnant Gardens (NT) – 32ha (80 acres) of the Conwy Valley, renowned for rhododendrons, camellias, magnolias, azaleas and a magnificent laburnum arch.

7 Soon after the gardens, and their large nursery, also on the right, the road enters the unmarked village of Pentrefelin. Turn second right in the village over a bridge, and almost immediately second right again up a very narrow, unsignposted lane. The lane rises and falls for 1½ miles to reach a T-junction. Turn left, and after 100m turn right on to the B5381. At a third T-junction, turn left on to the B5113 towards Colwyn Bay.

After 2 miles, turn right down Pen y Bryn Road, following the signs to Colwyn Bay. The road bends sharp left into King's Drive. At a 'no entry' sign, follow the route to the right and take the first left down Grosvenor Road, then turn left on to Conwy Road. At the roundabout, turn right over the A55. Take the fourth exit at the next roundabout, signposted to Rhos-on-Sea and the promenade.

8 At the seafront, turn left, following the coast road through Rhos-on-Sea and Penrhyn Bay. At a roundabout, continue ahead on the B5115, signposted to Llandudno, where the museum has artefacts dating back to Roman times. Continue along the seafront in Llandudno and park at the end of the promenade, near the ski centre – convenient for the cable car, tramway and pier.

The cable car is the longest passenger cable car in Britain, and it runs to the summit of the Great Orme, a 207m (679ft) hill, riddled with copper mine workings that date back to the Bronze Age. Uncovered in 1987, the tunnels and galleries are open to the public, including a huge chamber that is more than 3,500 years old.

Another way to reach the top of the hill, which has panoramic views and nature trails, is on the Great Orme Tramway. Opened in 1902, this is one of just three cable-operated tramways in the world that are still working (the other two are in San Francisco and Lisbon). The Victorian pier is Grade II listed and is unusual in having a 45 degree turn a little way along it.

Llandudno to Conwy

9 Return along the seafront. Turn first right at the war memorial, go straight on at the roundabout and left at the next roundabout on to the A546, signposted to Deganwy. Go through Deganwy and turn right at the roundabout over the bridge into Conwy.

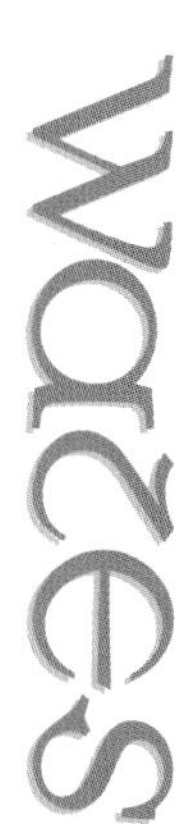

NORTH & MID WALES

14 RUTHIN

TOUR LENGTH 58 miles

A country drive, offering vistas that stretch from wild Wales to the Marches, and including the Horseshoe Pass, this route also takes in a lead mine, an ironworks museum and an aqueduct built by Thomas Telford.

Ruthin to Loggerheads

1 Tudor buildings around St Peter's Square and along the streets radiating from it characterise the peaceful market town of Ruthin, which is ringed by wooded hills. But today's serenity belies an often violent past. King Arthur is said to have had a rival in romance beheaded on the large stone block that stands in a corner of the square, while in 1400 the Welsh freedom fighter Owain Glyndwr laid a long but unsuccessful siege to the town's Norman castle. Cromwell had more success, defeating a Royalist garrison and razing the fortress – the modern Ruthin Castle is a hotel built in Victorian times.

To start the drive, take the A494 towards Mold. The road climbs steeply up the Clwydian hills, then descends more gently to Loggerheads. A country park is signposted to the left.

Loggerheads to Erddig

2 Return to the A494 and turn left to Gwernymynydd. Turn right immediately before the Swan Inn towards the village of Nercwys. Turn right at the T-junction on the edge of Nercwys and carry on to the crossroads in the centre of Eryrys. Then turn left and continue to a T-junction with the B5430 in Graianrhyd. Turn left. Continue through Rhydtalog to the crossroads with the A525 at Four Crosses.

Drive straight on, staying on the B5430 for another 1½ miles to a T-junction with the A525 on the edge of Coedpoeth. Turn right then take the first turn on the right, joining the B5426. The road passes an industrial archaeology trail, laid out around the restored engine house at Minera Lead Mine.

3 Less than a mile farther on turn left to Bersham, where a left turn in the village centre leads to a museum in the old Bersham Ironworks, a famous 18th-century cannon foundry.

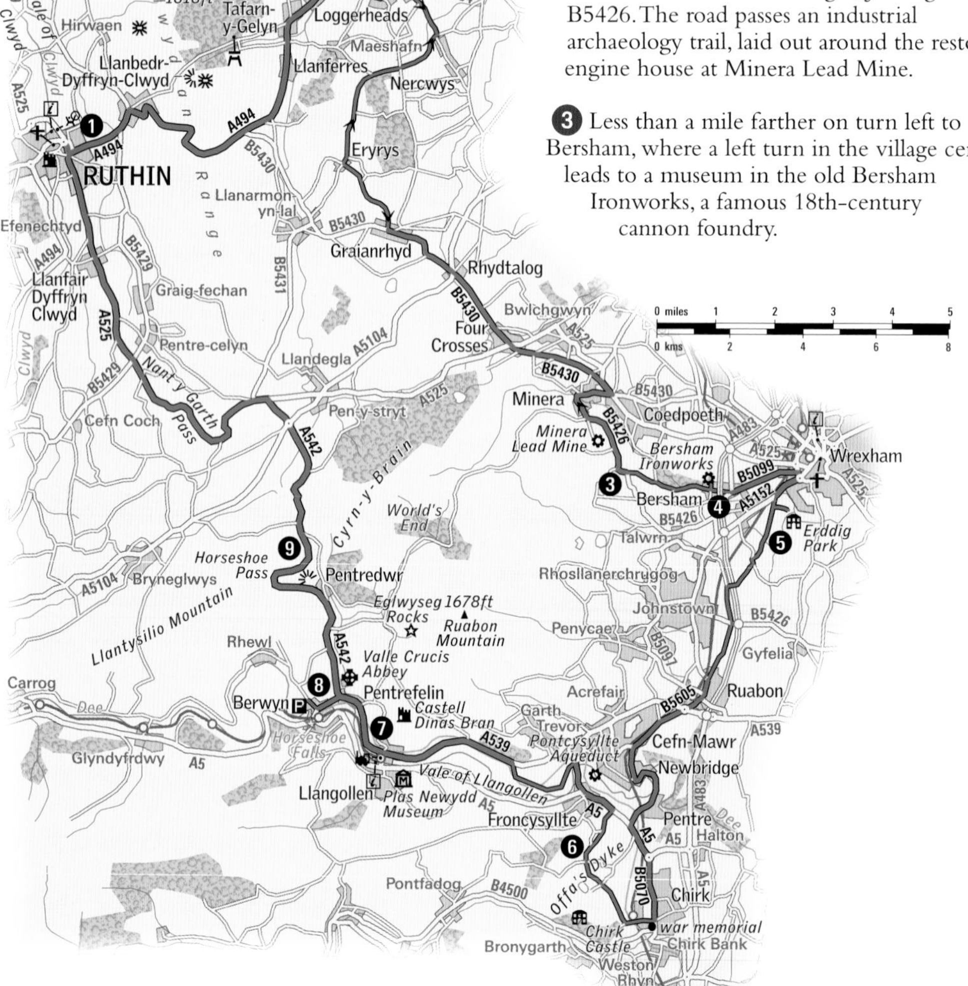

PONTCYSYLLTE AQUEDUCT

4 Return to the village centre, turn left and follow the road under the Wrexham bypass, past a junction with the B5098, and carry on along the B5099 to a junction with Victoria Road (the A5152). Turn right, then at the roundabout turn right again, still on the A5152, for a short distance before following a signposted turning on the left to Erddig Park (NT). The country park surrounds Erddig Hall (NT), which has a collection of 18th-century furniture and a walled garden, with a pond, rare fruit trees and an ivy collection.

Erddig to Horseshoe Falls

5 Go back to the road and turn left. Turn left at the next T-junction then immediately right across a bridge over the Wrexham bypass. On the far side of the bridge turn left and go on to join the B5605 and pass through Ruabon. At a roundabout beyond the village continue straight ahead on the B5605, through, through Cefn-Mawr and across the valley of the Dee to a T-junction with the A5. Turn left and follow the signs into Chirk, 2 miles distant.

In the centre of Chirk, turn right by the war memorial, a work by the 20th-century sculptor, engraver and typographer Eric Gill. Continue past the ornate wrought-iron gates of Chirk Castle (NT), on the left, and across a minor crossroads. Offa's Dyke, the earthwork constructed by an 8th-century king of Mercia to mark his frontier with the Welsh, can be seen in fields on the left.

6 Pass a left turn signposted to Nantyr and Pontfadog then fork right on the road marked as unsuitable for long vehicles. Continue downhill to the A5. Turn left and after less than a mile turn right towards Trevor. The road drops steeply in the shadow of the Pontcysyllte Aqueduct, built by master engineer and canal builder Thomas Telford. Cross the bridge over the Dee and immediately turn left to a junction with the A539. Turn left to Llangollen, where the bridge on the left leads into the town.

7 Continue on the A542 towards Ruthin. At Pentrefelin turn left on to the B5103. Fork right where the road divides and stop in the car park on the left. To see the Horseshoe Falls – an elegant curved weir built across the Dee by engineer William Jessop to siphon water into the canal system – walk along the road for a short way and turn off at St Tysilio's Church.

Horseshoe Falls to Ruthin

8 Return to the A542 and turn left. The road climbs the Horseshoe Pass – a long, unfenced section of road giving marvellous views of the Eglwyseg Rocks, an impressive limestone escarpment.

9 Continue beyond the pass to a roundabout and go straight on to a T-junction on the A525. Turn left and drive down the wooded Nant y Garth Pass to return to Ruthin.

KEY

1 Main entry
County boundary
Motorway
Principal A road

Scotland

The scenic drives of Scotland begin in some of the country's great historic towns, before heading out past mountains, monuments, lochs and coastal fringes. Breathtaking landscapes and a rich heritage make touring an unforgettable experience.

NORTH HIGHLANDS & ISLANDS 222-231
CENTRAL 202-221
SOUTHEAST 194-201
SOUTHWEST 188-193
Durness
Thurso
Wick
Lairg
Ullapool
Dornoch
Gairloch
Strathpeffer
Skye
Portree
Kyle of Lochalsh
Loch Ness
Inverness
Nairn
Elgin
Banff
Fraserburgh
Peterhead
Tomintoul
Cairngorms National Park
Aberdeen
Kingussie
Ballater
Braemar
Mallaig
Fort William
Grampian Mountains
Montrose
Pitlochry
Dunkeld
Forfar
Dundee
Mull
Oban
Crianlarich
Crieff
Perth
St Andrews
Loch Lomond & The Trossachs National Park
Callander
Stirling
Kirkcaldy
Lochgilphead
Dumbarton
Linlithgow
Edinburgh
Dunbar
Glasgow
East Kilbride
Irvine
Kilmarnock
Troon
Ayr
Brodick
Peebles
Coldstream
Jedburgh
Hawick
Moffat
Dumfries
Stranraer

SOUTHWEST SCOTLAND

Gentle hills, rocky shores and fabulous coastal scenery are the hallmarks of southwest Scotland, romantic homeland of poet Robert Burns, while in the firth, the Isle of Arran combines serene beauty with rugged charm.

1 DUMFRIES

TOUR LENGTH 57 miles

In this region's mild climate, trees grow tall and forests clothe the foothills of granite mountains. To the south is the sea and the Solway estuary – a place of sandy bays, salmon nets and smugglers' tales.

Dumfries to New Abbey

❶ A compact town of old red sandstone buildings and bridges, Dumfries is the only large settlement in this pastoral corner of Scotland. Robert Burns lived here in the last years of his life, and his favourite hostelry, the Globe Inn, has changed little since his death in 1796.

To start the drive, take the A756 and cross the River Nith by St Michael's Bridge. At the T-junction turn left on to the A710 towards New Abbey, passing through open country on the edge of the Nith valley.

After 2 miles cross a humpback bridge over Cargen Pow and go through Islesteps. The landscape soon becomes more rugged with granite hills covered in bracken and conifer forests. After another 2 miles, turn right to Mabie Forest for its walks and picnic areas. There are also mountain-biking trails.

❷ Continue on the A710 for 2½ miles to the Shambellie House Museum of Costume, on the right. Book illustrator Charles Stewart built up a collection of European fashions as references for his work and donated the costumes and his

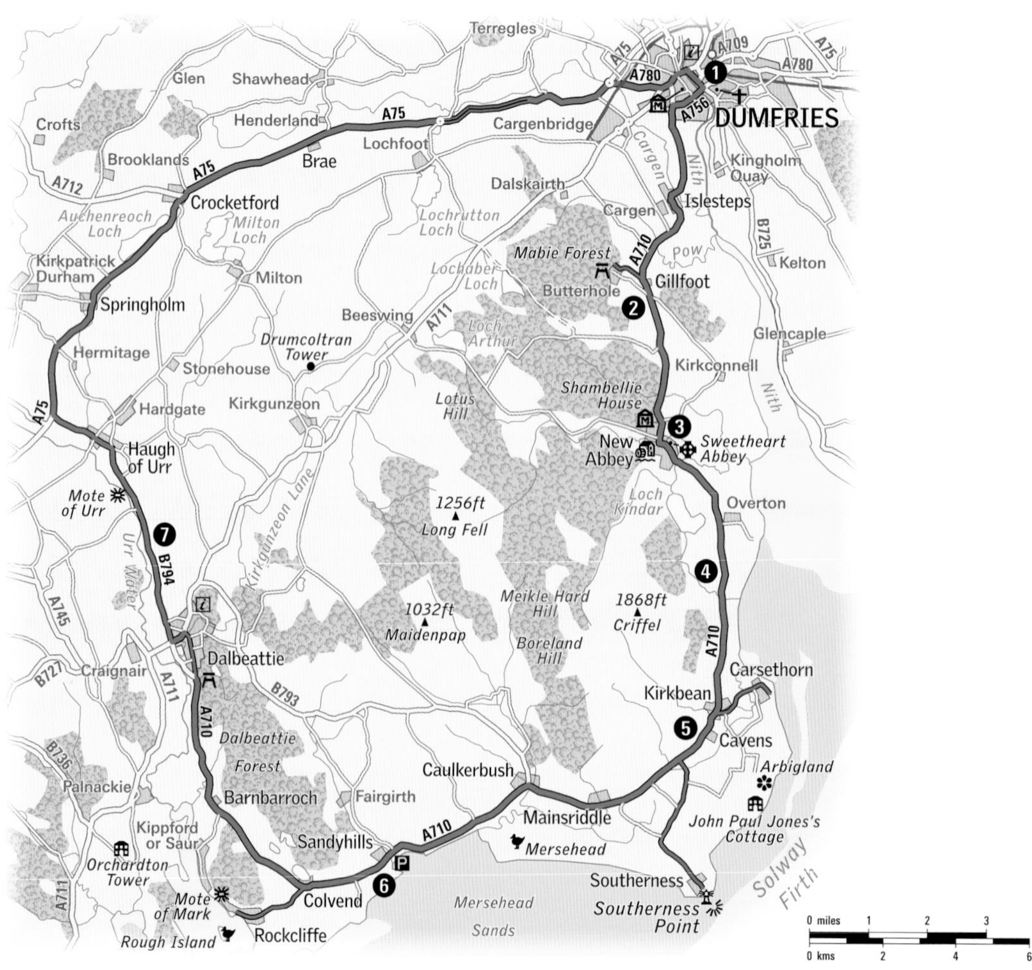

19th-century mansion to the National Museums of Scotland in 1977. The house is open during the summer months.

3 About ½ mile beyond the Shambellie House Museum of Costume is the picturesque village of New Abbey, which has a cobbled square and a working corn mill (HS). Nearby are the ruins of Sweetheart Abbey (HS), where its founder, Lady Devorgilla, lies buried with a casket containing her husband's heart.

New Abbey to Sandyhills

4 Continue on the A710. Drystone walls crisscross the fields and for 3 miles the Solway estuary dominates the view to the left, and the 570m (1,868ft) high Criffel mountain looms to the right. On the other side of the village of Kirkbean, turn left on to a side road. On the right is a turning to the exotic gardens of Arbigland and the birthplace of John Paul Jones, a gardener's son who became an American naval hero. The cottage is now a museum, open during summer. The side road from Kirkbean ends by the sea in the small village of Carsethorn, where the local hostelry is the Steamboat Inn.

5 Return to the A710 and continue for 1 mile. Turn left for Southerness Point, a rocky viewpoint and winter haunt of purple sandpipers. Its old lighthouse is no longer in use. Rejoin the A710 and continue through Caulkerbush, passing, just before the village, a single track road on the left to the RSPB's Mersehead reserve and visitor centre, notable for thousands of wintering barnacle geese, grazing the surrounding fields, and pintail ducks. There are fine views of the estuary across Mersehead Sands, where the tide can sweep into creeks with treacherous speed. Continue to Sandyhills Bay where there is a car park on the left and access to the sandy beach.

Sandyhills to Dumfries

6 Continue on the A710 to Colvend, and turn left for 2 miles to the village of Rockcliffe, which has fine 19th-century buildings dating from its Victorian tourism boom. Return to the A710 and turn left, passing the road to Kippford, a yachting village separated from Rockcliffe by the Mote of Mark, a granite outcrop topped by an earthwork. Regattas are held there in summer.

Go through Barnbarroch, pass Dalbeattie Forest and turn right into Dalbeattie at the confluence of two rivers, Urr Water and the oddly named Kirkgunzeon Lane. Dalbeattie's older houses were built from local granite, which was widely exported until about a century ago. Eddystone Lighthouse is among the many enduring Dalbeattie granite structures.

7 From Dalbeattie take the B794 to Haugh of Urr and on past tall trees. At the T-junction turn right on to the A75. After 4 miles the road passes Auchenreoch Loch. At Crocketford, stay on the A75 past the A712 on the left, which leads to the remote heart of Dumfries and Galloway. Continue for 8 miles as trees and mountains give way to rolling pasture, then take the second exit at a third roundabout on to the A780 back to Dumfries.

KIPPFORD

SOUTHWEST SCOTLAND

2 TROON

TOUR LENGTH 69 miles

Long sandy beaches form a golden fringe to a string of famous golf courses, including Royal Troon, while crumbling castles and are reminders of less peaceful times.

Troon to Straiton

1 Troon was one of Scotland's busiest ports in the 19th century, exporting coal. Today, ships are still built in the town at the Ailsa Shipyard, by the yachting marina. Troon's otherwise sedate pace of life is reflected in the elegance of its stone villas and hotels. To start the drive, follow the A759 then the B730 to Dundonald, where a 14th-century castle stands on a hill. Carry on to the junction with the A77, and continue ahead on the B730.

2 After almost 2 miles turn right and fork left uphill to the Barnweil Monument. A Gothic tower commemorates the 13th-century Scottish leader Sir William Wallace, and allegedly marks the spot where he stood during one battle, watching Ayr burn. Return to the B730 and turn right.

3 At the T-junction turn right, then left to Tarbolton, where, in a 17th-century thatched house, Robert Burns founded a debating society, which he called Burns's Bachelors' Club (NTS).

4 Continue on the B730 for about 5 miles to a T-junction. Turn right on to the A70, then left on the B730 between hedged fields. At the A713, turn left, passing the former mining communities of Polnessan, Patna and Waterside. In Waterside, two tall towers of a former ironworks identify the location of the Dunaskin Heritage Centre.

5 Before Dalmellington, turn right on to the B741 and continue to Straiton on the banks of the Water of Girvan. Turn right opposite the Black Bull Inn, and go through the village. After a right-hand bend, look out for a car park on the left. Around 20 miles of paths and tracks lead from this tranquil village, which has a turbulent history. In the late 17th century, government troops garrisoned nearby hunted down Covenanters, who were opposed to the Stuart kings interfering in Presbyterian affairs. The tomb of one 'martyr' can be found in the village churchyard. St Cuthbert's is also noted for its beautiful interior carvings.

CULZEAN CASTLE

Straiton to Alloway

6 Turn left on to the B741, signposted to Crosshill and Maybole, passing historic Blairquhan Castle on the right. The privately owned house and garden are open to the public, but check times before visiting.

After 3 miles, turn right on a minor road to Crosshill then, in the village centre, continue on the B7023 to Maybole, where the 17th-century castle has been restored, but the 14th-century church is in ruins.

7 Follow the B7023, signposted to Maidens. At the junction, keep straight on for Maidens on the A719, and after 2 miles turn right to Culzean Castle (NTS), which started as a medieval tower house and was transformed into a clifftop masterpiece by Robert Adam in about 1780.

8 Return along the A719, passing a junction with the B7023. Soon Ailsa Craig, out to sea, comes into view. A little farther on, the hillside known as the Electric Brae creates the illusion that the road is ascending as it descends. Beyond the brae, turn left to Dunure, where a mainly 13th-century ruined castle remains a forbidding landmark. Here, in 1570, the 4th Earl of Cassillis reputedly suspended the Abbot of Crossraguel Abbey over a fire to force him to sign away his lands.

9 Follow the road to the A719 and turn left towards Ayr, passing a view of the Heads plunging more than 60m (200ft) to the sea. Sandy beaches, three golf courses and a racecourse make Ayr Scotland's main west-coast resort. Continue over a roundabout on the outskirts of the town and, after ½ mile, turn right up Greenfield Avenue to Burns Cottage (NTS), which was built by the poet's father, William. Robert was born there on 25 January 1759 and spent much of his early life in Alloway and Ayr. The surrounding area is being transformed into a Burns National Heritage Park and a new museum is being built.

10 Return to the A719 and turn right. Follow the road across the River Ayr and right to a roundabout. Turn left on to the A79 past Prestwick airport, and just beyond a right-hand bend turn left on to the B749 to return to Troon.

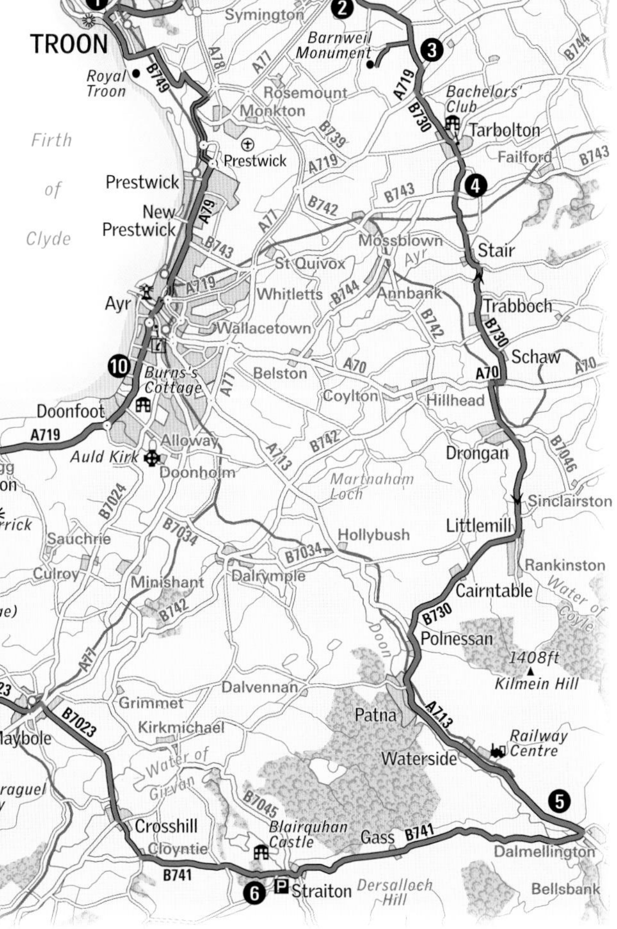

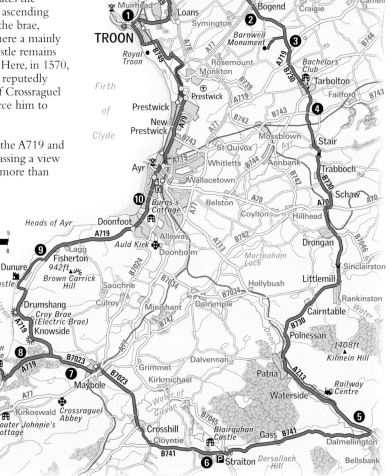

SOUTHWEST SCOTLAND

3 BRODICK

TOUR LENGTH 57 miles

Arran is a divided island, as this scenic journey shows. On one side, gently rolling hills melt away into the distance, while on the other, massed mountain peaks and ridges rear up beyond the sweep of its broad bays.

Brodick to Lamlash

❶ On a map, the Isle of Arran resembles a giant ship anchored in the Firth of Clyde, close to the long quay-like shape of the Mull of Kintyre. The island's capital, the little port of Brodick, lies on the Highland Boundary Fault – the geological fracture that separates Scotland's Lowlands from its mountainous north. Snow-capped in winter, the mountains protect the town from the icy north wind and so contribute to its unexpectedly balmy climate.

The drive starts with a visit to Brodick Castle (NTS), which dates from the 13th century. The castle is open from April to October. Check times before visiting. Leave the centre of town on the A841 towards Corrie. The road runs along the side of a golf course backing the beach, then follows the Glenshurig Burn upstream for a short distance before turning sharp right over a bridge. Continue for 1 mile before turning into the castle's main entrance, and follow the driveway to the car park.

Return to the centre of Brodick and stay on the A841, signposted to Lamlash. The road turns inland, climbing the forested slopes of Meall Buidhe before descending towards the broad sweep of Lamlash Bay, which is almost landlocked by the 305m (1,000ft) high whaleback shape of Holy Island. A cave on the isle's near shore is said to have been the cell of St Molaise, a disciple of St Columba.

Lamlash to Blackwaterfoot

❷ Continue through the centre of Lamlash, past its rows of whitewashed cottages and little pier, to the small seaside resort of Whiting Bay, where Glenashdale Burn flows into the sea.

❸ Continue on the A841 through Largybeg and take the first minor road on the left beyond the sharp hairpin bend in Dippen. The narrow road leads to Kildonan Castle – a crumbling ruin on the shore, with views across rock ledges to the nearby isle of Pladda and, in the distance, Ailsa Craig, no more than a blue cone on the horizon. Curling stones used to be made from rock quarried on this island. Those used by the Scottish women's curling team, who won gold at the winter Olympics in 2002, came from Ailsa Craig. The island is now a haven for seabirds.

❹ Continue along the minor road for a mile to rejoin the A841. Turn left to Kilmory, where Arran cheese is hand made in the traditional manner at the Torrylinn creamery.

❺ Carry straight on along the road, through the narrow, wooded valley at Lagg and across a bridge over the evocatively named Sliddery Water. The countryside becomes wilder as the road

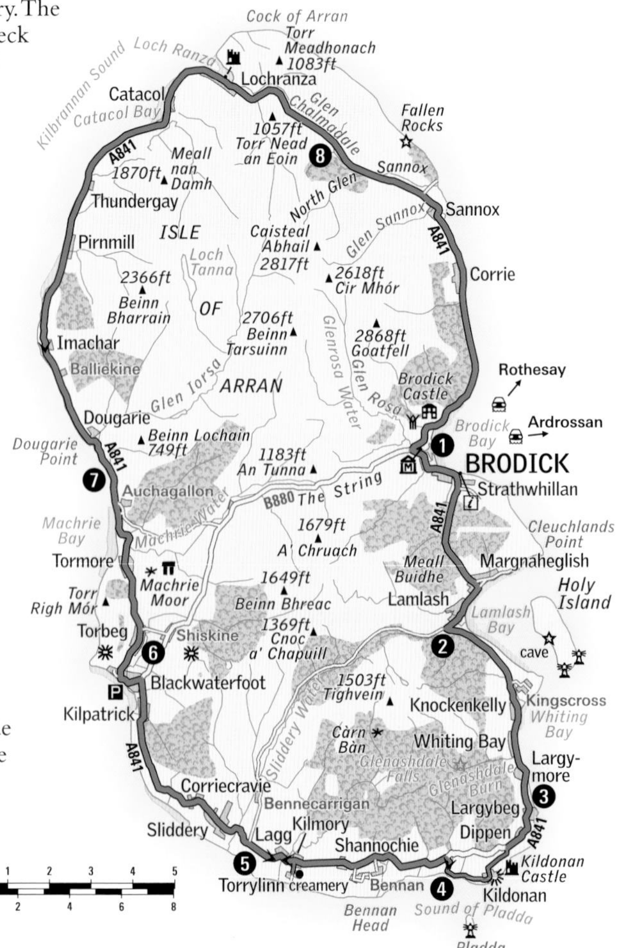

progresses from Sliddery along Arran's exposed west coast. To the right, rock-strewn, heather-clad hillsides sweep down to the roadside; to the left, across Kilbrannan Sound, the rocky shore of the Mull of Kintyre stretches as far as the eye can see. The seaside village of Blackwaterfoot lies at the bottom of a long descent. The car park is next to the tiny harbour, which is just big enough for two or three small boats, and here Clauchan Water flows over steps of rock, under a stone bridge and into the sea.

Blackwaterfoot to Brodick

6 Return to the A841 and turn left towards Machrie. Just before Machrie Bridge, a track on the right is signposted to Machrie Moor, where there is a rich concentration of Bronze and Iron Age monuments. Six stone circles stand close together, and chambered cairns, a standing stone and more stone circles spread out across the surrounding landscape.

7 Beyond Machrie, Arran's northern mountains squeeze the road against the shingle shore. Continue for 15 miles to the ferry port of Lochranza, where a forbidding medieval fortress (HS) stands on a shingle spit in the sea loch. The only malt whisky distillery on Arran was opened at Lochranza in 1995, although in the 19th century there were reputedly more than 50, mostly illegal, distilleries sending their wares to the mainland. The whisky produced on the island was discreetly referred to as the 'Arran waters'. Lochranza marks the northern extent of the road – and almost of the Isle of Arran itself.

8 Continue inland, along Glen Chalmadale and across a stretch of wild moorland to reach Sannox on the east coast. The road shadows the shore below the steep forested slopes and bare rocky ridges of Goatfell, the highest mountain on Arran. Continue through the village of Corrie to return to Brodick.

SOUTHEAST SCOTLAND

Ancient towns and cities, historic monuments and old fishing villages vie with world-famous golf courses and salmon rivers as the region's main attractions. Thick forests and wildlife havens have an appeal of their own.

4 LINLITHGOW

TOUR LENGTH 53 miles

This tour around the Firth of Forth takes in ruined castles, stately houses and an architectural folly. A Victorian rail bridge overshadows the old inn where Robert Louis Stevenson set a scene in one of his greatest adventure stories.

Linlithgow to South Queensferry

❶ The ancient burgh of Linlithgow was forged in the crucible of English–Scottish rivalry. Edward I set up military headquarters here in the early 14th century only to see the base overrun by the Scots a few years later. But the town's chief claim to fame lies in Linlithgow Palace (HS). It was here that one of history's great tragic figures, Mary, Queen of Scots – heroine to some, dangerous plotter to others – was born in 1542.

Leave Linlithgow on the A803, signposted to the Forth Road Bridge. Continue across the M9, then almost immediately turn right on to the A904. The driveway leading to the House of the Binns (NTS), where collections of furniture and porcelain are on show, lies about 1½ miles along the road on the left, immediately beyond the B9109 junction.

❷ Three miles farther along the A904, just past a right-hand junction with the B8020, is the road to Hopetoun House, a huge 18th-century stately home that was largely built by William Adam and his architect-decorator sons, Robert and John.

South Queensferry to Linlithgow

❸ Back on the A904, at the approach to South Queensferry, turn left on to the B924. Drive through the town, under the approach road to the Forth Road Bridge and follow the shore road to a car park on the left, near the inshore rescue boat station. The Forth Rail Bridge, which was opened in 1890, dwarfs all its surroundings, its huge girders casting a latticework of shadows over the road.

❹ Return along the B924 and turn left on to the A904. A short distance along turn left on to the A90 over the Forth Road Bridge, which was the longest suspension bridge in the world when it opened in 1964. On the far shore of the firth turn left on to the A985. Just beyond Rosyth naval base, turn left on to a minor road to Limekilns.

❺ Continue through Charlestown to rejoin the A985. Turn left and at the next roundabout turn left again on to the B9037. Follow the road through Low Torry and, from Low Valleyfield continue on a minor road to reach the small

FORTH RAIL BRIDGE

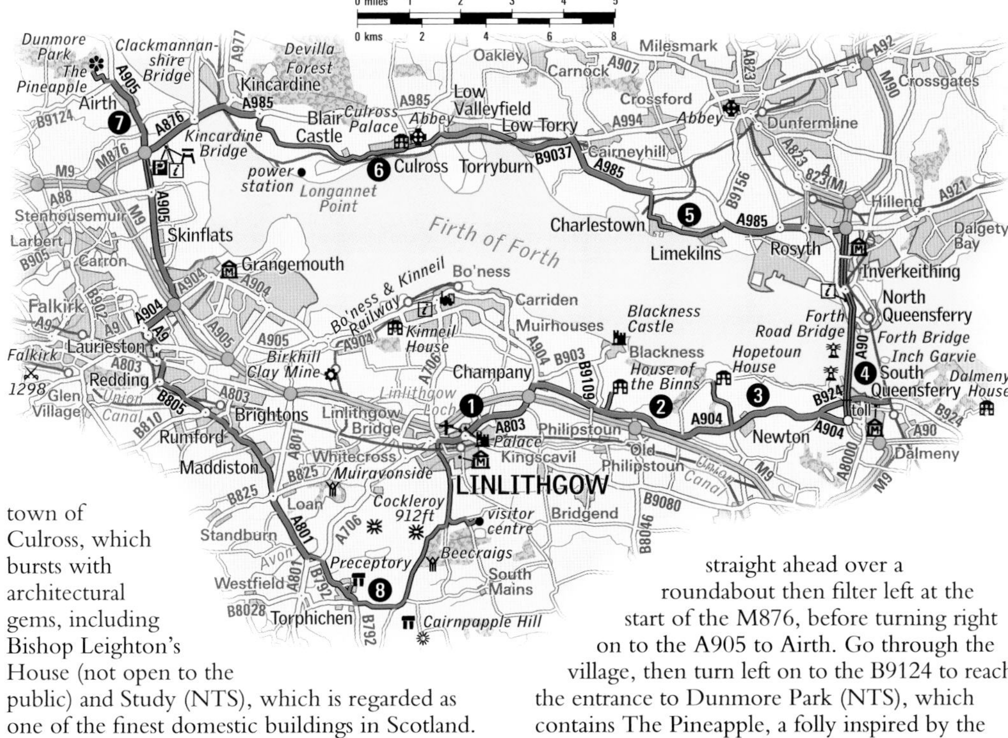

town of Culross, which bursts with architectural gems, including Bishop Leighton's House (not open to the public) and Study (NTS), which is regarded as one of the finest domestic buildings in Scotland.

6 From Culross, continue past the massive bulk of Longannet power station on the left. Originally built to burn coal brought from seams deep beneath the Firth of Forth, it is still Europe's third largest coal-fired power station and has a visitor centre. At a roundabout, turn left on to the A985, then left again to recross the Firth of Forth on the Kincardine Bridge, with views of the new Clackmananshire Bridge to the right. Continue straight ahead over a roundabout then filter left at the start of the M876, before turning right on to the A905 to Airth. Go through the village, then turn left on to the B9124 to reach the entrance to Dunmore Park (NTS), which contains The Pineapple, a folly inspired by the shape of the tropical fruit, and a walled garden. Cottages originally built to house the gardeners are in the care of the Landmark Trust and available for holiday lets.

7 Return to the A905 and turn right towards Skinflats and Grangemouth. Go through Skinflats and at a major roundabout on the edge of Grangemouth, turn right on to the A904. At the next roundabout turn left on to the A9 to Laurieston, then at the next second roundabout turn right (2nd exit) on to the B805, following this for some 5 miles to the Bowhouse roundabout, there taking the A801 (3rd exit) towards Bathgate. Immediately after crossing the River Avon, turn left on to a minor road, left again at the T-junction with the A706, and almost immediately right on to the B792 into Torphichen, where the Preceptory, to the left at the crossroads in the village centre, is a fascinating mixture of church and fort.

8 From the village continue on the B792 for ½ mile, forking left on to a minor road immediately beyond a junction with the B4087 on the right, and continue bearing left to reach a forestry plantation. Turn right at the far edge of the plantation, on to a minor road signposted to Beecraigs Country Park visitor centre and car park. From there, return to the minor road through the forest and turn right to reach a T-junction just beyond a caravan park. Turn left and continue along the road to a second T-junction. Turn right and follow the downhill road to return to the centre of Linlithgow.

5 PEEBLES

TOUR LENGTH **47 miles**

A famous salmon river, the Tweed, flows through the old mill town of Peebles. This trip follows its winding course as far as Melrose, over undulating, sometimes thickly wooded hills and past Sir Walter Scott's old home at Abbotsford.

Peebles to Traquair

1 The name Peebles may come from the word 'pebyll', meaning tent, used by the first Celtic settlers more than 2,000 years ago. These Celtic origins are celebrated every June in the week-long Beltane Festival, which culminates in the crowning of the Beltane Queen. The market town retains its historic layout, with many fine buildings dating from the 19th century.

To start the drive, cross the river over the 15th-century Tweed Bridge. At the roundabout, turn left on to the B7062.

After 3 miles the road passes Kailzie Gardens, an estate 213m (700ft) above sea level facing north and east and particularly susceptible to severe weather. Hardy plants have been used to create lovely displays of flowers and shrubs, designed to withstand the cold.

2 Continue on the B7062 with the Tweed to the left and the wooded hills of Cardrona Forest to the right. After 5 miles turn left to the white-painted, many-storeyed Traquair House, an old hunting lodge said to be the oldest continually inhabited house in Scotland, with a history that stretches back more than 1,000 years. The house is privately owned but open to the public from Easter to October. Check times before visiting. Since 1965, potent Traquair Ale has once again been produced in the 18th-century brewery, which used to make beer for house and estate workers.

Traquair to Melrose

3 Return to the B7062 and continue to the crossroads in Traquair. Turn left on to the B709. After ½ mile, where the road bends sharp left towards Innerleithen, go ahead on a minor road beside the Tweed, which climbs through the Elibank and Traquair Forests, the largest stretch of woodland in the Tweed valley. The forests, which include a well-regarded mountain biking centre, are mainly coniferous.

4 Continue through Peel and cross a lovely old bridge over the Tweed to reach the A707. Turn right to Yair, a popular spot for salmon fishing. Do not cross the bridge, but go ahead on the B7060, climbing steeply with grand views back across the river and up the Tweed valley. The road then winds down to reach the A7 at another bridge. Turn right across the bridge. After ½ mile, turn left on to the B6360, driving through woodland to Abbotsford, the romantically fanciful home of Sir Walter Scott for 20 years until his death in 1832. The Scottish baronial style main block was built in 1822 and is crammed with mementoes of Scott's life, including his outstanding library. In the care of a charitable trust, the house is open from March to October. Check times before visiting.

5 From Abbotsford, follow the B6360 to meet the A6091 at a roundabout. Turn right and follow the signs into Melrose, a town inhabited since the Bronze Age. The Ormiston Institute, which is also the Registrar's Office, in the Market Square has an exhibition on the fort of Trimontium, which was the Roman headquarters for southern Scotland. Near the town are the ruins of Melrose Abbey (HS), dedicated to the Blessed Virgin in 1146 and rebuilt after an attack by Richard II's forces in 1385. Many delicate stone carvings can still be seen among the standing remains. Nearby Priorwood Gardens (NTS) has an historic collection of apple trees, descended from the originals grown by monks from Melrose Abbey.

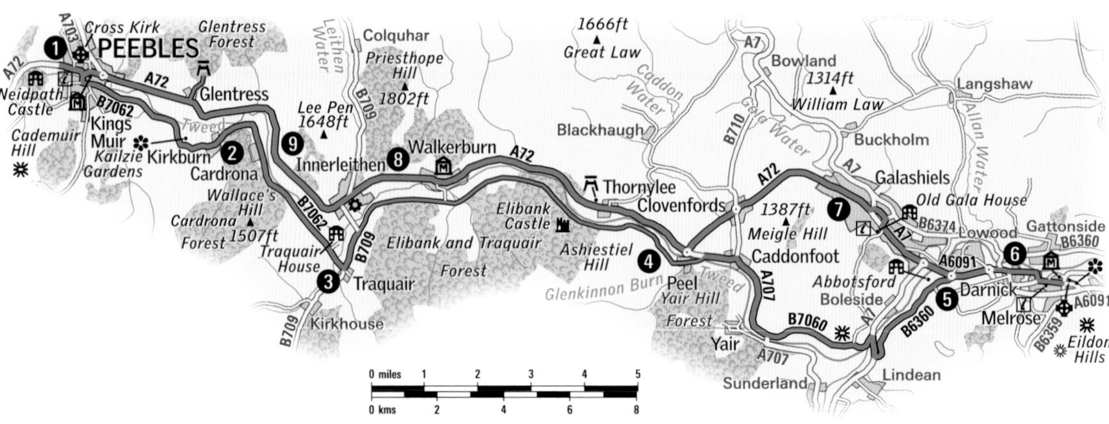

ABBOTSFORD

From the flowers grown in the gardens, some are selected for their special drying properties and are sold in the garden's shop.

Melrose to Peebles

6 Return to the roundabout near Abbotsford and follow the A6091 west to cross the Tweed by the high Galafoot Bridge. Then join the A7 into Galashiels. Like many Border towns, Galashiels was once a major manufacturer of textiles. The Lochcarron of Scotland Cashmere and Wool Centre at Waverley Mill has tours and a museum. Old Gala House dates from 1583 and houses the Christopher Boyd Gallery, which stages art exhibitions in summer.

7 Leave Galashiels by the A72, dropping down beside the Tweed to the former tweed-milling village of Walkerburn. The cloth-making history of the community is remembered in the Scottish Museum of Woollen Textiles, with fascinating displays of the craft's history and working life a century or more ago.

8 Continue on the A72 to Innerleithen, where the Leithen Water joins the Tweed. Formerly a thriving textile centre, Innerleithen now has just one textile mill, specialising in cashmere. The other reason for the town's rise to prosperity in the 18th and 19th centuries was the discovery of sulphurous, and reputedly curative, springs, St Ronan's Wells. Robert Burns described the place as a 'famous spa' in 1787, and Sir Walter Scott's novel *St Ronan's Well*, published in 1827, was widely assumed to be based on the town. As a result, Innerleithen became a popular Victorian watering hole. A fascinating glimpse into the 19th-century printing industry is provided by Robert Smail's Printing Works (NTS), which was set up in 1866 and remained virtually unchanged until it closed in 1985.

9 From Innerleithen follow the A72. After 3½ miles, turn right to Glentress Forest, which has a network of waymarked walks offering fine views over the Tweed valley. Return to the A72 and back to Peebles.

SOUTHEAST SCOTLAND

6 DUNBAR

TOUR LENGTH 87 miles

Medieval strongholds and historic towns give way to a nuclear power station via a country park, the gannetry on Bass Rock and a trip through the heather-clad Lammermuir Hills. A tranquil fishing village makes a welcome detour.

Dunbar to Gullane

❶ A sandstone tower and a few scattered stones are all that remain of the 13th-century castle at Dunbar. The ruins overlook a harbour backed by cobbled quays and restored warehouses built for a long-gone shipping trade. Dunbar has been a Royal Burgh for centuries. The 17th-century Town House in the main street lays claim to be the oldest civic building in Scotland in continuous use. Dunbar was the birthplace of conservationist John Muir, who founded the National Parks movement in the USA.

Leave Dunbar on the A1087 towards East Linton, passing the John Muir Country Park, a wildlife sanctuary covering 712ha (1,760 acres) of pine woods, grassland and coastline, with 8 miles of beaches. At the roundabout, turn right on to the A199 for 1½ miles, then turn right on to the A198 to Whitekirk. The road reaches the coast 5 miles farther on, and commands excellent views of Bass Rock, an island populated by seabirds. One of the best-known, and oldest, gannetries in Britain, the rock often appears to be snow-white as thousands of the birds flock to the colony.

At Castleton, turn right to visit the ruins of Tantallon Castle, a former fortress of the Douglas family (HS). The castle – renowned for its curtain wall, nearly 4m (12ft) thick – withstood several seiges during its history, but was finally overcome by Oliver Cromwell in 1651. It took a force of 3,000 men to defeat a mere 100 or so who were defending the castle.

❷ Continue on the A198 to North Berwick, a popular holiday destination since the arrival of the railway in 1850. Inland, the short, steep climb up the conical North Berwick Law is rewarded with spectacular views.

Follow the A198 out of North Berwick to Gullane, well known for the three golf courses that surround it, one of which is the championship course of Muirfield. Follow the sign to Gullane Bents car park. The sandy beach is backed by heathland.

Gullane to Cranshaws

❸ Continue on the A198 past Aberlady Bay, then turn left on to the A6137. On the outskirts of Haddington, go straight on at the roundabout. The town has many buildings of historical interest, including William Adam's Town House of 1748 and the Church of St Mary, known as the 'Lamp of Lothian'.

❹ Continue on the B6369 towards Gifford, passing the 14th-century Lennoxlove House, home of the Duke of Hamilton. The building

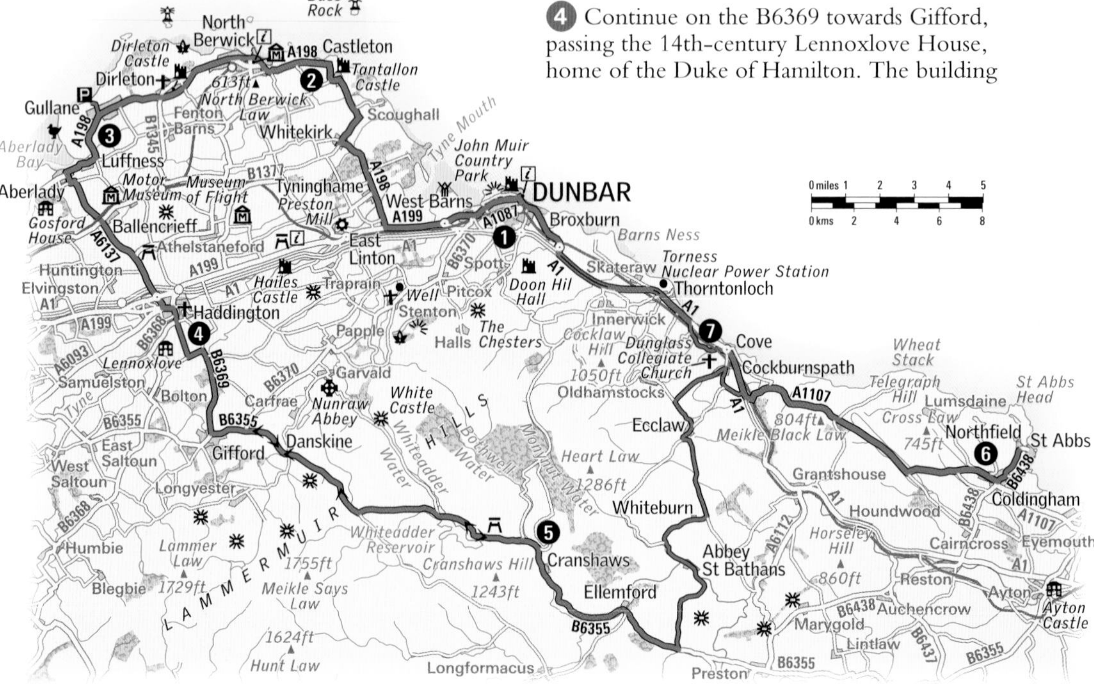

received its present name in the 17th century in honour of the Duchess of Richmond and Lennox, a favourite of Charles II's. At Gifford turn left on to the B6355 to climb into the Lammermuir Hills, which rise to more than 518m (1,700ft). About 5 miles beyond Gifford keep left at the junction, continuing on the B6355 to Whiteadder Reservoir (pronounced Whit-adder). The reservoir has a riverside walk and trout fishing.

Cranshaws to St Abbs

5 Continue through Cranshaws on the B6355 along Whiteadder Water, crossing the river at Ellemford Bridge. About 2 miles farther on, turn left on a minor road to Abbey St Bathans, continuing alongside the river. Fork right to Whiteburn. Turn left to Ecclaw at a T-junction and follow the road, ignoring forks, to the outskirts of Cockburnspath. Before reaching the village, turn right, signposted to Berwick. At the next junction, turn right on to the A1 and take the next left on to the A1107 coast road to Coldingham. Turn left in Coldingham on to the B6438 to St Abbs, a small village tucked away at the foot of the cliffs, with a harbour for small fishing and dive boats. Although the village is named after a convent that was built on the crags in the 7th century, it dates from the 19th when Ushers, the Edinburgh brewery, built a fishing station here.

St Abbs to Dunbar

6 Return along the B6438, turning right on to the A1107 and right again on to the A1. At Cockburnspath roundabout, take the first exit for Cockburnspath, then turn immediately right to Dunglass Collegiate Church (HS), founded in the 15th century by Sir Alexander Home.

7 From the church, turn left along a minor road back to the A1. Follow the signs to Dunbar, passing Torness Nuclear Power Station on the right, which has a visitor centre and coastal walkway. Follow the A1 back to Dunbar.

ST ABBS

SOUTHEAST SCOTLAND

7 ST ANDREWS

TOUR LENGTH 59 miles

The bare hills, sloping farmland and sandy shores encompassed by this route led James VI to describe the old kingdom of Fife as 'a beggar's mantle fringed with gold'. Pretty fishing villages enhance the effect, while Scotland's nuclear bunker at Troywood adds a chilling touch.

St Andrews to Falkland

1 The historic university city of St Andrews was once Scotland's ecclesiastical capital. In the Middle Ages its cathedral was the largest church north of the border. Today the city is better known as the home of golf – already popular when the university was founded in 1413 and played on the common ground, or links, that back the local beaches. The Society of St Andrews Golfers, which was formed in 1754, evolved into the famous Royal and Ancient Golf Club.

Leave St Andrews on the B939 signposted to Strathkinness. Continue through Pitscottie, home of 16th-century historian Robert Lindsay, who wrote the first history of Scotland in Scottish, rather than Latin. His book, *The Historie and Cronicles of Scotland, 1437–1575,* was used as reference by Sir Walter Scott, among others. Carry on to the village of Ceres, a pretty settlement with a village green. Here, the Fife Folk Museum, open during the summer, has displays of Victorian costume and farm implements showing local ways of life and work over the past two centuries.

2 At Craigrothie turn right on the A916 towards Cupar and Tay Bridge. Less than a mile farther on, turn right at a minor crossroads to the Edwardian mansion, Hill of Tarvit (NTS). House and gardens are open to visitors.

Return to the A916 and turn right, then take the first minor road on the left to a crossroads. Turn left on to the A914 and continue along the road for 6 miles. A mile beyond Kettlebridge turn right on to a minor road to Freuchie. Continue under a railway bridge and at the junction with the A92 go straight ahead, joining the B936. Follow the road into Falkland, where the 16th-century palace (NTS), once a royal hunting lodge, is surrounded by beautiful gardens.

Falkland to Lower Largo

3 Return through Freuchie to the A914 junction. Turn right then immediately left on to a minor road towards Kennoway. The road climbs past a forest plantation before descending, with commanding views over the Firth of Forth. At Kennoway turn right on to the A916 then immediately left towards Leven and the coast. At the A915 crossroads go straight on to reach the centre of the Edwardian resort of Leven.

PITTENWEEM, EAST NEUK

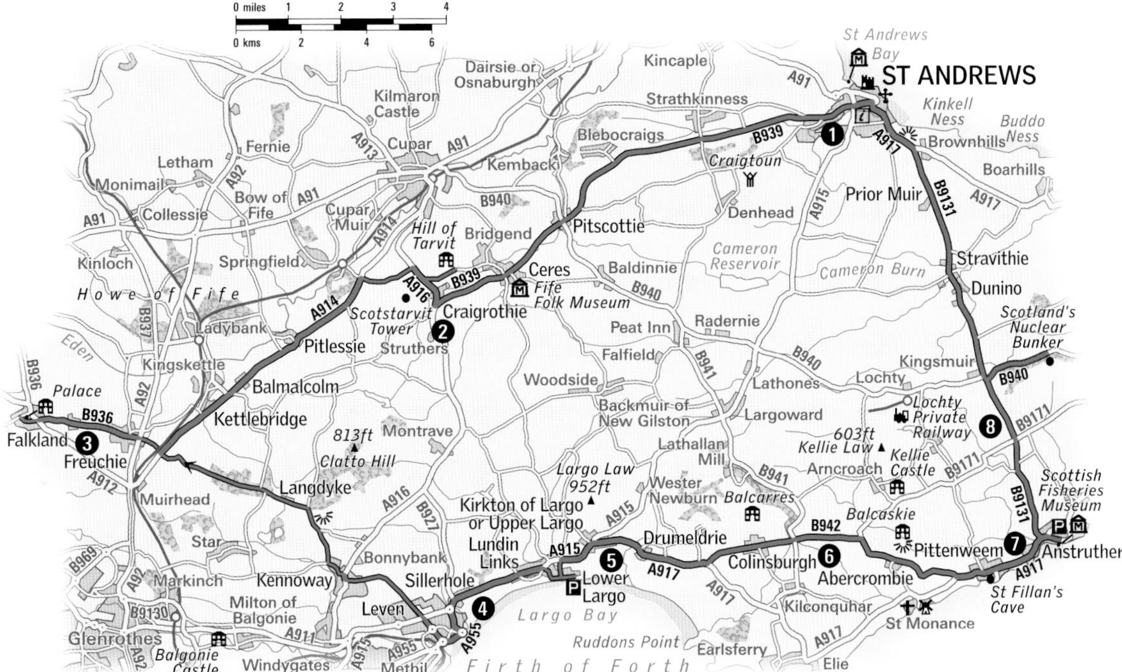

❹ At a roundabout in the town centre turn left on to the A955 to a T-junction with the A915 coast road. Turn right to Lundin Links, where a sign welcomes visitors to the East Neuk of Fife – the name for this stretch of coast, which has a collection of attractive fishing villages stretching along the firth to Crail. A short distance farther on turn right, off the main road, and continue on a minor road through Lundin Links town centre to the neighbouring seaside settlement of Lower Largo, where the celebrated castaway Alexander Selkirk was born in 1676. Selkirk was the inspiration for Daniel Defoe's novel *Robinson Crusoe*, having spent four years marooned on the Juan Fernández Islands, 400 miles from the coast of Chile. A lifesized statue of the shipwrecked mariner, who died in 1721, adorns some cottages on Main Street, on first-floor level – the site of his birthplace.

Follow the shore road past the harbour to the beachfront car park. The pier was constructed in 1827 and provided a working base for a large herring fleet. Coal was also exported from here, but today the craft that sail from the pier are mostly used for pleasure.

Lower Largo to Anstruther

❺ Drive away from the seafront to a T-junction on the A915 and turn right. In Upper Largo fork right on to the A917. After a little more than 2 miles, turn left on to the B942 to Colinsburgh, a small, grey stone village built in 1705 by Colin Lindsay, the 3rd Earl of Balcarres, to house disbanded Jacobite soldiers who had supported him in the 1689 Jacobite uprising.

❻ Continue on the B942 and where the road rejoins the A917, turn left to Pittenweem, an active fishing port with Dutch-style houses that today hosts an annual arts festival. St Fillan's Cave, the entrance of which is off a steep street overlooking the harbour, commemorates a 7th-century Irish monk.

❼ Continue to the fishing port of Anstruther, home of the Scottish Fisheries Museum, which is located on the harbour front. The collection includes 19 historic boats and 66,000 artefacts, telling the story of Scottish fishing and fishing life from the earliest times to the present day.

At a mini-roundabout in the town centre turn right on to the B9131 to reach the car park near the harbour.

Anstruther to St Andrews

❽ Take the B9131 towards St Andrews. After 4 miles a right turning on to the B940 leads to Scotland's Nuclear Bunker, a Cold War relic that has been preserved as a tourist attraction. A 150m (nearly 500ft)corridor leads down from what purported to be an unassuming farmhouse – in reality, the bunker's guardhouse – into a structure designed to shelter 300 people underground. Built on two levels, each the size of a football pitch, the bunker's quarters are more than 30m (100ft) below the surface, and protected by thousands of tonnes of blast-proof concrete.

Return to the B940 and turn left to a T-junction on the B9131. Turn right and follow the road as it descends towards St Andrews, giving views across the city and along the coast beyond.

CENTRAL SCOTLAND

From craggy western shores across moor and mountain to the smoother eastern coast, this is a land of lochs and soft peaty burns, where malt whisky distilleries abound and reminders of past tensions are plentiful.

8 MONTROSE

TOUR LENGTH 85 miles

This varied route leads past the vast tidal Montrose Basin, a haven for birds, through fertile farmlands in the Vale of Strathmore to Glamis Castle and the hills that frame the beautiful Angus glens. The fabulous beach at Lunan Bay is on Montrose's doorstep.

Montrose to Edzell

1 Bounded on three sides by water, Montrose is a resort, a sailing centre and a busy harbour used by ships servicing oil platforms offshore. Narrow twisting streets lead from the gable-ended houses of the High Street, which is dominated by the graceful steeple on the town's fine Old Church. Built in 1834, the steeple is 67m (220ft) high.

To start the drive, take the A935 towards Brechin, along the north side of the Montrose Basin. After 3 miles turn right to the House of Dun (NTS), an imposing mansion designed in 1730 by William Adam for David Erskine, Lord Dun. The gardens are open all year but check opening times for the house before visiting.

From Bridge of Dun, to the south, a steam train operates to Brechin on a restored section of the Caledonian Railway. In Victorian and Edwardian days royal trains would stop at Bridge of Dun to allow the monarch to take breakfast.

2 Continue on the A935 to Brechin, rising in red sandstone above the River South Esk. Its cathedral church was founded by David I in 1150. Near the church is the rocket-like Round Tower (HS), built 1,000 years ago.

From the centre of Brechin, take the B966 to Edzell, passing under the A90. At the south end of the village, the Dalhousie Memorial Arch spans the road. It was erected in memory of the Earl and Countess of Dalhousie, who both died in 1881. A mile to the west is Edzell Castle and Garden (HS). The castle was built in the 16th century by the Lindsays of Glenesk as a fortified house. In the magnificent Pleasance, or walled garden, is a box hedge spelling out the Lindsay motto *Dum spiro spero* – 'While I breathe, I hope'.

EDZELL CASTLE

Edzell to Glamis

3 Return to Brechin and turn right on to the A935. Beyond the Brechin Castle Estate, which has woodland walks, turn left on to the B9134, with views northwest to the hills rising gracefully above the Angus glens. Follow the road to the village of Aberlemno, which is noted for its Pictish sculptured stones. Two large stones stand at the roadside, and in the churchyard is another (HS), with 8th-century carvings that include entwined beasts and a battle scene.

4 After 3 miles, just before Lunanhead, turn left on a minor road to a T-junction and then right on to the B9113 to the red sandstone ruins of Restenneth Priory (HS). The priory was founded in the 8th century and then refounded by either David I or Malcolm IV in the 12th century, coming under the auspices of Jedburgh Abbey.

5 Continue on the B9113 to Forfar, the county town of Angus and once a textile, jute and carpet-weaving centre. A 17th-century octagonal turret marks the site of the long-demolished castle, where, it is said, Malcolm III held a parliament in 1057.

6 Leave Forfar on the A94 and, passing under the A90, continue to Glamis. North of the village is Glamis Castle, the seat of the Earl of Strathmore. The majestic multi-storeyed castle, built in the 17th century in the style of a French chateau, was a childhood home of Queen Elizabeth, the Queen Mother.

Glamis to Arbroath

7 Return along the A94 for 2 miles, then turn right on to the B9127, passing under the A90. Continue through Inverarity, Whigstreet and Kirkbuddo. At Carmyllie follow the B9127 left then right above Elliot Water to Arbroath. An ancient port, the town's origins date back to Pictish times. The abbey (HS) was the setting in 1320 of the Declaration of Arbroath, signed and sealed by Scottish nobles, which affirmed their commitment to an independent Scotland. From the abbey ruins, it is a short walk to the harbour, still used by fishing boats. The town is also home to the Arbroath smokie, a haddock smoke-cured over smouldering oak chips.

Arbroath to Montrose

8 Leave Arbroath on the A92. Follow the road for about 5 miles then turn right to Inverkeilor. Turn right in the village and follow the road to Lunan and a wonderful sweep of sand stretching around Lunan Bay. A walk south along the beach leads to the scant 15th-century ruins of Red Castle. Traditional fishing still takes place from the beach, with nets strung from poles. Follow the country lanes back to Montrose, driving past the once-thriving fishing village of Usan.

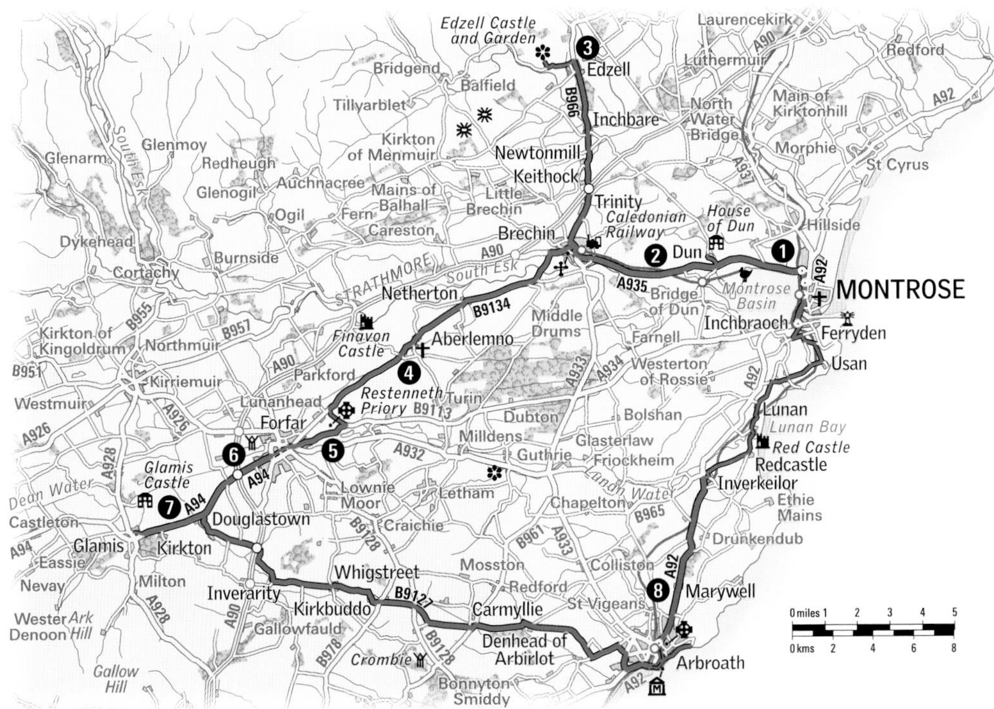

CENTRAL SCOTLAND

9 DUNKELD

TOUR LENGTH 71 miles

Starting from a once razed city and taking an old military road to the scene of a famous battle, the route also passes a peaceful loch where the same view attracted royal admiration twice, five centuries apart.

Dunkeld to Fortingall

1 The Jacobite rebellion of 1689 ran out of steam at Dunkeld when 5,000 Highlanders failed to take the town from 1,200 Lowland Cameronians, who had been drafted in to hold the line against supporters of the deposed James II. The cost of the siege was enormous, with old Dunkeld, including its 14th-century cathedral, sacked and burned. But a new town soon sprang up from the ashes. Dunkeld's 'Little Houses', lining streets near the restored choir of the cathedral, are a wonderfully preserved record of the rebuilding.

To start the drive, take the A923 out of Dunkeld, crossing Thomas Telford's stone bridge over the River Tay. Turn right at the T-junction on to the A9, then immediately left on to the A822. Follow the road along Strathbraan for about 8 miles to a T-junction and turn right on to the A826. Continue uphill through Glen Cochill. The route of today's highway deviates little from that of the military road built by General George Wade during his campaigns to suppress the Highlands after the 1715 Jacobite uprising. Continue to Aberfeldy.

Turn right at a T-junction for the town centre. Wade's Bridge over the Tay, a graceful five-arched structure, strikingly decorated with obelisks, was designed by William Adam. Leave Aberfeldy on the B846, crossing Wade's Bridge, and turn left at the T-junction in Weem. Castle Menzies, an unusual 16th-century fortified mansion, is a short distance along the road. Seat of the Menzies clan for more than 400 years, the building has been restored by the clan society and visitors are welcome. Check times beforehand.

2 The road bends right, leaving the Tay's flat valley floor. Continue to Keltneyburn, where a minor road on the left leads to Fortingall, a beautifully sited village with a churchyard yew tree reputed to be 3,000 years old. The present church was built in the early 1900s.

Fortingall to Killiecrankie

3 Back on the B846, the road climbs steadily, revealing views of the rocky summit of Schiehallion to the left. The mountain's symmetrical shape led the 18th-century Astronomer Royal, Nevil Maskelyne, to use it as a model in calculations aimed at discovering the Earth's mass.

Beyond Loch Kinardochy the road twists downhill to a T-junction at Tummel Bridge. Turn right on to the B8019 beside Loch Tummel. The scene from Queen's View was admired by Queen Isabella, wife of Robert Bruce, in the 14th century, and by Queen Victoria in the 19th.

4 Follow the road to Garry Bridge and turn left at a T-junction on to the B8079 towards Killiecrankie. Just before reaching the village, turn left into the Killiecrankie visitor centre (NTS) car park. The visitor centre has information about the area and tells the story of the 1689 Battle of Killiecrankie, when rebel Highlanders led by Viscount 'Bonnie' Dundee defeated a much larger government force. A path from the rear of the car park leads down some steps to the River Garry. A short way to the right, Soldier's Leap is named after a fleeing English soldier who saved his life by jumping the 5.5m (18ft) chasm.

Killiecrankie to Dunkeld

5 Leaving the visitor centre car park, turn left on to the B8079 and carry on to the granite-built estate village of Blair Atholl, a short distance beyond Killiecrankie. A regal avenue of lime trees

leads from the village to the privately owned Blair Castle, which is open to visitors in summer. Check times before visiting.

6 Return through Killiecrankie to Garry Bridge and carry straight on, following the A924 to the Victorian spa town of Pitlochry, better known today for whisky than it is for water.

7 Continue on the A924 to Ballinluig, then bear left on to the A9 down the Tummel valley towards Dunkeld. A mile or so before reaching Dunkeld, turn right into the car park for The Hermitage (NTS), where delightful walks are to be had beside the river and along forest tracks.

Rejoin the A9 and turn right, continuing past the village of Inver towards Dunkeld, which can be seen across the flat valley floor. At the junction with the A923 turn left and follow the road through Little Dunkeld back into the town.

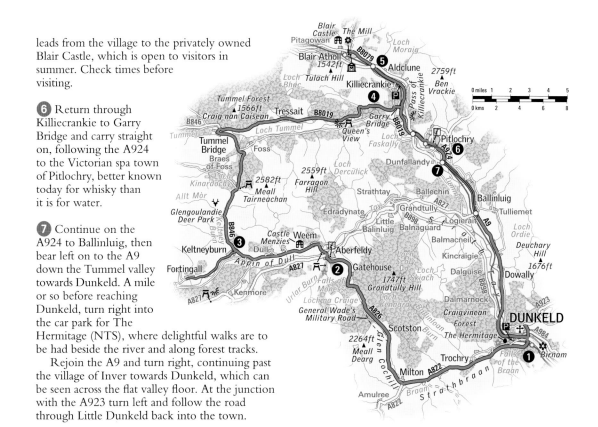

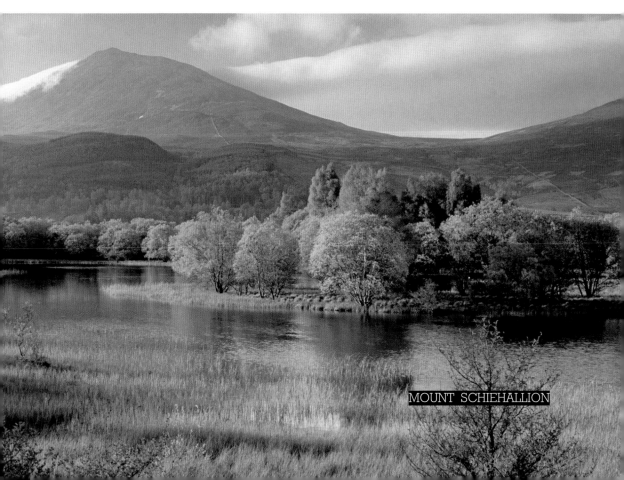

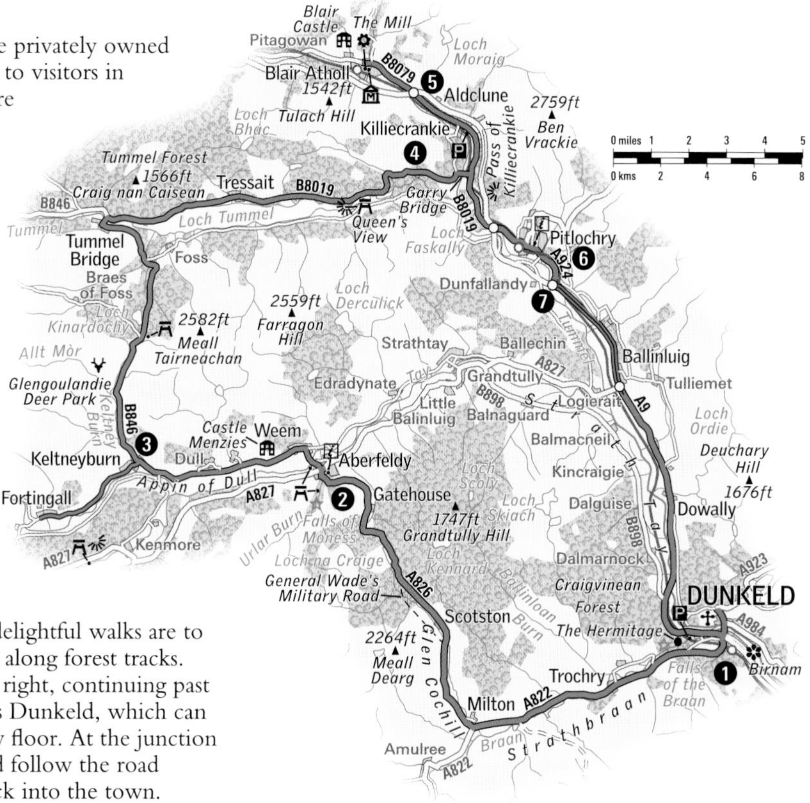

MOUNT SCHIEHALLION

CENTRAL SCOTLAND

10 CRIEFF

TOUR LENGTH 69 miles

From formal 17th-century gardens, this gentle meander through an historic landscape culminates in a visit to the Highland boundary fault and its earthquake-measuring equipment.

Crieff to Kinnoull Hill

1 Crieff and its surroundings are steeped in history and legend. In AD 79, Julius Agricola built a Roman fort on the outskirts of Comrie, and the area later became one of the greatest Celtic earldoms in Scotland. To the east, Scottish kings were crowned at Scone Palace from 1153–1488. To the west, in Balquhidder's glens and hills, the outlaw Rob Roy spent his last days. Bonnie Prince Charlie stayed at Crieff on his way to defeat at Culloden in 1746.

To start the drive, take the A822 towards Stirling. Just beyond the Pond of Drummond on the right, turn right for the magnificent Drummond Castle Gardens (open to the public in summer). These were laid out in the early 17th century for the 2nd Earl of Perth.

2 Continue on the A822 to Muthill, a small town known for its ruined medieval church. The tower, which would have been all there was of the church originally, may have been built for protection as much as worship, and probably dates from the 1000s. About 1½ miles beyond Muthill, turn left on to the A823, signposted to Dunfermline, and continue for 4 miles.

3 Shortly before the turn-off to the Gleneagles Hotel, turn left on to a minor road to Auchterarder. Turn left again at the junction with the A824 to reach the centre of the straggling village. The long main street gave rise to its local name, Lang Toon. Auchterarder was burnt down in 1716 by the Jacobite commander, the Earl of Mar, following the Battle of Sheriffmuir at the end of the previous year. The reason was to prevent English troops still in the area from obtaining shelter and supplies there.

4 Leave Auchterarder on the A824 and then turn right on to the B8062 through farmland to Dunning, another village put to the torch by the Earl of Mar. A stone cross just outside the village is a memorial to Maggie Wall, reputedly the last witch to be burned in Scotland, in 1657.

5 Just past Dunning's church, take the first turning left on to the B934 towards Forteviot, an important centre of the Pictish kingdom in the 8th and 9th centuries. The burial site of an early Bronze Age ruler has also been uncovered there. Do not turn left over the railway crossing but bear right on the B935 through Forteviot and along the twisting road to Forgandenny.

About 2 miles farther on, follow the road as it bends sharply to the left and enter Bridge of Earn along Station Road. At a crossroads, turn right on to the A912 along the main street. Just after the built-up area turn left and filter on to the M90. Where it divides, in about 2 miles, follow the sign to Dundee, Forfar, Aberdeen and Braemar, crossing Friarton Bridge, high above the River Tay, with fine views.

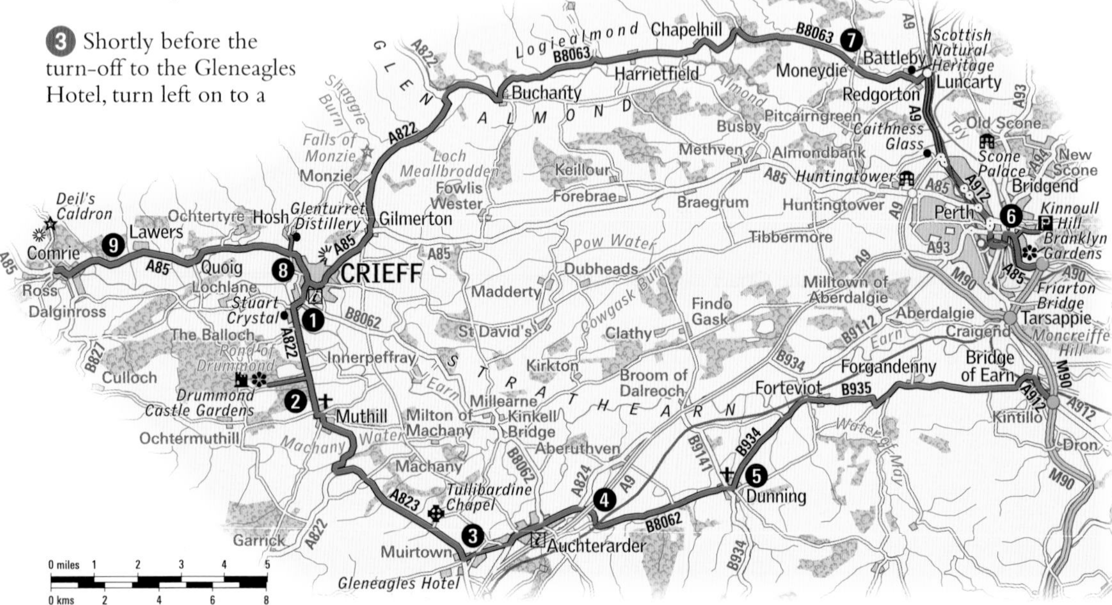

DRUMMOND CASTLE

At the far side of the bridge, take the filter left signposted A85 to Perth, Braemar and Coupar Angus. The road drops to river level with Friarton Bridge high above, and swings into the outskirts of Perth with Branklyn Garden (NTS) on the right – 0.8ha (2 acres) of beautiful alpines, shrubs and other plants. To visit Kinnoull Hill, which has paths and tracks up to the tower on the summit, turn right on to Manse Road 90m before the next traffic lights, just before the Isle of Skye Hotel. Drive up the hill and go straight ahead at the mini-roundabout. At the next mini-roundabout turn right to the Quarry car park.

Kinnoull Hill to Crieff

6 Return along Manse Road and turn right. Turn left at the traffic lights by the Isle of Skye Hotel. Cross the bridge, follow Perth's inner ring road and follow the signs for Inverness, joining the A9 at a major roundabout. After 2 miles take a left filter, following the signs to Luncarty and Stanley. At the next junction turn left on to the B8063, signposted to Logiealmond and Redgorton, and turn right at the crossroads, continuing on the B8063. At Battleby, the road passes the offices of Scottish Natural Heritage, the countryside agency. Open on weekdays, the offices have a small visitor centre and a reserve of 14ha (35 acres) with paths and walks.

7 Continue on the B8063 through a pastoral area to Buchanty. Just beyond the village, take a left filter on to the A822. At the junction with the A85 turn right to return to Crieff.

Crieff to Comrie

8 For an extension of the drive to Comrie, follow the A85 through Crieff. Just outside the town turn right to the Glenturret Distillery, the oldest distillery in Scotland, established in 1775.

9 Return to the A85 and continue for 7 miles to Comrie, which sits astride the Highland boundary fault and has recorded more earthquakes than anywhere else in Britain. Earthquake House, just west of the town, displays a replica of the first scientific equipment for measuring the phenomenon, used here in the 19th century. New seismometers have also been installed. Return to Crieff by the same route.

CENTRAL SCOTLAND

11 CALLANDER

TOUR LENGTH 41 miles

On the Trossachs Trail, in the shadow of Ben Ledi, loch succeeds stunning loch, and the road through a verdant forest leads to a ruined priory that once gave sanctuary to the young Mary, Queen of Scots.

Callander to Loch Katrine

1 The busy town of Callander, dominated by the 854m (2,883ft) Ben Ledi, has long been a centre for those drawn to the mountains, crags and glens of the Trossachs, a Highlands in miniature and a magnet for walkers. Long before that, the Romans built a fort here in the 1st century AD, and a road through the area was constructed in 1743 as part of the attempt to quell Highland rebellion. The writer Sir Walter Scott sparked off public interest in this beautiful spot in the early 19th century with his poem 'The Lady of the Lake' and his novel *Rob Roy*, based on the 18th-century outlaw Rob Roy MacGregor, whose simple grave is to be found in Balquhidder, just to the north of Callander. It stands in the churchyard, by the ruins of the old church, alongside the graves of his wife and two of their sons. The folk hero's story is told in the Rob Roy and Trossachs Visitor Centre in Callander. More recently, the town has become inextricably linked to the 1960s TV series *Dr Finlay's Casebook*, in which it appeared as 'Tannochbrae'.

To start the drive, leave Callander on the A84 going west towards Kilmahog, where there is a working woollen mill and shop. Originally built in 1758 to process flax, the mill still has its old waterwheel.

2 From Kilmahog, take the A821 towards Aberfoyle on the Trossachs Trail, a signposted tourist drive. The road passes Loch Venachar on the left to reach Brig o' Turk, a small village that was popular with 19th-century artists, including

LOCH SUCCEEDS STUNNING LOCH

LOCH VENACHAR

John Everett Millais. Poet, artist and social thinker John Ruskin also spent time here, and William Wordsworth's visit was recorded by his sister, Dorothy. The stone bridge, built in the early 1800s, replaced an earlier wooden one, while the 'turk' element of the village's name is thought to derive from *tuirc*, Gaelic for wild boar. The beasts were almost certainly once hunted in the region.

3 Continue on the winding road alongside Loch Achray to a junction at the head of the loch. Turn right to Loch Katrine, from which water is pumped to Glasgow. This was the place that inspired Sir Walter Scott to write 'The Lady of the Lake'. After it was published in 1810, the gentry came flocking to the area and its popularity was endorsed by a visit from Queen Victoria and Prince Albert. Boat trips on SS *Sir Walter Scott,* a steamer of 1900, run in summer to Stronachlachar, at the western tip of the loch.

Loch Katrine to Doune

4 From the loch, return to the A821 and carry on towards Aberfoyle through the Queen Elizabeth Forest Park, a huge timber-growing area that stretches into the heart of the Trossachs. Follow the twisting road along the Duke's Pass to the Queen Elizabeth Forest Park Visitor Centre on the left, which has displays on the park and details of a network of designated trails for walkers and cyclists to follow. The wealth of wildlife in the park includes red squirrels, and a walk along the Trossachs Bird of Prey Trail offers a good chance of seeing ospreys, buzzards and peregine falcons.

5 Follow the A821 to Aberfoyle on the edge of the Menteith Hills. The Scottish Wool Centre in the town tells the story of the industry. Several breeds of sheep are on show in the centre's fields, dogs can be seen at work with sheep and ducks, and there are seasonal shearing demonstrations.

6 Keep on the A821, round a sharp left bend, signposted to Stirling and Glasgow. After ¾ mile turn left on to the A81/A873, signposted to Callander. The Lake of Menteith comes into view on the right. At the end of the lake, turn right on to the B8034 to a jetty at Port of Menteith, from where boat trips can be taken to the island ruins of Inchmahome Priory (HS), a 13th-century Augustinian monastery. Inside the surviving chapter house is a fine collection of carved stone memorials, including a rare double effigy. Walter Stewart, who died in 1295, and Countess Mary are touchingly turned towards one another. Mary, Queen of Scots, was once hidden at the priory as a child, after the Scots defeat at the Battle of Pinkie in 1547.

7 Continue on the A81 to the next junction. Turn right on to the A873 towards Stirling. In the hamlet of Ruskie, turn left to Dunaverig Farmlife Centre, a working farm with displays on farming, past and present.

8 Follow the A873 through Thornhill and turn left on to the B826 towards Doune. At the next junction turn left on to the A84 to Doune. The town was once a centre of gun manufacture, and crossed pistols appear on its coat of arms. The name 'Doune' probably derives from 'dun', the Gaelic word for hillfort. On such a hill site stands the 14th-century Doune Castle (HS), which has a car park. There is also a nature reserve nearby, and for this turn right into the town and then left just before the church, signposted 'Nature Trail'. Then take the second left to Doune Ponds Nature Reserve car park.

Doune to Callander

9 Leave Doune on the A84, signposted to Callander, and follow the road all the way, with the River Teith to the left and Ben Ledi clearly visible on the skyline ahead.

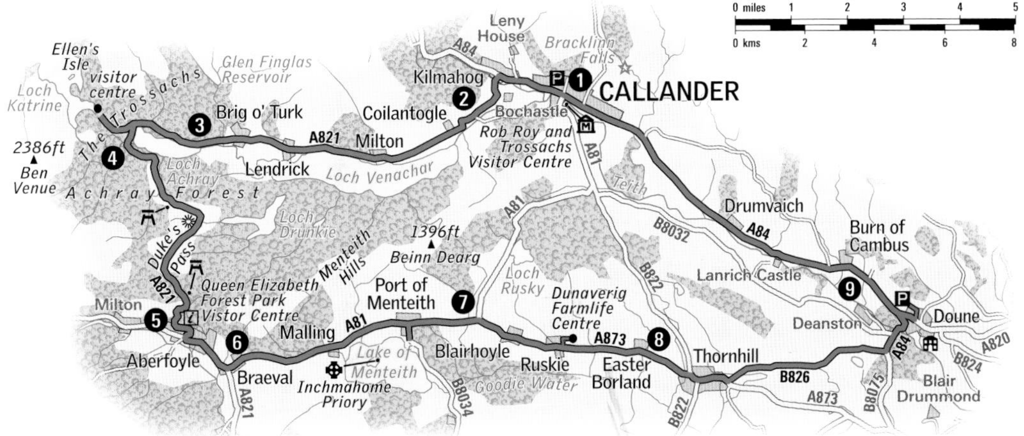

CENTRAL SCOTLAND

12 OBAN

TOUR LENGTH 78 miles

Through territory dotted with lochs and rivers, wooded valleys and Forest Enterprise land, the route leads past ruined castles and old villages to a wild and ragged coastline, which protects a tranquil garden.

Oban to Benderloch

❶ Rising in tiers behind a sheltered bay, Oban is a popular holiday resort, and the terminal for ferries to Mull, Coll, Tiree, Barra and South Uist. Its many visitors may lend the town a modern bustling character, but a Victorian charm still permeates its streets. McCaig's Tower, a hilltop folly that resembles an ancient Roman amphitheatre, is the town's most prominent landmark. It was built in 1897 by a local banker, anxious to ease Oban's unemployment and to perpetuate the memory of his name. The folly, together with Pulpit Hill, rising above South Pier, offers wide views towards the mountains of Mull. Leave Oban on the A85 towards Connel.

After 2 miles turn left on a minor road through Dunbeg to 13th-century Dunstaffnage Castle (HS), which guards the seaward approach to Loch Etive.

❷ Return to the A85, turn left, continue to Connel, then turn right on to the A828. The road bends left and leads across the Connel Bridge, which spans the Falls of Lora – the narrow outlet linking Loch Etive with the Firth of Lorn. Continue for 2 miles to the village of Benderloch. Forest Enterprise has a car park on the right.

Benderloch to Kilchrenan

❸ Return to Connel and rejoin the A85, turning right along the shore of Loch Etive. Turn left into the popular holiday village of Taynuilt, which is bypassed by the main road. The area's once-thriving iron-smelting industry is commemorated in the restored Bonawe Furnace.

❹ Leave Taynuilt towards Kilchrenan on the B845. This is a narrow road through the wooded valley of Glen Nant, which was once a rich source of charcoal. About 2½ miles from Taynuilt, there is a Forest Enterprise car park on the right.

❺ Continue on the B845 to Kilchrenan, where the graveyard surrounding its post-Reformation church contains early sculpted headstones.

Kilchrenan to Oban

❻ Beyond the village turn right towards Ford on a single-track road. For most of the 15 miles to Ford the road runs close to Loch Awe's forested shore. A mile beyond the lochside village of Dalavich the road passes the tiny ruined settlement of Newyork, established by the York Building Company of London in the 18th century. There are views across the loch to the castle-crowned island of Innis Chonnell, one of Argyll's many Campbell strongholds.

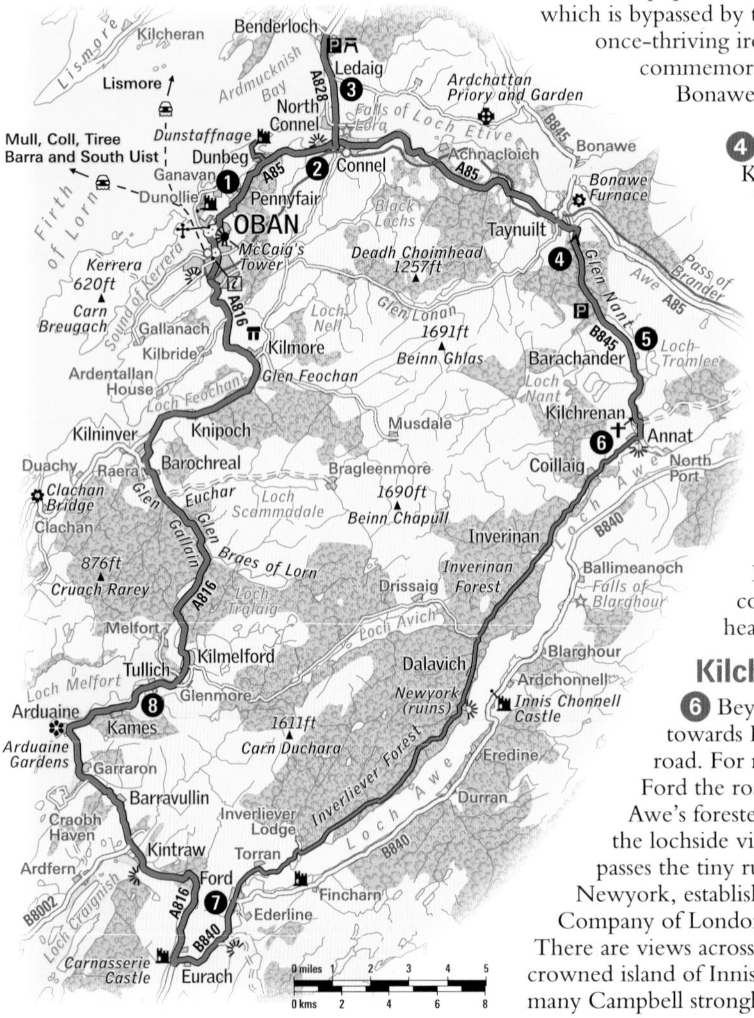

7 At Ford, bear right on the B840 alongside tiny Loch Ederline to a T-junction with the A816 at Carnasserie. The ruined 16th-century castle (HS), which is really a combined tower house and hall, has some fine architechtural detailing. It was built by John Carswell, the first Protestant Bishop of the Isles, who translated John Knox's liturgy into Gaelic in 1567.

Turn right to descend to the head of Loch Craignish, where a large, solitary standing stone on the right is flanked by the remains of two neolithic burial cairns. Continue to Arduaine, where a peaceful 8ha (20 acre) garden (NTS) thrives on Asknish Bay. The garden benefits from the North Atlantic Drift, bringing a mild climate and plenty of rain. Tender plants from all over the world are grown here, in the shelter of specially planted trees and shrubs, and it is particularly good for rhododendrons, azaleas, camellias and magnolias in the spring.

8 From Arduaine to Kilmelford the road hugs the shores of Loch Melfort, then winds through the forested Pass of Melfort and Glen Gallain to reach Kilninver on the shores of Loch Feochan. Continue on the A816 through Kilmore to Oban.

CENTRAL SCOTLAND

13 KINGUSSIE

TOUR LENGTH 52 miles

Scenery and wildlife dominate this drive through the Cairngorms National Park, from the misty Insh marshes and the RSPB's famed osprey-watching centre to lochs, hills and dense woodland where remnants of the old Caledonian Forest survive.

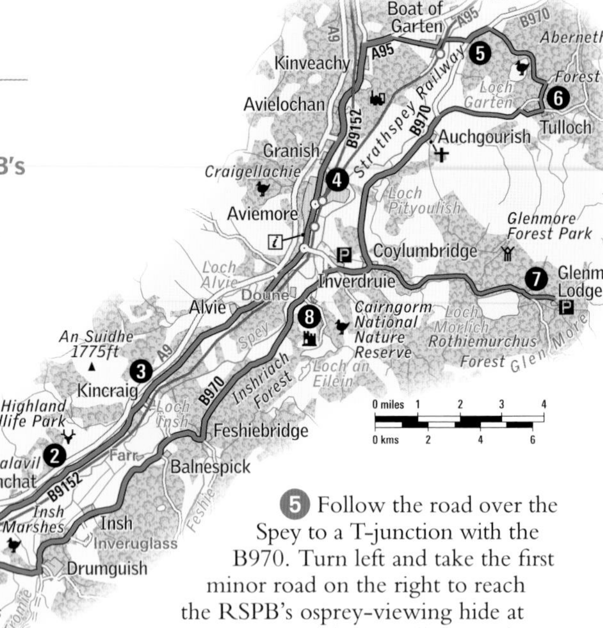

Kingussie to Glen More

❶ With the heady turpentine aroma of the surrounding Caledonian Forest blowing through it, Kingussie was once a place where invalids came to take advantage of the natural inhalant. These days the great natural forest is nearly all gone and visitors are attracted to Kingussie as a centre from which to watch birds and explore the surrounding Grampian Mountains, and to visit the fine Highland Folk Museum. Leave Kingussie on the B9152 signposted to Kincraig.

❷ Immediately beyond the hamlet of Lynchat the road passes Balavil, an imposing mansion on a slope to the left that was the home of James MacPherson, an 18th-century man of letters who claimed to have translated the manuscripts of the Celtic bard and warrior Ossian. Later research revealed the work to be a fraud.

On the opposite side of the road lies the RSPB reserve of Insh marshes, an important wintering ground for whooper swans, which fly south from Iceland and Greenland. The Highland Wildlife Park, on the left a short distance farther along the road, has bears, bison, beavers and wolves – animals that were once indigenous to the Highlands of Scotland.

❸ Continue through Kincraig to Loch Alvie where, during building work on the kirk in 1880, the bones of 150 people were discovered under the floor – a gruesome find for which no explanation has come to light.

Stay on the B9152 to the holiday resort of Aviemore, the principal centre for winter sports in Britain.

❹ Go through the centre of Aviemore and continue on the B9152, turning right on to the A95 to Grantown-on-Spey. After another 4 miles, turn right on a minor road to Boat of Garten. The Strathspey Railway, which uses steam trains, stops at this village.

❺ Follow the road over the Spey to a T-junction with the B970. Turn left and take the first minor road on the right to reach the RSPB's osprey-viewing hide at Loch Garten, which is usually open from April to the end of August.

❻ Continue along the lochside then turn right on to the road signposted to Tulloch and Tulloch Moor. After ½ mile the road divides. Fork right and continue downhill to a T-junction on the B970. Turn left to Coylumbridge, then turn left again on a minor road to Glenmore Lodge, the national outdoor training centre. Follow the road past Loch Morlich to the car park. Plenty of demanding hill walking is available from here.

Glen More to Inverdruie

❼ Drive back down the minor road to Coylumbridge and turn left on to the B970. Follow the road over the bridge, towards the village of Inverdruie. The broad rocky summit of Craigellachie, a National Nature Reserve, looms ahead, on the far side of the Spey. Turn right into Rothiemurchus Centre car park in Inverdruie. The Rothiemurchus Estate, in the centre of the Cairngorms National Park, offers many outdoor activities, including fishing and pony trekking as well as walking through spectacular scenery.

Inverdruie to Kingussie

❽ Continue on the B970 from Inverdruie to Feshiebridge, passing a minor road on the left to Loch an Eilein. Beyond Feshiebridge, the road runs above the Strathspey marshes, descending through Insh to the ruins of Ruthven Barracks – destroyed by the clan army after defeat at Culloden to prevent it falling into English hands. Stay on the B970, which passes under the A9 and over the Spey to reach Kingussie.

14 FORT WILLIAM

TOUR LENGTH 57 miles

This odd-shaped route commands such fabulous views across Loch Linnhe that it uses the same road twice, hugging the eastern shore before veering sideways to skirt Loch Leven. Driving along the Glen Nevis valley makes an impressive finale.

Fort William to Inchree

1 William of Orange lost no time in massively enlarging the strategic fortress at the head of Loch Linnhe, aware of the threat posed by Highland forces loyal to the deposed James II. Christened Fort William after the new king from Holland, it withstood sieges during the 1715 and 1745 rebellions and extended its name to the settlement nurtured under its walls, which had originally been called Maryburgh – these turbulent times are remembered in the town's West Highland Museum. The fort itself was demolished in 1855, although some remnants of it can still be seen by the side of the loch. Today's Fort William is a gateway rather than a gatekeeper – a bustling centre straddling the 'Road to the Isles' and the highway north. The huge bulk of Ben Nevis, the highest mountain in Britain, rises on one side of the town and the wilderness of Lochabar rolls away northwards.

Leave Fort William on the A82, driving south alongside Loch Linnhe, a sea loch that stretches just over nine miles into the Firth of Lorne, by the Isle of Mull. This is a busy road but a delightful one, with constantly changing views across to the hills of Ardgour on the western side of the loch. There are several large laybys on the right from which the full splendour of the scene can be appreciated.

About a mile beyond the tiny settlement of Corrychurrachan, turn right at a signpost to a picnic site, where views from the lochside are quite breathtaking.

2 Continue on the A82, passing a right turn signposted to the Corran Ferry. Ferries ply daily at roughly half-hour intervals across the Corran Narrows, a stretch of water that was held by Jacobite forces prior to the 1745 Rebellion. At Ardgour on the western side, the crossing is guarded by the Corran lighthouse, which was built in 1860 by Thomas and David Stevenson, writer Robert Louis Stevenson's father and uncle. It was one of several on the way to the Caledonian Canal.

Inchree to Kinlochleven

3 Continue on the A82 for about ½ mile to the small hamlet of Inchree, where there is a Forest Enterprise car park and, near it, some lovely ornamental gardens situated by one of the forestry houses. Half an hour's walk, mostly uphill, leads to the spectacular Righ waterfalls, which cascade over a series of rocky steps, through a wooded gorge and into a deep pool.

About ½ mile beyond Inchree, close to the pier in Onich, is a standing stone or monolith called Clach a'Charra, which is pierced by a hole.

Carry on to the junction with the B863 at North Ballachulish, where the mountains rise from the sea to more than 914m (3,000ft) and the hills of Glencoe loom over the landscape, their summits often disappearing into the clouds.

Kinlochleven to Fort William

4 Turn left on to the B863 and follow the road along the north shore of Loch Leven to Kinlochleven, the village at the head of the loch. Edward VII used to stay near here, for the shooting, and during the First World War, a prisoner of war camp was established in the woods above the village. The site can still be visited. From Kinlochleven plenty of walking is available on good, but sometimes muddy, paths and tracks. ▷

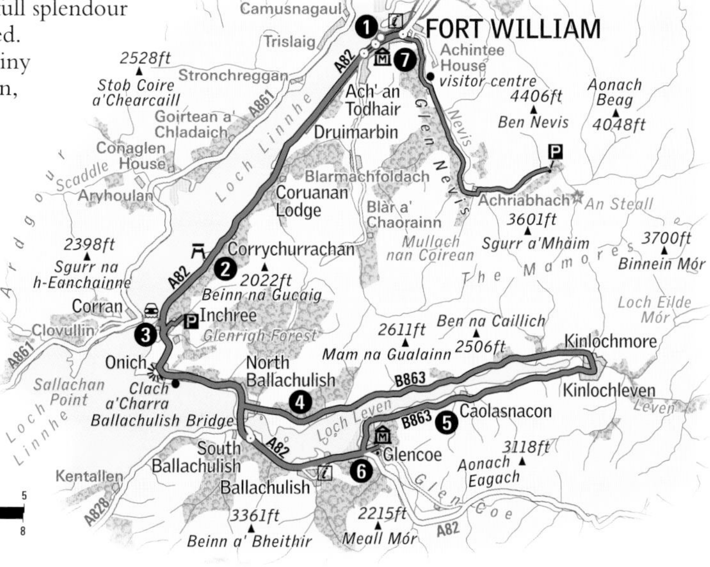

Follow the B863 as it climbs out of Kinlochleven with fine views across the loch below. After about 3 miles, at Caolasnacon, the loch narrows appreciably. In times gone by, drovers made their herds swim across the water here, on cattle drives south to the great markets, known as trysts, at Crieff and Falkirk. The mountains that can be seen across the loch include Mam na Gualainn, 796m (2,611ft), and Beinn na Caillich, 764m (2,506ft).

5 Continue along the south shore of Loch Leven, following the road as it bends left to cross the bridge over the River Coe. Beyond the bridge, turn left to the village of Glencoe, where the North Lorn Folk Museum is located in the middle of the main street.

6 Return to the B863 and turn right on to the A82 to Ballachulish. The old quarries on the left supplied the slate industry, and supported the village from the 17th century until the demise of slates as a roofing material in the 1950s.

Beside the hotel on the right, Highland Mysteryworld explores the myths and legends of Highland folklore. At the roundabout 2 miles beyond Ballachulish, go straight on, keeping to the A82 across Ballachulish Bridge. Carry on through North Ballachulish and Onich, and back along the side of Loch Linnhe to Fort William.

Fort William to Glen Nevis

7 For a scenic extension to the drive along the Glen Nevis valley, with the formidable masses of the Ben Nevis mountain range looming over the grassy slopes, leave Fort William again on the A82 towards Inverlochy. The old castle in Inverlochy, dating back to the 13th century and now ruined, was the site of a significant battle in 1645, followed by a notorious massacre. The castle was taken by the royalist Marquis of Montrose, whose forces drove out the defending Campbells and slaughtered all 1,300 of them.

At the roundabout at Nevis Bridge, take the road signposted to Glen Nevis, passing the Glen Nevis visitor centre at the foot of the main walkers' route to the summit of Ben Nevis, which soars steeply on the left. The road continues for another 5 miles around the base of the mountain as the glen narrows. From the car park at its end, a short but splendid walk further up the glen, on a good track, brings the spectacular An Steall waterfall in to view as the valley opens up again. Access to the foot of the falls across the river Nevis is by a wire bridge, one wire to walk on and two for handrails – not for the faint hearted. There is a car park at the head of the glen from where some quite strenuous walking is available on rocky footpaths. Sturdy footwear is essential.

LOCH LEVEN

SCOTLAND

CENTRAL SCOTLAND

15 BALLATER

TOUR LENGTH 78 miles

Bounded by the wild heights of Lochnagar to the south and the soaring peaks of the Grampian mountains to the north, this route leads through the wooded hills of Deeside, across bleak moorland and old bridges to Braemar and the royal retreat of Balmoral.

Ballater to Braeloine

❶ The pretty village of Ballater was developed as a spa in the late 18th century, and the area's popularity was assured from the 1850s, when Queen Victoria and Prince Albert built Balmoral Castle less than 10 miles to the west. From Station Square, take the A93 towards Aboyne. At a sharp left bend, continue over the Royal Bridge and turn left on to the B976 to Pannanich Wells Hotel. The tiny hamlet of Pannanich became widely known in 1760 when news spread that an old woman had been cured of scrofula (a form of tuberculosis) after drinking from a nearby spring, turning Ballater into a popular resort. Continue on the road, which follows the meandering River Dee through the wooded valley.

At Bridge of Ess, just before the bridge, turn right on to a narrow road signposted to the Braeloine Centre, a craft and nature venue. Follow the road as it climbs along the Water of Tanar to the car park.

Braeloine to Braemar Castle

❷ Return on the B976 towards Ballater and turn right on to the B9158 over the River Dee and through Dinnet on to the A97. After 1 mile, an unmarked track on the left leads to the Muir of Dinnet national nature reserve, an area of reedbeds, woodland, bogs and heaths, centred on two lochs. Some 140 bird species have been recorded there.

❸ Continue on the A97 through undulating farmland and moorland for some 7 miles. Past an outdoor centre to the right, turn sharp left on a narrow road towards the hamlet of Heugh-head. Just before the houses, the Old Semeil Herb Garden, established in 1820, is to be found.

❹ Drive on through the hamlet and follow the road sharp right, then turn left on to the A944 to Strathdon. At Bellabeg, where the Lonach Gathering is held each September, a sign marked 'Lost' stands beside the road. This is a signpost to a nearby farm, the name of which is derived from the Gaelic for 'productive fields'. Follow the road past Candacraig Gardens, formerly part of a large estate. The gardens are private but open to the public in summer.

❺ After 3 miles, branch right on to the A939 to Corgarff. Corgarff Castle (HS), originally a 16th-century tower house, is 1 mile farther on at Cock Bridge, at the foot of the Lecht Pass. Set

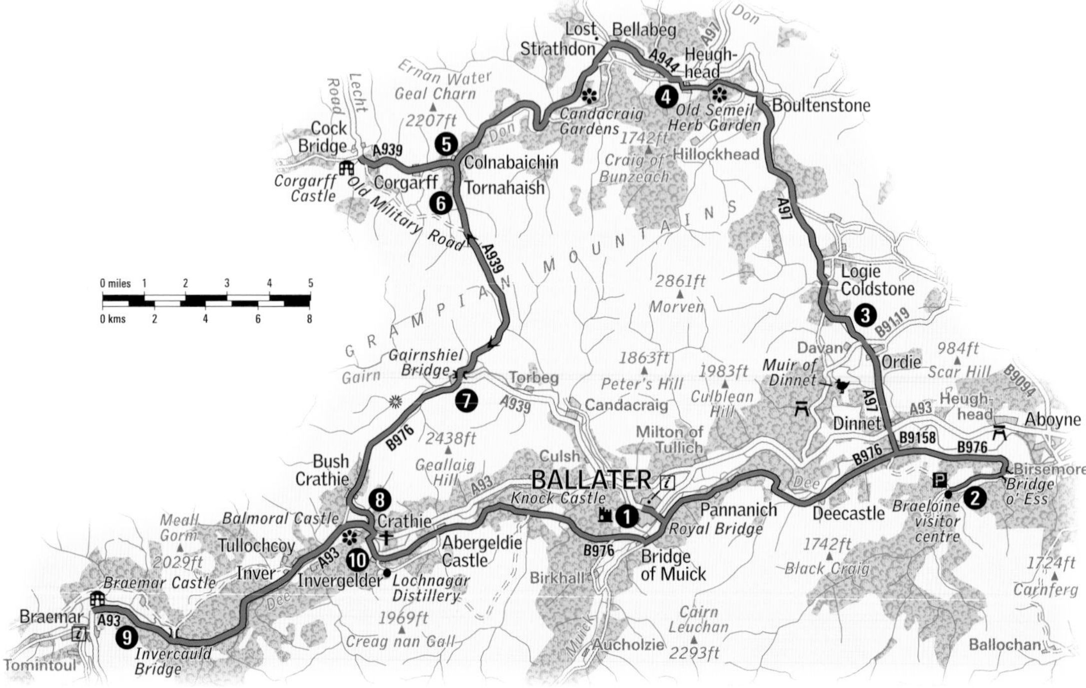

SET IN A WILD, ISOLATED SPOT
CORGARFF CASTLE

in a wild, isolated spot, Corgarff was once of strategic importance and has a violent history, including being burnt down twice. It was converted into a fort in the 18th century, when the distinctive star-shaped outer wall was built. The castle was restored in the 1960s, and a barrack room reconstructed.

6 Return to the junction with the A944 and continue on the A939 south towards Ballater, climbing steeply through desolate moorland on the old military road, which originally went directly to Corgarff. Its former course is marked by a track on the right. Cross the great humpback bridge at Gairnshiel, built in 1751.

7 Turn right on the B976. The narrow road twists through heather-clad moorland to a viewpoint near several cairns. The road passes Crathie, where Queen Victoria's faithful servant John Brown was born in 1836. Members of the royal family worship at Crathie Kirk.

8 Turn right on to the A93 towards Braemar. The road crosses the Dee at Invercauld – from the bridge, or brig, of 1752 the river can be seen flowing through wooded hills. Carry on to visit community-owned Braemar Castle, which also has a star-shaped outer wall. Check times first.

Braemar Castle to Ballater

9 Return on the A93 to Crathie, then turn right on the B976 towards Ballater. Across the bridge is Balmoral Castle. The grounds and their 16th-century tower house were bought by the Prince Consort in 1852, and the present castle was built a few years later. The grounds and gardens are open to visitors from April to July.

10 Follow the B976, passing a road to Lochnagar Distillery's visitor centre on the right. After about 7 miles a signposted track on the left leads to the ruins of 17th-century Knock Castle (HS). Continue through Bridge of Muick then turn left into Ballater.

CENTRAL SCOTLAND

16 TOMINTOUL

TOUR LENGTH 63 miles

Great swathes of heather moor sweep to the north and east, pure mountain streams tumble down to the Spey, and peat moss is dug nearby. This is malt whisky country, and the distilleries have visitor centres.

Tomintoul to Clash Wood

1 The Duke of Gordon envisaged Tomintoul as a centre for flax-growing and the linen trade when he set out its gridiron of streets in 1776, but it was the combination of golden barley and local streamwater, infused with the smell of peat smoke to make malt whisky, that made the region prosperous.

Take the B9008 towards Dufftown, driving through farmland and woods and across moors. After about 2 miles the road passes Tomintoul peat moss, on the left, a source of fuel for the kilns in surrounding malt whisky distilleries.

2 Follow the road, through Knockandhu to the centre of Tomnavoulin. Cross the bridge over the burn, the Allt a' Choire, pass Tomnavoulin Farm, on the left, then turn left on a minor road. After a short distance turn left into Clash Wood. The mature coniferous woodland is enclosed to keep out the deer, and supports red squirrels, badgers, wood mice, hares and many species of birds.

Clash Wood to Aberlour

3 Return to the B9008, turn left and at Auchbreck turn right on to the B9009 towards Dufftown. The road passes Morinsh Woods. Paths lead to the site of the Battle of Glenlivet, where in 1594 a force loyal to the Gordons defeated a much larger one owing allegiance to the Campbells.

4 Continue through the moorlands and rough pastures of Glen Rinnes, with Ben Rinnes, an 840m (2,755ft) high mountain with distinctive twin peaks, to the left. A golf course, on the left, marks the approach to Dufftown, founded in 1817 by James Duff, 4th Earl of Fife. The clock tower in the square houses the tourist information centre, and there is a small local history museum in Fife Street.

5 From the square, follow the A941 towards Craigellachie, passing the Glenfiddich Distillery on the right, where guided tours are given to the public. Near the distillery are the ruins of 13th-century Balvenie Castle (HS), occupied by the Duke of Cumberland ('the Butcher') in 1746 during his bloody suppression of the Highlands in the year following the Battle of Culloden.

BALLINDALLOCH CASTLE

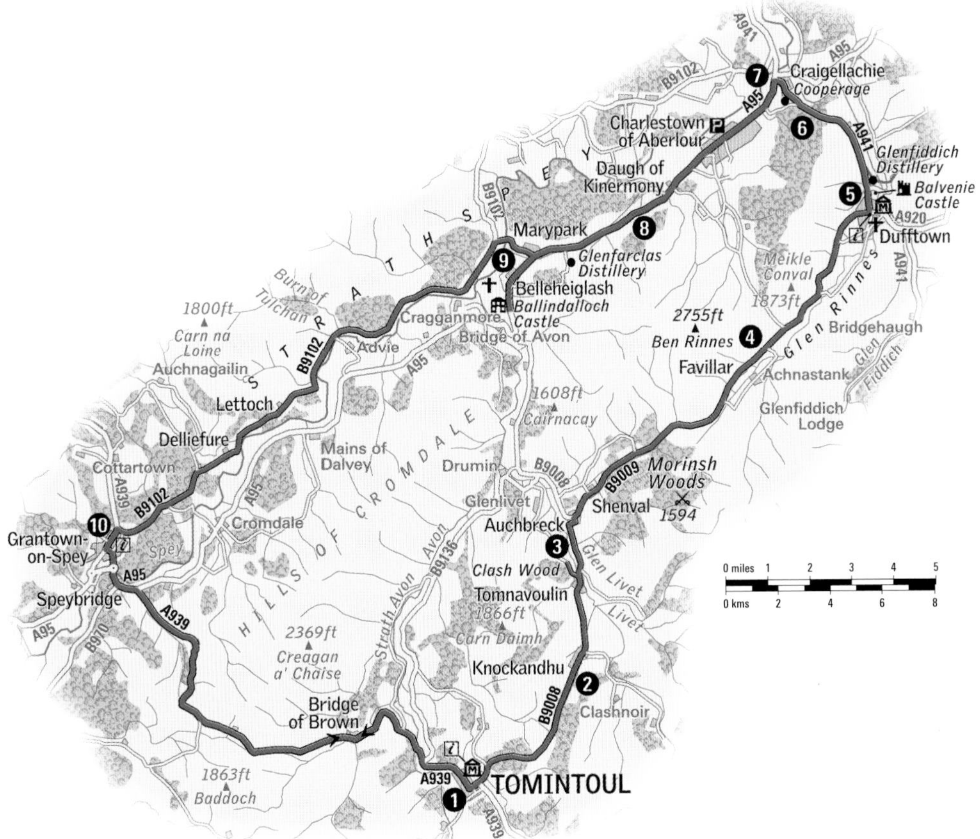

6 The Speyside Cooperage, where there are displays of barrel making, is conspicuously signposted on the approach to Craigellachie. The great Scots engineer Thomas Telford's elegant single-arched iron bridge over the Spey at Craigellachie is now bypassed by a new crossing, although it is firmly on the itinerary of walkers on the Speyside Way, a 50 mile long-distance trail, which passes through the town on its way from Spey Bay at the mouth of the river to Tomintoul.

Aberlour to Grantown-on-Spey

7 From Craigellachie turn left on to the A95 to Charlestown of Aberlour, usually referred to simply as Aberlour, following the course of the Spey upstream. At the Old Pantry tearoom, on the right-hand side of the main street by the square, turn right to reach the riverside car park. The Victoria Bridge, a suspension footbridge, used to be nicknamed the penny bridge because of the toll once claimed by a local landowner.

8 Continue on the A95, passing the Glenfarclas Distillery and visitor centre on the left and the B9138 junction on the right, to reach Inveraven Kirk, where the kirkyard contains Pictish stones. A short distance farther on, a minor road on the right leads to Ballindalloch Castle, which is privately owned and open from Easter to the end of September (but closed on Saturdays). Originating in the 16th century, many additions have been made since then.

9 From the castle return to the junction with the B9138 and turn left. Cross the Spey and turn left on to the B9102. The narrow road winds along the side of the Spey for all but the final 3 miles into Grantown-on-Spey, founded in 1776 by Sir James Grant as a centre for the Highland linen industry.

Grantown-on-Spey to Tomintoul

10 Turn left at the T-junction with the A939 to reach the town centre, then turn left on to the A95 towards Speybridge to join the A95 at a roundabout, taking the second exit to go straight on over the Spey. The village of Speybridge and the original three-span bridge, built in 1754 and now closed to traffic, can be seen downriver.

A mile beyond the bridge, turn right on to the A939 towards Tomintoul. Some of the route follows the old military road that was carved in the aftermath of Culloden. After Bridge of Brown, the road descends to Urlarmore, crossing the River Avon upstream from Bridge of Avon, a military crossing built in 1754. The road follows the river for a short way, then climbs uphill to reach Tomintoul.

CENTRAL SCOTLAND

17 BANFF

TOUR LENGTH 79 miles

North of the Grampian mountains, a fringe of red sandstone along the Moray Firth provides spectacular coastal scenery. The route passes secluded coves and fishing villages, and diverts inland, where a whisky distilling industry thrives.

Banff to Balloch Wood

1 In the port and resort of Banff, many houses belonging to 17th and 18th-century landed families have been preserved, and fine silver and armoury displays can be seen in the town's museum. Duff House (HS), seat of the Earls of Fife, is also a cultural arts centre with a regular programme of exhibitions, music and lectures. It is jointly run with National Galleries of Scotland and Aberdeenshire Coucil. From its car park, take the A97 towards Huntly.

Continue through farmland to Aberchirder, where the church, built in 1842, was the first Free Church of Scotland. The Free Church was recognised at a general assembly in 1843 following the Disruption, a schism that led to the resignation of 451 Presbyterian ministers from their livings. Their protest was against the nomination of ministers by patrons, such as the Crown or landowners, rather than by church congregations.

2 Continue on the A97 for 3 miles and turn left to Inverkeithny, entering the valley of the River Deveron. Turn right in the village opposite the Old Schoolhouse and continue ahead on the narrow road. Then turn right on to the B9024 and take the next right on to the B9001 past the Glendronach whisky distillery, which is open to visitors in summer.

3 Drive on to the junction with the A97 and turn left to the market town of Huntly, which, from the 14th century, was the powerbase of the Gordon family. Their old stronghold, Huntly Castle (HS), beside the Deveron, dates from the 12th century, but has a largely 16th and 17th-century palace and court. The castle fell into ruins when the Gordons later moved to Fochabers.

4 Take the A96 out of Huntly to Keith. In the town, turn right from Moss Street into Bridge Street. Continue ahead to Wester Herricks. Pass Herricks water treatment works on the left, and turn left on to a forestry track where the road bends right. Park at the side of the track to explore the mature conifer plantation of Balloch Wood. A network of paths crisscross the forest.

Balloch Wood to Cullen

5 Continue through Keith, passing the Strathisla Distillery, the oldest working distillery in the Highlands, and one of eight on a 70 mile Malt Whisky Trail through the foothills of the Grampians. Outside the town, turn right across

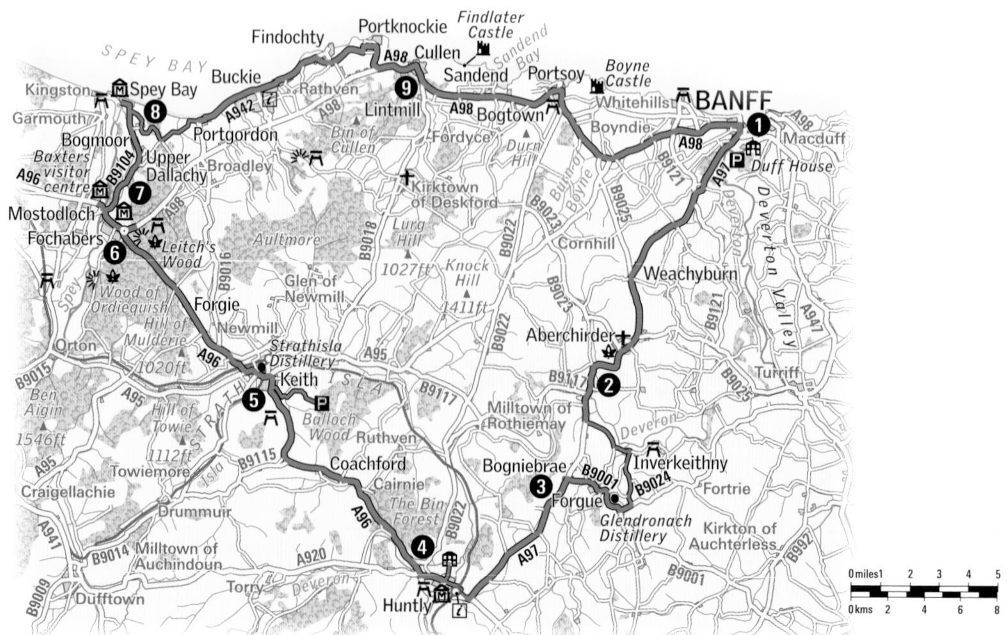

FINDOCHTY HARBOUR

a railway bridge on to the A96 towards Fochabers. At a roundabout, the junction with the A98 turn right and follow the signs for a forest car park. Leitch's Wood has walks and a viewpoint.

6 Return to the A96 and continue to Fochabers where the Georgian church has a clock tower dated 1798. Another church has been converted into a folk museum, telling the history of the town, which was founded in 1776. Prior to that, the old town of Fochabers was located a short way to the north, too near Gordon Castle for the 4th Duke's liking, so he had it moved. Just outside the town, Baxters soup factory has a visitor centre. George Baxter, once a gardener at Gordon Castle, started his food business in 1868. From Fochabers, take the B9104 on to the Speyside Way.

7 Continue through Bogmoor to Spey Bay. The Tugnet Ice House, owned by the Whale and Dolphin Conservation Society, is open to the public, but check times before planning a visit. Built to serve the fishing industry in 1830, it is the largest industrial ice house in Britain; just one third is visible above ground. It was filled with ice gathered from the Spey, and used to keep salmon fresh until shipping.

8 Returning to the outskirts of Spey Bay, fork left on minor roads to the former fishing village of Portgordon and follow the A942 coastal road through Buckie and Findochty – a big church is prominent on a rocky bluff – to Portknockie. Here there are unusual rock formations and lovely clifftop views. The harbour is sheltered by a rocky promontory, known as Green Castle, where a Pictish fortress once stood and traces of an Iron Age site have been found. Continue inland to the A98 and turn left for Cullen, where 19th-century railway viaducts are a reminder of the age of steam.

Cullen to Banff

9 Leave Cullen on the A98, passing Sandend on the way to Portsoy, a former coastal trading community. There, painstakingly preserved warehouses were once filled with greenish or reddish serpentine Portsoy marble, quarried nearby. The stone was particularly popular in 17th and 18th-century France and used in the chimney pieces at the Palace of Versailles.

A coastal walk east of the harbour leads to the ruins of late 16th-century Boyne Castle, a seat of the Ogilvies until their ownership was forfeited for supporting Bonnie Prince Charlie in the 1745 rebellion. Continue on the A98 to Banff.

NORTH HIGHLANDS & ISLANDS

Amid the untamed beauty of the mountains beyond the Great Glen, unexpectedly fertile coastal lowlands support tender plants. Deserted crofts scatter the uplands while eagles soar above the lofty peaks.

18 DORNOCH

TOUR LENGTH 90 miles

From the sandy shore of the Dornoch Firth, follow the route of the salmon upriver into a vast landscape of low hills dotted with crofting communities. Then turn back to wooded lowlands and the Tarbat peninsula.

Dornoch to Invershin

1 Extensive sands and a renowned golf course flank the compact town of Dornoch, which in the 13th century became an important place of worship after a cathedral was built here by Gilbert de Moravia, bishop of Caithness. To start the drive, take the A949 signposted to Inverness. Turn left on to the A9 and continue for about a mile, then turn right on to the A949 towards Bonar Bridge and Lairg.

2 The road winds downhill through woods and fields close to the Dornoch Firth. Just before Ospisdale, on the left, is a standing stone some 3m (10ft) high. At Spinningdale, nestling in a narrow river valley below wooded hills, castle-like ruins are all that remain of an early industrial venture, a cotton mill built in the 1790s. Apparently, it burnt down in 1806.

3 Continue to Bonar Bridge, where a distinctive bow-shaped bridge crosses the southern tip of the Kyle of Sutherland, then turn right on to the A836 signposted to Lairg.

4 Continue to Invershin, passing under a railway viaduct. A footbridge over the river leads to 19th-century Carbisdale Castle (now a youth hostel), which has 365 windows. Nearby Culrain was the scene, in 1650, of the Battle of Carbisdale, in which the Covenanters defeated the royalist General Montrose.

Invershin to Littleferry

5 About ½ mile through Invershin, turn left at the junction signposted to Lochinver, the A837, then turn right on to the B864 to Lairg. The road follows the course of the River Shin, which flows through a wooded ravine below. From the Falls of Shin visitor centre paths lead down to the river, where every summer salmon struggle against the torrent to reach their spawning grounds.

BONAR BRIDGE

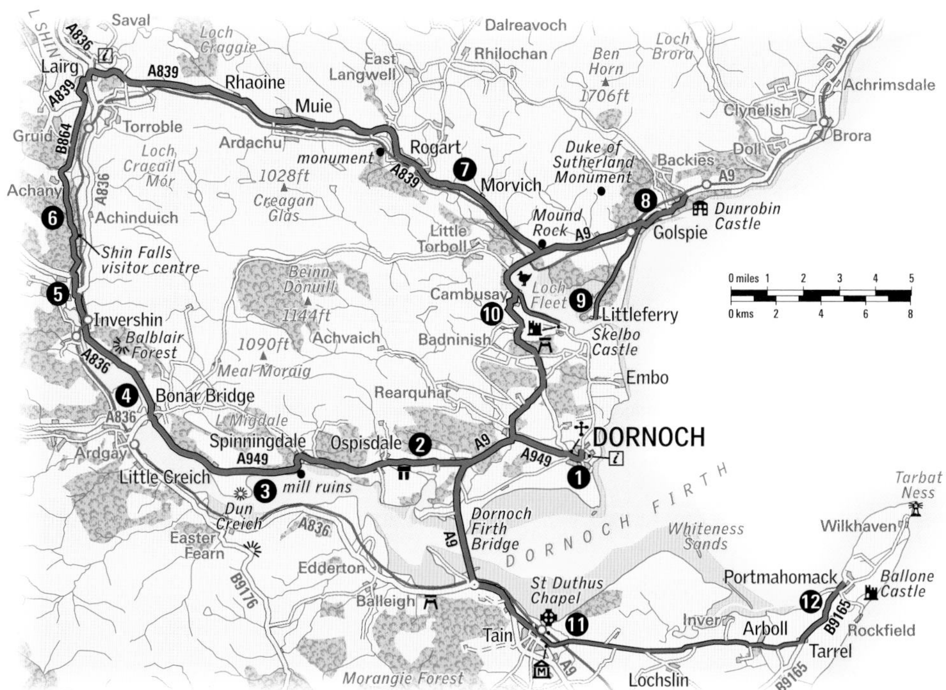

6 Carry on following the signs to Lairg, a large village at the centre of a vast crofting and farming hinterland. From Lairg turn right on to the A839 towards Rogart, climbing to the scattered crofts at Rhaoine then descending to the sprawling crofting community of Rogart. Across the valley to the right of the road, a cairn marks the birthplace in 1815 of Sir John Alexander Macdonald, the architect of the Canadian confederacy and Canada's first prime minister in 1867.

7 Continue along wooded and heather-clad foothills to the head of Loch Fleet, dominated by Mound Rock. Turn left on to the A9 to Golspie and Dunrobin Castle, turreted seat of the dukes of Sutherland. Far-reaching views can be had from the castle's luxuriant formal gardens, laid out in the style of Versailles, and also from the nearby hilltop statue of the 1st Duke of Sutherland, who played a leading role in the 19th-century Highland clearances.

8 Go back through Golspie and, before crossing the railway, bear left on a minor road to Littleferry. A steam ferry once used to cross the mouth of Loch Fleet from the old pier, despite the tide racing through at great speed.

Littleferry to Tain

9 Return to Golspie and turn left on to the A9. Go over the causeway crossing the head of Loch Fleet, then fork left towards Embo, following the shore to a car park by the ruins of Skelbo Castle (not open to the public). Loch Fleet is a nature reserve, where common seals, kittiwakes, terns and cormorants can often be seen. When the rising tide shuts the sluice gates in the causeway, salmon moving in from the sea to spawn gather in a pool until the way upriver is open. Their main run is in July.

10 Return to the A9 and follow the signs to Dornoch and Inverness. Stay on the A9 and carry on over the Dornoch Firth Bridge, which was opened in 1991. At the roundabout follow the signs into Tain. The town was established by St Duthus as a place of pilgrimage in the 11th century. The Heritage Centre and District Museum explain the area's history.

Tain to Dornoch

11 From Tain, follow an unclassified road signposted to Portmahomack, on the Tarbat peninsula. In this picturesque village, neat rows of whitewashed houses line the harbour, and at low tide, rock pools appear, scattered across the broad sandy bay. A Discovery Centre, housed in the Old Tarbat Parish Church, tells visitors about the area's Pictish past. Since the village faces west, unusually for this coast, sunsets witnessed from here may be spectacular.

12 To complete the drive, return to Tain and retrace the route across the Dornoch Firth Bridge, turning right, off the A9 on to the A949, for Dornoch.

NORTH HIGHLANDS & ISLANDS

19 STRATHPEFFER

TOUR LENGTH 77 miles

The mild climate and gentle landscape of the Black Isle contrast with the Highlands that surround it. Rolling fields cascade to the coast, popular coastal villages are known as 'the Riviera of the north', and Pictish stones indicate long habitation.

Strathpeffer to Cromarty

1 The Victorian spa village of Strathpeffer lies at the foot of Ben Wyvis. Visitors can still take the waters or travel back in time at the old railway station, which houses the Highland Museum of Childhood (open in the summer).

Start the drive from the tourist information centre in the square, taking the A834 towards Dingwall, a market town on the shores of the Cromarty Firth. The town's heritage trail includes the Town House Museum of local history and the Hector MacDonald Memorial tower, which commemorates a general who was aide-de-camp to Queen Victoria.

2 From Dingwall follow the A862 towards Inverness, and turn left at the roundabout on to the A835 towards Cromarty. Take the first left after the bridge over the Firth, the B9163, towards Findon. From the road there are lovely views towards Ben Wyvis. Keep following the signs to Findon and Cromarty. From the coast road around Urquhart, wildfowl and waders can be seen feeding on the mudflats below.

3 Turn right on to the busy A9, and then immediately left back on to the B9163. After 2 miles turn left at the junction towards Cullicudden. After Balblair, the road is single track for ½ mile. Continue on the B9163 to Udale Bay, where seabirds, such as greylag and pink-footed geese, can sometimes be observed from an RSPB hide.

4 Continue along the shore for 5 miles to Cromarty, from where boat trips leave to view the marine life of the Firth. The only thatched building left in Cromarty is Hugh Miller's house (NTS) in Church Street. Hugh Miller was a stonemason who went on to become a geologist, author and church reformer. The house has been restored to look as it would have done when he lived there in the early 19th century.

Follow the shore road through Cromarty, and take a single-track road towards McFarquhar's Bed – a sea stack with two arches, once used as a salmon fishing station. Turn left at the Cromarty Mains junction and park at the end of the road near the old coastguard lookout. Nearby are the Sutors of Cromarty, headlands on either side of the entrance to Cromarty Firth. 'Sutor' is the Scottish word for shoemaker and the legend is that two giant 'sutors' used the headlands for workbenches.

Cromarty to Beauly

5 From Cromarty, take the A832 towards Fortrose. At Rosemarkie, the history of the Picts is recorded at Groam House Museum, and a Pictish cross slab stands outside. Inland is the RSPB's Fairy Glen nature reserve.

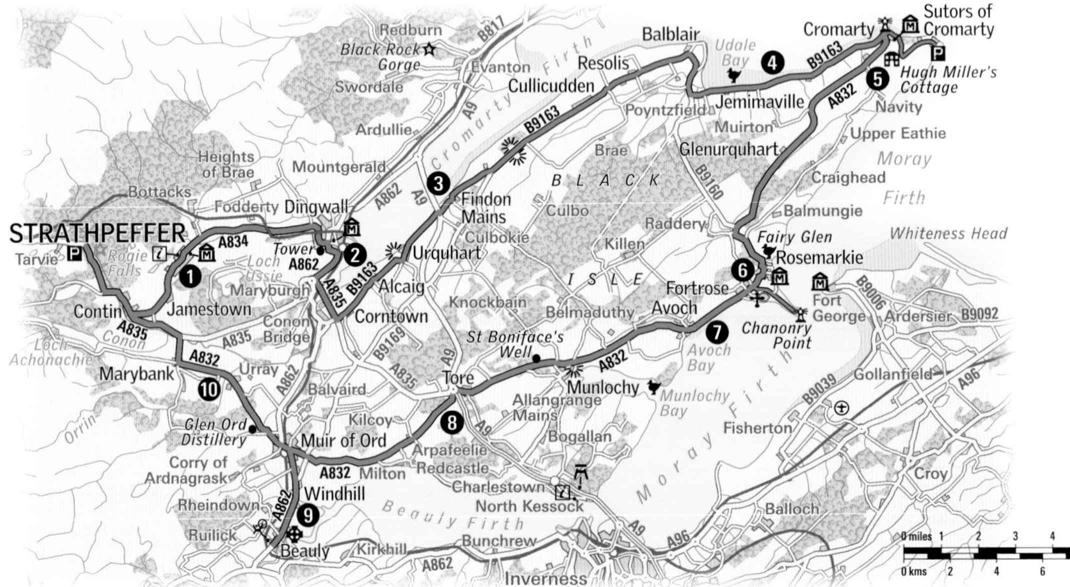

6 Continue to Fortrose, where the ruins of a 14th-century cathedral still stand in Cathedral Square. From Chanonry Point, outside the village, bottle-nosed dolphins can sometimes be seen in the Moray Firth.

7 Continue on the A832 through Avoch (pronounced 'Och'), passing St Boniface's Well. The trees around the well are covered in 'clouts' – rags left as an offering for the granting of a wish, a tradition created from a mixture of Celtic and Christian beliefs.

8 At the Tore roundabout, take the second exit, the A832, to Muir of Ord. At the junction in Muir of Ord, turn left to Beauly, which has a craft centre and a 13th-century priory (HS), which once had a fine orchard.

Beauly to Strathpeffer

9 Return to the Muir of Ord junction, turn left on to the A832, cross a railway bridge and take the first left towards Marybank, still on the A832. The Glen Ord Distillery and visitor centre are on the left.

10 Follow the A832, bear right at Marybank and cross the Moy bridge – the road narrows to a single track. At the junction, turn left on to the A835 to Contin and continue ahead to the Rogie Falls in the mainly coniferous Torrachilty Forest. From the suspension bridge near the car park, salmon can sometimes be seen leaping the high falls between June and October. Wild cats and pine martens live in the forest, and otters inhabit its small lochs. Return to Contin and take the first left on the A834 to return to Strathpeffer.

ROGIE FALLS

Take the high road

Following the coast road north is a trip back to a time when life was hard amid the stark beauty of the empty land and rocky shore.

The drive along the great right-angled sweep of the Caithness coast is a trip through some of the emptiest-seeming landscape in the world. But it wasn't always this forsaken. It was emigration, following the forced clearance of the local population to make way for more lucrative and less argumentative sheep, that emptied much of the far north of Scotland in the 19th century. From Strath Halladale to the Strath of Kildonan, the hills and moors still lie largely untenanted, as they have done for the past two centuries. By contrast, the bare, bleak coasts of the region, dramatic in their rocky isolation, lie studded with the settlements that came into being, or were developed from lonely fishing hamlets, at around the time of the clearances. Like so many grey stone commas, they punctuate the long road that curls for 90 miles from Helmsdale all the way north and west to the estuary of the Halladale River in Melvich Bay.

These dour little stone-built towns and villages of Scotland's northeasternmost coast mostly date from the late 18th or early 19th centuries. Some were created by landlords to receive the tenants they had cleared from their inland estates. Others were built by the splendidly named 'British Society for Extending the Fisheries and Improving the Sea Coast of this Kingdom' (soon shortened to 'British Fisheries Society') in a praiseworthy drive to provide employment and exploit the natural resources of mainland Britain's most back-of-beyond region. Helmsdale, Dunbeath, Wick, Castletown, Thurso – they go about their self-contained business above their fortress-like harbours, amid craggy cliffs and long strands of cream-coloured sand. This is wonderful country for village-to-village, bay-to-bay sauntering, and the north coast road encourages just that with its gentle curves and gradients, its glimpses of empty beaches and rugged headlands that seduce the traveller off the main route and down little side roads where no-one ever seems to venture.

Project abandoned

The formidable harbour walls of Helmsdale face into the North Sea some 50 miles south of Duncansby Head. On the cliffs just north of the grey little fishing town lie the ruins of Badbea, reached via a boardwalk from a car park alongside the A9. It was Sir John Sinclair who established Badbea for his displaced tenants. He intended them to grow oats, to find employment in the coastal industries he founded – distilling, weaving and fishing. But Badbea proved an impossible place to thrive and bring up a family. The village stood on poor, thin soil at the edge of 90m cliffs, a situation so wind-blasted and dangerous that the women had to tie their children to sticks and bushes while they worked. Now a few poignant ruins among the gorse bear witness to the life and death of Badbea.

North again, the A9 morphs into the A99 to Ulbster, where an obscure path to the cliff edge leads to the rough stone stairway of Whaligoe Steps, which plunge and zigzag down the face of 60m crags. Another local benefactor, David Brodie, paid £8 early in the 19th century to have the flagstone stairs built so that fishermen and their wives could carry creels of fish on their backs, up from the jetty deep in the black cleft of Whaligoe ('whale inlet') to the fish-curing shed

on the cliff. It must have been a tiring and tricky climb in the best of conditions; dangerous in driving rain; little short of deadly in the ice, snow and gales so common along this exposed northern coast.

Northernmost point

Around the time that Whaligoe Steps were built, the great engineer Thomas Telford developed huge harbour basins in the town of Wick in order to exploit the glut of herring then swarming off the Scottish coast. The A99 sweeps through the town, then forges north to the tourist village of John O'Groats through windy farming country where the fields are hedged with black flagstones. Most people think John O'Groats is the most northerly point of the British mainland, or the most northeasterly. It's neither. The northeastern-most point is Duncansby Head and to reach it necessitates turning aside off the main coast road. This is a weather-beaten spot, remarkable for the huge cleft of the Geo of Sclaites that cuts into the cliffs south of the lighthouse, and the twin sea stacks that taper like turbans out of the bay of Thirle Door as if a pair of Turkish giants had left their spare headgear behind.

At John O'Groats, the A836 takes over from the A99 and the coast swings to the west. Thurso lies 20 miles farther along, a fishing town with a narrow harbour and a windy, Norse feel to its grey stone streets. Before reaching Thurso, however, turn north at Dunnet village and follow a country road for 5 miles across bleak, loch-bespattered moorland right up to the stubby white lighthouse on Dunnet Head. Perched there, it's possible to stare across the white horses of the Pentland Firth to the cliffs of the Orkney island of Hoy in the rather splendid knowledge that, here and now, no other person is standing farther north in mainland Britain.

The bare, bleak coasts of the region are dramatic in their rocky isolation

DUNBEATH CASTLE, CAITHNESS

NORTH HIGHLANDS & ISLANDS

20 GAIRLOCH

TOUR LENGTH 69 miles

Beautiful Loch Maree and a national nature reserve, sub-tropical gardens and stunning views of the Western Isles from a rocky coast are the focal points of this Highland jaunt, based on three separate routes radiating out from the scattered village of Gairloch.

Gairloch to Kinlochewe

1 Even by Scottish standards Gairloch has a stunning setting, attracting holidaymakers ever since Victorian families braved the steamer trip up the west coast to the town's little harbour. The waters of a sea loch – warmed by the Gulf Stream – stretch away to a horizon punctuated by the darker blue shapes of Skye and Lewis. Behind the town, the rock-and-lake country of Wester Ross rolls upwards to the bare, rocky domes of the Torridons – a haunted landscape of desolate beauty, dotted with the ruins of crofts abandoned during the Highland clearances.

To start the first drive, head south on the A832 from Gairloch, with the sea to the right. Beyond Charlestown the road turns inland, along the wooded glen of the Kerry, and continues to the river's source in Loch Bad an Sgalaig.

2 A mile beyond the loch the road leaves the rocky open country for the dark and brooding pines of Slattadale Forest, which extends all the way down to the shores of Loch Maree. Turn right near the bottom of the hill into a car park and picnic place. A short stroll leads to a viewing platform over Victoria Falls, a lovely cascade on the burn flowing into Loch Maree.

SHIELDAIG

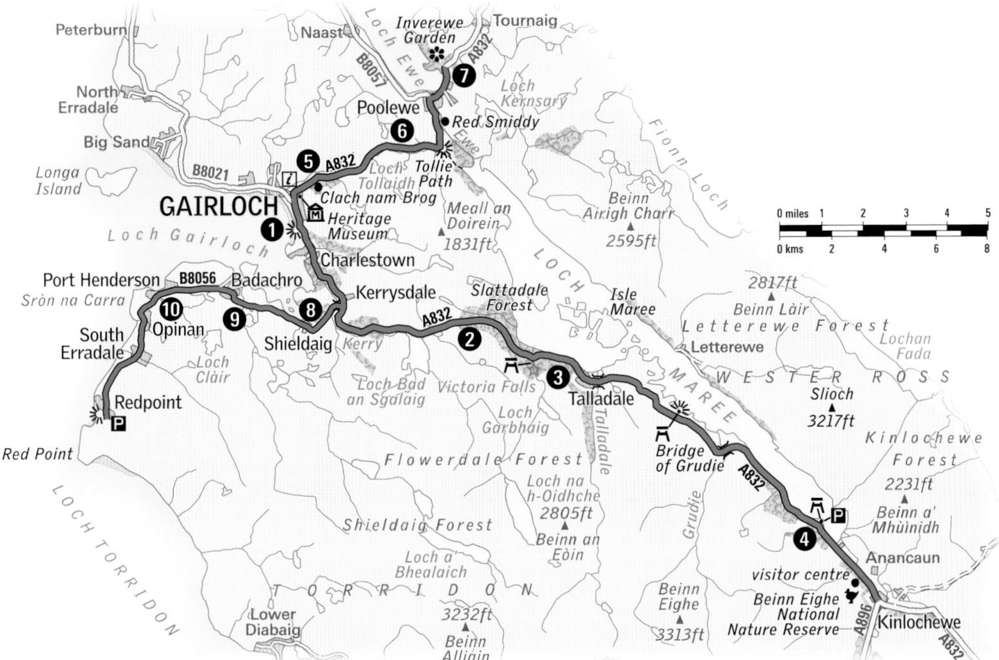

3 Rejoin the A832, turn right and continue down to the shore of Loch Maree. Across the water lies a group of more than 50 islands – including Isle Maree, on which stand the remains of a chapel built by a 7th-century Celtic saint.

The road continues through Talladale and over the Bridge of Grudie. The landscape across the water is dominated by the dramatic, buttressed summit of Slioch.

4 One mile before the head of the loch, there is an easily missed car park for Beinn Eighe Trails on the left. Mountain and woodland trails start from here. Continue along the road for the visitor centre at Kinlochewe, 2½ miles farther on.

Gairloch to Poolewe

5 For the second drive from Gairloch, take the A832 heading northwards. The road bends inland, crossing a cattle grid on to open moorland scattered with rocks – including a huge roadside stone on the right called Clach nam Brog, or Shoe Stone. This is where, until well into the 20th century, women would pause to put on their stockings and shoes on their way to church.

6 Less than a mile beyond Loch Tollaidh the road passes a layby on the left, from where there is a view down the Tollie path to Loch Maree. The road meets the banks of the River Ewe opposite the remains of Red Smiddy, where the first ironworks in Scotland was established in the early 17th century.

7 Continue on the A832 for ½ mile beyond Poolewe to the entrance to Inverewe Garden (NTS), where the area's microclimate allows the cultivation of sub-tropical plants and flowers.

Gairloch to Redpoint

8 For the third drive from Gairloch, take the A832 southwards and continue for 2 miles to a junction with the B8056. Turn right, following the signpost to Redpoint. The road immediately crosses a stone bridge over the River Kerry, then winds through deciduous woodland before returning to the sea loch at Shieldaig, a hamlet on a little island-sheltered bay. Shieldaig island is densely forested with Scots pines, thought to have been planted in the 1800s.

9 Continue to Badachro, the model of a remote west coast settlement with its small harbour and peat cuttings. The village is situated on an inlet from Loch Gairloch, and protected by the small rocky island of Eilean Horrisdale. Locally caught cod used to be dried at Badachro, but the boats moored there now are mainly leisure craft.

10 Drive on through Port Henderson, Opinan and South Erradale. The road climbs past a layby that offers magnificent views of the Western Isles, and soon comes to an end at the scattered village of Redpoint. From the parking area, there is a path to the beach and it is also possible to walk on to Red Point itself – a low promontory to the south with wonderful views of the Isle of Skye.

NORTH HIGHLANDS & ISLANDS

21 PORTREE

TOUR LENGTH 75 miles

Reminders of Flora Macdonald are never far away on this trip around the rugged coast of Skye's northern peninsula, where dramatic waterfalls and surprising rock formations are set amid superb scenery.

Portree to Uig

❶ Bright, colour-washed houses overlook the harbour of Skye's capital, Portree. It was at McNab's Inn, on the site of the Royal Hotel, that Bonnie Prince Charlie bade farewell to Flora Macdonald in 1746 before he returned to France.

To start the drive, follow the A855, signposted to Staffin. Go past Loch Fada and Loch Leathan on the right, with sea views opening up over the Sound of Raasay. On the far edge of a pine plantation on the left, a footpath leads to the Old Man of Storr rock pinnacle. These weirdly shaped rocks stand at the foot of the Storr, cliffs that rise up to 719m (2,358ft) and dominate the area.

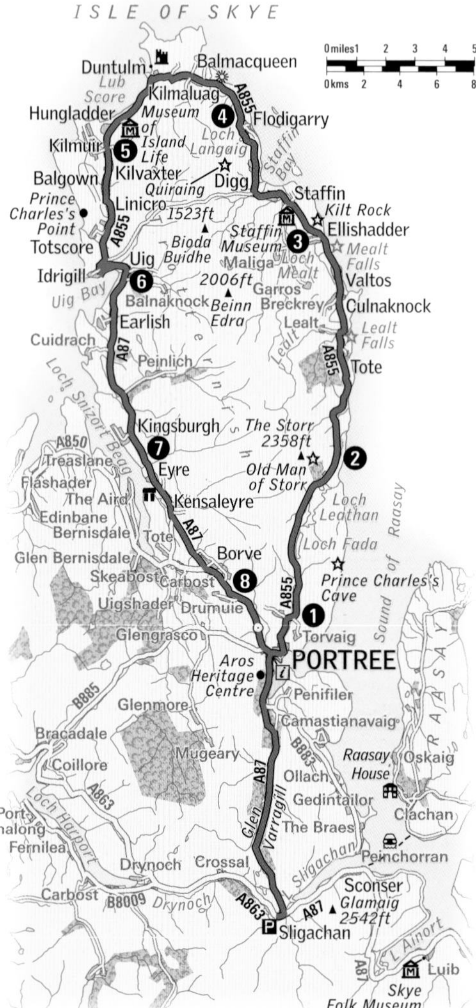

❷ Carry on along the A855 and just after a bridge over the River Lealt, turn in to a car park. From there a footpath leads to a headland, with views back to the dramatic Lealt Falls, where the river drops into a gorge.

Continue to Loch Mealt. Opposite the loch, take a minor road on the right to a car park with views of Mealt Falls, plunging 52m (171ft) to the sea, and Kilt Rock, where bands of light and dark dolerite in the basalt rock cliff face resemble the pleats of a kilt. Next to the Kilt Rock viewpoint is the Staffin Museum, which displays a collection of dinosaur fossils, plus local geological samples that tell the history of Skye's northern peninsula, the Trotternish.

❸ Drive on to Staffin, a crofting community that backs on to broad Staffin Bay. Follow the A855 out of Staffin. After 3 miles the road reaches Loch Langaig on the left, where a footpath leads to the strange ancient rock towers of the 543m (1,781ft) high Quiraing, which is Gaelic for 'pillared stronghold'. Among the pinnacles is The Table, a grassy area that was used for hiding cattle from raiders in the 15th and 16th centuries. After less than a mile the road comes to tiny Flodigarry, where Flora Macdonald lived when she returned to Skye in 1751 after her imprisonment in London, and bore five of her seven children. Her former cottage is now part of a hotel.

❹ Follow the A855 to Duntulm. On the headland above a sheer cliff are the ruins of Duntulm Castle, once a Pictish fortress and in the 16th and 17th centuries the stronghold of the Clan Donald.

Follow the A855 as it turns south towards Kilmuir. On the left is the Skye Museum of Island Life, recalling crofting over the past 100 years. Nearby is a memorial to Flora Macdonald, who was buried here in 1790, wrapped in a sheet from Bonnie Prince Charlie's bed.

❺ Continue on the A855 around a hairpin bend and drop towards Uig Bay. At the next junction, the A855 becomes the A87. Turn right to the fishing port of Uig. Ferries leave from the pier for the Outer Hebrides.

Uig to Sligachan

❻ Leaving Uig, turn right on to the A87. After 5 miles cross over the River Hinnisdal and continue for 1¼ miles to Kingsburgh, on the shores of Loch Snizort Beag. Bonnie Prince

STRANGE ANCIENT ROCK TOWERS

THE QUIRAING

Charlie spent a night at Kingsburgh House in 1746, when the price on his head was £30,000. Flora Macdonald moved to the house in 1756, and here in 1773 she met Dr Johnson and James Boswell on their tour of the Highlands.

7 Follow the A87 to Kensaleyre, the site of two standing stones said to be almost 4,000 years old. Legend tells that they once supported the cooking pot of Fionn, king of the Feinne, and his warriors, who would tuck into venison after a day's hunting.

8 Go ahead at a junction with the A850. Return to Portree and turn right on the A87 towards Sligachan. Just beyond Portree on the right is the Aros Heritage Centre, with displays on Skye's history from 1700 onwards. Follow the A87 to the remote Sligachan Hotel, situated by a loch and at the head of Glen Sligachan, which runs south to the sea. The hotel, standing between the jagged mountains of the Black Cuillin and the slightly more rounded Red Cuillin, has a climbing museum, and a micro brewery. Return to Portree by the same route.

Index

Index entries in bold refer to touring bases. Page numbers in italic refer to pictures.

C

D

I

J

K

L

Acknowledgments

Front cover Getty Images/Steve Allen (Isle of Skye); **Back cover** www.ntpl.org.uk/©NTPL/Joe Cornish (Brecon Beacons); **1** www.ntpl.org.uk/©NTPL/Joe Cornish (Winnat's Pass, Derbyshire and Peak District); **2-3** Getty Images/Travelpix Ltd (Forest road, Hampshire); **6-7** Photolibrary.com/David Noton (Road to Milborne Port, Somerset); **8-9** naturepl.com/John Waters; **11** Photolibrary.com/Ben Pipe; **12-13** Photolibrary.com/Britain on View; **15** www.ntpl.org.uk/©NTPL/Rupert Truman; **17** naturepl.com/Ross Hoddinott; **19** naturepl.com/Adam Burton; **20-21** naturepl.com/Ross Hoddinott; **23** Photolibrary.com/Lee Frost; **24** Collections/© Barry Beattie; **26-27** Photolibrary.com/Adam Burton; **28-29** Photolibrary.com/Guy Edwardes; **30-31** naturepl.com/Adam Burton; **32-33** Caroline Wood; **34** Photolibrary.com/Peter Lewis; **37** www.ntpl.org.uk/©NTPL/Derek Croucher; **40-41** Photolibrary.com/Tony Howell; **42** Photolibrary.com/Adam Woolfitt; **44-45** naturepl.com/David Noton; **46-47** Photolibrary.com/Dave Porter; **49** Photolibrary.com/Britain on View; **50** www.jasonhawkes.com; **53** Photolibrary.com/ Roy Rainford; **54-55** Photolibrary.com/Adam Burton; **57** Photolibrary.com/Martin Brent; **58** Photolibrary.com/Britain on View; **61** Photolibrary.com/David Sellman; **62** © David Sellman; **64** Jo Bourne; **67** Alamy Images/© John Woodworth; **68-69** Photolibrary.com/Simon Winnall; **72-73** Photolibrary.com/Pearl Bucknall; **75** www.jasonhawkes.com; **76-77** Photolibrary.com/Britain on View; **78-79** www.ntpl.org.uk/©NTPL/David Noton; **81** Photolibrary.com/Dave Porter; **82-83** Photolibrary.com/Britain on View; **84** Photolibrary.com/Lee Beel; **87** Photolibrary.com/Alan Novelli; **90-91** Photolibrary.com/David Noton; **92** Photolibrary.com/Britain on View; **95** Photolibrary.com/Lee Frost; **96** Photolibrary.com/Peter Packer; **98-99** Skyscan.co.uk/W.Cross; 101 Photolibrary.com/Dave Porter; **102** Photolibrary.com/Jon Gibbs; **105** Photolibrary.com/Dave Porter; **106-107** Photolibrary.com/Justin Foulkes; **109** Pictures Colour Library/Paul Isles; **110** www.ntpl.org.uk/©NTPL/Nick Meers; **113** Photolibrary.com/Rod Edwards; **114** www.ntpl.org.uk/©NTPL/John Miller; **117** Photolibrary.com/Rod Edwards; **119** www.lastrefuge.co.uk/Dae Sasitorn & Adrian Warren; **120-121** Photolibrary.com/Jon Allison; **123** Photolibrary.com/Doug Pearson; **124** Photolibrary.com/Britain on View; **127** Photolibrary.com/AlanNovelli; **128-129** Photolibrary.com/Dave Porter; **131** Photolibrary.com/Jason Friend; **133** Photolibrary.com/Britain on View; **134-137** Photolibrary.com/Roger Coulam; **138** Photolibrary.com/Rod Edwards; **140-145** Photolibrary.com/Joe Cornish; **146** www.lastrefuge.co.uk/Dae Sasitorn & Adrian Warren; **149** Photolibrary.com/Rod Edwards; **150** Collections/© Mike Kipling; **153** Photolibrary.com/Andy Stothert; **154-155** Photolibrarywales/Allen Lloyd; 156 Photolibrary.com/Britain on View; 159 Photolibrary.com/Andy Stothert; 160-161 Photolibrary.com/Britain on View; **163** Photolibrary.com/David Noton; **164** Photolibrary.com/Britain on View; **167** Photolibrary.com/Graham Bell; **168** Photolibrary.com/Britain on View; **170-171** naturepl.com/David Tipling; **172** Collections/© Alan Greeley; **174-175** Photolibrarywales/Pierino Algieri; **176-177** Photolibrary.com/David Noton; **178-181** Photolibrary.com/Steve Lewis; **182-183** Photolibrary.com/Flight Images LLP; **185** Photolibrary.com/Steve Lewis; **186-187** Scottish Viewpoint/Iain McLean; **189** Photolibrary.com/Andy Stothert; **190** Photolibrary.com/Marc Bedingfield; **193** Photolibrary.com/Derek Croucher; **194-195** Photolibrary.com/Joe Cornish; **197** Photolibrary.com/Britain on View; **199** Collections/© Dennis Barnes; **200** Collections/© David Cairns; **202** © Crown Copyright reproduced courtesy of Historic Scotland.www.historicscotlandimages.gov.uk; **204-205** naturepl.com/David Noton; **207** Scottish Viewpoint/Peter Scott; **208** Scottish Viewpoint/VisitScotland; **211** SCOTLANDSIMAGES.COM/© The National Trust for Scotland; **214-215** Photolibrary.com/Dennis Hardley; **217** Photolibrary.com/David Sellman; **218** Pictures Colour Library/Edmund Nagele; **221** Collections/© Dennis Barnes; **222** Photolibrary.com/Duncan Shaw; **225** Collections/© Phil Crean; **226-227** Scottish Viewpoint/Richard Clarkson; **228** Photolibrary.com/Dennis Barnes; **231** Photolibrary.com/Adam Burton

With thanks to Ruth Binney, Amy Dibden, Susie Hallam and Steve and Marilyn Tait for route checking.

Contributors

Project Editor Jo Bourne
Art Editors Julie Bennett, Kathryn Gammon
Sub Editor Marion Paull
Cartographer Philip Storey
Cartographic Consultant Alison Ewington
Feature Writer Christopher Somerville
Additional material Marion Paull, Philip Storey
Picture Editor Caroline Wood
Proofreader Barry Gage
Indexer Marie Lorimer
Maps European Map Graphics Limited

FOR VIVAT DIRECT
Editorial Director Julian Browne
Art Director Anne-Marie Bulat
Managing Editor Nina Hathway
Picture Resource Manager Sarah Stewart-Richardson
Pre-press Account Manager Dean Russell
Product Production Manager Claudette Bramble
Production Controller Jan Bucil

Origination by FMG
Printed in China

Every reasonable care has been taken to ensure that the information in this guide is accurate at the time of going to press, but the drives described may be subject to change. The publishers and copyright owners accept no responsibility for any consequences arising out of use of this book, including misinterpretation of the maps and directions and those arising from changes taking place after the book was finalised. We are always pleased to hear from readers who wish to suggest corrections or improvements. Contact us on **08705 113366** or email us at **gbeditorial@readersdigest.co.uk**

The Most Amazing Scenic Journeys in Britain is published in 2011 in the United Kingdom by Vivat Direct Limited (t/a Reader's Digest), 157 Edgware Road, London W2 2HR

The Most Amazing Scenic Journeys in Britain is adapted from **Country Walks and Scenic Drives** published by The Reader's Digest Association Limited in 1998.

We are committed both to the quality of our products and the service we provide to our customers. We value your comments, so please do contact us on **08705 113366** or via our website at **www.readersdigest.co.uk**

If you have any comments or suggestions about the content of our books, email us at **gbeditorial@readersdigest.co.uk**

ISBN 978 0 276 44584 2
Book Code 400-477 UP0000-1
Oracle Code 250014571S.00.24